- Take notes from your sources. **10a–10e**
  - Use note cards, paper, computers, or photocopies and printed materials. **10a**
  - Record complete information.
  - Follow a consistent format.
  - Transcribe information accurately.
  - Include facts in brief form.
  - Condense information in summaries.
  - Restate ideas in paraphrases.
  - Transcribe quotations to use an author's exact words.
  - Recognize information that is common knowledge. **10d**
  - Avoid plagiarizing information, ideas, or wording **10e**
- Plan your paper carefully. **11a–11e**
  - Review your research. **11a**
  - Rework your thesis statement. **11b**
  - Develop an informal outline. **11c**
  - Organize your notes according to your outline. **11d**
  - Construct a formal outline, when needed. **11e**
- Draft your paper. **12a–12e**
  - Reflect on the writing process. **12a**

  - Blend facts and summaries into your own sentences.
  - Paraphrase ideas when appropriate.
  - Quote material selectively.
  - Document your research using parenthetical notes. **12d**
  - Create an interesting, effective title.
  - Draft an interesting, appropriate introduction and conclusion.
- Revise your paper with care. **13a–13d**
  - Reconsider your content. **13a**
  - Rework your style. **13b**
  - Eliminate technical errors. **13c**
  - Seek reactions from others. **13d**
- Follow the requirements of your chosen documentary style. **14–17**
  - Include required information in citations.
  - Follow format requirements.
  - Model your citations on similar samples.
  - Combine information from several forms when necessary.
  - Prepare your manuscript carefully.

HANDBOOK

for

College Research

THIRD EDITION

Robert Perrin

Indiana State University

HOUGHTON MIFFLIN COMPANY   Boston   New York

Vice President and Publisher: Patricia A. Coryell
Executive Editor: Suzanne Phelps Weir
Editorial Assistant: Peter Mooney
Associate Project Editor: Lindsay Frost
Senior Art and Design Coordinator: Jill Haber
Composition Buyer: Sarah Ambrose
Manufacturing Manager: Florence Cadran
Marketing Manager: Cindy Graff Cohen
Marketing Assistant: Wendy Thayer

Acknowledgments
Chapter 5
Figures 5.1, 5.2, 5.3, 5.4, and 5.5: Screenshots from LUIS System Online Catalog are reprinted with the permission of Indiana State University.
Figures 5.6, 5.7, and 5.8: Images produced by ProQuest Information and Learning Company. Inquires may be made to: ProQuest Information and Learning Company, 300 North Zeeb Road, Ann Arbor, MI 48106-1346 USA. Telephone (734) 761-7400; E-mail: info@il.proquest.com; Web-page: www.il.proquest.com.

Chapter 7
Figure 7.1: Google is a trademark of Google Inc. and used with permission.
Figure 7.2: © 1998–2004 InfoSpace, Inc. All rights reserved. Reprinted with permission of Infospace, Inc.
Figure 7.3: Image © Board of Trustees, National Gallery of Art, Washington.

Chapter 9
Excerpt from "The Gold Standard" by Cullen Murphy, *Atlantic Monthly*, January 2002: 16–17. Reprinted by permission.

Chapter 12
"Poem (1)" from *The Collected Poems of Langston Hughes* by Langston Hughes. Copyright © 1994 by The Estate of Langston Hughes. Used by permission of Alfred A. Knopf, a division of Random House, Inc.
Bruce Springsteen, "Streets of Philadelphia." *Philadelphia* Soundtrack. Epic. © Bruce Springsteen. ASCAP. All Rights Reserved. Reprinted by permission of John Landau Management, Greenwich, CT.

Chapter 14
Architectural terms for parts of the Lincoln Memorial. Modified from Einhorn Yaffee Prescott (1994).

Printed in the U.S.A.
Library of Congress Control Number: 2003115595
ISBN: 0-618-44133-6

23456789-VHG-08 07 06 05

Contents

Preface

In many ways, researching is already a part of your life. When you pick up *TV Guide* to find out what programs are on, you research. When you scan the nutritional label on a cereal box to find the number of calories in a single serving, you research. When you check the Internet to find the average price of a car, truck, or SUV, you research. When you read a review of a film to decide whether or not to see it, you research. When you ask a friend about his or her response to a teacher's class before enrolling, you research. In situations like these, you gather, read, listen to, and evaluate ideas and information to make informed decisions—all of which constitutes research.

But research extends beyond these everyday activities. When you read about, talk about, and ask questions about a topic that interests you, you research in a broad, thorough way. Whether your interests involve science fiction, hip-hop music, sharks, auto racing, or the stock market, you can use systematic researching techniques to learn more about the subject—and once you learn more, you can compare information and reach conclusions.

In the academic setting of a college class, research becomes more comprehensive, more thorough, and more varied than most personal research. Nonetheless, college research builds upon the informal research that you have done in the past. It still involves gathering ideas and information to learn about a subject, even though it is more systematic, more demanding, and more clearly oriented toward an academic goal than is informal research.

The Content and Contexts of *Handbook for College Research*

Handbook for College Research (HCR) is designed to introduce the standards required for college research and writing. In sequential fashion, its chapters describe the research process, offering strategies, hints, and recommendations to help you become a successful researcher and writer. A number of features make *HCR* both comprehensive and easy to use:

- *A Handbook Format.* To make information easy to find, *HCR* presents major principles in each chapter as numbered precepts (statements of key ideas).
- *Alternative Documentary Styles.* To meet varied research needs, *HCR* includes four up-to-date documentary styles—Modern Language Association (MLA),

American Psychological Association (APA), University of Chicago (Chicago, also known as Turabian), and Council of Biology Editors (CBE)—in Chapters 14–17. *HCR* also includes sample papers in each documentary style.

■ *Information on Electronic Sources.* Acknowledging advances in research technology, *HCR* offers advice about using Internet search engines and interpreting information in Internet sites, discussion groups, and CD-ROM sources. Of special value is a section on evaluating Internet sources.

■ *Information about Online Catalogs.* Recognizing that computers have revolutionized libraries, *HCR* addresses the challenges and benefits of using an online catalog to locate materials in the library's collection and of using periodical databases to locate articles in magazines, journals, and newspapers.

■ *Field Research.* Recognizing that not all research occurs in a library, *HCR* describes alternative sources, such as interviews, questionnaires, surveys, and audiovisual sources.

■ *Guidelines for Collaboration.* To acknowledge current trends in research, *HCR* includes discussions and advice about the special needs, challenges, and strategies of collaborative research.

■ *Student Samples.* Throughout its chapters, *HCR* follows the progress of students working individually and collaboratively, tracing the work that leads to the sample papers.

■ *Exercises.* In appropriate chapters, *HCR* includes exercises that correspond to the chapter discussions, providing incremental work leading to a research project.

■ *Supplementary Materials.* *HCR*'s appendixes include a discussion of document design (which includes manuscript preparation) and an extensive list of abbreviations and shortened forms of publishers' names, both necessary for completing accurate citations. In addition, *HCR* includes a brief glossary of computer terms.

■ *Web Site.* An accompanying Web site features a wide variety of materials that expand upon the student text. The "Student Resources" section features additional cross-curricular sample research papers demonstrating a variety of documentation styles, easily accessible sample citations in the four documentation styles, additional research exercises, questions for student writers to help them pinpoint research topics appropriate to their interests, links to URLs discussed in the book, chapter quick-reference features, and abbreviated versions of the book's electronic research chapters. The "Instructor Resources" section includes an overview of the book, advice on teaching research, sample syllabi, advice on grading/assessment, and suggested assignments.

Collaborative Work and Research

Applying examples from the workplace—whether a research laboratory on a college campus, the public relations division of a multinational business, or the offices of a law firm—many instructors provide opportunities for collaborative research. These experiences with collaborative research yield important dividends: you have opportunities to work and learn *with* others; you learn to use your strengths to a group's advantage (and your own); you learn to divide the responsibilities of research to complete tasks more quickly and more thoroughly than you could individually; and you learn to work with others, which allows you to monitor, encourage, and help other group members.

To encourage collaborative research, labeled sections throughout *HCR* provide suggestions for using collaborative work at each stage of the research process.

Acknowledgments

My work on *HCR* was made more pleasant and more productive because of the supportive, knowledgeable staff at Houghton Mifflin—thanks especially to Suzanne Phelps Weir, Peter Mooney, and Lindsay Frost.

I am also indebted to the following people for reviewing the manuscript of the *Handbook for College Research:*

Sandy Boyd, College of Marin
John C. Dobelbower, Ball State University
Sara W. Guthrie, Mississippi County Community College
Michael D. Harrold, Indiana State University
Daniel Hipp, Aurora University
Margaret Karsten, Ridgewater College
David McGrath, College of DuPage
Robert Delius Royar, Morehead State University
Sandra K. Vance, DeVry University

In addition, I would like to thank the students in my research-focused writing classes for their comments about the effectiveness of the explanations, samples, and exercises; the teaching assistants, instructors, and lecturers in the Department of English, Indiana State University, for their suggestions and recommendations; and the students who have allowed me to use their research materials and papers.

As always, I wish to thank my wife Judy, my daughter Jenny, my son Chris, and my daughter-in-law Kate for their encouragement.

R. P.

1

Moving from Subject to Topic: Where Research Begins

QUICK REFERENCE

Selecting a subject is the crucial first step in the research process, narrowing the general subject into a well-focused topic is an important second step.

- ▶ Be open-minded about potential topics.
- ▶ Consider a variety of subjects related to different aspects of your life or to diverse interests from your studies, as well as subjects from your general social observations.
- ▶ Before making a final subject selection, consider your interests, the length of the assignment, the availability of materials, the challenges involved, the uniqueness of the approach, and the potential perspectives you might have.
- ▶ Narrow your general subject to a specific topic by considering issues of time, place, or special circumstance.
- ▶ Work with assigned subjects, when appropriate, using the principles for selecting subjects and narrowing topics.

Research begins with a subject. In some academic contexts, you may choose the subject yourself, usually with the instructor's approval, but in other contexts you may be required to choose from a small number of topics. In yet other contexts, your instructor may assign a topic with a predetermined focus.

Each of these circumstances provides a distinct impetus for your research work, but after choosing a subject yourself or receiving an assigned topic, you are not ready to head for the library to check out books and photocopy articles or search the Internet for Web sites. You can certainly do that, and many people do; however, without preliminary work, you are likely to spend time in unproductive ways. To ensure that your early work is efficient and productive, employ some preliminary strategies for clarifying your topic.

1a   Choose a general subject.

When you select a subject with the instructor's approval, you have a great opportunity to expand your knowledge of a subject that interests you. Sometimes selecting a subject is challenging, especially with the pressure an assignment brings, so consider these ways of choosing a subject.

Strategies for Selecting Subjects

- _Learn more about a regular activity._ Make a list of things you do on a regular basis: listen to music, work, rebuild automobiles, shop, swim, work out, read, watch television. Then consider facets of those activities to learn about in greater detail. For example, if you listen to jazz or blues, you could research the life of a particular musician or the influence of a particular record label. Examine your daily life for elements that would be interesting to research.

  To explore subjects of general interest, go to the home pages of _Google_ at <http://www.google.com>, _HotBot_ at <http://hotbot.lycos.com/>, _Web Crawler_ at <http://www.webcrawler.com/>, or some other search engine and peruse their directories of subjects.

- _Explore possibilities in academic subjects._ Using a textbook for an academic course (perhaps in your major or minor area of study), leaf through the index, noting subjects that interest you. Skimming the index of a child psychology book, for example, could yield interesting topics such as moral development, birth order, sex roles, conflict resolution, self-paced learning, physiological development, and group dynamics.

  To consider subjects related to academic disciplines, go to the _WWW Virtual Library_ at <http://www.vlib.org/> for a fourteen-category set of links to specialized fields of study. Or consult the _Academic Guide to the Internet_ at <http://www.aldea.com/guides/ag/attframes2.html>, particularly using the sidebar links to discipline-specific subjects.

- _Consider subjects introduced in your classes._ Review notes and reading assignments from other classes. Notes and readings from an economics class might suggest topics like risk factors of mutual funds, the effects of tax cuts on family finances, or trade agreements. Provocative ideas—or information that challenges assumptions—can serve as a springboard for research. Completing research related to a subject you are studying broadens your learning experiences.

  To explore subjects related to your classes, ask your instructors for the names of professional organizations (and their acronyms). Then search the

Internet using the acronym, plus *.org*. The correlation is frequently clear: <http://www.acsm.org> reaches the American College of Sports Medicine site; <http://www.maa.org> reaches the Mathematical Association of America; <http://www.apa.org> reaches the American Psychological Association. Then explore the site for topics of interest.

■ *Consider geography.* Where you have been or where you want to go can guide your choice of subjects. If you enjoyed a trip to Dublin, research to learn more about the city or one of its particular features. If you want to visit China, learn about what you will find there. Consider towns, cities, counties, states or provinces, regions, countries, or continents.

To locate a convenient listing titled "Countries of the World," consult *Infoplease.com*'s online almanac at <http://www.infoplease.lycos.com/countries.html>. Or to explore geographical locations from a traveler's perspective, visit *Travel.com*'s "Destinations" at <http://www.travel.com>.

■ *Think in terms of people.* Consider learning more about an intriguing person, either living or dead: a performer, religious leader, politician, corporate figure, inventor, athlete, writer, historical personage, scientist.

To explore possibilities that focus on people, connect to *Biography.com*'s home page at <http://www.biography.com> to find profiles of over 25,000 people. Or consult *Infoplease.com*'s biography page at <http://www.infoplease.com/people.html> for listings by categories like "world rulers," "athletes," and "entertainers."

■ *Consider problems.* A research paper provides an excellent opportunity to learn about the scope of selected problems—personal, social, economic, religious, or political and about alternative solutions. If you research a personal problem, be certain that you are willing to discuss it with peer editors, perhaps tutors, and your instructor.

To identify problems that are worth exploring, connect with *Public Agenda Online* at <http://www.publicagenda.org> to link to issues categorized by twenty-two subject headings. Or go to *Lycos*'s directory of "Social Issues" at <http://dir.lycos.com/society/issues/> for an alphabetical listing of hundreds of subjects.

■ *Explore life changes.* Through research you can learn a great deal about changes that have occurred or are occurring in your life, whether they include marriage, divorce, bankruptcy, births of children, going to college, joining the work force, the aging or death of a parent, or retirement.

Turn to a Web site called *Life: Outlined* at <http://www.lifeoutlined.co.uk> to find subjects grouped by these topics: "healthy life," "home life," "family life," "working life," "financial life," "learning life," and "later life."

■ *Examine subjects that generate strong opinions.* Assuming that you explore both sides of the issue without bias, researching subjects such as censorship, birth control, immigration policies, deforestation, campaign finance reform, welfare policies, talk radio, or gun control can be informative and enlightening. However, be aware that one-sided discussions of controversial subjects are usually ineffective.

To identify subjects that have prompted serious debate, go to *DebatingSociety.com* at <http://www.debatingsociety.com/> to explore this week's subjects and those of previous weeks. Or explore the Concordia

College Library's "Controversial Issues Series" at <http://library.cord.edu/reference/researchguides/controversialissues.pdf> to see a list of sources on discussion-provoking subjects.

■ *Analyze social, political, or cultural events.* Consider especially events that you follow (or have followed) on a regular basis, whether the antismoking movement, the Super Bowl, presidential campaigns, the ongoing turmoil in the Middle East, or the Olympics.

To explore subjects of social, political, or cultural concern, go to the home pages of *Excite* at <http://www.excite.com/>, *Google* at <http://google.com>, or some other search engine and peruse their directories of subjects.

■ *Explore special interests.* Consider your special interests or hobbies: skiing, doll collecting, scuba diving, weight training, cooking, photography. Though you already know a great deal about subjects that interest you, research provides an obvious opportunity to learn even more.

To explore subjects of special interest, go to the home pages of *Galaxy* at <http://www.galaxy.com/>, *C/NET Search* at <http://www.search.com>, or some other search engine and peruse their directories of subjects.

With these strategies in mind, brainstorm for possible subjects, eventually choosing three to five alternative ones. Even if you are intently interested in researching one subject, having several backup subjects is useful. Beginning a major research project with only one potential subject can be disastrous if, for example, another person has chosen the same topic and has checked out the major sources ahead of you. Further, you may discover that research materials provide only limited perspectives on your chosen subject. With alternative subjects, you can change focus immediately, without a lengthy and frustrating delay.

COLLABORATION

Your first challenge in collaborative writing is selecting a person (or perhaps several people) with whom to work. If you know classmates already, you can choose easily. If you do not, take time to "interview" prospective collaborators. Some instructors create questionnaires or allow class time for students to discuss their needs, goals, and preferences. In either context, choose someone with whom you have or can establish good working relations. Consider the following criteria:

Selecting Collaborators

■ *Compatible personalities.* Select collaborators with whom you get along—but remember that you will be *working* together, not socializing.

■ *Compatible work habits.* Select collaborators whose work habits are similar to your own. If you ordinarily start early on a project or assignment and work steadily, you will be frustrated by working with someone who procrastinates.

- *Compatible strengths and weaknesses.* Select collaborators whose abilities complement your strengths and compensate for your weaknesses, providing balance in your combined research effort.
- *Compatible schedules.* Select collaborators who share similar school and work schedules. No matter how compatible you are otherwise, if you and your collaborators are unable to meet on a regular basis, your work will be more difficult.
- *Compatible goals.* Select collaborators who want similar results. If you will be satisfied only with an *A* or a *B* on a project, avoid collaborators who will be satisfied with a *C* or *D*. If your goals are not similar, the commitment to the work will not be, either—and you may do a disproportionate share of the work to achieve your own goals.

Effective collaboration requires balanced contributions from all members of the group. Keep these factors in mind as you choose the person (or people) with whom you will work.

As you select potential subjects for your research, keep these important and practical principles in mind.

Guidelines for Assessing General Subjects

- *Interest.* Select a subject that interests you enough to spend hours thinking, reading, and writing about it. Choosing a topic that does not genuinely interest you is counterproductive. Take full advantage of this opportunity to enjoy your learning.
- *Length.* Select a subject that can be adequately treated in the length requirements of the assignment. Discussing a broad subject such as federal funding of the arts in only five pages will lead to a hopelessly general paper. So make sure that the scope of your subject can be covered within the recommended number of pages.
- *Materials.* Select a subject for which you can find enough material. Check with your instructor or a reference librarian to determine whether your school's library has sufficient print sources related to your topic; however, remember that you can also research at other libraries or get materials from other schools through interlibrary loan. In addition, complete a preliminary Internet search to see whether a broad range of material is available.
- *A challenge.* Select a challenging subject, but not one that requires technical or other specialized knowledge that you do not possess and do not have time to acquire. Researching should be a learning process, but you can learn only so much within a given time period.
- *Uniqueness.* Select a subject that is not overused. Overused or overly familiar topics are weak choices because readers are likely to feel as if they know about the subject already.

■ *A special perspective.* Select a subject that you can approach in a fresh way. Consider a new angle for discussing the subject, realizing that readers will find your special approach interesting because it is not overly familiar.

Having selected a general subject that meets these criteria, confer with your instructor to ensure that it meets the requirements of the assignment. Getting advice at this preliminary stage is wise, since you can forestall some potential problems.

Jarah Estes-Cooper, a history education major, considered a variety of topics related to her major. She considered writing about Eleanor Roosevelt because she had always been fascinated by the first lady's independent spirit. She thought about exploring the way Internet sites made historical documents available to people everywhere. But she also thought that perhaps this topic might require her to describe the preparation of electronic documents. That, she decided, was probably too technical for her to manage well.

Finally, she decided to research Washington, DC, specifically focusing on the monuments and memorials that are part of the National Mall. Because she had visited the capital recently, she had some materials already, and because of her university's large history program, she assumed that she would find many sources on the topic. Further, she could take advantage of the many online sources that she knew were available. Consequently, the subject seemed to be a workable one.

COLLABORATION

Elissa Allen and Jeremy Reynolds, both psychology majors, decided to work together on their research project because they shared the same general interests. Since their research subject had to treat family relations in some way, they considered these options: single-parent families, sibling rivalry, and multigenerational families.

They agreed that Elissa's strong opinions about single-parent families would interfere with their objectivity, and they decided that multigenerational families might be either too difficult to define or too broad as a topic. Even sibling rivalry, they decided, was potentially negative. Consequently, they modified sibling rivalry to focus on birth order and its effects on children.

EXERCISE 1.1   *Preliminary Internet Search*

Explore at least three electronic sources to begin your search for a subject. Then write a brief paragraph describing not only your process but also any interesting results.

EXAMPLE

I had some fairly good ideas about subjects that came from my brainstorming on general interests, academic subjects, and life changes. So I decided to move in different directions with my Internet searching. My exploration of *Biography .com* was entertaining and informative—and I'm afraid I got sidetracked and read several of the brief biographies, even about people I wouldn't consider writing a paper about. I found people of all kinds who might prove interesting choices for a paper: Mohandas Gandhi, Charlie Chaplin, Babe Ruth, Dolley Madison, Wilbur Wright, Catherine the Great, and others. Then I shifted my search to controversial topics and connected with *DebatingSociety.com,* which was equally interesting but, for me, less promising. The subjects—from gun control to medical testing—were widely varied, but I had a hard time imagining that I could cover most of them well in a brief paper. Therefore, I think I'll consider subjects from my personal brainstorming and from my exploration of *Biography.com.* ■■

EXERCISE 1.2 *General Subjects*

List five possible subjects for your research paper. Use the criteria above to determine how promising your subjects are. (Later exercises, all leading to a research paper, will draw upon these topics.)

EXAMPLE

1. Government subsidies
2. High-grossing films
3. Credit-card debt
4. Museums
5. Childcare ■■

1b Narrow your general subject to a specific topic.

A focused topic helps you determine a thesis (the main idea for the paper) and select, review, and read only the materials that are appropriate for your paper. Skimming reference materials for an hour or two and then narrowing the subject can save hours of work.

Consider alternative ways to begin your review of reference materials. If your library has shifted from a print reference collection to an electronic one, use the library's home page to locate electronic encyclopedias, fact books, dictionaries, and other general materials. Then simply connect to the sources you want and begin your preliminary work. If your library's collection is still in book form, go to the reference room and use either the online catalog to enter your subject or one of the subject lists many libraries post in the reference area. Either strategy allows you to locate print reference materials in the collection that relate to your subject. If you begin by searching the Internet, review those sites that offer the broadest overview of your subject, as opposed to those that focus on individual features.

When reviewing general reference materials, pay particular attention to recurrent themes, details, and ideas. Take notes on interesting items and use them to narrow your focus to single facets of the larger subject.

COLLABORATION

Divide preliminary reading to make the process of reviewing background information efficient. Then compare notes with collaborators to gain a broad understanding of the subject; try to reach a consensus about what facets of the larger subject are of most interest to all collaborators.

Once you have a general knowledge of your preliminary subject, limit it in one or more of the following ways.

Strategies for Limiting Subjects

- _Time._ Restrict the discussion to a specific, manageable time span. For example, the general subject of teenage pregnancy could be restricted to teenage pregnancy in the 1950s or 1990s. Such time restrictions focus research suitably, especially when time has altered the way in which some subjects are perceived.
- _Place._ Restrict the discussion to a single, specific location. For example, the general subject of wetlands preservation could be restricted to wetlands preservation in the Mississippi River basin or in Florida. Such narrowing allows you to control your reading and to focus the paper.
- _Special circumstance._ Restrict the discussion to a specific circumstance. For example, the general subject of achievement testing could be restricted to the primary grades or to college admissions.

Combine these strategies to achieve even greater focus. For instance, a student might research teenage pregnancy in rural communities or wetlands preservation in Florida during the last decade.

Jarah, for example, discovered through general reading in reference materials that there was a wealth of materials on Washington's monuments and memorials, so she began to consider ways to limit her subject. She considered restricting her discussions to late-twentieth-century memorials: the Vietnam Veterans Memorial or the Korean Veterans Memorial. Although her subject had already restricted her to a specific location—the National Mall—she considered focusing on monuments and memorials on the Mall itself or those adjacent to the Mall, like the Vietnam Veterans Memorial or the Grant Memorial. She also thought about special circumstances: the uses of the monuments, renovations and modifications, and so on.

Because of her special interest in the Lincoln Memorial, Jarah eventually decided to focus on it exclusively and to consider special circumstances related to its construction and use as a site for protests. She was not certain what she would discover, but she knew that these preliminary stages of narrowing her subject to a specific topic would help her to focus her research.

COLLABORATION

Through their separate reading, Elissa and Jeremy discovered that Western cultures show the most interest in birth order and that this interest has emerged most strongly since the early 1900s, when family structures began to change. The two students decided to limit their focus by location and time. However, because they also noted that many writers said that special circumstances influence the effects of birth order, Elissa and Jeremy decided to concentrate on the variables that could alter the normal effects of birth order.

EXERCISE 1.3 *Specific Topics*

Select three subjects from your response to Exercise 1.2 and rewrite them to identify a particular time, place, or special circumstance. In parentheses, identify the limiting factor of each one.

EXAMPLE

1. Government subsidies for the dairy industry (special circumstance)
2. Museums and innovative programs of the last twenty years (special circumstance and time)
3. Childcare in the inner city (place)   ■■

1c   Work with assigned subjects, when appropriate.

When you cannot choose your subject, accept the situation without too much grumbling and consider these benefits: (1) You do not need to spend time considering and reconsidering subjects; (2) if materials were not available, your instructor would not have assigned the subject; and (3) you will gain experience in completing directed writing, the kind most often done in the workplace.

Different Kinds of Assigned Subjects

A research paper with an assigned subject may allow for extensive choices or provide no choices at all. The degree of choice determines how you should proceed, so consider these options:

■ *General category only.* Some instructors identify a *type* of subject to control the general direction of your research but, within that restriction, allow you to select the specific subject for the paper. For instance, in a philosophy class, you might be required to write a research paper on a twentieth-century philosopher. Such a pattern establishes some crucial limits—you cannot, for instance, write about a medieval philosopher; it also allows you considerable freedom—you *can* write about a French or German or American philosopher, and you *can* choose which one.

When presented with only general categories, work within the general restrictions but follow the strategies just discussed in sections **1a** ("Choose a general subject") and **1b** ("Narrow your general subject to a specific topic").

■ *General subject only.* Other instructors predetermine the subjects you can write about but allow you to select the subject (from a list of choices, for example) and decide how to narrow it. In a music appreciation class, for instance, you might be given a list of composers from which to choose.

When given a general subject, proceed according to the guidelines presented in sections **1a** and **1b;** you still have sufficient freedom to justify a full exploration of alternative subjects and narrowed topics.

■ *Specific subject.* Still other instructors assign specific subjects to write about. For example, in a British drama class, each student might be assigned to research a particular non-English playwright whose work influenced the British theater. Because the playwrights are assigned, one phase of the work is eliminated. Yet students are free to establish the specific focus of their research.

When assigned a specific subject, begin your exploration process at the stage identified in **1b** ("Narrow your general subject to a specific topic").

■ *Specific subject with limitations.* Some instructors eliminate almost all choices, from selecting the subject to determining the focus or topic. In a geology class, each student might be assigned a well-known geological formation like the Grand Canyon or the Devil's Kitchen and be required to discuss how the formation represents an important geological pattern.

When you are given a limited, specific subject, move directly into preliminary research, since both the subject and the focus have been provided.

Although assigned-topic research papers may seem restrictive, they still allow you to bring a special focus to the work. Kristin Garfield, a student in an honors life sciences course, had to prepare a brief research report to share with her classmates. The instructor provided a list of subjects to choose from, and among them was "communicable diseases." Because her grandmother had contracted polio as a child, Kristin had long been interested in the disease; in addition, she had recently read that polio had been eradicated in the Western Hemisphere. Because of her personal interest and the possibility of getting recent information on the subject, Kristin narrowed her topic with relative ease.

As you work with assigned subjects, remember that you must develop a commitment, whether personal or strictly academic, to the research. The best research comes when you combine those goals.

EXERCISE 1.4　*Assigned Subjects*

To gain practice in working with assigned subjects, review this list of optional subjects that might be used for a brief research paper in an American history class. Select one subject and narrow it to a specific topic. Then, in small groups or as a class, discuss the numerous ways to narrow these broad subjects.

EXAMPLE

1. Alaska	6. Nebraska
2. Arizona	7. New Hampshire
3. Florida	8. Oregon
4. Louisiana	9. Tennessee
5. Missouri	10. Wisconsin

2

Planning Thesis Statements and Stated Objectives

QUICK REFERENCE

Focus the ideas of your research paper—for yourself and your readers—by presenting a thesis statement, research question, or statement of a problem, depending on the nature of your paper.

▶ Use a thesis statement to guide a persuasive paper.

▶ Make sure that your thesis statement clarifies your narrow topic, expresses your opinion about it, and conveys a tone appropriate for the paper.

▶ When helpful, qualify major ideas, clarify major elements, and acknowledge your readers' knowledge of the topic.

▶ Use a research question or a statement of a problem or objective to guide an informative paper.

▶ Make sure that your question, statement, or objective is focused, concise, and well worded.

To clarify the central goal of your writing, present your ideas in one of the following ways. For a persuasive paper, express the major idea through a thesis statement. For an informative paper, express your purpose as a question (that the paper will answer), a statement of a problem (that the paper will describe), or as a research objective (that the paper will fulfill).

2a   Write a working thesis statement, when appropriate.

A working thesis statement guides the planning and drafting of a persuasive research paper. Because research involves substantial reading and thinking, the working thesis statement also helps you select and evaluate materials, thus directing you to explore a specific, narrow facet of the subject.

Having narrowed your research subject and having thought about the paper's purpose, you can write a working thesis statement: a brief statement of the topic and your opinion about it. Plan to refine the working thesis statement later in the researching and writing process, to produce a final statement to guide readers of the paper.

A working thesis statement has three essential characteristics and may include several optional ones.

Essential Characteristics

- *A specific, narrow topic.* An effective thesis statement (working or final) directs readers' attention to a focused topic.
- *A clear opinion on the topic.* To ensure that readers understand your perspective, a thesis statement unambiguously states your analysis of the topic, not merely facts about it.
- *An appropriate tone.* To achieve balance, the tone of the thesis statement should be appropriate for the topic, purpose, and audience of the paper.

The following example illustrates how these elements can be incorporated:

> A basic understanding of how special effects are achieved in film enhances viewers' filmgoing experiences.

The topic "special effects in film" is clearly stated; the opinion, that understanding how special effects are achieved affects viewers positively, is stated unambiguously and is clarified by the word *enhances*; the tone is straightforward and serious.

To create a context for the statement of topic and opinion, a working thesis statement may also include one or more of the following characteristics.

Optional Characteristics

- *Qualification of major ideas.* To ensure that the discussion is reasonable and balanced, qualify the topic in any way that may be necessary, acknowledging opposing opinions.
- *Clarification of important elements.* Identify key elements of the topic, perhaps indicating major points of discussion or organizational patterns.

■ *Acknowledgment of readers' knowledge.* Acknowledge what readers probably know about the topic; this helps establish a common perspective for
discussion.

Incorporating at least one optional characteristic further improves the thesis statement, as is illustrated in this example:

> Although many filmgoers seem uninterested in the technical aspects of
> filmmaking, a basic understanding of how special effects are achieved in
> film enhances their filmgoing experiences.

This example uses a qualification (acknowledging an opposing perspective) to create balance. Alternatively, the thesis statement could have
mentioned the special effects most often used, or it could have acknowledged that readers may know something about special effects because
of informative programs or special features on DVDs. Which kind of optional element or elements to include depends on the emphasis you wish
to create with a thesis statement.

When drafting a working thesis statement, remember that it guides
but does not control research. Consider a working thesis statement as an
idea to be confirmed, refuted, or modified on the basis of research. Exploring materials in this fashion makes research a process of discovery, allowing new ideas and unexpected information to lead you in promising
directions.

On the basis of her general reading and discussions with other history
students, Jarah decided to research the ways in which the Lincoln Memorial was used as a location for protests. Before searching for specific,
relevant materials, however, she reviewed her preliminary notes and for-
mulated the following working thesis statement:

> The Lincoln Memorial originally was built as an impressive monument to a
>
> beloved president, but it has since become a symbol of American protest.

With this working thesis statement to guide her research, Jarah could
eliminate sources that treated unrelated aspects of the topic and search for
those that were suitably connected to her approach. She knew, however,
that the working thesis statement might change as she learned more about
the topic.

▶

COLLABORATION

Writing collaboratively—in pairs or in larger groups—is a challenge,
but early attempts to devise a working thesis statement provide a useful beginning. Establish a balanced relationship by keeping these
strategies in mind:

- *Decide on roles.* Whoever writes (or types) most quickly or fluently should transcribe ideas, to ensure that you work with reasonable speed. Other collaborators should actively contribute ideas and respond to questions.
- *Decide on a working style.* Consider working in independent stages—with one person writing a first draft, followed by other collaborators revising the draft. Or consider working in tandem, with an ongoing discussion of ideas followed by a quick transcription of agreed-upon phrases. Determine which style—or variation—works best for you and your collaborators.
- *Share the work.* Maintain equity during the writing process to ensure that neither you nor your collaborators dominate. A collaborative relationship is established during early stages of your work, so experiment and practice with working arrangements.

Elissa and Jeremy devised their working thesis statement together, with both "thinking out loud" while Jeremy hurriedly transcribed the sentence on paper. Then they read and reread that working thesis statement, making substitutions and changes in the wording, and finally settled on this version:

> Although the effects of birth order are always evident to some degree, other variables also affect personality, intelligence, and socialization.

With the statement to guide them, Elissa and Jeremy began their research, looking for information about the variables that alter the general effects of birth order.

▶ EXERCISE 2.1   *Working Thesis Statements*

Using the narrowed topics from Exercise 1.3, write three working thesis statements that might guide your research. Discuss them with other students in class or with your instructor to determine which one promises the most productive research and the best paper.

EXAMPLE

1. Although the federal government first subsidized the dairy industry during the Great Depression to ensure its survival, the threat is long past, and the time has come for the dairy industry to operate without subsidies.
2. Although museums have long been seen as formidable, formal institutions, today's curators challenge this assumption by hosting unique programs and arranging innovative exhibits.
3. Before government agencies can fairly expect parents on welfare to work, they must provide affordable, acceptable childcare.   ■■

2b   State your objectives, when appropriate.

Informative research papers (often presented as reports) convey information. When producing an informative research paper is the goal, ask a useful research question, articulate a problem to be researched, or state an objective of the research, depending on your purpose.

A Research Question

A research question focuses research, determining which materials are useful and which are not. When devising a working research question and, later, when revising it to create a final research question, consider these points:

- *Focus on a single topic.* Address a narrow topic, not a general subject. (The principles discussed in section **1b** apply.)
- *Limit the scope of the question.* Limit the question to a single idea that includes only a few secondary elements.
- *State the question succinctly.* Express the question directly and clearly so that readers understand the focus of the paper.
- *Ask an answerable question.* Ask a question that can be answered by using available materials and within the limits (research time, paper length) you have.

The following ineffective examples illustrate the importance of writing clear and workable research questions.

Have sales of foreign-made cars, appliances, electronics, clothes, and toys continued to affect the trade balance?

(Although "foreign trade" can be seen as a single topic, the question contains too many elements. Limit the discussion to one major product.)

What do divorce statistics tell us about American culture?

(This question, though valid, is far too expansive to be treated effectively in a brief paper. Focus the question on a more limited feature of the larger subject.)

With the increase in cable systems, which make it possible for children of all ages to view programs and films in unsupervised situations at home, it seems futile to maintain the current film rating system for theaters, so this question arises: should the current film rating system, which was developed in the late 1950s, be changed or simply abandoned?

(This question is far too wordy to be clear. State the question more concisely.)

How can we restore American waterways to their previously unpolluted condition?

(Because we can never completely return our waterways to their previous condition, this question is unanswerable. Pose a question for which there are possible answers.)

A working research question guides but does not control research. During research, if you discover that your question is inexact or inappropriately focused, revise the question.

► EXERCISE 2.2   *Research Questions*

Write three research questions that might guide your work. Discuss them with other students in class or with your instructor to determine which is likely to lead to the most promising paper.

EXAMPLE

1. Has the increase in postal rates affected the greeting card industry?
2. Do nontraditional students take advantage of support services on college campuses?
3. How costly is closed-captioned television?   ■ ■

A Research Problem

A statement of a research problem is a declarative sentence that describes a problem to be analyzed in a research paper. Because it guides research, the statement should do the following things:

■ *Define the problem.* Distinguish the problem from similar or related problems. To serve as a useful guide for research, the statement must be detailed enough to be clear.
■ *Identify the people affected.* Narrow the statement (and subsequent research) to a single group or a very small number of groups.
■ *Establish an appropriate time frame.* Place the problem within a context of time: two months, one year, five years, the 1960s, 2000 to the present.
■ *Describe the location, when applicable.* Place the problem in a physical or geographical context: in Utah, in cities with more than 500,000 people, in the Middle East, in multifamily dwellings.

The elements included in a statement of a research problem determine the direction the paper takes. For example, you could explore a problem such as homelessness from many perspectives. You could define *homelessness* in a general way, as pertaining to anyone without permanent shelter, restrict it to those who are homeless by choice, or narrow it to people discharged from government-run mental institutions. You could concentrate on men, women, children, or entire families. You could deal with homelessness in the last twenty years, ten years, or two years. You could deal with homelessness in major metropolitan areas, moderately sized cities, or small towns. To write an effective, detailed paper, rather than a superficial one treating too many issues too briefly, work with a problem that is narrowly defined.

A working statement of the research problem provides direction for research and determines the focus of the paper. By stating the problem well, you begin your work effectively.

EXERCISE 2.3   *Research Problems*

Write three statements of research problems that might guide your research. Discuss them with other students in class or with your instructor to determine which is likely to lead to the most promising paper.

EXAMPLE

1. The producers of American films are so intent on making popular films that they continue to remake successful old films.
2. Elementary class sizes in _____ (your local school district) now exceed national averages.
3. Laboratory animals are still used to test cosmetics.   ■■

A Research Goal

A research goal—a brief, well-focused sentence—describes the purpose of a research paper that simply presents information. When devising a research goal, consider these steps:

■ *Define the topic.* Clearly identify the topic, to determine the direction of the research. For example, if you are writing about prayer in public schools, identify voluntary or mandatory prayer as your topic.
■ *Narrow the topic when necessary.* Restrict the subject so that research is manageable. For example, if your topic is geothermal systems, narrow your focus to either heating or cooling or concentrate on features such as cost, efficiency, or environmental advantages.

Directly stated research goals are unsubtle: for example, "I will present information about Hillary Clinton's major speeches to humanitarian groups, both before and during her service in Congress." However, they provide an excellent focus for certain kinds of researched writing.

Kristin knew that her primary interest was polio in the United States; she needed only to clarify her approach to the topic. After several attempts, she produced this research goal:

> I will share a brief history of polio in the United States, ranging from early epidemics to the last recorded American case.

By setting geographic limits, as well as establishing Kristin's intention to provide an overview, this statement would usefully guide her research.

EXERCISE 2.4   *Research Goals*

Write three research goals that might guide your research. Discuss them with other students in class or with your instructor to determine which is likely to lead to the most promising paper.

EXAMPLE

1. I plan to collect and share information about slang used in the 1950s, including original sources and current meanings.
2. I will gather information on price variations between brand name and generic drugs, concentrating on the ten most widely used drugs.
3. I will share information on the construction of the Sears Tower (America's tallest building) in Chicago.   ■ ■

Defining Research Goals and Evaluating Sources

Consider the varied goals that you can achieve through researching and writing a paper. Also evaluate the kinds, quality, and number of sources you might need to complete your research work.

▶ Think broadly about what you might achieve through your research.

▶ Consider the course-related, professional, and personal goals you plan to achieve through your research.

▶ Recognize that your topic, in some ways, determines what kinds of sources are most useful during your research.

▶ Use a broad range of sources during your research: books, periodicals, audiovisual sources, and electronic sources.

▶ Consider whether currentness is important in evaluating the usefulness of your sources.

▶ Consider the availability of the research materials you want to use.

Most often, academic or job-related requirements prompt your research, but at other times, you may want to know something for reasons of your own. In the best of circumstances, these two contexts merge, and while meeting someone else's expectations, you satisfy your personal curiosity. This interplay of goals and purposes enriches research.

3a   Acknowledge the goals of your research.

Your research should be guided by both general and specific goals; understanding them will help you sense the value of research. First, consider academic goals related to your general education.

Course-Related Goals

- *Learning to use the library.* You need to know how to locate and use library facilities and materials: the online catalog, the reference area, the book and periodical collections, and the microforms.
- *Learning to use the Internet for academic purposes.* Although you probably have used the Internet for personal reasons, you need to learn how to locate, evaluate, and use the Internet's academically focused resources.
- *Learning to assess source materials.* After locating materials, you need to evaluate them effectively. Research provides necessary practice in determining which sources are worth using in a paper and which are not.
- *Learning to take notes.* You need to know how to gather material from your sources systematically, clearly, accurately, honestly, and selectively.
- *Learning to deal effectively with opposing views.* Each researching experience exposes you to multiple views on a subject; the more you read, think about, and respond to contradictory perspectives, the more sophisticated your reasoning skills can become.
- *Learning to synthesize ideas.* You need to gain experience in reading, reviewing, interpreting, and synthesizing ideas to reach an understanding of a subject. Research provides a broad range of experiences in thinking about topics.
- *Learning to incorporate material in your writing.* After taking notes, you need to know how to incorporate information from them in your writing with clarity, accuracy, and style.
- *Learning to present information to support your claims.* You need to know which materials to use in supporting your ideas, and you need to explore options for presenting ideas effectively. Writing a research paper provides an extended opportunity to practice selecting and presenting ideas and information.
- *Learning to cite sources accurately in the paper.* You need to know how to document the sources of ideas, information, and quotations in the expected form.

These general goals relate to courses with the research paper as the major project. For you as a student in one of these courses, these broad goals are the foundation of your research work.

    In discipline-specific courses, research projects continue to follow from the goals noted above, but they also add the following ones.

Professional Goals

■ *Learning to use specific source materials.* Each subject area depends upon materials that professionals in the discipline have found particularly valuable. When researching in a discipline-specific course, you are expected to learn how to use those sources.

■ *Learning to use specialized writing formats.* Writing in each subject area is specialized, and you must learn to write in appropriate formats including reports, précis, abstracts, proposals, explications, or other specialized modes.

■ *Learning to use the specialized style of the discipline.* Each subject area has its own special concerns about style, and these relate to vocabulary, the use of present or past tense to describe the work of others, the use of active or passive voice, the amount of creativity that is expected, the use of specialized materials, and formatting.

■ *Demonstrating a basic knowledge of the discipline.* In specialized courses, you must demonstrate a working knowledge of the field. In researched writing for such a course, expect to demonstrate an understanding of the general principles upon which the field is based.

These professional goals are particularly important because completion of the requirements for a college degree implies a working knowledge of a major field of study, and that includes knowing how research is completed in that field.

In addition, individual goals should guide research. The best researching experiences generally come when you want to learn something that goes beyond course requirements.

Personal Goals

■ *Learning about the subject.* Whether you selected your subject on your own or not, wanting to learn more about it provides extra motivation.

■ *Learning to use sophisticated methods of research.* As you move from one research experience to another, your researching skills should improve, becoming progressively more sophisticated.

■ *Improving writing skills acquired in earlier research experiences.* With each research paper, you should improve upon earlier work, eliminating mistakes and improving style.

■ *Expanding educational experiences.* Each new research project is another opportunity to become a better student and a more knowledgeable individual, and it provides for personal growth.

Personal goals concentrate on degrees of knowledge, improvement, sophistication, and experience. Although they are less easily quantifiable than goals matched to courses, they are equally important.

Jarah understood her course goals—they were clearly described in the first-day materials from her class—but she had to consider what her personal goals were. One, of course, was learning about the Lincoln Memorial. Another was increasing her fluency with the online catalog in her university's library, as well as with the periodical databases. Yet another goal was to learn to explore Internet sites more critically than she had in the past. A final goal—a very forward-looking one—was to produce a high-quality paper that she could share with her future students.

COLLABORATION

When working collaboratively, first prepare individual goals to share with your collaborators. Discuss common goals and individual goals. If collaborators' individual goals seem incompatible—for example, if one person wants to use electronic sources heavily, but another would be satisfied with traditional print sources—discuss the differences from the outset of the project and reach a compromise as soon as possible. Learning to work collaboratively—sharing responsibilities, arguing productively, reaching consensus, and writing together—is an important goal in itself.

Neither Elissa nor Jeremy had worked collaboratively since high school, and those situations had involved extra-credit projects, not writing. Consequently, among their goals was learning to work together equitably to produce a paper that would be better than the ones they could produce individually.

EXERCISE 3.1   *Research Goals*

To gain insight about your research goals, make two lists, one presenting assignment-specific or professional goals and one presenting your personal goals for your research paper. Discuss these goals with your instructor.

EXAMPLE

Assignment-specific Goals

1. Use the Internet selectively
2. Conduct an interview
3. Incorporate research with personal style
4. Use personal experience, too

Personal Goals

1. Figure out citations once and for all
2. Get at least a *B*
3. Complete everything early or on time
4. Get comfortable with using the library's online catalog

3b   Consider the kinds of sources you need.

Before beginning your research, consider the range of materials needed to develop the paper. Follow these guidelines:

■ *Let course or project requirements guide selections.* When assignments specify the required sources for a project—the numbers of books, magazine articles, journal articles, newspaper articles, audiovisual sources, and electronic sources—the choices are made for you. When source requirements are unclear, consider other factors.

■ *Consider the strengths books have.* Books frequently are more comprehensive than other sources. Written (or compiled) after the events they discuss, books often achieve a degree of critical distance.

■ *Consider the strengths periodicals have.* Periodicals—magazines, journals, and newspapers—provide very current information.

■ *Consider the strengths audiovisual sources have.* Audiovisual sources such as television and radio provide instantaneous coverage of events. Other audiovisual sources—film, recordings, interviews—may provide unexpected and fresh perspectives.

■ *Consider the strengths electronic sources have.* Electronic sources provide access to a broad range of material that otherwise may be unavailable. Further, electronic sources are updated frequently—in some cases, daily—and, therefore, may provide the most current information on a topic.

■ *Let the topic guide you.* Many times, the topic determines the sources to use. If the topic requires very recent information, periodicals, audiovisual sources, and electronic sources will dominate; if you are doing a study from a historical perspective, books may dominate.

Jarah began with specific course requirements: she had to use a minimum of two books, three periodicals, three electronic sources, and one audiovisual source as the basis for her paper. However, given her topic (and its connection with her history major), Jarah also wanted to make sure that she used a variety of government sources, both print and electronic.

COLLABORATION

As you and your collaborators decide what kinds of sources to use, discuss the value of books, periodicals, audiovisual sources, and electronic sources. The varied perspectives (and researching experiences) of collaborators will allow all of you to benefit from the contributions of each individual.

Elissa, for example, had discovered a recent book on birth order effects, while Jeremy had noticed an article in a recent issue of a professional journal. Beginning with those sources, they planned to expand their list to include a larger number of books and journal articles. They suspected, however, that popular magazines would not discuss birth order in depth, so they did not consider popular magazines as credible sources.

As you gain researching experience, work to achieve a broad balance of sources, making subtler distinctions among them. For example, include different types of periodicals—such as a weekly magazine, a monthly magazine, and a quarterly—to represent variety even within the larger categories of books, periodicals, audiovisual materials, and electronic sources.

▶◣ **EXERCISE 3.2**   *Kinds of Sources*

To provide an overview of research on your subject, write a brief paragraph describing available sources.

EXAMPLE

> With a topic like childcare benefits to allow parents on welfare to work, I think I'll have many choices. The issue of welfare has been a long-standing problem, so I know there are books available; however, I don't know if they focus on the problem in the way I need. With all the talk of government cutbacks, I know periodicals must have recent discussions of the topic. Also, since we've got a good social work department here at school, I'm almost certain I can get someone to give me an interview. Finally, with the range of Web sites on the Internet, I surely will find some current and helpful information.   ∎∎

3c   Consider the currentness of your sources.

Whether your sources must be current or not depends on the subject of the paper. Subjects related to science, technology, or the medical professions generally require current sources. A paper about tuberculosis, based on twenty-year-old materials, is not sufficiently up-to-date. Yet a source published in 1920 might adequately discuss classical Greek architecture, since critical opinions about the design of the buildings did not change much in the twentieth century. Consider whether your topic requires current sources, keeping the following points in mind:

- *Currentness is not everything.* Because of recent developments in electronic publishing, many assumptions about books' being comprehensive, analytical, and thorough may not be valid. Today, publishers can produce a book on a sensational subject in a matter of weeks or months. Consider sources carefully; the most recent book may not be the best one.
- *Be aware of editions.* Normally, use the most recent version of a book with multiple editions because it incorporates changes based on responses to earlier editions, and it is up-to-date.
- *Older sources can provide perspective.* Use an old book or an early edition of a book to share an early perspective on a subject. Such insights are sometimes useful.
- *Interpretations and theories change.* All subject areas evolve, not just the sciences. Core information may not change, but opinions do. For example, the texts of Shakespeare's plays are the same today as they were twenty years ago, but scholars and critics have changed their views on several plays and

have reassessed many of Shakespeare's dramatic techniques. So be aware that all disciplines are changing, no matter how stable they appear to an outsider.

Jarah knew that some elements of her research—the information on the design and construction of the Lincoln Memorial—could come from sources of any period; for the most part, these basic facts are unaffected by time. However, she also knew that to discuss the uses—including the most recent uses—of the Lincoln Memorial for protests, she would need to use periodicals and electronic sources to establish currency.

COLLABORATION

Acknowledging that their paper was essentially a "background report" about a facet of developmental psychology, Elissa and Jeremy needed to provide an overview of the subject but did not need to emphasize very recent developments. Consequently, they could include a range of both old and new materials.

EXERCISE 3.3   *Currentness of Sources*

Write a brief paragraph discussing whether or not very current sources are required for your paper. Then write a second paragraph explaining how you might use an out-of-date source.

EXAMPLE

The topic of childcare benefits for people on welfare who want to work requires me to use very up-to-date information. I need current childcare costs in a typical city, to match with current amounts for welfare benefits. Any data more than two years old won't make the point I need. On the other hand, some of my background information can come from older sources, and the quotes I need can come from just about any time period.

I could use old welfare statistics—maybe from the 1970s or 1980s—side by side with current statistics to show how the problem has gotten worse. Old information would provide an excellent contrast.   ■ ■

3d   Consider the availability of your sources.

To avoid being caught off guard or being frustrated during subsequent stages of research, consider the availability of sources. Libraries have extensive collections of materials on a surprising number of subjects, but they may not have everything you want or need. Consider the likelihood of finding materials.

- *Your school's library.* Unless you are at one of the nation's major research institutions, your college or university library has its limitations. Library acquisitions frequently are determined by the strongest disciplines at a school: if the criminology program is outstanding, the library's collection in criminology is probably strong; if the anthropology program is small, the library's collection in anthropology is probably limited. Instructors and librarians can help you assess the library's holdings related to your topic. (See Chapters 4 and 5.)

- *Online sources.* Use the Internet to locate a great deal of information, much of it available in full-text form that you can download onto a work disk. (See Chapter 7.)

- *Your public library.* Most public libraries have a broad spectrum of sources, intended for general-interest reading and moderate research. The public library is a resource, but its value for academic research may be limited.

- *Interlibrary loan.* Through the college or university's interlibrary loan department, you have access to materials at other schools. Go online to review the catalogs at other institutions and request material. Also be aware that many public libraries now have interlibrary loan departments.

- *Checked-out materials.* Because students, faculty, community members, and people working through other libraries have access to your school library's materials, you may discover that sources have been checked out. When researching, be aware that sources may not always be available instantaneously; you may need contingency plans.

Jarah's chances of finding sufficient materials were good: the department of history at her university was large, so she could assume that the library's collection in that area would be equally large. She also knew that periodical databases with full-text features would give her access to a wide range of periodicals. Further, the Internet would allow her to extend her research far beyond her campus library, providing her with many, many options.

COLLABORATION

Elissa and Jeremy were somewhat concerned about the availability of sources on birth order. They knew that the library had books on the subject, but with two child psychology courses being offered that semester, courses for which papers were required, they feared that some of the books would be checked out. Consequently, they planned to check out and use books first, knowing that they could use noncirculating periodicals and Internet materials at any time.

Learning about Your Library

QUICK REFERENCE

Explore your library so that you know what resources are available and how to use them.

▶ Locate the "operational" areas where your preliminary research begins: the circulation area, the reference area, the catalog area, the interlibrary loan area, and the reserve area.

▶ Explore the collections of materials: the stacks, the current periodicals area, the government documents area, the microform area, the media area, the new-book area, the preshelving areas, the special collections area, and the special libraries.

▶ Locate "support" areas that can make your work in the library easier: computer clusters, photocopy areas, and group study rooms.

Some college and university libraries offer group tours as part of new-student orientation; many libraries, however, prefer to link orientation to the activities of research-based undergraduate courses such as freshman composition or introductory communication; still other libraries offer students self-paced tours of the facilities. Following the appropriate orientation pattern, explore your school's library and locate the primary research areas discussed below.

4a Locate the circulation area.

Usually near the main entrance, the circulation desk is the place where you check out and return books. Policies about the length of time you can keep books, procedures for requesting a "recall" on a book, and information about fines and replacement charges for overdue or lost books are usually posted at the circulation desk.

When libraries have special collections, interlibrary departments, or discipline-specific libraries, each such facility often has its own circulation desk.

4b   Explore the reference area.

The reference area, normally located on the main floor, provides a wealth of general source materials: dictionaries, almanacs, fact books, encyclopedias, indexes, guides, bibliographies, and yearbooks; additionally, such collections often include subject-specific reference books.

Located nearby, the reference desk is generally staffed by specially trained reference librarians who answer (or help find answers to) most of your research questions. Recognize them as resources in your search for materials.

Many libraries have begun to shift from print-based reference collections to electronic ones, so you can expect the physical space of the reference collection to diminish over the next few years, even if the collection itself (in electronic form) remains the same size or increases. Though an electronic reference collection does not offer the advantages of browsing, it enhances research by providing continually updated materials that can be accessed from any online computer, as well as from in-library computers. When you explore your library's print-based reference collection, ask about its electronic collection.

4c   Familiarize yourself with the catalog area.

Generally located on the main floor of the library—most often near the circulation desk or reference area—the catalog area provides access to informational records of library materials. Look for clusters of computer terminals that are specifically programmed to retrieve information about sources in the library's collection (print, audiovisual, and electronic). Chapter 5, "Learning to Use Online Catalogs and Periodical Databases," describes the use of cataloging systems (see pages 35–54).

4d   Explore the stacks.

The stacks, bookcases that store the library's collection of books and other bound materials (volumes of periodicals, proceedings from conferences, dissertations), are arranged according to the library's classification system (the Library of Congress or Dewey decimal systems are the most common). Since the stacks contain most print research materials, learn how they are arranged. Most libraries post an extensive array of floor plans and listings for your convenience.

4e   Familiarize yourself with the current periodicals area.

The current periodicals area is easy to find: look for display racks holding recent issues of popular magazines, journals, and newspapers, surrounded by reading chairs and tables. In addition to recent issues in the browsing area, however, current issues of research-focused periodicals are often arranged alphabetically on special display shelves.

The current periodicals area provides access to very recent materials. Because these materials usually have not yet been indexed, the success of research done in this area depends, to some extent, on resourcefulness, patience, and luck.

4f   Locate the government documents area.

Government documents often are separated from the general library collection. Even though they sometimes have their own cataloging system, government documents are usually included in the primary catalog as well. The government documents area is frequently staffed by specially trained reference librarians because the variety and complexity of government documents make many of these materials somewhat difficult to find and use; take advantage of the help that reference librarians can provide.

Recognizing the power of the Internet, an increasing number of government departments, agencies, and units are making their documents available online. As these electronic documents become more common, print collections of government documents will grow smaller. However, the advantage of working with a specially trained librarian will remain.

4g   Explore the microform area.

The microform area houses the library's collection of both microfilm materials (wide spools of film containing reduced-size photographic images of source materials) and microfiche materials (small, transparent cards with similarly reduced images). To make these materials usable, the area also includes microfilm and microfiche readers, projectors that enlarge the images and allow you to photocopy these materials.

Until recently, libraries made extensive use of microforms to maintain collections of special materials. Back issues of newspapers have been regularly kept in microforms because the poor-quality paper on which they are printed and their awkward size make binding them impractical. Some periodicals have typically been kept only in microform to conserve space in the library.

Currently, most libraries subscribe to online services that make many sources once maintained in microforms available electronically, but until *all* materials are accessible online, you may need to use the microforms area.

4h   Find the media area.

A collection of audiovisual sources is usually housed in an area identified by a title such as "Audiovisual Resources," "Media," "Multimedia," or "Nonprint Materials." This area includes films, filmstrips, records, audiotapes, videotapes, CD-ROMs, CDs, and DVDs.

4i   Browse in the new-book area.

In some libraries, new books are kept in a special area for several months before being added to the general collection. This area (if your library has one) contains the most up-to-date sources available, so remember to browse there to see what books have recently been added to the library's collection.

4j   Find the preshelving areas.

In each section of the library or on each floor, locate the preshelving areas, where books are placed temporarily before being returned to the primary collection. Preshelving works this way: a book is first checked in through the circulation department; then it is taken to the preshelving area nearest the book's classification in the stacks, where it is placed with other books (even in this temporary location, books are arranged according to classification). Then, at a later time, these preshelving books are returned to their permanent positions in the stacks. When a book has not been checked out but you cannot locate it in the stacks, always check preshelving.

4k   Locate the library's computer clusters.

In addition to the computers in the catalog area, locate additional computers in other parts of the library; in most libraries, additional terminals are located on each floor and in each special section, collection, and specialty library.

Computers that provide Internet access are often clustered together, frequently near the reference collection. These computers provide access to a wide range of electronic services. In addition, many libraries provide computer labs for students' word processing needs.

4l   Search out the special collections.

Many libraries have special collections of rare books, archival materials relating to local events or history, or books donated by or purchased by patrons or groups; these may serve your research needs.

Most libraries also have special collections of materials and equipment for the visually impaired: Braille editions of many materials, equipment to magnify texts, special reading areas with controlled lighting, books on tape, and other aids.

4m   Locate any special libraries.

When discipline-specific collections are large enough, they may be housed in specialized libraries. At large, research-focused universities, almost every major field of study has its own specialized library; at smaller institutions, however, only a few disciplines have special libraries.

When comprehensive libraries are subdivided into smaller libraries, their holdings are generally cross-listed in their catalogs. For instance, a computer in the education library would list materials from the primary collection and from the English library, just as a computer in the main library would list sources found in the sublibraries.

4n   Find the interlibrary loan department.

The interlibrary loan department is often located near the circulation desk or the reference area. In this area, librarians process requests to borrow materials from other libraries, and when the materials arrive, sign out interlibrary loan materials at their special checkout desk.

At many libraries, you can now e-mail your requests for materials from other libraries, but you still must pick up materials at the interlibrary loan department.

4o   Locate the reserve area.

Usually located near the circulation desk or the reference desk, the reserve area is a holding place for materials—books, articles, collections—that faculty members, committees, and other groups want to make available for limited checkout periods. For example, if an instructor wants every student in a class to read a single chapter in a particular book, he or she can place the book on reserve; students then check out the book for the specified amount of time (one hour, three hours, one day, or whatever the instructor indicates).

4p   Find the photocopy areas.

Most libraries now have photocopy centers, specific locations with varied photocopying equipment and functions: for example, making enlargements, reductions, and transparencies. If your library is large enough to have such a center, you may find machines that make change, machines that create and credit photocopy cards, and a variety of photocopy machines with different capabilities. Other photocopy machines (usually with fewer capabilities) generally are available at other locations throughout the library.

When a book or periodical has not been checked out but you cannot locate it in the stacks or preshelving areas, always check the photocopy areas. You may find it there.

4q   Locate the group study rooms.

Most libraries offer students small rooms for group study. These moderate-sized rooms frequently contain a conference table and chairs, so that members of a group can gather to confer about their work. These rooms are excellent locations for collaborative work: they are private, which allows you to discuss work openly without disrupting other patrons, yet they are near research materials. While these rooms are generally available on a walk-in basis, you can reserve them in advance at many libraries.

Libraries are multifaceted facilities, providing patrons with a remarkable range of services and materials. To make the best use of the library, become familiar with not only the source materials at your disposal but also the support services that members of the library staff provide.

▸ EXERCISE 4.1   *Library Orientation: Option A*

If an introduction to your school's library has been part of student orientation, or if you have had a library orientation as part of class activities, devise and answer a series of five questions relating to the library's facilities, policies, and services.

EXAMPLE

1. When periodicals are being bound, for how long are they unavailable? (For two to three weeks)
2. Is there a limit to how many books I can check out? (Twenty-five)
3. Why does my book bag sometimes set off the alarms when I try to leave the building? (The metal buckles sometimes set off the alarms.)
4. Is it possible to get interlibrary loan materials in less than the regular amount of time? (Yes, but only by reserving the source through interlibrary loan and then picking it up yourself)
5. Why do the computers lock up sometimes, and what should I do when that happens? (Overloads and miskeying information are the most common problems; seek help at the desk and avoid pounding randomly on the keyboard.)   ■ ■

EXERCISE 4.2   *Library Orientation: Option B*

If an introduction to the library was not part of student orientation, or if you do not have a library orientation as part of your class activities, go to the library on your own. Ask at the circulation desk or the reference desk whether the library offers guided tours or provides maps or self-paced tour booklets. If neither is available, create your own tour by searching for the areas described in this chapter.   ■ ■

Learning to Use Online Catalogs and Periodical Databases

To find the print sources that you need, take advantage of the features of your library's online catalog.

▶ Familiarize yourself with your library's online catalog (electronic search system); review the opening screen, explore optional search patterns (author, title, keyword), and review the help screens.

▶ Use keyword searches unless you want to search for a specific author's work or know the title of a source.

▶ Use Boolean search logic to combine key terms to create a targeted search.

▶ Review source records using the Long View, since it provides the most comprehensive information about potential sources.

▶ Print pages selectively, making hard copies of only the sources that seem well matched to your topic.

▶ When helpful, have copies of selected records e-mailed to your account to review at a later time.

▶ Familiarize yourself with your library's periodical databases for locating articles in magazines, journals, and newspapers; review the opening screen, experiment with limiting your searches by date and type of periodical, and review the help screens.

▶ Read abstracts of articles before deciding whether to review an entire article.

▶ Use the full-text and page-image features of your library's periodical databases to review articles whose abstracts suggest that their content matches your topic.

▶ Print articles selectively, making hard copies of only the most promising sources.

Online catalogs (also called electronic search systems) have replaced traditional card-based catalogs and now provide a wide range of search capabilities. To take full advantage of these features, you must learn to use them well. Some search techniques are easy to learn, while others are somewhat complicated. Nevertheless, learning to use an online catalog provides tremendous research dividends. It creates opportunities for sophisticated, targeted searches that help you find materials that fit your specific research needs.

5a   Remember what all online catalogs have in common.

The cataloging system at your school is unique because individual libraries modify basic systems to fit their collections and to meet the needs of their patrons. Consequently, the identifying information for each source may vary from library to library, or the display screens for your library's online catalog may look quite different from those of a nearby school. However, the cataloging system at your library, no matter what its format and visual design, can provide you with the information you need to locate materials in the library's collection.

Information about Sources

All online catalogs provide standard information about each source in the library's collection. Whether it appears in the Brief View (also known as the Short Record) or the Long View (also known as the Long Record), this information is available for each source, although not necessarily in this order:

Brief View (Standard Information about Each Source)

- *Author*. The full name of the author is included. When works have multiple authors, sometimes only the first author's name appears in the Brief View; however, the record can be retrieved by using an additional author's name. (In the Long View, all authors' names appear.)
- *Title*. The work's full title, including subtitles, is always included.
- *Facts of publication*. The city and state or country (place of publication), publisher, and copyright date are included.
- *Technical description*. A wide range of information may be included: the number of pages devoted to prefatory material, the source's total number of pages, the size, information about illustrations, and other specific features.
- *Location*. Information about the location of the source—"Main Library," "Science Library," "Reference Collection," "Special Collections," and other similar descriptions—allows you to find the source in your library.
- *Call number*. The classification number assigned to the source (most often

the Library of Congress classification number) helps you locate the source within the library's collection.

■ *Number of items.* When a source includes more than one item (2 volumes, 1 volume and CD-ROM, 2 filmstrips and 1 audiotape), that is indicated.

■ *Status.* The record indicates whether the source has been checked out, whether it is overdue, whether it is on reserve or on loan, and so on.

■ *Database information.* Records frequently indicate the database from which the record is retrieved.

Long View (Includes All Information from the Brief View, plus Additional Information about Each Source)

■ *Editions.* Editions (2nd, 4th; revised, enlarged) are noted.

■ *Notes.* Special features may be described—for example, the inclusion of a bibliography, an appendix, or specialized index—and the number of pages for each is frequently provided.

■ *Table of contents.* A listing of chapter or section titles provides a compact overview of the source's contents.

■ *Subject classification.* A listing of primary and secondary subject classifications from the Library of Congress system is included.

These comprehensive, technical descriptions familiarize you with a source before you search for it in the library's collection. (See pages 77–89 for a discussion of evaluating sources.)

Multiple "Access Points"

Online catalogs provide alternative ways to locate sources within a library's collection, saving you both time and energy.

■ *Author.* If you know an author's name but do not know any specific titles, retrieve records by completing an author search. Most online catalogs require you to present the author's name in last-name/first-name order (*Sagan, Carl,* not *Carl Sagan*) but do not require either capitalization or a separating comma (*sagan carl* often works). You can also search using last names only (for example, *Browning*), but the system then provides you with an alphabetical list of all authors with the same last name, from which you can choose the appropriate one (ranging, for example, from Al Browning to Elizabeth Barrett Browning to Robert Browning to William C. Browning).

■ *Title.* When you know the title of a book but not the author, retrieve records by typing in the source's title. Most online catalogs require you to omit articles (*a, an, the*) that begin titles (*Unheavenly City,* not *The Unheavenly City*) but do not require capitalization (*unheavenly city* works). Importantly, title searches require exact matches, so misspellings or slight variations in word order do not secure a record for a source.

■ *Subject.* Online catalogs allow you to access records by subject, but such searches are often complicated because they require the use of Library of

Congress subject headings, which may or may not match popular phrasing. For example, a search for "auto racing" leads through a series of stages, to the Library of Congress subject "auto rallies," while a search for "welfare reform" only leads to the general subject of "public welfare." Of course, you can then search "public welfare" for subclassifications by subject, but such a process is somewhat inefficient.

■ _Keyword._ The computing capabilities of online catalogs now allow you to search for a subject using key words and phrases, a powerful research strategy. Because keyword searching looks for the designated word or phrase anywhere in the database—titles, subtitles, subject classifications—it provides the most comprehensive way to locate materials on your subjects.

These four approaches provide alternative ways to locate sources in your library's collection. Explore all of the options. You will certainly discover, through practice, your favorite approach, but you should be familiar with all of the strategies.

5b   Learn to locate and interpret information on search screens.

Familiarize yourself with the screen features of your library's online catalog. Practice and experiment, reviewing the major options available on the system. Keep in mind that libraries often have handouts available near the computer terminals. These point-of-use handouts usually are prepared by library staff to be used without tutorial help and are presented as step-by-step instructions, with very specific "check your progress" reminders and suggestions.

The following on-screen options—illustrated with screens from Indiana State University's online catalog (LUIS)—are representative of what you will find.

Library Home Page

The opening screen—the library home page—provides access to the full range of features available from your library. Presented with the now-standard library photograph or logo, the page frequently includes an electronically linked list of the library's features, including features like these: "About Us" (descriptions of the library's goals, initiatives, history, and so on), "Special Services" (explanations of tutorials, workshops, and other services related to library use), "Quick Reference" (direct links to the most commonly used encyclopedias, directories, manuals, statistical sources, dictionaries, and fact books), "Subject Browser" (links to subject classifications like humanities, social sciences, science, and technology), "Other Libraries" (connections to libraries within a region, state, or consortium), "Search Tools" (links to the Internet search engines provided through the library), "Databases" (linked listings of all databases available through the library, often arranged alphabetically and by subject), "Online Catalog" (links to the online catalog that you use to retrieve records for sources in the library's collection), and "University Home Page" (necessary links to your school's major Web site).

Although your library's home page may include somewhat different information—more or fewer links with similar or different titles—take a few minutes to familiarize yourself with the opening screen because it provides access to the library's full range of features.

Author or Title Search Screen

On the author or title search screen (they may be combined; see Figure 5.1), you can begin your search for materials in the library's online catalog. Most screens provide a window—called a free-text field—in which you type either the author or title, but special drop-down screens help you to narrow your search. For instance, a "Search by" screen allows you to select among options like these: search by "title," "journal title," "author," "call number," "subject," or "keyboard boolean and relevance." Additionally, a "Quick Limit" screen provides options like these: "none" (which means you set no limits), "last ten years," "videorecordings," "schools" (if the catalog database in linked to other institutions), or "special libraries" (if your library has any). Further, a "Records" screen allows you to identify the number of records you would like displayed at one time: "10 records per page," "20 records per page," and so on.

Taking full advantage of the options available on an author or title screen improves your chances of retrieving the specific information you need in the most helpful format.

Keyword Search Screen

On the keyword screen (see Figure 5.2), you can begin your search for sources in the online catalog. In a window, you type a word or phrase, and drop-down screens allow you to restrict the search. For example, one screen option allows you to designate the way in which the search system interprets the word or phrase: a descriptor like "any of these" searches the database for records that use *any* words you include, together or in isolation, anywhere in the record; a descriptor like "all of these" searches for records in which all the words are included, though it does not distinguish either phrasing or word order; a descriptor like "as a phrase" searches for records that include the phrase in the exact form you present. Using these alternatives can produce widely varied results, so consider carefully what kind of search you want to initiate.

The phrase "Gulf of Tonkin Resolution" provides a workable sample. To enter this phrase with the "any of these" feature would produce unwieldy results because the system would search for all database records that include

FIGURE 5.1

Author/Title Screen

Help instructions

Standard search strategies

Free-text field

Standard limiters ("last ten years," "video-recordings," and so on)

Record selection (10, 20, 25, 50 records)

System identification

Online options

Category search

Specialized limiters

Library systems

FIGURE 5.2
<u>Keyword Search Screen</u>

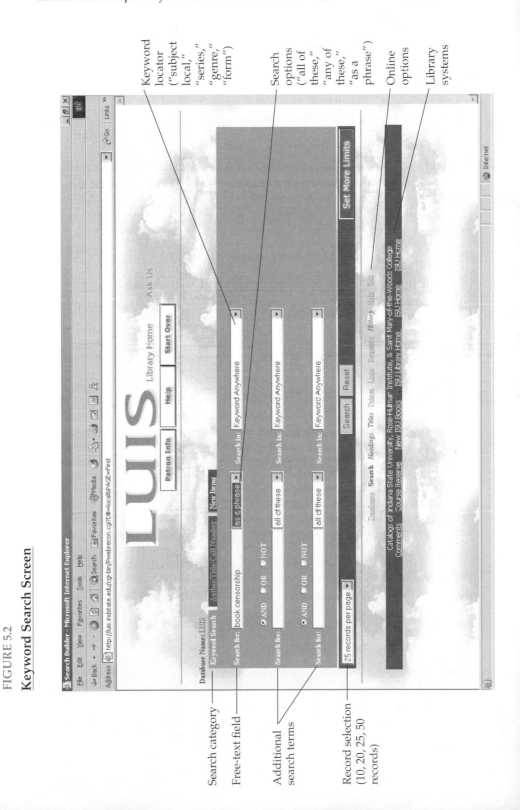

the word *gulf* or *tonkin* or *resolution,* either singly or in combination—producing a list of thousands of records. Entering the same phrase with the "all of these" feature would narrow the search considerably because the system would then search for records that included all three terms, though they could appear in separate portions of the records; consequently, the results could still include a very large number of sources. Using the same phrase with the "as a phrase" feature would produce the most helpful results because the system would search the database for records that include these three words together in the exact order you have given; the search results, then, would be narrow and selective.

Using other drop-down screens, further restrict searches by setting other useful, common limiters: "subject local," "series," "genre/form," and so on. Or you can set additional but less common limiters like these: "language," "location," "date," "medium" (map, CD-ROM, electronic file), "item type" (book, periodical, manuscript), "place of publication," or "publication status." Although these specialized limiters probably are not necessary for most of your searches, it is helpful to know that these possibilities exist.

Search Results Screen

After you type in your search term—author, title, or keyword—the online catalog retrieves appropriate records from the database. They appear in tabular form and are identified by item number, title, author, publication date, and library or collection (see Figure 5.3); many systems, even in this early listing, include the call number, the checkout status, and the location of the source within the library collection. If there are more records than fit on one screen, the system divides the list into groups of ten, twenty, or more, according to the guidelines you provided on the earlier screens. If you do not indicate preferences, the system uses a default number, usually ten or twenty records per screen.

Once again, you have the opportunity to manipulate the information you receive so that you can use it easily. For example, the online catalog can arrange your materials according to a variety of principles: alphabetical order by title, alphabetical order by author, chronological order by publication date, and reverse chronological order by publication date. Although all of these arrangements serve specific research purposes, the most helpful are alphabetical by author (in those instances when you recognize authors by name) and reverse chronological order (in those instances when you wish to use the most recent sources).

Most online catalogs now provide alternative ways to use their records even at this early stage. You can mark the records you want and either print them, save them on a disk, or e-mail them to your account.

FIGURE 5.3

Search Results Screen

FIGURE 5.4
Brief View of a Record

Keyword with keyword locator

One-line title

Facts of publication

Library

Circulation information

"Find It" link reveals location within library

Search type

Degree of information

Author

Full title

Technical information

Call number with link to books with similar call numbers

Link to book reviews of selected source

LUIS Record View 1 - Microsoft Internet Explorer

File Edit View Favorites Tools Help

Back

Address http://luis.indstate.edu/cgi-bin/Pwebrecon.cgi?v1=28&ti=1,2&CNT=500&Search_Arg=book+censorship&Search_Code=FT*&PID=2259978&SEQ=20040205113606&SID=1

LUIS Library Home Ask Us

New Search | <- to Titles | Patron Info | Search History | Help | Start Over

<- Previous   Next ->

Brief View   Long View   MARC View

Banned in the U.S.A. : a reference guide to book censorship in schools and...

Database Name: LUIS
Search Request: Keyword Relevance Search = book censorship
Search Results: Displaying 2 of 10000 entries

Relevance:
Database: LUIS
Main Author: Foerstel, Herbert N.
Title: Banned in the U.S.A. : a reference guide to book censorship in schools and public libraries / Herbert N. Foerstel.
Published: Westport, Conn. : Greenwood Press, 1994
Description: xxii, 231 p. ; 25 cm.
ISBN: 0313285179 (alk. paper)
Location: ISU Main Library
Call Number: Z 658 .U5 F64 1994
Status: Not Charged
Find It   Z 658 .U5 F64 1994
Reviews   0313285179 (alk. paper)

<- Previous   Next ->

Done   Internet

Brief View of a Record

Once you select a record, a screen appears that provides basic information about the source (see Figure 5.4). This condensed record, called the Brief View or Short Record, provides a helpful range of information: author, title, facts of publication, technical description, location, call number, number of items, checkout status, and the database (see pages 36–37 for a detailed explanation).

Many online catalogs use the call number to provide a helpful electronic link from the Brief View (indicated by underlining or use of a second color). By clicking on the call number, you can get a sequential listing of sources that share the same beginning call numbers (those that identify the primary subject). By using this feature, you can secure an easily scanned list of the materials that would be shelved along with your initial source.

Most online catalogs now provide alternative ways to use these records: you can print them, save them on a disk, or e-mail them to your account.

Long View of a Record

If a source seems promising after you scan the Brief View of a record, click to the Long View to get comprehensive information on the source (see Figure 5.5). The Long View includes all of the information included in the Brief View, as well as this additional information: editions, notes, table of contents, and subject classification (see page 37 for a detailed explanation).

Many online catalogs provide additional electronic links from the Long View (you can also click on the call number from this screen). By clicking on the author's name, for example, you can secure a list of other materials in the library's collection that he or she has written. Since an author's interest in a subject usually extends beyond one work, this link allows you to scan other titles quickly to see whether any serves your research needs. By clicking the subject listing, you can retrieve the Library of Congress subjects that are most closely related to the one identified in a source's Long View. Because Library of Congress terminology is sometimes unusual, this gives you the chance to search pregrouped subject headings that you might not have considered otherwise.

Finally, from the Long View, you can print records, save them on a disk, or e-mail them to your account.

Because online catalogs vary widely, not all of the features described in this handbook may be available to you. However, these options are now fairly common on most online catalogs, where they provide an impressive range of researching possibilities.

FIGURE 5.5

Long View of a Record

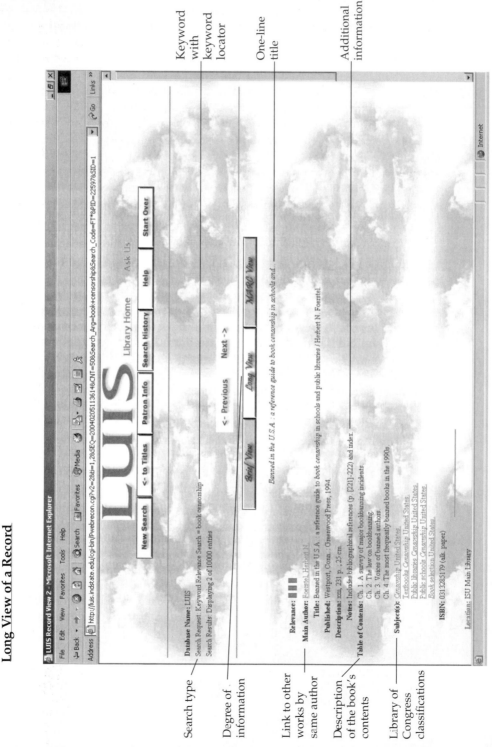

Search type

Degree of information

Link to other works by same author

Description of the book's contents

Library of Congress classifications

Keyword with keyword locator

One-line title

Additional information

Printed Records

At most libraries, computer terminals are linked to nearby printers so that you can print information from search screens (and, of course, you can print them from your personal computer if you access the library's online catalog from your residence). However, rather than indiscriminately printing every screen or record that seems related to your search, review the Long View of the record. If the source is appropriate for your research, print the record. If it is not, save yourself from having sheaves of extra and useless printed records—and save printing costs.

► **EXERCISE 5.1**   *Interpreting Search Results: Online Catalog*

Using a keyword term or phrase related to your research topic, complete a search using your library's online catalog. Once you have your search results, select a source. Print out both the Brief View and the Long View of the source and label the elements of the displayed record.   ■■

5c   Consider the benefits of online periodical databases.

Today's online periodical databases provide access to articles in magazines, journals, and newspapers. Comprehensive periodical databases— such as EBSCOhost, FirstSearch, JSTOR, Lexis-Nexis, ProQuest, and others—make available sources in many general-interest magazines, selected professional journals, and assorted national newspapers. Additional, more specific databases—ERIC (Educational Resource Information Center), MEDLINE, MLA (Modern Language Association), PsycARTI-CLES, ScienceDirect, SPORTDiscus, and others—provide access to articles within disciplinary specialties. Whether comprehensive or specialized, however, these online databases have notable advantages over the print-based indexes that researchers once used:

- *Currentness.* New information is added regularly to these databases— daily, weekly, monthly—so that the information is always up-to-date.
- *Multiple use.* Records exist in electronic form, so many people can access them simultaneously.
- *Convenience.* Because they are available online, database searches can be conducted at any time.
- *Search capabilities.* New systems for indexing periodicals match the capabilities for online library catalogs; of particular importance is the ability to conduct keyword searches.
- *Text versions.* Many databases now provide articles in alternative forms, from simple citations to full-text typed versions of articles to full-page images of original sources.

5d Consider what all comprehensive periodical databases have in common.

Your library undoubtedly subscribes to one or several major periodical databases and probably subscribes to a number of subject-specific databases. Although each one has a slightly different design, format, and features, these databases provide you with access to sources in magazines, journals, and newspapers.

Information about Articles

All periodical databases provide standard information about current articles in a wide range of sources, although not necessarily in this order:

- _Article title._ The article's full title, including subtitles, generally is included first because some periodical articles have no attributed authors.
- _Author._ If there is an attributed author, his or her full name is included.
- _Magazine, journal, or newspaper title._ The periodical's full title is included.
- _City._ To provide extra clarity, the city of publication is included.
- _Date of publication._ The publication date is presented in alternative forms, depending on the periodical: (1) month, day, and year; (2) month and year; or (3) season and year.
- _Volume and issue numbers._ Both volume and issue numbers are provided for magazines and journals; they are not always provided for newspapers.
- _Start page._ The page on which the article begins in the original source is always included.
- _Number of pages._ If the article extends to a second or subsequent page, the total number of pages is included.

These comprehensive, technical descriptions of articles provide basic information to help you decide whether you want to examine one or more articles closely.

Access to Articles

Periodical databases provide access to sources through keyword searching by subject ("tax cuts," "nutrition," "investment banking," "art auctions," "energy conservation," "health care," "photography"). In rare instances when you wish to locate the work of a selected author, you can still enter his or her name as a keyword search, presented in normal order.

5e Learn to locate and interpret information on search screens.

Familiarize yourself with the features of your library's periodical databases. Explore their features on your own, but keep in mind that most libraries provide instructional handouts or post directions near computer terminals.

The following on-screen options from the ProQuest database are representative of what you will find.

Start Page/Keyword Search Screen

Because a comprehensive periodical database merges the information provided in widely varied, discipline-specific indexes and databases, it often opens with a start page that displays the options you have (see Figure 5.6). Among your choices are databases that index popular magazines, professional journals, a balanced selection of national newspapers, and articles by broad subjects (education, science, humanities, and so on). Brief descriptions accompany the name of each index or database, but links lead you to more thorough descriptions and many times allow you to see full lists of the periodicals that are indexed.

Most comprehensive periodical databases allow you to select among the databases so that your search results best suit your purposes. For example, if you need a newspaper article, you could proceed with your search using only that portion of the database; similarly, you could search only journals that are peer reviewed; or, of course, you could run a search using all databases available. The choice is yours.

A keyword search in a periodical database works just like a keyword search in an online catalog: you type in a selected word or phrase, and the system then searches for records that match. On-screen features with links help you improve the quality of your search. For example, you may select a date range for the sources you want; ProQuest, for instance, provides nine options: "All dates" (everything in the database), "Last 7 days," "Last 30 days," "Last 3 months," "Last 12 months," "On this date" (you supply the date), "Before this date," "After this date," and "Specific date range" (you supply starting and stopping dates). Because currentness is one of the strengths of periodical sources, this feature provides maximum benefits. In addition, usually you can select among types of publications to search. Many periodical databases provide simple yet helpful options like "All publication types," "Scholarly journals," "Magazines," "Trade publications," "Newspapers," and "Reference/Reports"; other systems provide narrower classifications by type. Further, many databases allow you to select where you want the keyword to appear: "Citations and Abstracts" (the keyword would then appear in *only* those areas) or "Article Text" (the keyword would appear in the text of the article, which would

FIGURE 5.6

Start Page/Keyword Search Screen: Periodical Database (ProQuest)

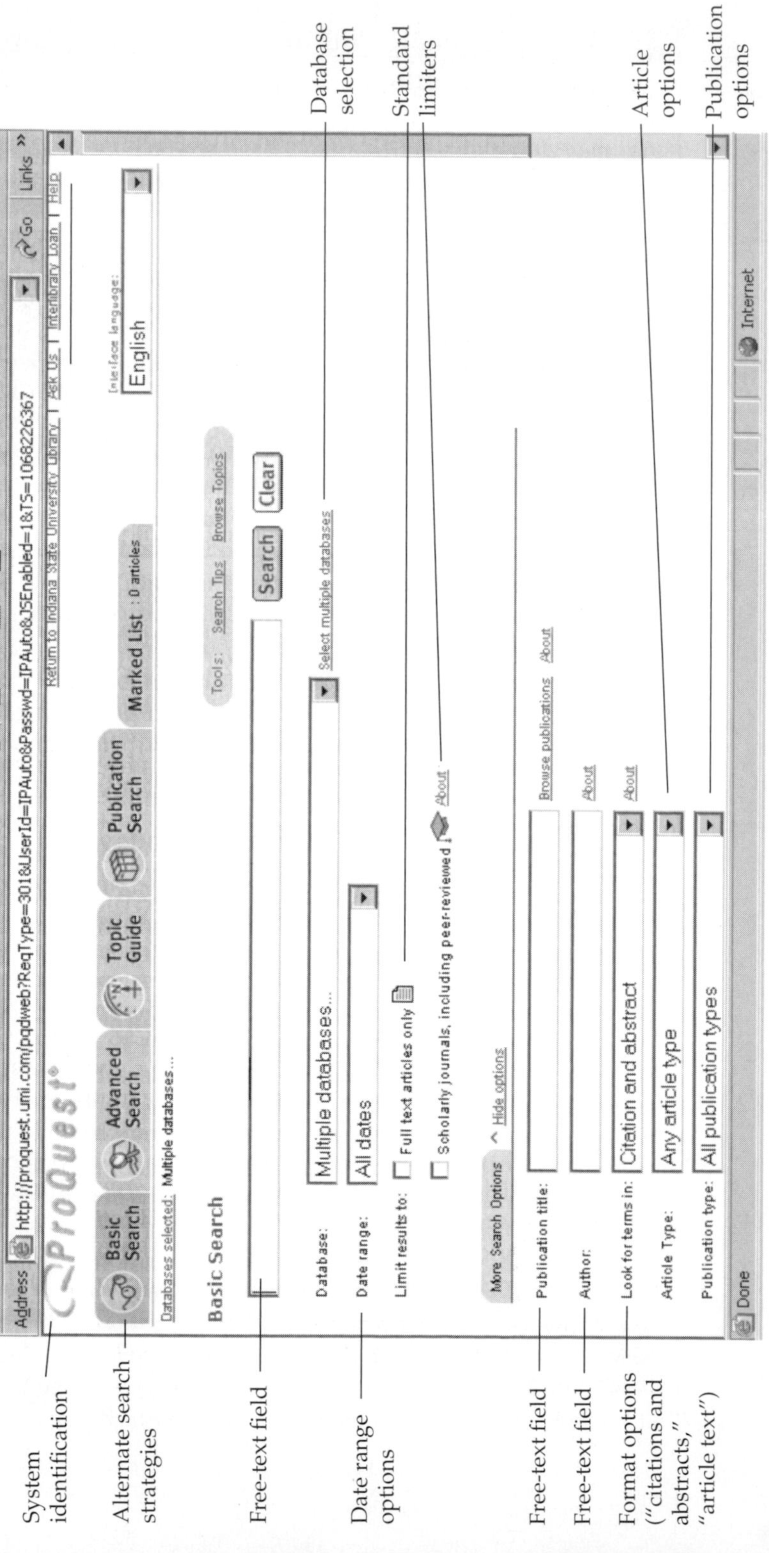

Image published with permission of ProQuest Information and Learning Company. Further reproduction is prohibited without permission.

include its title). You can also restrict searches by format (only full-text articles) or publication pattern (only peer-reviewed articles).

To enhance their search capabilities, most databases also provide links to specific help pages, offer optional search strategies, and list on-screen suggestions for using the system.

Results Screen

After you type the search term, the database retrieves appropriate records. They appear in tabular form, in reverse chronological order (with the most recent sources listed first), and are identified by item number (see Figure 5.7). This preliminary record for each source includes key information: article title, author (if there is one), the periodical title, the city of publication, the publication date, volume and issue numbers, and page information; in short, the record provides most citation information. If there are more records than fit on one screen, the system divides the list into groups of approximately ten records.

When alternative versions of the articles are available, databases also identify which formats are available for each source. Generally using icons (visual symbols), databases indicate whether articles are available in "Citation/Abstract" form, "Full-Text" (a citation, abstract, and typed version of the article), "Text plus Graphics" (a citation, abstract, and typed version of the article, along with illustrations, graphs, charts, and other visual elements), or "Page Image" (a scanned reproduction of the article as it originally appeared in the periodical).

Article Screen

Once you select a record in the format you want, an appropriate screen appears (see Figure 5.8). The simplest screen—Citation/Abstract—includes all of the technical information on the article, plus an abstract, a brief summary of the major ideas of the piece. The Full-Text screen includes the same information, followed by the typed text of the article. The Page Image screen provides scanned images of pages from the original source.

Once you find an article that fits your research needs, you can either print it directly from the screen or e-mail it to your account to use later. Because printing from screens is relatively slow, e-mailing records is sometimes preferable. However, Page Image documents must be printed from screens.

Because periodical databases vary, not all of the features described in this handbook may be available to you. However, these options are now common in most databases, where they provide efficient ways to search for articles in periodicals.

FIGURE 5.7

Search Results

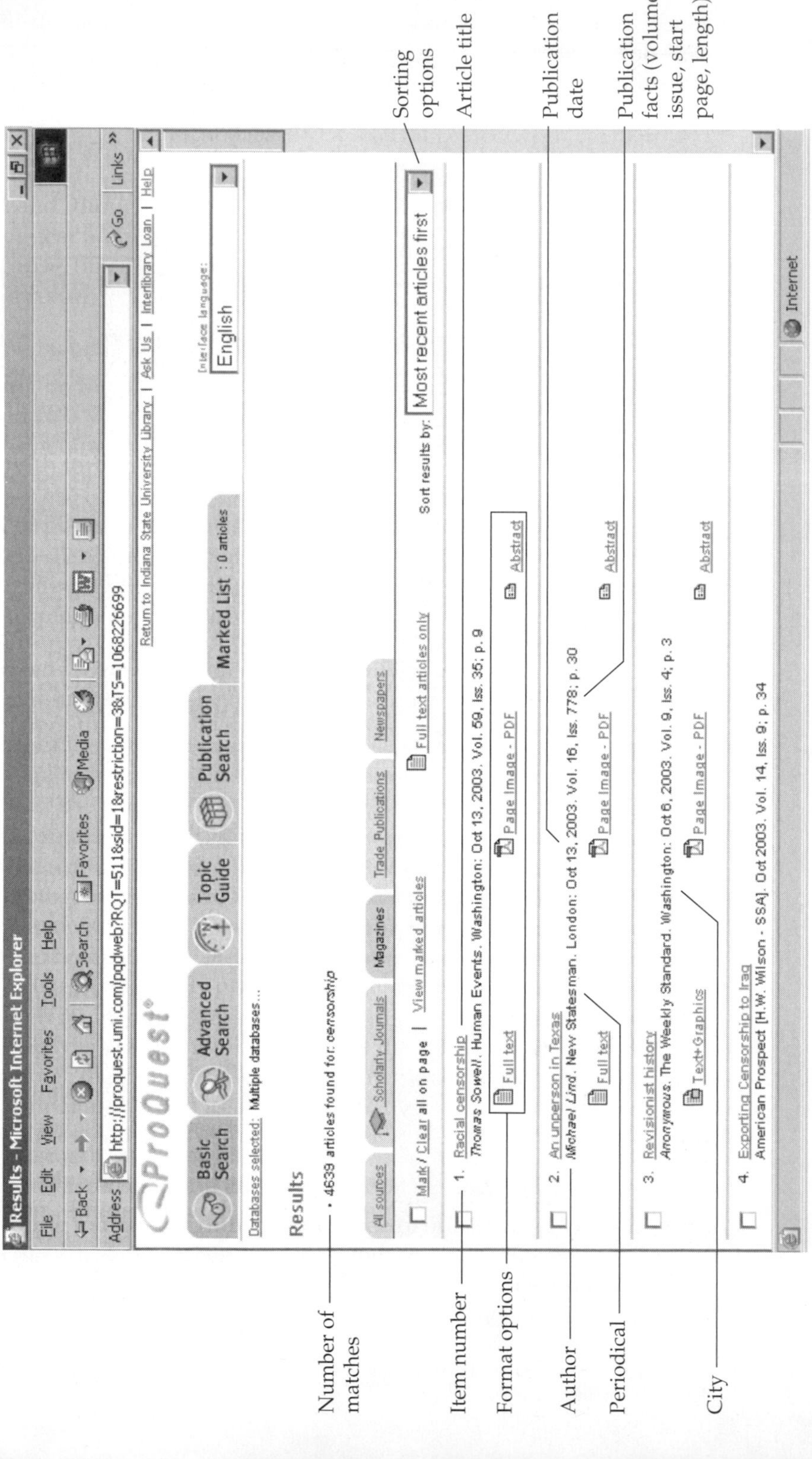

Number of matches

Item number

Format options

Author

Periodical

City

Sorting options

Article title

Publication date

Publication facts (volume, issue, start page, length)

Image published with permission of ProQuest Information and Learning Company. Further reproduction is prohibited without permission.

FIGURE 5.8

Article Screen

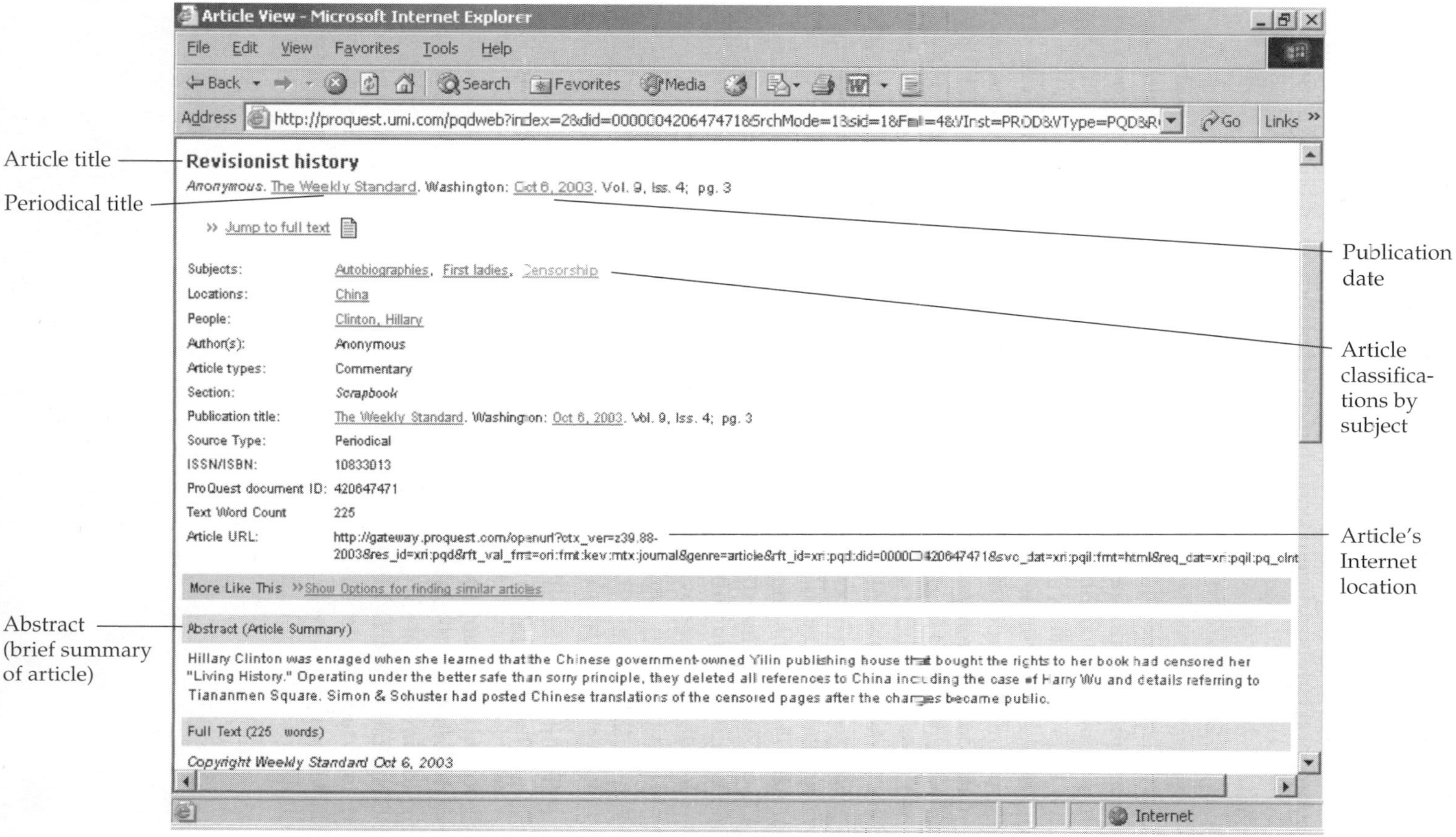

Labels (with leader lines pointing to the screen):

- Article title
- Periodical title
- Publication date
- Article classifications by subject
- Article's Internet location
- Abstract (brief summary of article)

Screen content:

Article View - Microsoft Internet Explorer

File Edit View Favorites Tools Help

Back Search Favorites Media

Address http://proquest.umi.com/pqdweb?index=23&did=000000420647471&SrchMode=1&sid=18&Fmt=4&VInst=PROD3&VType=PQD3&... Go Links »

Revisionist history

Anonymous. The Weekly Standard. Washington: Oct 6, 2003. Vol. 9, Iss. 4; pg. 3

» Jump to full text

Subjects:	Autobiographies, First ladies, Censorship
Locations:	China
People:	Clinton, Hillary
Author(s):	Anonymous
Article types:	Commentary
Section:	Scrapbook
Publication title:	The Weekly Standard. Washington: Oct 6, 2003. Vol. 9, Iss. 4; pg. 3
Source Type:	Periodical
ISSN/ISBN:	10833013
ProQuest document ID:	420647471
Text Word Count	225
Article URL:	http://gateway.proquest.com/openurl?ctx_ver=z39.88-2003&res_id=xri:pqd&rft_val_fmt=ori:fmt:kev:mtx:journal&genre=article&rft_id=xri:pqd:did=000000420647471&svc_dat=xri:pqil:fmt=html&req_dat=xri:pqil:pq_clnt

More Like This »» Show Options for finding similar articles

Abstract (Article Summary)

Hillary Clinton was enraged when she learned that the Chinese government-owned Yilin publishing house that bought the rights to her book had censored her "Living History." Operating under the better safe than sorry principle, they deleted all references to China including the case of Harry Wu and details referring to Tiananmen Square. Simon & Schuster had posted Chinese translations of the censored pages after the changes became public.

Full Text (225 words)

Copyright Weekly Standard Oct 6, 2003

Internet

▶ EXERCISE 5.2   *Interpreting Search Results: Periodical Database*

Using a keyword term or phrase related to your research paper, complete a search using one of your library's periodical databases. Once you have your search results, select a source. Print both the Citation/Abstract record and the Full-Text record and label the elements.   ■ ■

6

Conducting Field Research and Using Audiovisual Sources

QUICK REFERENCE

Take advantage of the sources of information that exist outside your library by conducting varied kinds of field research and by using audiovisual sources.

► Use sources—interviews, discussions, and news stories—from television and radio.

► Contact local experts on your subject to gather information; remember that people have different kinds of expertise.

► Remember that informed nonspecialists may provide useful information and commentary.

► If you conduct an interview, prepare thoroughly and conduct the interview in a professional manner.

► If you create and administer a questionnaire or survey, design it carefully, conduct it fairly, and tabulate the results systematically.

► Consider a full range of audiovisual sources to broaden your research: film, television, recordings, visual art, and performances.

Although most research makes use of library or online sources, the people in the community around you can provide unique kinds of information and insights. It is worthwhile to discover who and what they are and to recognize their value.

6a   Consider experts from radio and television.

When experts give interviews on radio and television programs—on news broadcasts, for example, or on interview shows or talk shows—the programs provide a context for discussions. You can take advantage of these recent broadcasts to discover current thinking on a subject.

Locating copies of the broadcasts may be a challenge, however. Transcripts or tapes of local programs are readily available; call the station or network to acquire a transcript, audiotape, or videotape. Locating transcripts of national broadcasts (for instance, an interview on national radio or on cable) has become relatively easy: simply go to the Web site of the broadcast station or network (electronic addresses are usually the call letters and the abbreviation *.com,* as in <http://www.nbc.com>). Once you've reached the home page, look for links to the program you want— *Washington Week, Meet the Press, Firing Line,* and so on—to locate the appropriate transcript.

6b   Consider local experts.

Your community includes knowledgeable people who may be willing to provide additional information and insights on your topic. As specialists in their disciplines, members of college faculty make good interview subjects because they are comfortable explaining concepts and responding to questions. In the wider community, consider interviewing not only people with scholarly training but also people with practical experience. (See **6d** for a full discussion of planning and conducting an interview.)

EXERCISE 6.1   *Experts on Your Topic*

List at least five "experts" whom you might interview. Include brief descriptions of their areas of expertise and then describe what they might know about the topic. These people and their comments will supplement, not replace, other sources. In groups of three or four students, discuss your choices and brainstorm for other possibilities.

EXAMPLE
Subject: Gun Control
1. Gerald Jenkinson, Sheriff of Madison County: Jenkinson is aware of county patterns for crimes using guns.
2. Jake's Gun and Ammo—the owner or a salesperson: Gun store workers support a pro-gun position and have practical experience with guns.
3. National Rifle Association—local chapter president: An NRA officer could talk about gun advocacy programs.
4. Emergency Room supervisor at the local hospital: An ER supervisor could address the medical issues that result from the misuse of guns.

5. Dr. Carrol Bennett, principal of East Central High School: A principal is aware of safety issues in public facilities where guns are not allowed.
6. Dr. Edward Lee, professor of criminology: A criminology professor could discuss theories of criminal behavior involving guns.   ■ ■

6c Consider responses from informed nonspecialists.

People who are affected by but not directly involved in the study of your research topic can provide useful information, insights, and reactions, illustrating the "common view" of people in general. The most effective way to gather people's reactions to a topic involves the use of questionnaires and surveys. (See section **6e** for a full discussion of planning questionnaires and surveys.)

▶
▼ EXERCISE 6.2   *Questionnaire or Survey Groups*

List at least five questionnaire or survey groups you could use to gather responses to questions on your topic. Put asterisks (**) next to those groups that would probably be the easiest to query and briefly describe the kinds of topics you might address with them.

EXAMPLE
Subject: Gun Control
1. Students in three Criminology 120 classes ** (I would ask Crim. students about principles of law enforcement, especially concerning gun-related crimes.)
2. Students at the union
3. Students in my English class
4. Students living in my residence hall ** (I would ask residents questions about personal safety and rules for multistudent housing.)
5. People at the local mall   ■ ■

6d Prepare thoroughly for interviews.

An interview is an excellent way to gather information and to get reactions to ideas. Prepare for an interview by selecting a suitable interviewee, by strengthening your knowledge of the topic, and by planning the interview itself. Consider these guidelines as you prepare:

■ *Save the interview until late in the research process.* To ensure that you are knowledgeable enough about your topic to conduct an effective interview, delay it until you have done a substantial amount of reading.
■ *Select a knowledgeable person to interview.* Consider professionals who have studied the subject, as well as people whose experience has made them informed nonspecialists.

- *Arrange the interview in advance.* Call or write the interviewee a week to ten days in advance to arrange a mutually convenient time for the interview.
- *Agree to a place and a time limit for the interview.* Meet the interviewee at his or her place of business or home, but be flexible. If meeting for a personal interview is not possible, arrange for a telephone or an e-mail interview. Generally, a twenty- to thirty-minute interview is sufficient if you are well prepared.
- *Do background reading to prepare for the interview.* To develop intelligent, thought-provoking questions, first research your topic well. You need not understand all aspects of it, but you must understand it well enough to ask pertinent questions.
- *Plan primarily interpretive questions.* Although you can ask specific, factual questions during an interview ("How many patients do you see a day?"), interpretive and evaluative questions ("What issues of health-care reform trouble you most?") elicit the most interesting and useful responses.
- *Prepare a written set of questions.* Develop a set of questions and arrange them in a logical order. Leave space to write between questions. Using note cards for questions—one question per card—is also a good method.
- *Be flexible.* Even though you have arranged questions in a logical order, follow the interviewee's lead and add related questions or change the order of questions as the interview takes place. Being well prepared, yet flexible, helps you get the best information possible.
- *Take careful notes.* Record information and ideas quickly but carefully as your interviewee responds to questions. Double-check any detailed information for accuracy before leaving. If the interviewee does not object, consider taping his or her comments, but also take written notes.

Since it provides an expert's personal perspectives, clarification of ideas and issues, and responses to ideas and information, an interview is an especially helpful way to supplement traditional research.

Jarah thought that an interview would be a promising way to gather additional information about and reactions to her ideas on the Lincoln Memorial, but she had some difficulty deciding whom to interview. She considered interviewing Mr. McFarlan, one of her high school history teachers, because of his special interest in Washington, DC. She thought perhaps she would interview one of the American history professors on her campus. She even considered trying to arrange an e-mail interview with someone from the National Park Service—providing she could use the Lincoln Memorial Web site's links to identify someone both knowledgeable and willing to respond. She wrote some possible questions but decided to postpone her prospective interview until later in her research, when she would be well informed and when she had unanswered questions.

▶ EXERCISE 6.3 *A Person to Interview*

Select a person to interview as part of your research process. Then write a brief paragraph (25 to 50 words) describing the person's qualifications to discuss the topic. Consider his or her education, work experience, personal experience, special interests, and reputation within the community.

EXAMPLE
Subject: Gun Control

John "Jake" Andrews, owner of Jake's Gun and Ammo, is an excellent source because he provides an on-the-street perspective. He's worked at JG&A for thirty-five years, having taken over the business from his father; he's sold guns to many people; he obviously believes in the "right to bear arms" and represents the pro-gun position.   ■■

▶ EXERCISE 6.4 *Questions for an Interview*

Compose five or more questions prompted by your preliminary reading. These questions should encourage your interviewee to share his or her thoughts, not merely provide "yes" or "no" responses.

EXAMPLE
Subject: Gun Control

1. As the owner of a gun shop, you must have some ideas about the role guns play in our society. Could you explain your ideas?
2. How effective have the "wait periods" been in preventing or controlling crimes involving the use of guns?
3. As the owner of a gun shop, what is your reaction to the Brady Bill?
4. Why has the NRA been so successful in blocking legislation to control the sale of guns?
5. Have you ever had misgivings about selling a gun to someone? Why or why not?   ■■

6e Plan questionnaires and surveys carefully.

Both questionnaires and surveys solicit responses to questions about selected subjects; however, they differ because questionnaires require participants to write down responses on printed forms, whereas surveys ask for oral responses. Collated responses to either questionnaires or surveys indicate the percentages of people who responded in certain ways. (The opinion polls so frequently mentioned on the news are usually telephone surveys.)

When planning a questionnaire or survey, consider these guidelines:

■ *Ask a small number of questions.* Limit the number of questions. Asking ten to twenty questions generally provides an acceptable number of responses.

- *Ask for demographic information only if it is likely to be helpful.* Unless demographic questions have a bearing on your results, limit the number of questions about age, sex, race, income, and education. Many people find such questions intrusive.

- *Match questions to your research needs.* When useful, ask questions with "yes" or "no" responses (Should Union Board funds be used to finance a student literary journal?). At other times, solicit responses with a small range of alternative choices (Psychological counseling should be available to students at no cost: Always, Frequently, Sometimes, Never). At still other times, provide a broad range of responses.

It is acceptable to display Christmas decorations in government offices.

1	2	3	4	5	6	7	8	9	10

Strongly   Strongly
Agree   Disagree

- *Keep your language clear.* Phrase your questions clearly so people can complete the questionnaire or survey quickly.

- *Establish a logical order.* Since there is no give-and-take in a questionnaire or survey (which differentiates one from an interview), arrange questions in a coherent order.

- *Select a consistent response pattern.* If responses are first listed "yes," then "no," maintain the order throughout. If a response sequence is "Always," "Frequently," "Sometimes," and "Never," maintain the order with each question.

- *Administer the questionnaire or survey yourself.* Administer the questionnaire or survey yourself to ensure that the explanations and procedures are always the same—an important element of questionnaire and survey methodology.

- *Expect limited participation.* Unless you have connections with a class, an organization, a student group, or some other gathering of people, expect only a small number of people to complete the questionnaire or survey.

- *Tabulate the results carefully.* Use a blank copy of the questionnaire or survey to record the number of people who gave each response. Make a clear notation on the original form to indicate that the information has been tallied in order to avoid confusion later on.

- *Interpret your results.* Expect one of several patterns when evaluating the results of questionnaires and surveys. If results differ from what you expected (or from what research suggested would be normal), use the results to demonstrate that, at least locally, the responses to the topic are not predictable. If the results are similar to what you expected (on the basis of research or personal experience), use them as verification of patterns that exist elsewhere. If you find surprises and perhaps even conflicting responses, use them to assert the varied reactions to the topic.

Questionnaires and surveys are unique and potentially useful forms of field research. Based on local responses to specific topics, they create a unique perspective that supplements traditional research.

Jarah was not completely convinced that a questionnaire or survey would match her research needs. She could certainly ask people how they felt about the Lincoln Memorial, whether they had visited the site, or whether they had noticed that the Memorial was often the backdrop for protests. However, since she could not predict whether people had visited the site, seen it in the news, or held reasonably strong opinions on the subject, she might get inconsequential or even unhelpful results. However, with a narrow survey group—history teachers, for example—she could get excellent results. Consequently, Jarah did not dismiss a questionnaire from her research plan.

EXERCISE 6.5 *Questions for a Questionnaire or Survey*

Having done some preliminary reading, compose five or more questions for a questionnaire or survey. These questions should be directed to your response group and should allow them to clarify their views easily. Include demographic questions only if necessary. Arrange the questions in an effective order, establishing a logical sequence for the questions.

EXAMPLE

1. _____ Male _____ Female
2. Do you own a gun? _____ Yes _____ No
3. Do members of your immediate family own guns? _____ Yes _____ No
4. Have you ever fired a gun? _____ Yes _____ No

Circle the numeral that most clearly indicates your response to each statement:
1 = Strongly Agree, 2 = Agree, 3 = No opinion, 4 = Disagree,
5 = Strongly Disagree.

5. All guns should be registered with the local police.
1 2 3 4 5
6. Classes in gun safety should be required for gun owners.
1 2 3 4 5
7. Gun users should be licensed, in the same way drivers are.
1 2 3 4 5

6f Consider audiovisual sources.

Audiovisual sources—film, television, music, art, performances—provide unique perspectives when they are part of research. Consider these potential uses of audiovisual materials:

- *Films.* Use films to illustrate the issues presented in your research. *To Kill a Mockingbird* illustrates racial inequity in a way that statistics cannot.
- *Television programs.* Use television programs to expand research, perhaps demonstrating how popular culture has embraced your topic. *M*A*S*H* both reflected and perpetuated America's cynical view of war, while at the same time honoring those in the military.
- *Recordings.* Use song lyrics to include artistic treatments of your topic. Eminem's "Without Me" is an aggressively upbeat commentary about his place in the rap and pop communities.
- *Visual art.* Use visual art—paintings, drawings, and photographs—to create impact within your research. Picasso's *Guernica,* with its horrific images of destruction, creates a strong emotional message that could reinforce a paper on the Spanish Civil War or any other war.
- *Performances.* Although it is unlikely that all readers would have seen or heard the same live performance, including information from or reactions to a performance can offer a unique perspective.

By providing popular or aesthetic perspectives, audiovisual sources suggest fresh ways in which to think about research topics. In doing so, these sources usefully expand the parameters of research.

Jarah was excited by the audiovisual options that were available to her and only had to consider which ones could be most effectively incorporated in her paper. Films provided a rich source, since the Lincoln Memorial has been used as a setting in many commercial films: *No Way Out, A Few Good Men, Forrest Gump, Dave, JFK,* and *The American President.* In addition, television programs—most available on videotape and DVD—have recorded some of the famous Lincoln Memorial events Jarah wanted to discuss, particularly Martin Luther King Jr.'s "I Have a Dream" speech. Even television programs like *West Wing* provide passing views of Washington's most familiar monuments and memorials. Visual art provided Jarah with another wealth of possibilities, from drawings and paintings and models of the Memorial to thousands of photographs in which the Memorial appears. She could even include the familiar image from the back of a five-dollar bill. With so many options to choose from, Jarah was sure that she would include audiovisual materials in her final paper. She simply had to decide which kind and how many to include.

▶ EXERCISE 6.6   *Audiovisual Sources*

List at least three audiovisual sources that could be used as part of your research paper. Following each item, identify why or how the source could be used.

EXAMPLE

Subject: Gun Control

1. *Boyz N the Hood* (film): The drive-by shootings show why gun control is needed.
2. *Pulp Fiction* (film): The holdup scene in the restaurant shows innocent people being terrorized by gun-toting lunatics.
3. Aerosmith's "Janie's Got a Gun" (recording): The song illustrates how pervasive violence with guns is.

Using the Internet and Other Electronic Sources

Take full advantage of the Internet, discussion groups, and CD-ROMs to broaden your research.

▶ Explore a variety of search engines and choose the one that best matches your researching preferences.

▶ Familiarize yourself with search engines, using a general-interest topic to practice gathering information.

▶ Learn to interpret search results to select the best Web sites.

▶ Consider the alternative kinds of Internet sources available to you.

▶ Use the links between Web sites to broaden your search.

▶ Print information selectively, making copies of only the sources that are well matched to your topic.

▶ Use e-mail to gather information from discussion groups.

▶ Use CD-ROMs when they prove helpful.

▶ Print copies of Internet materials because the specific content of Web sites changes regularly.

The Internet and other electronic sources have altered dramatically the ways in which researchers work. No longer restricted to materials available locally, researchers can now access a remarkable range of materials in electronic form. Although the possibilities that exist because of these new and easily updatable forms are wonderful, they also can be somewhat daunting, especially when you consider that, according to recent estimates, 800 million documents now exist on the Internet.

As a researcher, however, you need to learn to secure the broadest range of electronic sources and learn to use them critically. Such a challenging task takes both time and effort, but it is worth the effort because it increases the scope of your research dramatically.

7a   Explore a variety of Internet search engines.

The Internet is a complex, high-speed network of computers that allows users to send and collect electronic information. Using computer software called browsers (for example, Netscape or Microsoft Internet Explorer), individual computers connect with the electronic network through search engines, Internet programs that locate individual sites using keyword searching techniques.

Most search engines provide the same basic features:

- *Keyword searching.* All systems allow you to enter words or phrases—your search terms—in a window called a free-text field and then display a list of Internet sites that correspond in some way to the keywords.
- *Linked directories.* On their opening pages, most systems provide directories of general-interest topics that you can explore.
- *High-interest links.* Most systems also provide links to high-interest, often commercial topics.
- *Help.* Most systems provide links to instructions, often giving not only basic operating instructions but also suggestions to improve your searches.

Beyond these basic features, however, individual search engines provide unique features and capabilities. Therefore, you should explore several alternative search engines to see which one provides the capabilities you require, in the format that best meets your needs. Consider these representative search engines:

AltaVista <http://www.altavista.com/dir/default>

In addition to keyword searching, *AltaVista* provides a sixteen-topic, high-interest directory (ranging from the Arts to Health to Science), as well as links to Web sites related to news and shopping, popular Web sites, and multimedia. Further, *AltaVista* allows you to customize searches by language.

C/NET <http://www.search.com/>

In addition to keyword searching, *C/NET* provides a twenty-three-topic, general-interest directory (ranging from Business and Money to Government), as well as links to the most popular Internet searches.

Excite <http://www.excite.com/>

In addition to keyword searching, _Excite_ provides an eighteen-topic, high-interest directory (ranging from Careers to Lifestyle), as well as links to news-related Web sites (national, technology, sports).

Galaxy <http://www.galaxy.com/>

In addition to keyword searching, _Galaxy_ provides a sixteen-topic, general-interest directory (ranging from Business and Commerce to Medicine), as well as a thirteen-topic, high-interest directory (ranging from Career to Health). Further, _Galaxy_ allows you to customize your search by choosing among alternative subdirectories.

Google <http://www.google.com/>

In addition to keyword searching, _Google_ provides a sixteen-topic, high-interest directory (ranging from Business to Computers to Recreation). (See Figure 7.1.)

Lycos <http://www.lycos.com/>

In addition to keyword searching, _Lycos_ provides an eighteen-topic, high-interest directory (ranging from Autos to Travel), as well as a nine-topic, general-interest directory (ranging from College to Society and Beliefs) and links to news-related Web sites.

WebCrawler <http://webcrawler.com/>

In addition to keyword searching, _WebCrawler_ provides a sixteen-topic, high-interest directory (ranging from Autos to Travel), as well as links to news-related Web sites.

Yahoo! <http://www.yahoo.com/>

In addition to keyword searching, this personally focused site provides a thirty-six topic, high-interest directory (ranging from Autos to Maps to Horoscopes).

Because of their varying options and formats, not all search engines work well for all searches. Therefore, explore and compare at least several of them before choosing the one (or ones) best suited to your needs. Remember, as well, that even your preferred search engine may not always provide the best search results on a specific topic, so consider the advantages of using multiple search engines for Internet research.

FIGURE 7.1

Google: Opening Page

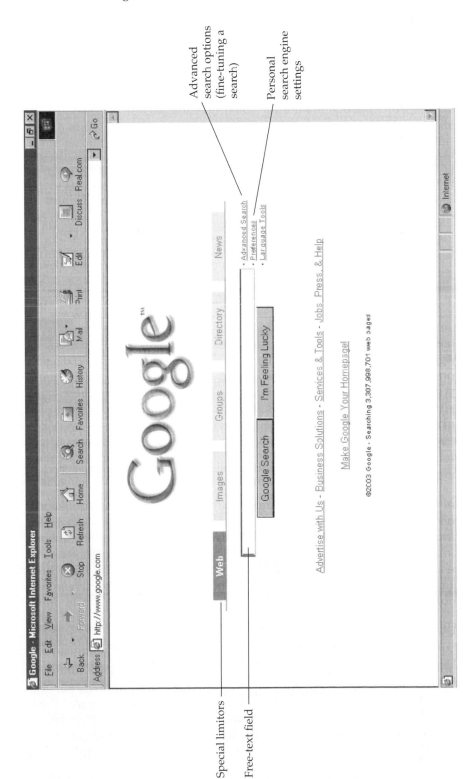

▶
▼ EXERCISE 7.1   _Becoming Familiar with Search Engines_

Connect to the opening page of at least three search engines to examine their features and formats. Examine all parts of the page: note the page layout, review the directories of topics, explore the help options, and notice any special features. Then select the search engine that seems best matched to your needs and write a brief paragraph explaining the reasons for your preference.   ■ ■

7b   Learn to interpret Internet search results.

Once you select the search engine that best suits your needs, begin your search process. Experiment with the system using a high-interest topic with which you are relatively familiar. Such an experimental search allows you to become familiar with the process without the added pressure involved with formal research.

Begin at the opening page of the search engine, type in a keyword term (a word or phrase), click the search button, and wait for your results. Once the system displays the list of records, examine them to see what they contain. (See Figure 7.2.) The display lists and records in most systems contain basic information and features like these:

■ _Web results._ Many search engines identify how many records have been retrieved using your keyword search. The numbers are often shockingly large—frequently in the thousands—since Web sites may be included multiple times because of the recurrent use of the keyword in their electronic records.

■ _Web site names._ Most search engines provide the names of the Web sites in which related materials can be found; if the sponsoring group, corporation, or individual is not evident from the Web site name, some search engines provide that information as well. If the title of the specific source is underlined, it provides the link to the Web site.

■ _Electronic addresses._ The electronic address—the Universal Resource Locator (URL)—is frequently provided; when the record applies to an item featured within the Web site, the URL may indicate the general site or the specific item. Because the link to the Web site is most often provided through the source's title, the URL is usually for informative purposes only. Infrequently, however, the URL provides the link to the Web site.

■ _Brief descriptions._ Many systems provide very brief—one- or two-sentence—descriptions of the source identified in the record.

In addition, different search engines provide specialized information or options. _Excite_ and _Google,_ for example, list search results hierarchically, with the most popular Web sites listed first. _C/NET_ provides Search Partners, selected Web sites that highlight features of the keyword. _WebCrawler_ identifies news stories related to the keyword. _Galaxy_ includes subject-

FIGURE 7.2

MetaCrawler: Keyword Search

Free-text field

Electronic address

Web site summary or description

List of search engines utilized

Search links to related subject headings

Web site name with link

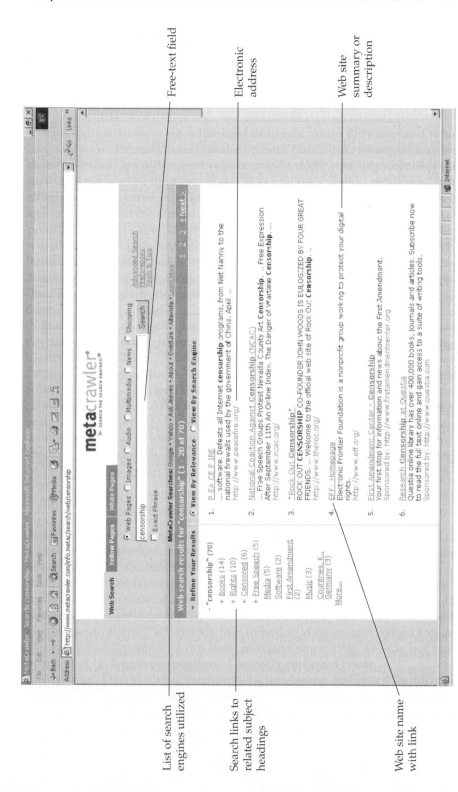

related links for further searching. *AltaVista* identifies additional terms to broaden the search. Because this information can make you a more informed researcher, use these features to enhance your search techniques.

▶ EXERCISE 7.2   *Interpreting Search Results*

Using three different search engines, enter a keyword and conduct a search. Print the initial pages of each of the three searches and label the elements: Web results, Web site name, URL, description of the source, and special information or options.   ■ ■

7c   Consider the kinds of Internet sources available.

Because any person, group, organization, institution, or corporation can post information on the Internet, not all of the material is of equal quality. Nonetheless, you have access to a broad range of potentially useful sources.

Scholarly Projects

Through universities and other educational institutions, scholarly projects of enormous scope and size flourish on the Internet. Whether they are efforts to share hundreds of full-text books online, to make available satellite photography of the earth, or to chronicle art through the centuries, these scholarly projects provide important scholarly materials for researchers everywhere.

Information Databases

To make available the vast statistical resources of governmental departments and agencies, research institutions, and corporations, these databases provide a wealth of technical information—whether it is census information from 2002, data on grain exports, or the operating budget of the Smithsonian Institution.

Web Sites

Whether designed to share information, forward a political agenda, promote a product, advocate a position, or share ideas, Web sites have proliferated. They may be developed by individuals or groups, may function independently or be affiliated, may be simple or complex, or may be silly or sophisticated. Nonetheless, they provide a rich resource for researchers, particularly when you consider the range of Web sites that exist:

- *Professional Web sites* <.org>. Most professional organizations have Web sites where they share membership information, as well as articles, documents, position statements, reports, advertisements, and other professional materials.
- *Corporate Web sites* <.com>. Almost all commercial entities—businesses, affiliated groups, and corporations—have Web sites where they report policies, practices, and profits, as well as share information and sell products.
- *Government Web sites* <.gov>. All government departments, agencies, and institutions have Web sites where they post mission statements, goals, data, policies, and initiatives.
- *Educational Web sites* <.edu>. Most schools and educational support groups have Web sites where they provide information about their policies, resources, programs, faculty, facilities, standards, and initiatives. Further, academic Web sites on almost any topic imaginable are created by individuals affiliated with educational institutions.
- *Military Web sites* <.mil>. All branches of the military have Web sites where they post enlistment procedures, operational information, reports, policies, and initiatives.
- *Museum Web sites* <.museum>. Many museums have Web sites where they post operating schedules, as well as describe collections, exhibits, seminars, fund raising, and community services.

Add to these the Web sites developed by nonaffiliated individuals and groups, as well as those developed in other countries, and you get a sense of just how many Web site resources are available.

7d   Learn how to find information on home pages.

When your Internet search process leads you to the home page of a scholarly project, information database, or Web site (see Figure 7.3), explore the site thoroughly, looking for these features:

- *Electronic address (URL)*. Scan the URL for basic information, particularly the domain (the portion of the address that indicates the kind of site, noted in an abbreviation): *.edu, .gov, .org, .mil, .com, .museum*. The domain suggests the focus of the individual or the group that developed the Web site. (See section **8d**, "Evaluate Internet sources," for more discussion of domains.)
- *Official title*. Look for an official title for the Web site, including subtitles; it usually is presented in large display type and, through its wording, suggests the focus of the Web site.
- *Author, host, editor, or Web master*. Search for the name of the person or people responsible for developing or maintaining the Web site. In those cases in which an individual has developed the entire Web site, his or her name will be clearly displayed. When the Web site has been developed by a variety of

FIGURE 7.3

National Gallery of Art Home Page

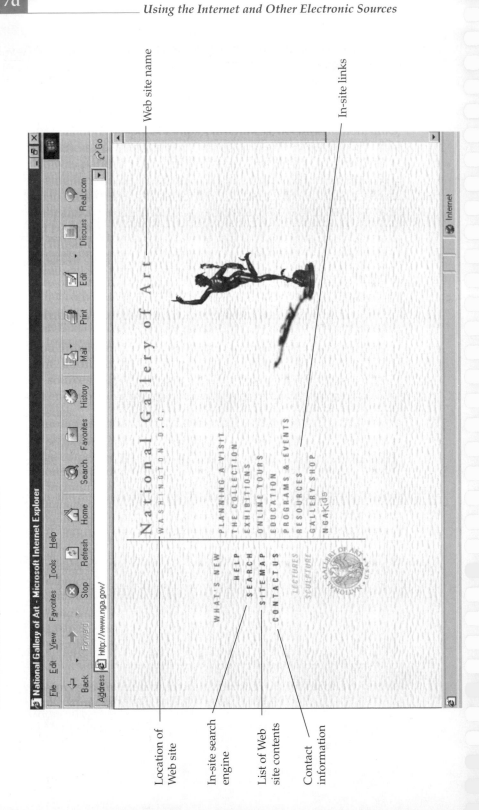

Location of
Web site

In-site search
engine

List of Web
site contents

Contact
information

Web site name

In-site links

people, one individual usually maintains the site; he or she is referred to as editor, host, or Web master.

- *Affiliation or sponsorship.* Locate any references to affiliation or sponsorship. Many times this information appears in an obvious position, for example with the Web site title; at other times, this information is located in the "small type." You may have to be resourceful to find it.

- *Location.* Identify the place where the Web site originates. When cities are listed, this is easy. When institutions—schools, organizations, corporations—are listed alone, you may have to gather this information from a reference source.

- *Posting date or date of last update.* Find the date on the Web site. Many Web sites provide a statement of when the site was first posted and when it was last updated. In those instances when this is not done, explore the Web site for dates of any kind: a copyright date may be the only date you can find.

- *About this site.* It is sometimes helpful to read the brief material that explains the site's development. You may discover useful information about authors, editors, or hosts and their backgrounds and sometimes their affiliations.

- *Site directory.* When a Web site directory is provided, use it. Functioning like a table of contents, it provides an overview of the Web site's features.

Web sites vary dramatically in the ways they are designed and presented, which makes them interesting to work with. However, because you need to cite information from them, learning how to find important identifying information saves you time in later stages of your work.

EXERCISE 7.3   *Finding Information in a Web Site*

Complete two Internet searches that lead you to two Web sites. Print the home page of each site and any related informational pages ("About This Site," "Site Directory," and so on). Then label the primary features: URL, official title, author (host, editor, or Web master), affiliation (or sponsorship), location, posting date (or date of last update), and other special links. If information is missing from a Web site's home page, provide an explanatory note.   ■■

7e   Use Web sites judiciously.

It is easy to use Web sites quickly—sometimes too easy. Therefore, avoid a hasty and random print-and-move-on approach to Internet research, opting instead for a thorough and careful approach. In particular, consider two important options:

Using Internal Links

Many Web sites provide links to related Web sites. Sometimes they appear within documents as hyperlinks (direct connections); sometimes they appear in bibliographic entries that are themselves links; sometimes they appear in lists of resources. Wherever you find these links to other sources, consider using them, for they provide additional resources that have been recommended either explicitly or implicitly.

Printing Materials

Before printing a document from the Internet, scan it to make sure that it truly fits your research needs. Does it provide the level of detail that you need? Does the source provide balance among your entire range of sources? Does it provide any useful comments from informed specialists? Does it include useful graphic materials, like maps, charts, tables, or illustrations? Does it contain information or ideas that you have not found elsewhere? Does it include current data or interpretations? If it does not add to your research in some significant way, it wastes both time and paper to print copies of the pages. Yet if it is promising, then printing copies is worthwhile. If you print copies for later use, be sure to record the URL carefully, perhaps at the top of the first printed page; you will need this information to prepare citations for your works-cited list.

7f   Consider discussion (or interest) groups.

Linked through Listservs (software programs that manage e-mail exchanges among groups of people), discussion groups allow people with similar interests to communicate. To join a discussion group, use an Internet directory like *Delphi Forums* <http://www.delphiforums.com/> to find an interest group related to your topic or complete an Internet search using "discussion groups" as your search term to locate the ones you want to join.

After reaching the discussion group and adding your electronic address to its distribution list, expect to receive *all* mail sent by all members of the discussion group. Because discussion groups allow for unrestricted discussion, expect the contributions to be of uneven quality: some are likely to be thoughtful and well-reasoned comments, while others may be less helpful. As a result, be selective in using information.

When exploring a discussion group, be prepared for these patterns:

■ *Discussions are in progress.* Because long-term subscribers to interest groups have been discussing subjects for a while (sometimes for years), you join them in "mid-conversation." Do not feel overwhelmed by discussions you cannot understand, at least initially; instead, search for the FAQ (Frequently Asked Questions) files that answer commonly asked questions.

■ *Expect a flood of messages.* Since most groups draw members from across the country—indeed, from around the world—and since you will receive every message directed to the group, expect a large number of messages, sometimes hundreds a day.

■ *Discussion groups have unique communication styles.* Because discussion group "conversations" are "faceless," they sometimes seem abrupt, slightly combative—or, infrequently, hostile. Be aware of the communication style, but concentrate on gathering valuable information.

Discussion groups allow people with similar interests, no matter where they are, to share ideas and information. Take advantage of the technology to broaden your research.

7g Consider CD-ROM sources.

CD-ROM (compact disc, read only memory) sources provide digitally formatted information. Most libraries no longer use CD-ROM technology to provide primary access to indexes, bibliographies, abstracts, encyclopedias, or statistical collections because the Internet delivers such materials more conveniently. However, many libraries continue to maintain sizeable CD-ROM collections.

If you locate a CD-ROM source using your library's online catalog (a notation about form will appear in the Long View), consider using it—particularly if it provides interactive material. Otherwise, you may be better served by Internet sources.

7h Be aware of special concerns about using electronic sources.

Electronic sources provide a wide range of materials for your research. Yet the benefits are offset by some complications—which can, nonetheless, be addressed by careful planning.

Changes in Sources

Because electronic sources are modified more easily than print materials, they change frequently. Internet sites, for example, may be updated or changed from one day to the next. If your research occurs over a short period of time—such as one semester, as is typical for most research projects—this may be less important than research for long-term projects that extend over several semesters. Knowing that electronic source materials change, however, will keep you from being caught unaware.

Source Verification

Once they have received research papers, many instructors verify sources. With traditional print materials, this is a straightforward process: instructors locate books and periodicals to confirm information and to double-check the accuracy of citations. Such procedures yield uneven results with electronic sources. The appropriate use of CD-ROM sources, for example, is easy to confirm. However, Web sites and other kinds of electronic sources change, and instructors may be unable to locate the information you have used.

The difficulty in verifying some kinds of electronic sources should not, of course, prohibit taking advantage of this ever-expanding source of information. However, in the early stages of research using electronic sources, discuss with your instructor how he or she wants to address this matter; often, turning in printouts of electronic materials will suffice.

Printing Copies of Materials

To ensure that you have the material for your later stages of work, always print copies of electronic materials. Also, remember to record full citation information.

Electronic sources are a promising addition to the traditional sources available to researchers. Although it takes time to learn how to gain access to these sources and use them to their fullest potential, the time is well spent.

Evaluating Sources and Writing a Research Proposal

QUICK REFERENCE

To ensure that the sources for your paper are suitable, evaluate them critically; then prepare a research proposal to describe briefly the direction you plan to take with the paper.

▶ Evaluate books by the author, the focus, the coverage, the publisher, and the date of publication.

▶ Evaluate periodicals by the credibility of the publication, the author, the focus, the coverage, and the date of publication.

▶ Evaluate audiovisual sources to ensure that they add interesting and varied perspectives in your paper.

▶ Evaluate Internet and other electronic sources by the credentials of the author, the sponsoring group or affiliation, the nature of the Web site (business, governmental, professional, and so on), and the date of electronic publication.

▶ Evaluate your combination of sources to ensure a balanced treatment of your topic.

▶ Clarify your plans for the research paper by preparing a research proposal; describe the context for your research, explain your specific focus, and provide a list of potential sources.

Because not all sources are equally useful, you should analyze sources and select the best ones. This is an ongoing process, with continued assessments and reassessments.

8a   Compile a preliminary list of sources.

Compile a list of potentially useful sources, basing it on online catalog, periodical database, and Internet searches, as well as on exploration in audiovisual areas. As you move to the library stacks to locate books, to the shelves to locate periodicals, and to special collections to gather other materials, select only those sources that show promise. Avoid hauling ten books home from the library, if only three may be useful; resist printing or photocopying sixteen articles when only eleven may be helpful; avoid printing documents from twelve Web sites if only eight seem promising.

8b   Evaluate print sources.

Assess each print source, using the guidelines noted below:

- _Author's credentials._ Determine whether an author's credentials show him or her to be an authority on a subject or to have a special perspective on it. An author's academic degrees (M.D., Ph.D., M.B.A., R.N.) suggest having specialized education in the field, while affiliations (with a university or organization) help establish authority. Search for other works the author has published. Read the entry about the author in a discipline-specific _Who's Who._

- _Appropriate focus._ Determine whether the source addresses the topic in a helpful way. Examine the subtitle to see whether it suggests a particular and useful point of view that is matched to your emphasis. A book titled _Latin American Civilization: Colonial Period_ may be too general, while another, _The Colonial Heritage of Latin America: Essays on Economic Dependence in Perspective,_ may be suitably specific. Because an author usually states his or her goals, emphases, and interpretations in a preface, introduction, or first chapter, skim these sections to get an idea of the author's approach.

- _Sufficient coverage._ Determine whether the source covers the topic sufficiently. In a book, examine the table of contents. If the book's focus seems somewhat removed from yours, review the index; look under appropriate topic headings (remember to think of alternative headings) to see how many entries appear and how many pages are noted. Skim a portion of the text to see how material is presented.

- _Reputable publisher._ University, academic, educational, or trade presses publish most of the books you will use, and this generally ensures appropriate, effective materials. In addition, publishers often specialize in certain kinds of books, so learn to recognize the important publishers in your field. For example, Grove Press publishes many important modern plays, while Van Nostrand Reinhold publishes many books in the sciences.

- _Publication date._ For many topics, sources older than five or ten years have limited value. However, consider establishing a historical context by using old sources. For example, articles from the 1950s reported physicians' recommendation that patients smoke to control their weight and to ease tension; such outdated information could be useful in describing society's changing perception of tobacco use.

■ *Respected periodicals.* Examine the masthead and the list of staff of magazines: a large staff suggests a comprehensive operation and multiple points of view, both good features. Generally, use specialized periodicals: *Sport*, a general-interest magazine, covers tennis, but not as thoroughly as *Tennis* does. Examine the masthead, the list of editorial staff, and the organizational affiliations of journals—the more prestigious the organization, the more prestigious the journal; look for national or international affiliations. However, smaller, less important journals also serve research needs. Read the entry for a periodical in *Magazines for Libraries.* Choose newspapers on the basis of your focus: for topics of international or national importance, use major publications such as the *New York Times*, the *Washington Post*, or the *London Times;* for issues of regional or local importance, use regional or local newspapers.

■ *Useful supplementary materials.* Examine special sections of books, including in-text illustrations, tables, charts, graphs, or diagrams; bibliographies; and sections containing special supporting materials, such as case studies or collections of additional readings. In a journal, check for related materials within the same issue. Sometimes entire issues are organized in whole or in part around a theme, in which case several articles from the same issue may relate to your topic.

■ *Appropriate writing style.* Skim a potential source to see how it is written. Is it developed with examples and facts or narration and description? Does the author explain and support claims, document facts, and present a balanced discussion? Is the style varied, lively, and interesting? Does the author use technical and other vocabulary that you understand?

8c   Evaluate audiovisual sources.

Because of the range of audiovisual sources, you need to assess each kind individually. However, many of the techniques for evaluating audiovisual sources correspond to those of print and Internet sources.

■ *Lectures and speeches.* Use criteria similar to those for print sources: speaker, relationship to your topic, coverage, sponsoring group or organization, and date.

■ *Works of art, photographs, cartoons, recordings, performances, and exhibits.* Because these sources are used primarily to create special interest in most researched papers, consider how well the image, exhibit, recording, or performance illuminates the topic. Does it provide a cultural parallel? Does it offer a popular perspective? Is the image reproducible in the paper, or can your description of a performance enhance the paper?

- _Maps, graphs, tables, and charts._ Consider these visual sources as you would traditional print sources. Consider authorship (that is, who created these materials?), presentation of information, sponsoring group or location of the material, and date.

- _Film, television, and radio._ When these sources are used creatively—a commercial-release film, a situation comedy, or a radio talk show—evaluate them in the same way you would art and other creative audiovisual forms. When these sources serve informative purposes—documentary films, news specials, radio interviews—evaluate them as you would print sources.

- _An interview, questionnaire, or survey._ Treat these in the same way you would treat print sources, establishing the credibility of the respondents, the thoroughness of the questioning techniques, the date, and the quality of the responses.

8d Evaluate Internet sources.

Because of the number of Web sites available, the Internet poses special problems when you assess sources. In addition, the standards often associated with the evaluation of print sources do not always apply to Internet sources, since virtually anyone can post a Web site.

To ensure that your Internet sources are worthwhile, assess them using the following criteria. Also review the sample evaluation of Web sites related to the topic "censorship" (pages 82–88).

- _Author, editor, host, or Web master's credentials._ A Web site may or may not have an author, editor, host, or Web master. If it does, explore the site for information about his or her credentials or qualifications to discuss the topic. In many instances, descriptions of academic experience (suggested by degrees or current positions) or work experience (suggested by job or work title, past or present) indicate his or her theoretical or practical knowledge of the topic.

- _Appropriate focus._ Skim the Web site to see whether it focuses suitably on your topic. Sometimes the Web site title makes the focus clear. For example, three Web sites titled _Banned Books and Censorship, Internet Censorship,_ and _Myths, Misrepresentations, and Misconceptions: Censorship in Comics_ approach the general subject of censorship in three distinct ways; therefore it is easy to decide which one best approaches the issues important to your research. However, at other times, an entire Web site has a general focus, but its internal links allow you to locate material on a narrower aspect of the larger subject. Consequently, you may have to explore the subsections of a Web site before you can decide whether it has the focus you need.

- _Sufficient coverage._ Review documents in the Web site to see whether the coverage is thorough enough for your purposes. Although not every site must provide substantive coverage, some should. How long are the in-site documents? How many documents (subsites) are included? How thoroughly is the information presented? How specific is the information? How balanced is the material? Answers to questions like these can help you discover the depth of coverage that a site provides.

■ *Domains.* Examine the Web site's electronic address (URL) to see how the site is registered with the Internet Corporation for Assigned Names and Numbers (ICANN); a Web site's "top level domain" provides useful clues about its focus and function:

.*aero*   Indicates an air-transportation industry site. Representing national and international business interests, these sites focus on forwarding the agendas of multinational transportation conglomerates.

.*biz*   Indicates a site with a business affiliation. Like sites identified with its corollary, .*com,* a business site's primary function is to make a profit.

.*com*   Indicates a commercial site. Although materials found on commercial sites can be extremely helpful, keep in mind that the primary function of commercial groups is to make money. What you find on a commercial site is part of a sales-driven organization, so you should use it critically.

.*coop*   Indicates a site for a nonprofit cooperative. Since cooperatives are groups of smaller organizations that band together for mutual benefit, you need to consider the nature of the benefits to decide how to use the information these sites provide.

.*edu*   Indicates a site affiliated with an educational institution. Although this implies a reasonable level of sophistication and trustworthiness, you need to consider that affiliated individuals can construct private pages.

.*gov*   Indicates a government site. These sites present consistently trustworthy information (statistics, facts, reports, and so on). They are less useful in interpretive matters, since there is often a sense of self-justification in government rationales.

.*info*   Indicates an unrestricted site. Without a unifying principle or goal, these sites are difficult to assess except on an individual basis.

.*mil*   Indicates a military site. The technical information on these sites is consistently useful, but interpretive material frequently justifies—as you would expect—a single, pro-military position.

.*museum*   Indicates a site for a museum. Since museums can be nonprofit institutions affiliated with nations, states, counties, cities, and schools or for-profit institutions affiliated with organizations and businesses, you need to consider the purpose each museum serves to decide how to interpret the information that you find.

.*name*   Indicates a name-registry site. It is unlikely that you will use these sites in your academic research.

.*net*   Indicates an independent, unaffiliated site. Use the materials on these sites only after considering them carefully. The possibility of finding useful information is balanced by the possibility of finding questionable material.

.org   Indicates an organizational site. Since the nature of organizations is to advance political, social, financial, educational, and other specific agendas, you need to review these materials with care.

.pro   Indicates a professional site. Since these sites are used to establish registries among professional groups, it is unlikely that you will use them.

Don't automatically discount or overvalue what you find on any particular kind of Web site. Rather, consider, when appropriate, the biases that influence the ways in which the information in a site is presented and interpreted.

- *Affiliation or sponsorship.* Examine the site to see whether it has an affiliation or a sponsorship beyond what is suggested by the site's domain. Sometimes sites have multiple affiliations and sponsorships—for example, with an organization (National Council of Teachers of English) and a government agency (the Department of Education). In such cases, the focuses of the individual sponsors generally are subsumed by the broader, shared goals of the sponsorship partners.

- *Posting or revision date.* Consider the date of original posting or the date on which information was updated. Since currentness is one of the benefits of Internet sources, look for sites that provide recent information.

- *Documentation.* Review Internet materials to see how thoroughly authors have documented their information. From what sources does the information come? How current is that information? Is it appropriately and clearly acknowledged? How much of the information comes from secondary sources (other people's material) and how much comes from primary sources (the writer's own work)? If facts, statistics, and other technical information are not documented appropriately, it suggests shoddy work, at best, and dishonest work, at worst.

- *Links to or from other sites.* Consider the "referral quality" that Internet links provide. If a Web site is linked to a wide range of other sites, that suggests that it has been found consistently valuable to a wide range of people. Conversely, if a Web site provides a wide range of links to other sites, that suggests that the author or editor is broadly informed about other useful sources, which is always a good sign.

- *Appropriate writing style.* Skim the Web site to see how it is written. Is the style varied, lively, and interesting? Does the writer use a traditional, fluent prose style, or does he or she use a disjointed, journalistic style that is increasingly popular in Web sites? All sources do not have to be written in the same style, of course, but it is an issue worth considering when you evaluate a source.

Sample Evaluation: Web Sites Related to "Censorship"

Devon, a student preparing a paper for a communications class, began his Internet research by conducting an *MSN.com* search using the term "censorship," which yielded a total of sixty-eight matches. These eleven sites were displayed on the first search screen:

1. Censorship *Encarta* <http://encarta.msn.com/find/concise.asp?ti= 761559522>
2. *MSN Encarta—*Censorship <http://encarta.msn.com/find/concise.asp?ti= 761559522>
3. Censorship <http://www.serendipity.li/cda.html>
4. *Free Expression Network Clearinghouse* <http://www.freeexpression.org>
5. *Censorship and What We Can Do about It* <http://a-ten.com/censorship>
6. *Free Speech Movement Archives* <http://www.fsm-a.org>
7. *EFF Censorship and Free Expression Archive* <http://www.eff.org/censorship>
8. *HotWired: Cyber Rights under Attack!* <http://www.hotwired.com/special/indecent>
9. *Freedom of Expression* <http://insight.mcmaster.ca/org/efc/pages/chronicle/censor.html>
10. *Freedom Forum* <http://www.freedomforum.org>
11. *American Library Association Challenged and Banned Books* <http://www.ala.org/bbooks>

Devon made two initial observations after reviewing the opening screen: first, sixty-eight seemed to be a very small number of matches for a high-interest subject like censorship, and second, the results were clearly not arranged by number of "hits," since the first two matches were to *Encarta*, an online encyclopedia (which the URL indicated was part of the *MSN.com* system). Devon planned to use an additional, more powerful search engine, but he began by linking to these eleven Web sites to assess their value for his research.

Matches 1 and 2: *Encarta* (an online encyclopedia)

A click on the first or second link (http://encarta.msn.com/find/concise.asp?ti=761559522) took Devon to a visually busy opening page on censorship: it contained a large picture with a link to *MSN*'s "Fitness and Recreation" pages and included sidebar information on book sales and study guides, as well as a promotion for winning a trip to Paris. These commercial features made Devon somewhat skeptical about the academic value of the site, but he continued to explore the site more fully before abandoning it.

After a close look, Devon found an article outline that included these promising topics: "Introduction," "Early History," "Church Censorship," "Censorship in the Modern World," "Censorship in the United States," and "Current Problems and Trends." By scrolling through the article's sixteen screens, he discovered an easy-to-read, informative, and reasonably detailed treatment of censorship (even though it was cluttered by advertisements for credit cards, books, study aids, and Internet services).

Devon was pleased to discover the name of the author and a brief summary of his academic credentials at the end of the article; this allowed Devon to assess the author's credibility. Milton R. Konvitz's authority was clearly established: he has a Ph.D. and two law degrees; he is a retired professor from Cornell University; he has written a book on constitutional law and civil rights.

Even though Devon initially found the Web site's design visually distracting and thought unrelated commercial material (advertisements) might suggest a nonacademic site, he was glad that he reviewed it carefully because, on closer examination, it proved to be a credible source that he would return to during his research.

Match 3: _Censorship_

By clicking on the third link (http://www.serendipity.li/cda.html), Devon connected to a Web site simply called _Censorship_ (sponsored by _Serendipity_). The opening page was uncluttered, included an opening paragraph on the scope of censorship around the world, a small graphic element ("Say NO to Net Censorship"), and a bulleted list of twenty-five featured topics.

Looking through the list of topics, Devon wondered about their suitability for his research: a number focused on censorship in other countries, some focused on particular legal cases that he did not recognize, and a few related to political-action groups. Yet several internal links seemed promising, so he explored the site further. A link to a subpage titled "The Bill of Rights" provided him with the complete text of the first ten amendments to the Constitution in easily readable form; "The Bill of Rights" subpage also included an additional link to another subpage, titled "Thomas Jefferson on the Bill of Rights." This subpage provided a wide range of quotations related to civil liberties, each carefully documented (with yet another link called "Sources").

By clicking on "Sources," Devon linked to a University of Virginia page, created by Eyler Robert Coates for the Alderman Library, that cited the critical editions of Jefferson's work from which the quotations were taken.

Although much of the _Censorship_ site was beyond the scope of Devon's research, he was pleased to find a copy of the Bill of Rights and some useful quotations; the care with which the material was cited (and the University of Virginia affiliation) assured him that the information was carefully prepared and well worth using in his later work.

Match 4: Free Expression Network Clearinghouse

A click on the fourth link (http://www.freeexpression.org) took Devon to the home page of the Free Expression Network. The page was divided into blocks of information with headings like "FEN Newswire," "Topics,"

"Connections," "News," "Headlines," and "Trends and Analysis." He observed that most of the page's links included sources that were recognizable: Associated Press, American Civil Liberties Union, First Amendment Center, *Baltimore Sun*, Student Press Law Center, and others. He also noted that the page had been updated within the past month and that it included an "About FEN" link.

In hopes of discovering what kind of organization FEN was and what its goals were, Devon clicked on the "About FEN" link, where he learned that FEN was "an alliance of organizations dedicated to protecting the First Amendment right of free expression and the values it represents, and to opposing governmental efforts to suppress constitutionally protected speech." This direct statement of FEN's goals clarified the group's purpose and, importantly, assured Devon that the site's materials would represent multiple perspectives (even though they were all free-speech) because membership included the American Civil Liberties Union, the American Library Association, the Association of American Publishers, the Electronic Privacy Information Center, the National Coalition Against Censorship, and others.

Returning to the home page, Devon selected the link "Censorship" and connected to a subpage providing additional links to "Art," "Books, Magazines, Etc.," "Music," "Television," and "Video Games." By clicking on "Books, Magazines, Etc.," Devon found twenty-eight additional links to full-text articles, arranged in reverse chronological order.

Devon's exploration of this site reassured him that even though FEN was a political-action group with an agenda, the diversity of its members would ensure his finding articles representing many perspectives. Further, the links to full-text articles, as well as links to the individual sites of FEN member groups, would provide him with a broad range of research materials.

Match 5: Censorship and What We Can Do about It

A click on the fifth link (http://a-ten.com/censorship) connected Devon to a site titled *Censorship and What We Can Do about It*. The left third of the home page was a column of linked advertisements for books available at *Amazon.com*; the right two-thirds of the page included a two-paragraph comment on the state of censorship in the United States and a list of eighteen often-censored books by Steinbeck, Salinger, Twain, Blume, Dahl, Huxley, and others. Each book's title linked to *Amazon.com*. When Devon observed that the site had not been updated since 1998, he was not surprised that he found no mention of recently censored books.

Although Devon found the comment interesting and noted familiar titles in the list, this site did not provide him with any new or unique information. He doubted that he would return to it for his later research.

Match 6: Free Speech Movement Archives

By clicking on the sixth link (http://www.fsm-a.org), Devon connected to the home page of the Free Speech Movement Archives. His review of the home page at first confused him: phrases like "The FSM didn't happen in isolation" and references to the "FSM 40th Reunion" and "FSM Vets' News and Views" made him wonder about the content and purpose of the site.

By linking to a few subpages ("Narratives of the FSM," "the outside world," and "Berkeley campus developments"), Devon discovered that the FSM Web site was, in a sense, a historical site, rather than a site that focused on the free-speech principles for which the organization was founded. Unless Devon's research plans changed—to focus on the actions of free-speech groups, rather than on the larger issues of censorship—it was unlikely that he would return to this site.

Match 7: EFF Censorship and Free Expression Archive

A click on the seventh link (http://www.eff.org/censorship) connected Devon to the Electronic Frontier Foundation's *Online Censorship and Free Expression* home page. The well-designed page provided an uncluttered site directory on the left, an easy-to-interpret column of related links on the right, and a wide middle column identifying "Featured Materials," "Featured News," "Archived Materials," "Subtopics," "Files," and "Subtopic Descriptions"; beneath each heading were lists of subpages presenting articles, position statements, policy definitions, and directories.

Although Devon was impressed by the clarity of the Web site's design and the thoroughness with which it presented information, the site's focus on Internet censorship did not match his research goals. As a result, Devon would probably not return to this site.

Match 8: HotWired: Cyber Rights under Attack!

By clicking on the eighth link (http://www.hotwired.com/special/indecent), Devon linked to *HotWired*'s *Cyber Rights under Attack*. Although the use of the word *cyber* in the Web site's name suggested that the site would probably not match his research needs, Devon nonetheless reviewed the site to see whether it contained general information on censorship or provided any useful links.

Devon was impressed by the site's clear graphic design and its lack of visual clutter, but he found that the site was true to its purpose and focused on only Internet censorship. After skimming several spirited articles that caught his attention, Devon concluded that the site, though interesting, would not meet his research needs.

Match 9: Freedom of Expression

A click on the ninth link (http://insight.mcmaster.ca/org/efc/pages/chronicle/censor.html) produced no results. Instead, the server displayed a *404 Not Found* page. Devon was both puzzled and frustrated that one of the top eleven matches produced no results, yet he had no choice but to move on with his preliminary research.

Match 10: Freedom Forum

By clicking on the tenth link (http://www.freedomforum.org), Devon connected to the Freedom Forum home page, which clarified that Freedom Forum was a "nonpartisan foundation dedicated to free press, free speech and free spirit for all people." In a column to the left, Devon found a site directory, and on the right, graphic elements that promoted the organization's museum (or *newseum*, as they called it), online exhibits, memorials, and featured columns (articles).

A middle column on the page asked for museum volunteers, congratulated recent institute graduates in journalism, and announced the electronic publication of the annual report. Finding no information relating to the principles of free speech on the home page, Devon nevertheless explored the subpages of the site, where he learned that the Forum was based at Vanderbilt University, information that was interesting but unrelated to his research.

When Devon linked to "Publications," he was at first disappointed to see item numbers next to each listed publication. He had seen such information before on sites that required users to order documents, a time-consuming and costly process. However, on closer examination, he discovered that some publications were also available in PDF format, so he scanned the list and found at least three PDF documents that appeared to relate to his research. Devon would return to this site as his research progressed.

Match 11: American Library Association
Challenged and Banned Books

A click on the eleventh link (http://www.ala.org/bbooks) took Devon to the home page of the American Library Association. With a site directory down the left (mostly treating organizational matters), the rest of the page was covered with what appeared to be stacks of boxes, each containing a topic. Some topics were easy to identify (like "The 100 Most Frequently Challenged Books"), while others were quite confusing (like "IF Issues"). Though somewhat confused by the clutter of the page and the titles of some topics, Devon knew that an organization like the American Library Association would address the issue of censorship completely—and do so from a position of authority—so he continued his search of the site.

Though the design of the subpages was no better than that of the home page, the information was widely varied and interesting. Devon found quotations about censorship from famous writers and political leaders; he found lists of reasons why books are challenged; he found lists of most-challenged books (the Harry Potter series topped the list in 1999); he found press releases for recently challenged books ; he found editorials. In short, he found a wealth of information, so he was pleased and knew that he would return to the site as he continued his research.

Devon's focused examination of the sites was based on essential criteria: credibility of the author, appropriate focus, thorough coverage, biases or special focus, affiliations or sponsorships, currentness, documentation, links, and appropriateness. Yet Devon's review also reveals several additional strategies. He was patient enough to explore each site thoroughly before either dismissing it or using it; he looked beyond surface features (design, color, layout) to see whether the site contained the information he needed; he followed the links throughout the sites to see whether additional information could be found. Devon's experience in searching for and evaluating Web sites illustrates the focused yet flexible approach that is needed to review the hosts of sites available on the Internet.

8e　Evaluate your combinations of sources.

Although you must first evaluate your sources individually—whether they are print, audiovisual, or Internet—your goal is to collect a set of high-quality sources that together provide a balanced treatment of your topic. To that end, you also need to evaluate your sources as a group. Consider these issues:

- *Alternative perspectives.* In combination, does the work of your authors provide a range of perspectives—academic and popular, liberal and conservative, theoretical and practical, current and traditional? Work to create balance by including works representing many positions.
- *Varied publication, release, or distribution dates.* Does your group of sources represent the information, ideas, and interpretations of different periods? Your sources should represent more than one time period and the point of reference it provides.
- *Different approaches to the topic.* In combination, your sources should range from the technical—including facts and statistics—to the interpretive—providing commentary and assessments.
- *Diversity of sources.* Incorporate in your work a wide range of sources—books, magazines, journals, newspapers, audiovisual sources, and electronic sources—to ensure that you have taken advantage of the strengths that each provides.

Evaluating sources is an inexact process. No matter how carefully you review materials, some later prove unhelpful. Yet early efforts to evaluate sources are likely to make later, more comprehensive work—reading and taking notes from the sources—more clearly focused and productive than it otherwise would be.

COLLABORATION

When evaluating sources collaboratively, you have the advantage of discussing each source's merits with other people to decide whether it is promising. Elissa and Jeremy, for example, reviewed their potential sources together. Glancing at Walter Toman's *Family Constellation: Its Effects on Personality and Social Behavior,* they each pointed out its positive qualities—noting that the book was in its fourth edition, observing that its publisher, Springer, was well recognized, and seeing in the biographical information about Toman that he had taught at Harvard and at Brandeis before teaching at several European universities. Elissa and Jeremy, because they concurred on the potential usefulness of Toman's book, considered it a "must" for their research.

As she began collecting materials, Jarah discovered a large number of Web sites related to Washington, DC, in general and the Lincoln Memorial in particular. Though the information was excellent, she was somewhat concerned about using too many electronic sources. Through discussions with a reference librarian who specialized in government documents, Jarah learned that many government agencies had begun to transfer print materials—pamphlets, booklets, and reports—into electronic forms. Reassured that many of her electronic sources were reformatted versions of earlier National Park Service materials, Jarah planned to use all of them in her paper.

EXERCISE 8.1   *Considering Sources*

Either alone or in small groups, consider the potential problems that would arise if you used the sources described below:

1. Five sources by the same author (for example, three books and two articles by Stephen Jay Gould)
2. Three articles, a table, and two charts from the same issue of *Time*
3. Sources from special-interest groups (for example, materials on birth control from either Planned Parenthood or the Christian Coalition)
4. An interview with your mother or father (for example, asking them about family-related issues)
5. Six books from the same publisher
6. A source you found in the checkout line of a grocery store (for example, *National Inquirer, People, TV Guide, Redbook,* or *Cosmopolitan*)
7. All of the subpages from a single Internet site (for example, using all twelve links from the *Victorian Web*)
8. A source published in 1985 (for example, for papers on the AIDS virus, the Japanese-American trade deficit, or Emily Dickinson's poetry)   ■ ■

8f   Prepare a research proposal.

A research proposal clarifies—for your instructor, your classmates, and you—why you intend to research a specific topic, how you intend to research it, and what purpose your work serves.

Writing a research proposal is a useful way to formalize the choices you have made up to this point. Think about it: you have selected a subject and narrowed it to a specific topic; you have created a working thesis statement (or research objective); you have considered what kinds of sources would be most useful; you have used the library, the Internet, and the community to locate materials; you have evaluated your sources. In short, you have completed the preliminary stages of your work. Applied researching, planning, and writing await you. So what better time is there to describe your research plan?

Use the following guidelines to prepare a research proposal:

- *Create a general framework.* First, describe the context for your research activities by answering several questions: (1) Why do you want to research your chosen topic? (2) What special experiences have prepared you for the research (work experience, reading, classroom work, hobbies)? (3) What will you learn through your research? (4) How much can you expect your instructor and classmates to know about the topic? By answering these questions, you clarify how and why you began your work.
- *Establish a specific focus.* Second, describe your narrowed topic, answering questions (many of which helped you narrow your working thesis statement) to establish the focus for your research: (1) How have you limited the time period of the topic? (2) How have you limited the topic geographically? (3) What special circumstances limit the topic? (4) What is its historical or critical context? (5) Is there a question or a set of questions you hope to answer through research? By answering these questions, you clarify the methods used in narrowing the topic.
- *Describe research sources and strategies.* Third, describe the sources and any special techniques you intend to use to gather information. Source materials may appear either in a list divided according to type (Books, Articles, Other Sources) or in a list with all sources arranged alphabetically. (See Chapters 14–17 for sample works-cited forms.) By presenting a list of potential sources, you establish the scope of your research.

The research proposal allows you to pause in the middle of your research to describe (and perhaps re-evaluate) your choices and to get a response to the plan from your classmates and teacher. Once you and your readers have confirmed that the proposal suggests a promising research project, you can proceed with primary research work.

► EXERCISE 8.2   *The Research Proposal*

Prepare a formal research proposal of approximately 750 to 1,250 words (three to five pages). Follow the manuscript style appropriate for your course (see Chapters 14–17 for alternative manuscript styles); provide your name and course information and a title for the proposal, probably a brief description of the topic.

Use headings (*A General Framework, A Special Focus, A List of Sources,* or similar descriptive labels) to divide the large elements of the proposal. Under the first two headings, provide answers to the questions noted above (see pages 92–95). Under the third heading (and perhaps under subheadings), include publication information about sources, presented according to accepted citation forms (see Chapters 14–17).   ■ ■

Estes-Cooper 1   *Paging*

Jarah Estes-Cooper

Dr. Robert Perrin   *Identifying information*

English 107

March 16, 2003   *Date*

A Research Proposal: The Lincoln Memorial   *Title, centered*

A General Framework   *Heading*

    I have been fascinated by Washington, DC, since I started
grade school. I loved the look of the huge government buildings and
was fascinated by the layout of the Mall, the area located between the
Capitol Building and the Lincoln Memorial and between the White   *Create a context in the opening paragraph.*
House and the Jefferson Memorial. Everything seemed so grand, and I
often imagined what it must be like to walk through the parks going
from one building to the next. I read books, looked at magazines, and
even paid close attention when these locales were the backdrops of
events I saw on the news.

    My dream of visiting Washington, DC, came true when the
band from our school marched in a parade. In the months before the
trip, I participated in fund-raising events and began a more earnest kind   *Discuss your special perspectives.*
of research about the city than I had done before. I read encyclopedia
articles, I checked out books (particularly the oversized ones with
beautiful pictures), and I talked to people who had been to the Capital.
And I became increasingly aware of the buildings, monuments, and
memorials and what they represent to different people. My mother, I
discovered, was a secret fan of the White House (she'd donated baby-
sitting money to Jackie Kennedy's restoration efforts); my dad was
very critical of the Vietnam Veterans Memorial, he said, until he visited
it while on a business trip; and Mr. McFarlan, my history teacher,
was fascinated by the presidential memorials. In the months before   *Provide interesting details.*
we traveled to Washington, I began to notice that these famous struc-
tures were used repeatedly in films: *No Way Out, A Few Good
Men, Forrest Gump, Dave, JFK,* and, of course, *The American
President.*

Estes-Cooper 2

When I and my fellow band members arrived in Washington, I think I was the most excited person on the bus, but it was worth the kidding from my friends when I finally got to walk on the Mall and see the places I'd only read and heard about. What surprised me was that my favorite place was not one of the ones I'd expected; instead, I found that the Lincoln Memorial made the greatest impression on me. I still remember walking up the giant staircase to face a building that I had seen in pictures a hundred times before, and I still remember how over-whelmed I felt.

Comment on early, informal research.

My interest in the Lincoln Memorial has increased since that Washington trip. I've scouted sites on the Internet, and I've even bought some Lincoln Memorial souvenirs from Web sites, but I've never had the chance to do serious research on the topic. Therefore, I want to use this opportunity to learn about this national memorial and share that information with readers who probably recognize the Lincoln Memorial—and perhaps have seen it—but know few of the interesting details about its history.

Acknowledge your readers' perspectives.

Heading

A Specific Focus

It is crucial for me to incorporate some history of the Lincoln Memorial itself, which was not built for decades after Lincoln's death. The information about its design and construction and restoration are helpful in clarifying for readers why the Memorial looks the way it does today. However, my special focus will be on the way the Memorial has been used over the decades as a location for many important historical events. Starting with Marian Anderson's singing on the Memorial steps in 1939 and continuing to recent events, I hope to show how the Memorial has become a symbol of protest and celebration.

Clarify your approach to the narrowed topic.

Heading

A List of Potential Sources

"Civil Rights: March on Washington." *Facts.com.* 2003. 22 Feb. 2003
<http://www.2facts.com/stories/index/h006707.asp>.

Estes-Cooper 3

"D. C. Rally Protests Racial Profiling." *Facts.com*. 2003. 22 Feb.
    2003 <http://www.2facts.com/stories/index/2000185360
    .asp>.

Glazer, Nathan. "Monuments in an Age without Heroes." *Public Inter-*
    est 123 (1996). *ProQuest*. 2002. Bell and Howell. 18 Feb. 2003
    <http://proquest.umi.com/pqdweb/>.

Griswold, Charles L. "The Vietnam Veterans Memorial and the Wash-
    ington Mall: Philosophical Thoughts on Political Iconogra-
    phy." *Critical Issues in Public Art: Content, Context, and*
    Controversy. Ed. Harriet F. Senie and Sally Webster. Washing-
    ton: Smithsonian Inst., 1992. 71–100.

"Lincoln Memorial." *eBay*. 30 Jan. 2003. *eBay*. 31 Jan. 2003 <http://
    ebay.com>.

McGee, Elaine S. *Acid Rain and Our Nation's Capital: A Guide to*
    Effects on Buildings and Monuments. US Geological Survey.
    Dept. of the Interior. Washington: GPO, 1997.

---. *Colorado Yule Marble: Building Stone of the Lincoln Memorial*. US
    Geological Survey. Dept. of the Interior. Washington: GPO,
    1999.

Roth, Leland M. *Understanding Architecture: Its Elements, History,*
    and Meaning. New York: Icon-Harper, 1993.

Sandage, Scott A. "A Marble House Divided: The Lincoln Memorial,
    the Civil Rights Movement, and the Politics of Memory, 1939–
    1963." *Journal of American History* 80 (1993). *ProQuest*.
    2002. Bell and Howell. 18 Feb. 2003 <http://proquest.umi
    .com/pqdweb/>.

United States. National Archives and Records Administration. "Civil
    Rights March on Washington, DC." Photograph. *National*
    Archives and Records Administration. 13 May 1998. College
    Park. 11 Mar. 2003 <http://www.nara.gov/cgi-bin/
    starfinder/17260/standards.txt>.

---. ---."The Unfinished Lincoln Memorial." *National Archives and*
    Records Administration. 13 May 1998. College Park. 11 Mar.
    2003 <http://www.nara.gov/education/teaching/memorial/
    memhome.html>.

*Provide full
citations for
the sources
you have
collected so
far.*

*Arrange
sources in
alphabetical
order and
follow citation
patterns
carefully.*

Estes-Cooper 4

---. National Park Service. "Lincoln: The Memorial." *Lincoln Memo-
    rial.* 8 July 2002. NPS. 5 Feb. 2003 <http://
    www.nps.gov/linc/memorial/>.

---. ---. "Stones and Mortar: The Statistics of the Monuments and
    Memorials on the National Mall." *National Park Service.*
    8 Aug. 2002. NPS. 5 Feb. 2003 <http://www.nps.gov/nama/
    mortar/ mortar.htm#linc>.

"Vietnamese War Protests: Washington Demonstrations." *Facts.com.*
    2000. 22 Feb. 2003 <http://www.2facts.com/stories/index/
    h01825.asp>.

Wiener, Jon. "Save the Mall." *Nation* 13 Nov. 2000. *ProQuest.* 2002.
    Bell and Howell. 18 Feb. 2003 <http://proquest.umi.com/
    pqdweb/>.

Give special attention to complicated citations, like those for government documents.

Thinking Critically

Evaluate the ideas and developmental methods in what you read to ensure that sources are systematic and fair; critique what you write to achieve similar results.

▶ Consider the assumptions implicit in both inductive and deductive reasoning.

▶ Examine warrant-based reasoning to determine whether the warrants (assumptions) establish appropriate connections between the claims and the evidence.

▶ Analyze your audience to ensure that you can meet their needs.

▶ Consider carefully the use of facts and statistics as evidence.

▶ Evaluate whether examples are relevant, representative, and complete.

▶ Recognize that writing can appeal to logic, ethics, and emotion.

▶ Recognize and avoid logical fallacies.

Critical thinking involves systematic and rigorous evaluation of ideas, both in what you read and in what you write. As a reader, examine books, articles, reports, and other sources, evaluating their claims and evidence to decide how each source serves your research needs. As the writer of a research paper, use critical thinking skills to present and support your claims.

9a Think critically, analyzing alternative methods of development.

Three basic patterns of reasoning—induction, deduction, and warrant-based reasoning—organize ideas and evidence in different ways, reflecting differences in thinking patterns. Be aware of these patterns during both researching and writing.

Inductive Reasoning

Induction builds from specific evidence (observations, experiences, examples, facts, statistics, testimony) and then, through interpretation, derives a claim (described as a conclusion or a generalization). The soundness of inductive reasoning depends on careful evaluation and description of evidence, reasonable interpretation, and clear expression of the claim.

Consider this evidence regarding Maxwell Elementary School:

- Children at MES have an absence rate higher than the school district average.
- Children at MES have the second-lowest standardized test scores in the school district.
- More children at MES receive suspensions because of fighting than do children at other elementary schools in the district.
- Fewer children at MES than the district average graduate from high school.

You could make several different claims based on a review of this evidence: (1) Maxwell Elementary School students face greater obstacles to success than do children at other elementary schools in the district; (2) Maxwell Elementary School students experience a disproportionately high amount of educational interference; (3) Maxwell Elementary School students are less likely to succeed than are students at other schools.

While reading and writing, analyze the cumulative evidence that leads to a claim or claims. As this example shows, slightly different interpretations of the same evidence can result in different, though related, claims.

Deductive Reasoning

Deduction begins with a general claim (or premise) and then clarifies or illustrates the original claim with supporting information. The effectiveness of deductive reasoning depends on a reasonable claim, thorough description of related evidence, and sound use of logic in reaching a conclusion.

For example, consider this general claim, which many people believe: children learn from the example set by the adults around them. Interestingly, the support for a general claim like this varies as much as the writers who support it. The supporting evidence could be presented positively, through examples related to work, education, human relations, good health, fiscal responsibility, and so on. Conversely, the same generalization could be supported negatively, through examples related to drug and alcohol abuse, physical violence, crime, compulsive behaviors, and so on.

While reading and writing, analyze the original claim and the evidence used to support it. As the previous example shows, different kinds of evidence can illustrate the same claim.

Warrant-based Reasoning

Warrant-based reasoning begins with an idea expressed as a claim (or conclusion); it is presented in conjunction with related evidence. The warrant is the underlying assumption, often unstated, that establishes a relationship between the claim and the evidence, in the same way a warranty (from the same root word) makes a claim (this product will work for at least one year) based on evidence (the product has been tested and has worked for at least one year).

Claim

Assisted living facilities provide the most beneficial medical care for the elderly.

Evidence

Assisted living facilities provide homelike settings with familiar living arrangements.

Warrant

Homelike settings, with more familiar living arrangements, are beneficial.

Carefully evaluate warrants, especially unstated ones. An invalid warrant, even an implicit one, leads to unreasonable claims.

Because college admissions tests are administered nationwide, they are an effective measure of student potential. (The implicit warrant is that widely used tests are effective. Because this notion is questionable, the conclusion is questionable as well.)

EXERCISE 9.1   _Patterns of Critical Thinking_

To practice applying the principles of critical thinking, complete the following arguments. Compare your responses with those of classmates to see the variations that occur when people interpret the same evidence.

Inductive Argument

Evidence
Tuition costs have increased, on the average, 5–15 percent yearly.
Books often cost $100–$150 per course.
Student fees average $300 per year.
School supplies can cost well over $500 a year.
Room and board now averages between $5,000 and $7,000.

Claim

_____

_____

Deductive Argument

Claim
We have become a society of complainers.

Evidence

_____
_____
_____
_____

Warrant-based Argument

Claim
Computers have improved people's lives.

Evidence
People keep records efficiently, conduct business quickly, and communicate speedily.

Warrant

_____
_____
_____

■■

EXERCISE 9.2   *Claims, Evidence, and Warrants*

Identify the claims, evidence, and warrants (both implicit and explicit) in the following paragraph.

It is not known whether any single vertebrate species is more or less immune to pain than another. A neat line cannot be drawn across the evolutionary scale dividing the sensitive from the insensitive. Yet the suffering of laboratory rats and mice is regarded as trivial by scientists and the public alike. These rodents have the dubious honor of being our No. 1 experimental animals, composing possibly 75 percent of America's total lab-animal population. As Russell Baker once wrote, "This is no time to be a mouse."
                    —*Patricia Curtis, "The Argument against Animal Experimentation"*

■■

9b   Analyze your audience.

Communication occurs within a context created by the writer, the reader, and the assumptions they bring to the process. Although no element within this context exists in isolation, looking at them separately can make you sensitive to the complexities of the process of communicating ideas.

To improve your work as a critical researcher and writer, evaluate the needs, assumptions, and challenges of your reading audience and assess how to meet their expectations.

Questions about Readers
■ What do they know about the topic?
■ How skeptical might they be about your claims?
■ What preconceptions or misconceptions might they have?
■ What kinds of evidence do they require?
■ What kinds of objections might they raise?
■ What needs do they bring to the reading?

To write a balanced, informed paper that clearly acknowledges the needs of varied readers, consider how the opposition might refute your claims. Similarly, how might you refute theirs? How might you reconcile these opposing views?

Freewrite about objections to your views or use two columns, listing your most important evidence on the left and an opponent's response on the right. Keep these opposing views in mind when writing, conceding points when necessary and countering objections when appropriate. You cannot accommodate all readers, but attempt to anticipate the needs, expectations, and objections of critical readers.

9c   Evaluate evidence.

Evidence is the illustrative material used to support a claim. As a researcher, analyze what kinds of evidence sources offer and how well they use it. As a writer, select and present evidence with care because critical readers examine your evidence to decide whether it substantiates your claims.

Evidence can be classified as facts and statistics, examples, and expert testimony.

Facts and Statistics

Facts are verifiable pieces of information (58,135 American soldiers died in the Vietnam War); statistics are mathematical data (approximately 65 percent of soldiers killed in Vietnam were in the U.S. Army). Well-chosen facts and statistics clarify and, consequently, support many of the claims made in researched writing. However, be skeptical about the use of factual and statistical information because authors with special interests may manipulate information to support their claims. The following sample paragraph supports a claim that the 2001–2002 recession was unusual in many respects.

> The recession of 1990–91 resulted in unemployment of 7.8%, and the one before that 10.8%. The rate today is confoundingly tame at just 5.7%.

Still, nearly 2 million jobs have been cut this year. That's triple any year in the last decade. So the low unemployment rate is masking painful job churn and insecurity.

> —*Daniel Kadlec, "Stumped by the Slump"*

Examples

Examples are individual cases that illustrate claims (the Watergate cover-up as an example of the abuse of executive power). Examples from personal experience are considered primary evidence, while examples from other people's experiences are considered secondary evidence. To be effective, examples must be relevant, representative, and complete.

Relevant Examples

Relevant examples illustrate a claim in a timely way and present single cases that correspond effectively with the larger issue presented in the claim. To illustrate the claim that Jimmy Carter was an ineffectual president, a relevant example might be his mishandling of the hostage crisis in Iran; such an example corresponds to the seriousness of the claim and illustrates it in an important way. However, an example about the embarrassments caused by President Carter's brother Billy ignores the important values presented in the claim and does not address President Carter's effectiveness as a leader. The following sample paragraph supports the claim that people are often depressed because they do not achieve goals—even unstated ones.

Many people subconsciously set goals based on past situations, and those goals can be triggered automatically when they find themselves in similar circumstances. For example, if you set out to make a good impression at parties when you were young—so much so that you carefully measured every gesture and word—it's likely that over time, you began expecting yourself to give a flawless performance at *every* party, without conscious thought or intent. Whether or not you live up to that unacknowledged standard could trigger a good or bad "mystery mood," according to a recent study at Ohio State University.

> —*"Demystifying the Blues"*

Representative Examples

Representative examples are neither extremely positive nor extremely negative. Extreme examples are ineffective because careful readers see them as exceptions and do not find them convincing. In a paper on the negative effects of state lotteries on family finances, for instance, a $6-million winner would not be representative, nor would a person who spent the family food money on lottery tickets. Neither extreme example supports the assertion convincingly. The following sample paragraph supports the claim that the so called "gold standard" applies to many areas of life.

Although obsolete in economics, the idea of the gold standard in other areas remains powerfully seductive—the Holy Grail of equivalence. Grade inflation is occurring everywhere, but at variable rates; grade comparisons are difficult. A student's class rank is often a more useful measure of relative achievement, but not all schools provide it. The Law School Admissions Council (the organization that administers the LSAT) has devised one way around the problem. Recognizing that absolute grade-point averages differ in value, it has plotted the historical distribution of GPAs for all students from a particular school who take the LSAT; it can then determine where the GPA of any given applicant would fall within this distribution, thus yielding an approximation of class rank. Presumably, it ought to be possible to go even further, by correlating the grade-point averages of applicants from particular colleges or universities with the average law-board scores of applicants from those institutions. Students with A averages from one college might have an average LSAT score of 160, say, whereas the same score might be typical of B students from some other college. In effect, the LSAT determines the exchange rate for many local currencies.

—_Cullen Murphy, "The Gold Standard"_

Complete Examples

Complete examples provide sufficient information to allow readers to see how the examples work as evidence. Incorporating responses to the journalists' questions (_who, what, when, where, how,_ and _why_) is one useful way to guarantee completeness. A summary can further clarify important connections. The following sample paragraph supports the claim that plastic surgery is both medically risky and costly.

Take, for instance, the face-lift. In a full-scale face-lift operation, the surgeon makes a long incision around the face: behind the ears, into the scalp, and below the chin. Then he or she delicately separates the skin from the flesh below it and the flesh from its underlying support structure of muscle and bone, pretty much the way a cook skins and debones a chicken breast. As the surgeon gently tugs the flesh toward the forehead or neck, deep furrows, such as naso-labial folds—those cheeky, matronly trenches that run from the sides of the nose to the mouth—become less noticeable. This is major surgery, requiring four or more hours in the operating room, general anesthesia, a month of recovery time, and a fat bank account (none of the cost, which can be upwards of $20,000, is covered by insurance).

—_Lisa Margonelli, "Gambling on Beauty"_

Expert Testimony

Expert testimony in written work, like expert testimony in court trials, is a statement of opinion or a judgment made by an expert or authority in a field. For example, a specialist in labor practices or a statistician working with government hiring data could speak authoritatively to support a claim about sexual discrimination in government hiring. A feminist critic of literature would not necessarily have any expertise in regard to hiring practices, even though he or she might have a reasonably informed opinion on the subject. The following sample paragraph supports the claim that the economy, though sluggish, is still healthy.

> Despite the tech bust, America's economy is still moving along at Internet speed. The boom-bust cycle now occurs so fast that companies are discovering they may have to add workers almost as soon as they've let them go. The pace not only augers a swift rebound from recession, but it also suggests the economy has undergone a profound change that will force economists to rewrite their textbooks. The old view: Hiring lags behind recovery by several months. The new theory: Skilled workers are so valuable that they're likely to be back on the job faster than ever before. "It may be that companies overreacted by laying off people more rapidly than they would have ordinarily," says Alice Rivlin, a former Federal Reserve vice chairman now at the Brookings Institution. Now, she says, companies may start hiring much faster than in past recoveries.
> —*Noam Neusner, "Back to Business"*

Appeals

Appeals to readers stress the logic of claims, emphasize the ethical nature of positions, and focus on the emotional nature of discussions. Most writing blends these appeals to emphasize multiple perspectives. As a researcher, you should analyze the techniques writers use to improve your understanding of their work; as a writer, you can recognize the techniques to employ in your writing.

Appealing to Logic

Appeals to logic emphasize evidence, providing facts and statistics to support a claim. The following paragraph emphasizes technical information—thereby appealing to logic—to emphasize why the product olestra required unique testing procedures.

> Olestra is probably the most studied of all food additives, and its market approval process was one of the costliest and the longest in history. But the case of Olestra is also remarkably different from that of other food additives because the decision process also took twists and turns equally different from the path of other food additives. For one thing, Olestra may replace a major portion of fat in the diet, a "macroingredient" that typically furnishes about 35 percent of calories in the diets of American consumers. This is not a coloring agent or sweetener that substitutes for minor ingredients in food. Because Olestra would be replacing such a large pro-

portion of the fat in the diets of some people, the [Food and Drug Admin-
istration] recommended that [Procter & Gamble] examine Olestra's nutritional and gastrointestinal effects, not just toxicity.

—*Laura S. Sims,* The Politics of Fat

Appealing to Ethics

Appeals to ethics stress the writer's trustworthiness, honesty, fairness,
clarity, and directness. The following paragraph establishes the writer's
role as a patriot and citizen, as well as his understanding of prejudice; by
providing a balanced description that even includes humor, he establishes
an ethical perspective.

After I was honorably discharged from the U.S. Air Force in 1975, the
FBI opened a file on me. It began with the ominous suggestion that I might
be involved in "suspected" terrorist organizations, but the investigation
concluded two years and 23 pages later that I was concerned only about
improving my community. The investigation seemed based on the assumption that because I was an Arab, I must be a potential terrorist. Most
of the juicy text was blocked out with heavy, black Magic Markered lines,
so it's hard to know for sure.

—*Ray Hanania, "One of the Bad Guys?"*

Appealing to Emotion

Appeals to emotion emphasize the needs, desires, hopes, and expectations
of readers, particularly sympathy and self-interest. The following paragraph, emphasizing the personal and emotional dimensions of health
care, appeals to readers' sympathy.

Obviously the decisions that must be made when an elderly patient
faces a medical crisis are difficult ones for everyone—patient, loved ones,
doctors, hospitals and health-care personnel alike. When a satisfying, although perhaps restricted, life is possible if treatment is successful, the decisions are easy: You do everything you can. But when someone has had a
medical crisis and is in failing health with little hope of recovery; when all
the painful, costly, possibly degrading though heroic measures may gain
no more than a few extra days or weeks or, maybe, months for a patient
who is probably miserable and often unconscious, the decisions are more
difficult and individuals may vary widely in their preferences—if, indeed,
they are given a choice.

—*Roy Hoopes, "Turning Out the Light"*

EXERCISE 9.3   *Evidence*

Identify the kinds of evidence used in the following paragraphs. Discuss with
class members why this evidence is effective and consider alternative ways to
support the claims in the paragraphs.

As the physical infrastructure [of America] erodes, the social infrastructure is being quietly starved, creating an emergency in the provision of affordable housing, jobs at a livable wage, basic health care, education, and the social services required to sustain the social fabric. The crisis of affordable housing has now yielded "over three million homeless people," writes journalist Michael Albert, "who wander our backstreets eating out of garbage cans and sleeping under tattered newspapers in bedrooms shared with alley rats." About 13 percent of Americans have fallen through the slashed social safety net and are poor, partly reflecting the unpleasant reality of an economy churning out a high proportion of extremely low wage jobs. More than 45 million Americans have no health insurance. This includes one-fifth of all American children, contributing to America's life expectancy being lower and the infant mortality rate higher than in all Western European countries and some Eastern European ones as well. Meanwhile, the collapse of American public education is yielding an average American high school student who not only has difficulty locating France, Israel, or the United States itself on a map, but scores lower across the board than students in virtually all the other advanced industrialized countries. This is well understood by American parents, who shun the public school system when they can afford to do so. An estimated 9 out of 10 Boston parents send their children to parochial school or any place other than a Boston public school.

—Charles Derber,
The Wilding of America: Greed, Violence, and the New American Dream
■■

9d   Avoid logical fallacies.

Logical fallacies are errors in thinking and writing that result from faulty logic. Analyze logical fallacies to determine the logic of what you read; strive to avoid logical fallacies in what you write.

Hasty Generalization

A hasty generalization is a conclusion based on too little evidence, suggesting a superficial investigation of an issue.

The recent increase in the numbers of tornadoes, hurricanes, heavy rains, and intense snow indicates that we are currently experiencing the effects of global warming.

(Although recent weather has been severe, it is illogical to assume that changes in weather are related solely to global warming. In addition, such a statement ignores the fact that weather patterns have always occurred in cycles.)

Oversimplification

Oversimplification ignores the complexities, variations, and exceptions relevant to an issue.

> Violence on television leads to violence in society.

> (Television violence may contribute to societal violence, but it is a single factor among many. Such a statement ignores the complex and multiple causes of violence.)

Either/Or

The either/or fallacy suggests that only two choices exist when, in fact, there are more. This type of thinking is not only illogical (because multiple alternatives are almost always available) but also unfair (because ignoring complexities and choices distorts a discussion).

> For the sake of learning, we must maintain the firmest kind of discipline, including corporal punishment, in our public schools, or we can expect chaos, disorder, and the disintegration of education as we know it.

> (The two alternatives presented are extremes: firm discipline resulting in order versus relaxed discipline resulting in chaos. The statement both ignores moderate methods of maintaining discipline and asserts that without firm discipline the worst will happen. It is highly manipulative.)

Begging the Question

Begging the question distorts a claim by including a secondary idea that requires proof, though none is given.

> Since wealthy doctors control health care services, Americans can expect the costs of medical treatment to escalate.

> (The writer has provided no evidence that doctors control health care services. Further, the use of the word *wealthy* implies that doctors' remunerations directly determine costs. Both of these issues muddy the logic of the argument.)

Sometimes begging the question is done very subtly, through word choice.

> The antiwar demonstrators of the 1970s should be remembered as the cowards that they were.

> (The writer uses the word *cowards* to define the groups without making any attempt to prove the implicit warrant that protesting is cowardly.)

Association

Fallacies of association suggest that ideas or actions are acceptable or unacceptable because of the people associated with them. Such a fallacy ignores the fact that ideas or actions should be evaluated on their merits.

> Arab terrorists repeatedly have threatened peace around the world; is it any wonder that people from the Middle East are viewed with suspicion?

> (This assertion links all people in the region with a small group of terrorists. Such reasoning ignores the fact that terrorists often act alone or as part of small, fanatical groups that do not represent the larger population.)

Non Sequitur

Non sequitur, a Latin expression meaning "it does not follow," presents a conclusion that is not the logical result of a claim or of evidence that precedes it.

> Japanese children spend forty percent more time in the classroom than, and outperform, American children. American parents should take more interest in their children's schooling.

> (Both statements may be true, but the writer does not establish any logical connection between them.)

Bandwagon

The bandwagon fallacy suggests that if a majority of people express a belief or take an action, everyone else should think or do the same. Such arguments give the weight of truth or inevitability to the judgments of the majority, which may not be justified.

> Over 70 percent of Americans favor tariffs on imports from China, and you should, too.

> (The argument falsely implies that the force of public opinion alone should sway undecided opinion. Such arguments are often bolstered by statistics from studies or surveys, but the use of numbers alone does not sufficiently support the writer's position. The advisability of tariffs should be decided on the basis of their effect on national and international interests, not on possibly uninformed or self-interested and emotional opinions.)

Red Herring

A red herring is an irrelevant issue introduced into an discussion to draw attention from the central issue.

> State boards of education should not vote to spend money for art and music programs when so many of our children fail to read at their grade levels.

(Deplorable as the children's poor preparation in reading may be, it has no bearing on the quality, or benefit to students, of arts education programs.)

Post Hoc, Ergo Propter Hoc

Post hoc, ergo propter hoc—a Latin expression meaning "after this, therefore because of this"—suggests a cause-and-effect relationship between two actions, even though one action simply preceded the other.

Since the artificial sweetener aspartame was introduced in 1981, cancer rates have risen in the United States.

(Although cancer rates rose after the introduction of aspartame, there is not necessarily a verifiable link between the two.)

Ad Hominem

Ad hominem, a Latin expression meaning "to the man," is an attack on a person involved with an issue, rather than on the issue itself. By shifting focus from ideas to people, writers fail to address the real issues.

Freedom of speech statutes should be restricted. After all, current law supports Larry Flynt, enabling him to publish *Hustler*, an offensive, degrading magazine.

(The issue of free speech statutes should be addressed on its own merits. The mention of Flynt, a visible and controversial publisher, sidetracks the discussion and fails to make any case against the statutes themselves.)

False Analogy

A false analogy is a comparison that is not based on relevant points of similarity. For an analogy to be logical, the subjects must be similar in several important, not superficial, ways.

Today's stock market, like the stock market in the 1920s, seems headed for trouble.

(Although it follows some similar procedures, today's market has many more checks and balances and regulations that make this analogy strained.)

EXERCISE 9.4   *Logical Fallacies*

Identify and explain the logical fallacies in the following sentences.

1. Jean Genet's plays should not be regarded so highly. After all, he was a thief and served time in prison.
2. Many Nobel Prize winners in science used animals in their experiments, so using animals in research must be acceptable.
3. I saw a man on a road crew sitting in the back of a truck reading a magazine and drinking a Coke. Obviously, road-crew jobs are extremely easy.

4. If the federal government stopped paying child support, fewer unmarried women would have children.
5. If business people can deduct the cost of their lunches, factory workers should have the same right.
6. To reduce the deficit, all we have to do is increase taxes.
7. Unless we outlaw all corporate donations to candidates, all our politicians will become pawns of business.
8. New York has exceptional museums, beautiful parks, varied entertainment, and fabulous restaurants. It is a great place to raise a family.
9. Any student who tries hard enough is sure to get an *A* in the introductory speech class.
10. Since smoking marijuana is immoral, we should punish anyone caught using it.

■■

CHAPTER 10

Taking Notes from Sources

QUICK REFERENCE

Careful and consistent note-taking is crucial during research: effectively taken notes simplify subsequent writing, while careless note-taking frequently leads to inaccuracies and wasted time.

▶ Consider the benefits and complications of alternative methods of note-taking: use note cards, the computer, or photocopied or printed texts; then select the pattern or patterns most compatible with your needs and working style.

▶ Always take complete, consistent notes, recording the author's name, the title (if needed for clarification), a category notation, and page references (when needed).

▶ Take notes of alternative kinds depending on the information: use factual notes for technical information; use summaries to present ideas in condensed form; use paraphrases to put ideas into your own words; use quotations to record other people's exact words.

▶ Consider which ideas and what kinds of information are common knowledge.

▶ Recognize the seriousness of plagiarism.

▶ Avoid plagiarism by acknowledging individual prose style, original facts, and personal interpretations and ideas.

10a Consider alternative techniques for taking notes.

Many options exist for taking notes. You can use 3″ × 5″ index cards to record citation information for sources and to take notes. Or you can use 4″ × 6″ cards for note-taking, while reserving smaller cards for citation information. You may want to take notes on legal pads or on other sheets of paper. You can photocopy entire articles or sections of books. You can use personal computers to type notes directly into computer files and thereby eliminate a subsequent stage of transcription. You can use online computers to download the full text of articles from electronic sources.

Before beginning your note-taking, analyze each note-taking system and choose the one most compatible with your specific project, library facilities, work habits, and instructor's expectations.

Note Cards

Note cards—3″ × 5″, 4″ × 6″, or 5″ × 7″—have the longest-standing tradition in library-based research. Before using or dismissing note cards, however, consider their advantages and disadvantages.

- *Advantages.* Note cards are easy to handle and can be bound together with rubber bands or placed in envelopes. They can be shuffled into different order without difficulty, making them ideal for experimenting with the arrangement of information in later stages of research. They are also easy to take into the library stacks or almost anywhere else.
- *Disadvantages.* Note cards hold a limited amount of information (a special problem if your handwriting is large). If you record information on a second and a third card, keeping them together is problematical.

Paper

Standard-, legal-, and steno-sized paper—each offers a readily available alternative to note cards. Think about the advantages and disadvantages of taking notes on paper.

- *Advantages.* Either standard- or legal-sized paper provides sufficient room for taking notes. Stacks of paper holding extensive notes fit easily into folders or large envelopes.
- *Disadvantages.* Taking paper into the library stacks is awkward because you need a firm writing surface. If you make multiple notes on the same sheet, arranging information is difficult during later stages of research.

Computers

Using computers (those in computer labs in the library, those available in another computer cluster on campus, or your own) to take notes is another option. This method of note-taking also has its advantages and disadvantages.

- *Advantages.* After taking notes on computers, you do not need to retype them, so there is less chance of transcribing notes incorrectly when you write the paper. Also, with disk copies of notes, you can print multiple versions to use at various stages of research.
- *Disadvantages.* Using computers for note-taking is awkward in some

libraries. You must either take materials to the computer cluster, check materials out and take them home, or use a laptop computer. Consequently, on-site note-taking is difficult.

Photocopies and Printed Texts

Photocopying (articles and sections of books) and printing (texts from electronic sources) are practical alternatives to traditional note-taking techniques. Before using these techniques, consider the advantages and disadvantages of these strategies.

- *Advantages.* Instead of taking notes, you can photocopy or print copies of entire articles to read and evaluate wherever and whenever it is convenient. Since they are personal copies, you can mark on them. You do not have to copy quotations and record facts; you can simply include them when typing the paper, thereby reducing errors.
- *Disadvantages.* Photocopying is expensive, especially if you are not selective. Further, because of binding formats for some periodicals, copies "fade" toward the center where the tightly sewn pages tend to curve. In addition, organizing your paper is difficult when your "notes" are simply highlighted portions of photocopied or printed pages.

Choose your note-taking strategy carefully, weighing the plusses and minuses of each method. Remember as well that during research you may need to use a combination of note-taking strategies.

EXERCISE 10.1   *Your Note-Taking Strategy*

Write a brief paragraph (50 to 75 words) explaining the note-taking pattern that you plan to use. Explain why the advantages of that system outweigh its disadvantages for you.

EXAMPLE

> Even though I griped about a card-based system when I was in high school, I think that it is probably the best system for me. My handwriting is small and neat, so the problem of space is not much of an issue. And since I have a tendency to lose track of familiar, everyday things like notebooks, the novelty of using cards will be a plus.   ▪▪

10b   Take complete, consistent, accurate notes.

Begin by recording an accurate citation for a source (see Chapters 14–17 for a discussion of works-cited forms). Recording citation information completely and clearly—either on a note card, on a separate written list, or in a separate computer file—saves time during later stages of research.

Whether you use note cards, paper, computers, or photocopies and printed texts, establish a uniform system as you begin reading and taking notes. The samples that follow provide a useful model. Modify this note-taking system as necessary to suit your particular needs.

Complete Information

Record complete identifying information with each separate note to avoid having to return to a source.

- *Author's name.* At the top of a note card or at the beginning of an on-paper note, record the author's last name. When several authors have the same last name, use first names or initials to distinguish them. For a source with more than one author, include only as many names as are necessary to identify that source. (See Chapters 14–17 for discussions of listing multiple authors in works-cited entries.)
- *Title, when necessary.* When using only one source by an author, omit the title. However, when using several sources by the same author, include brief forms of titles to distinguish among the sources. Key words—underlined (or italicized) or in quotation marks—work especially well: *Wounded Knee* for *Bury My Heart at Wounded Knee* or "Yerkes" for "Going Ape at the Yerkes Primate Research Center."
- *Category notation.* Near the beginning of each note, place a brief descriptive term clarifying the idea or subtopic that the information supports. Notes for a paper on wildflowers might include category notations like "regional differences," "landscape use," and "current popularity."
- *Page numbers.* Record the numbers of all pages from which you gather information; place page numbers consistently in notes to avoid confusion with other information.

Note card format

Author's name   Brief title   Category notation

Appleyard/Understanding   science vs. faith

Recorded ——"*Science [in the late 19th century] was the*
information;   *lethally dispassionate search for truth in the*
in this case,
a quotation   *world whatever its meaning might be; religion*
               was the passionate search for meaning
               whatever the truth might be."

p. 79 ———— Page number

Paper format

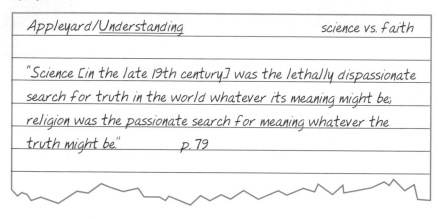

Appleyard/Understanding   science vs. faith

"Science [in the late 19th century] was the lethally dispassionate search for truth in the world whatever its meaning might be; religion was the passionate search for meaning whatever the truth might be."   p. 79

Computer format

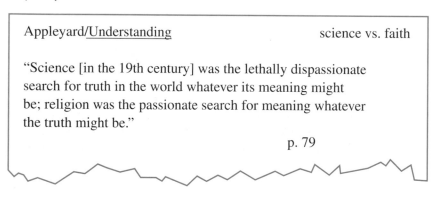

Appleyard/Understanding   science vs. faith

"Science [in the 19th century] was the lethally dispassionate search for truth in the world whatever its meaning might be; religion was the passionate search for meaning whatever the truth might be."

                                              p. 79

Consistent Format

Record notes in a consistent format to avoid confusion at later stages of research or writing.

- *Placement of information.* Where to place the author's name, title (when necessary), category notation, and page numbers is a personal choice, but be sure to establish a consistent pattern to use in *all* notes.
- *Abbreviations.* Use abbreviations selectively during note-taking. Using unfamiliar, spur-of-the-moment abbreviations to save time can actually waste time; when you work with notes days or weeks later, unusual abbreviations can be indecipherable or baffling.
- *Notations.* Note peculiarities or special qualities of a source. For example, indicate that a pamphlet has no page numbers or that a source has an excellent chart. Indicate where page breaks occur; a double slash (//) is an effective notation. (See sample notes on pages 116 and 119.)

Accurate Information

After completing a note, double-check its accuracy. Check the spelling of names and the wording of titles; check numbers, dates, and statistics; check quotations. Returning to sources to recheck the accuracy of notes (as opposed to looking for additional information) wastes valuable research time.

COLLABORATION

Because you and your collaborators share note-taking responsibilities and because during later stages of planning and writing, you will use the notes gathered by *all* researchers, use the same note-taking strategies. Having all notes from all collaborators in an agreed-upon format makes it easy for everyone to work without confusion or frustration at later stages of the research process.

10c Take different kinds of notes, depending on the material.

Few sources satisfy all researching needs. Some are well written but have few facts; others include excellent ideas expressed in unimpressive language. Because sources have different strengths and provide different kinds of information, take notes flexibly. Four common kinds of notes serve most purposes.

Facts

Factual notes record technical information—names, dates, amounts, percentages—to be incorporated in your own sentences. Record such information with minimal clarifying notations; double-check notes for accuracy.

Original Source

First read this brief excerpt from pages 27–28 of Lyle E. Schaller's *The Evolution of the American Public High School: From Prep School to Prison to New Partnerships* (Nashville: Abingdon, 2000). Then examine the note card that records facts from the excerpt.

> A major reason for [the] national debate in the 1890s over the ideal high school curriculum was the sharp increase in enrollment and graduate rates that began after the Civil War and the subsequent emphasis on graduation. The number of students graduating from high school was 16,000 in 1870, a year in which the number entering first grade was over a million. The number of high school graduates doubled to 32,000 in 1883, doubled

again to 65,000 in 1894, doubled again to 129,000 [*page break*] in 1908, [more than] doubled again to 1,068,000 in 1937, and doubled again to 2,290,000 in 1964. That 1964 number was 143 times the number of high school graduates 96 years earlier! Since 1980, the number of students graduating from high school each year has ranged between the high of 2.9 million in 1980 and the low of 2.4 million in 1990, with the 1990s averaging 2.5 million annually.

```
Schaller/Evolution                    enrollment numbers

High School Graduation Rates
—1870: 16,000                         —1937: 1,068,000
—1883: 32,000                         —1964: 2,290,000
—1894: 65,000                         —1980: 2.9 million
—1908: 129,000//                      —1990: 2.4 million

                                      pp. 27–28
```

Summaries

Summaries present the substance of a passage in condensed form. A useful means of recording examples, summaries must be written entirely in your own words, usually in abbreviated form. When taking notes, read the passage carefully, determine which information and ideas to record, and express them in your own words, phrases, or short sentences. Do not use any of the author's words without enclosing them in quotation marks.

Original Source

First read this brief excerpt from page 76 of Erik Larson's *The Naked Consumer: How Our Private Lives Become Public Commodities* (New York: Holt, 1992). Then examine the note card that summarizes the excerpt.

TRW [a credit-reporting company] won't provide a marketer with copies of any actual credit reports. This would be too brazen a violation of existing fair credit laws. Instead TRW compiles a list of consumer names that reflect the credit data. L.L. Bean, for example, could request a list of all consumers who possess a bank card with $5,000 or more of available credit. (TRW does not allow a search by specific brand of card; neither did Equifax.) TRW would then search its files and pull a few million names. The company, however, would not return the list directly to Bean, but rather to a third party printer, ostensibly to protect the privacy of consumers who fit the search criteria (but also a dandy way of keeping unscrupulous clients from running off with the names and using them again).

Larson/<u>Naked Consumer</u>   *mailing lists*

*Equifax and TRW (major marketing firms) compile
lists—the book's example is people with credit cards
with spending limits over $5,000—and sell them
to direct-market retailers. That way retailers can
target people with, the assumption is, large
discretionary spending habits—the $5,000 figure
would generatate a list of several million people.*
                                        p. 76

Paraphrases

Paraphrases restate a passage in your own words, but unlike summaries, they contain approximately the same amount of detail and the same number of words as the original. If a passage contains an important idea but does not meet the requirements for a quotation (see pages 118–119 for a discussion), restate the idea in your own words, sentence structure, and sequence. After finishing the paraphrase, check it carefully against the original passage to ensure that the idea has been completely restated. If you use any phrases or sentences from the original, place them in quotation marks.

Original Source

First read this brief excerpt from page 152 of Jessica Mitford's *The American Way of Birth* (New York: Dutton, 1992). Then examine the note card that paraphrases the excerpt.

Following up on the report by the Public Citizen Health Research Group, some metropolitan dailies highlighted its findings as related to their own communities. The *Atlanta Journal & Constitution* featured a chart showing the caesarian rates in several for-profit hospitals ranging from 42.5 percent to 32.6 percent, whereas Grady Memorial Hospital in Atlanta, which delivers babies to more indigent mothers than any other hospital in the state, had one of Georgia's lowest rates—18.7 percent.

> Mitford/*American Way*   c-sections
>
> The rates of caesarian sections increase or decrease
> depending on how doctors are paid and how patients
> pay their bills. When doctors bill separately for
> procedures and when patients have their own insurance,
> the rates of caesarian sections increase to roughly one-
> third of births (33-39%); hospitals with the lowest
> c-section rates are those where doctors do not receiove
> special fees and where bills are not itemized.
>
>   p. 152

Quotations

Quotations reproduce a writer's work word for word, maintaining original spelling and punctuation. Assess the value of the quotation before you
copy it by asking the following questions:

- *Style.* Is the author's language so distinctive that you cannot say the same
  thing as well or as clearly in your own words?
- *Vocabulary.* Is the vocabulary technical and therefore difficult to translate
  into your own words?
- *Reputation.* Is the author so well known or so important that the quotation
  can lend authority to your paper?
- *Points of contention.* Does the author's material raise doubts or questions or
  make points with which you disagree?

If you answer yes to any of these questions, then copy the quotation into
your notes. Enclose the author's words in quotation marks and double-
check the note against the original; the copy must be *exact.*

Indicate when the quotation comes from a comment or passage by
someone other than the author—for example, when an author has quoted
someone whom you also wish to quote.

Original Source

First read this brief excerpt from pages 270–271 in Paul Robinson's *Freud
and His Critics* (Berkeley: U of California P, 1993). Then examine the note
card that quotes from the excerpt.

> Michael Foucault has called Freud a "founder of discursivity," meaning by
> that someone who has created a new way of speaking, "an endless possi-
> bility of discourse."[1] Harold Bloom asserts, "No twentieth-century

writer—not even Proust or Joyce or Kafka—rivals Freud's position as the central imagination of our age."[2] Freud has fundamentally altered the way we think. He has changed our intellectual manners, often without our even being aware of it. For most of us Freud has become a habit of mind— a [*page break*] bad habit, his critics would be quick to urge, but habit now too deeply ingrained to be broken. He is the major source of our modern inclination to look for meanings beneath the surface of behavior—to be always on the alert for the "real" (and presumably hidden) significance of our actions. He also inspires our belief that the mysteries of the present will become more transparent if we can trace them to their origins in the past, perhaps even in the very earliest past we can remember (or, more likely, *not* remember).

Robinson/<u>Critics</u>   influence

"Freud has fundamentally altered the way we think.
He has changed our intellectual manners, often without
our even being aware of it. For most of us [,] Freud
has become a habit of mind —a // bad habit, his critics
would be quick to urge, but a habit now too deeply
ingrained to be broken. He is the major source of our
modern inclination to look for meanings beneath the
surface of behavior—to be always on the alert for the
'real' (and probably hidden) significance of our actions."
                                           p. 270-71

EXERCISE 10.2   *Taking Notes*

Record facts, summaries, paraphrases, and direct quotations from the books and articles on your preliminary list of sources; each note should accurately reflect the source and provide full identifying information.   ■■

10d   Consider the issues of common knowledge.

Determining whether information is common knowledge (which requires no documentation) or whether it is specialized knowledge (which must be documented) complicates note-taking.

Common Knowledge

Some facts and interpretations are known by many people and consequently are described as common knowledge. That U.S. presidents are elected to four-year terms is commonly known, as is the more interpretive information that the U.S. government is a democracy with a system of checks and balances among its executive, legislative, and judicial branches.

However, common knowledge extends beyond general information to more specific information within fields of study. In English studies, for example, it is commonly known that George Eliot is the pseudonym of Mary Ann Evans, and a commonly acknowledged interpretation is that drama evolved from a Greek festival honoring the god Dionysus. Documenting these facts in a paper *for an English course* would be unnecessary because they are commonly known, even though you might have discovered them for the first time.

Guidelines

As you research an unfamiliar subject, distinguishing common knowledge that does not require documentation from special knowledge that requires documentation is sometimes difficult. The following guidelines should help:

- *Historical facts.* Names, dates, and general interpretations that appear in many general reference books are considered common knowledge. For example, George Washington was the first president of the United States, and the U.S. Constitution was adopted in 1787.
- *Unattributed literature.* When literature cannot be attributed to a specific author, it is considered common knowledge. Two examples are *Beowulf* and the Bible. However, the use of specific editions or translations still requires acknowledgment. (When in doubt, ask your instructor for assistance.)
- *General observations and opinions.* Observations and opinions that are shared by many people are considered common knowledge. For example, a general observation is that children learn by actively doing, not just by passively listening; a commonly held opinion is that reading, writing, and arithmetic are basic skills to be learned by an elementary school child.
- *Unacknowledged information from multiple sources.* When information appears in multiple sources without special notation, consider it common knowledge. For example, it is common knowledge that the earth is approximately 93 million miles from the sun and that the gross national product (GNP) is the market value of all goods and services provided by a nation in a given year.

If a piece of information does not meet these general guidelines or if you are uncertain about whether it is common knowledge, always document the material.

COLLABORATION

Working with collaborators provides multiple perspectives on what information can be considered common knowledge. After all, you and your collaborators have all read substantial amounts of material. As a result, you have multiple points of reference when deciding whether certain facts or ideas are common knowledge—allowing you to make a more secure judgment than you might make alone.

EXERCISE 10.3 *Common Knowledge about Your Topic*

Make a list of ten facts, ideas, or interpretations that are generally known or held about your topic. Next to each item, identify the category of common knowledge into which it falls.

EXAMPLE

Subject: Academy Awards
1. *Gone with the Wind* (1939) was the first color film to win the award for best picture: historical fact.
2. If you give good performances long enough, you're bound to get an Oscar: general observation.
3. Katharine Hepburn won more acting Oscars than any other performer in a leading role: unacknowledged information from multiple sources.
4. Comedies and comic performances are less likely to win awards than dramatic films and performances: general opinion.
5. Whoever wins the Directors' Guild award usually wins the Oscar for best director: general observation. ■■

10e Recognize the seriousness of plagiarism.

Plagiarism—the word comes from the Latin word for kidnapping—is the use of someone else's words, ideas, or line of thought without acknowledgment. In its most extreme form, plagiarism involves submitting someone else's completed work as your own; a less extreme but equally unacceptable form involves blocking and copying entire segments of another writer's work into your own writing; and a third form involves carelessly or inadvertently blending elements (words, phrases, ideas) of a writer's work into your own.

In all of its forms, plagiarism is academically dishonest and unacceptable, and the penalties for its practice range from failing individual papers or projects to failing courses to being dismissed from college to having degrees revoked. The seriousness of plagiarism cannot be ignored, so you must make a determined effort to avoid this practice.

Whole-Paper Plagiarism

When students are foolish enough to submit the work of another writer as their own, they fail to consider a variety of factors that usually lead to their being discovered. First of all, instructors get to know their students well through class discussions and through the evaluation of previous writing. They learn what students are interested in; they learn how students express themselves; they learn students' sentence patterns; they learn the level of students' diction; they learn their students' technical fluency.

As a result, when a student whose interests have tended toward popular culture submits a highly scientific paper, the instructor is likely to be concerned. When a student whose language has been informal (with colloquialisms and contractions) submits a highly formal paper, the instructor takes note. When a student whose usual sentence style is of average complexity submits a paper with elegant, sophisticated sentences, the instructor is troubled. When a student whose word choices have been fairly average submits a paper with evocative or technical language, the instructor is justifiably surprised. When a student whose papers have been cluttered with technical errors submits a highly polished and technically flawless paper, the instructor is suspicious. In short, when a paper doesn't match a student's "writing profile," instructors notice.

Many instructors—being aware of the availability of papers on the Internet—use an Internet search engine like *Google* and type in a selected phrase (usually one with unusual or interesting language or a notable sentence pattern); with the sophistication of these search engines, instructors can usually locate the original source of the paper. Then the trouble for the student begins.

Avoid the serious problems that result from plagiarism. It is much more sensible to do your own work.

Copy-and-Paste Plagiarism

Though less extreme than whole-paper plagiarism, copy-and-paste plagiarism is equally unacceptable and unwise. It is equally evident, as well. Just imagine an instructor reading through a paper that illustrates a student's familiar expression and style and then noting an abrupt shift in sentence sophistication, diction, or technical fluency. When this happens, instructors immediately notice what is not the student's own work.

Resist the temptation to copy and paste segments of e-mailed articles from databases or from portions of Web sites; such use of others' work is both dishonest and easy to recognize.

Plagiarism due to Carelessness

In some cases, plagiarism is inadvertent, the result of careless note-taking, punctuating, or documenting. However, the writer is still at fault for dishonest work, and the paper is unacceptable.

To avoid plagiarism that is the result of carelessness in using words, ideas, or lines of thought, learn to recognize distinctive content and expression in source materials. The following qualities are most notable:

- *Distinctive prose style.* An author's writing style is determined by choices of words, phrases, and sentence patterns, as well as by his or her organizational patterns, use of headings, use of examples, use of specialized punctuation, use of illustrations, and other aspects of the writing.
- *Original facts.* Most authors include some factual material that is distinctly theirs—that is, based on individual research or experience. This material is easily distinguishable from any they attribute to other sources.
- *Personal interpretations and ideas.* Most authors evaluate, assess, and comment on information in a highly personal way—creating a unique perspective on the subject or information under discussion, and a unique order (sequence) or arrangement of particular ideas or concepts.

As you work with sources, be aware of these distinguishing qualities and make certain that you do not appropriate the prose (word choices and sentence structures), original research, interpretations, or ideas of others without giving them proper credit.

Look, for example, at these paragraphs from Joyce Appleby, Lynn Hunt, and Margaret Jacob's *Telling the Truth about History* (New York: Norton, 1994):

> Interest in this new research in social history can be partly explained by the personal backgrounds of the cohort of historians who undertook the task of writing history from the bottom up. They entered higher education with the post-Sputnik expansion of the 1950s and 1960s, when the number of new Ph.D.s in history nearly quadrupled. Since many of them were children and grandchildren of immigrants, they had a personal incentive for turning the writing of their dissertations into a movement of memory recovery. Others were black or female and similarly prompted to find ways to make the historically inarticulate speak. While the number of male Ph.D.s in history ebbed and flowed with the vicissitudes of the job market, the number of new female Ph.D.s in history steadily increased from 11 percent (29) in 1950 to 13 percent (137) in 1970 and finally to 37 percent (192) in 1989.
>
> Although ethnicity is harder to locate in the records, the GI Bill was clearly effective in bringing the children of working-class families into the middle-class educational mainstream. This was the thin end of a democratizing wedge prying open higher education in the United States. Never before had so many people in any society earned so many higher

degrees. Important as their numbers were, the change in perspective these academics brought to their disciplines has made the qualitative changes even more impressive. Suddenly graduate students with strange, unpronounceable surnames, with Brooklyn accents and different skin colors, appeared in the venerable ivy-covered buildings that epitomized elite schooling.

Now look at the following examples of plagiarized and acceptable summaries and paraphrases.

Summaries

Plagiarized

— a historian's focus is *partially explained by* his or her *personal background.*
— because of their experiences, *they have a personal incentive* for looking at history in new ways.
— Large numbers were important, but the change in viewpoint *made the qualitative changes even more impressive.*

The italicized phrases are clearly Appleby, Hunt, and Jacob's, even though the verb tenses are changed. To avoid plagiarism, place key words, phrases, or passages in quotation marks or rewrite them entirely in your own words and form of expression.

Acceptable

— a historian's focus and interpretation are personal.
— for personal reasons, not always stated, people examine the facts of history from different perspectives.
— Large numbers were important, but the change in viewpoint "made the qualitative changes even more impressive."

Here the words and phrases are the writer's, not Appleby, Hunt, and Jacob's. Quotation marks enclose a selected phrase by the authors.

Paraphrases

Plagiarized

Even though ethnic background is not easily found in the statistics, the GI Bill consistently helped students from low-income families enter the middle-class educational system. This was how democracy started forcing open college education in America.

Changing selected words, while retaining the basic phrasing and sentence structure of the original, is not acceptable paraphrasing. Appleby, Hunt, and Jacob's thought pattern and prose style are still evident in the passage.

Acceptable

> Because of the GI Bill, college wasn't only for middle-class children anymore.
> Even poor children could attend college. For the first time, education was accessible
> to everyone, which is truly democracy in action. The GI Bill was "the thin end
> of a democratizing wedge prying open higher education."

The revised paraphrase presents Appleby, Hunt, and Jacob's idea but does not mimic their sentence structure; the quoted material records a single phrase for possible use later. Remember that summaries and paraphrases, as well as facts and quotations, require full citations.

Avoiding plagiarism takes conscious effort, but through careful and complete note-taking and documenting, you can ensure that your work is acceptable.

EXERCISE 10.4   *Practice in Note-Taking*

For practice, take notes on the following paragraphs as if you were researching their subjects. Include a fact, a summary, a paraphrase, and a quotation from each set. (Check your notes to confirm that you have not inadvertently plagiarized any part of the paragraphs.) Then discuss with classmates your techniques for note-taking and the ideas and information gleaned from these passages.

A. Collier, James Lincoln. *Jazz: The American Theme Song*. New York: Oxford UP, 1993. [The following paragraphs appear on pages 22 and 23; a double slash (//) indicates the page break.]

> Furthermore, the feminism that was an integral part of the new spirit was critical to the acceptance of jazz. Until middle-class women were able to go out drinking and dancing, their boyfriends and husbands would not be able to do so either, more than occasionally. But now, by 1920, they could. So the middle class began visiting speakeasies, cabarets, roadhouses, and dance halls where the new music was played. Their financial support was critical, for it was only the middle class and the class above that could afford to patronize places // like the Cotton Club, where Duke Ellington developed his music and became celebrated; the Club Alabam, which provided the first home for the Fletcher Henderson Orchestra; Reisenweber's, where the Original Dixieland Jazz Band introduced jazz to mainstream America; the colleges where Beiderbecke, Oliver, and other groups got much of their employment in the early 1920s.
>
> We have to understand, then, that while a substantial proportion of the American middle class did not like jazz—was indeed threatened by it—probably the majority at least tolerated it, and a large minority were excited by it. Conversely, a great many religious blacks, and religious working people in general, were as hostile to the music as was the middle-class opposition. Jazz was astonishingly democratic: both its friends and its foes came from the whole spectrum of the American class system.

B. Worster, Donald. *An Unsettled Country: Changing Landscapes of the American West*. Albuquerque: U of New Mexico P, 1994. [The following paragraphs appear on page 27.]

Westerners of many stripes want to lay claim to [John Wesley] Powell, because they sense that he shared their interest in, their loyalty toward, the West. He was, in a sense, the father of their country. But today he would be a most bewildered old fellow if he came back to look at the West we have been making: a West that is now the home of 77 million people, ranging from Korean shopowners in Los Angeles to African-American college students in Las Vegas, from Montana novelists and poets to Colorado trout fishermen and skiers, from Kansas buffalo ranchers to Utah prison guards. How to make a regional whole of all that? And how turn the life and ideas of the nineteenth-century frontier dirt farmer become explorer-geologist become environmental reformer into a prophet for all those people today?

What those 77 million still have in common, despite the demographic and cultural changes, is the land itself. Even today questions about how that land ought to be used, exploited, or preserved continue to dominate western conversations and public-policy debates. Much of that land is still in public title, despite all the access that has been allowed to private users. Perhaps the most distinctive feature of the West, after aridity, is the fact of extensive public ownership of that land, hundreds of millions of acres in all, a feature that ties the past to the present. In New Mexico the federal government owns 33 percent of the state, in Utah 64 percent, in Nevada 82 percent, though in my own state of Kansas it owns about 1 percent.

C. Monmonier, Mark. *Air Apparent: How Meteorologists Learned to Map, Predict, and Dramatize Weather*. Chicago: U Chicago P, 1999. [The following paragraphs appear on page 47.]

Small compared to the Smithsonian's pre–Civil War telegraphic network, the Cincinnati weather service largely reflected the initiative of Cleveland Abbe (1838–1916), director of the Cincinnati Astronomical Observatory. An astronomer who had worked at the National Observatory, in Washington, Abbe moved to Cincinnati in 1868 to revive a small, privately financed observatory, which had deteriorated during the war. To stimulate public interest as well as collect data on atmospheric refraction (a personal research interest), he proposed a cooperative effort involving the Western Union Telegraph Company, the Associated Press, and Smithsonian weather observers in selected cities. Observers would telegraph reports to Cincinnati, Abbe would prepare a summary, Western Union would broadcast his synopsis to the Smithsonian and newspapers throughout the country, and the AP would defray telegraph charges.

A nice idea but not easy to organize, even by someone with Abbe's perseverance—only two distant observers (one in Leavenworth, Kansas, and the other in St. Louis, Missouri) contributed to his first summary, written by hand but posted prominently at the Cincinnati Chamber of Commerce on September 1, 1869. Within a week, though, the number of stations had increased to five, including Cincinnati, and on September 8, an optimistic Abbe printed the first issue of the *Weather Bulletin of the Cincinnati Astronomical Observatory.*

Abbe had hoped for reports from 22 stations, but his network grew erratically, with reports often delayed or missing, and many forecasts based on fewer than a dozen observations. Even so, a confident Abbe wrote his father that "I have started that which the country will not willingly let die."

D. Larkin, Susan. "From Scapegoats to Mascots." *Critical Issues in Public Art: Content, Context, and Controversy.* Ed. Harriet F. Senie and Sally Webster. Washington: Smithsonian Institution, 1992. 189–198. [The following paragraphs appear on page 189.]

If success of public art is measured by public recognition and affection, the lions flanking the grand staircase outside the New York Public Library are among the most successful examples in America. They have been featured in cartoons, children's stories, a Woody Allen monologue, and a play by John Guare. In the background of tourist snapshots or television news footage, they communicate instantly that the setting is New York, New York. Festooned with yuletide wreaths, they symbolize Christmas in the city. But these sculptures, now so cherished, were at first maligned. A reckless media onslaught spawned by a personal vendetta soured initial public reception of the library's most conspicuous art.

From the beginning, the construction of the New York Public Library was plagued by political controversy and labor disputes. When architects John Carrère and Thomas Hastings signed the contracts in December 1897, the work was expected to be completed in three years. Instead, it dragged on for fourteen. In that contentious atmosphere, the architects did not attempt a lavish art program like those for the Boston Public Library or the Library of Congress. They designated sculptures for only four locations on the building's facade. The most visible would be a pair of lions flanking the entrance stairs on Fifth Avenue. Probably on the recommendation of Augustus Saint Gaudens, the architects commissioned Edward Clark Potter to sculpt the lions.

CHAPTER

11

Planning the Paper

Invest time in systematically planning your research paper. Your writing will be easier, and the paper will be better if you do.

▶ Review your notes to ensure that you have the right kind and number of sources, that you have varied information to include, and that you have a broad working knowledge of your topic.

▶ Revise your working thesis statement or objective, as necessary.

▶ Create an informal outline for the paper to establish the general arrangement of sections.

▶ Arrange your notes by section.

▶ When necessary, prepare a formal outline, adhering to important conventions.

After gathering information, organizing the research paper is an exciting stage because you are ready to bring ideas together in a clear and logical form.

11a   Review your research.

Planning is an interesting, transitional phase of research. Some information is fresh and clear, having been recorded only recently, while other information may seem distant and inexact because it was recorded much earlier. For this reason, review your research materials before planning the paper.

Begin by rereading the assignment sheet and your research proposal, to re-examine the principles guiding your work. Then review your notes. Though time-consuming, rereading all notes allows you to see the range of materials and the connections among the ideas. A complete grasp of these materials is crucial for revising the working thesis statement (or objective), preparing an outline, and sorting notes.

Number and Kinds of Sources

While reviewing notes, be aware of the number and kinds of sources you have used. If the paper assignment requires three books, make sure you have sufficient information, ideas, or quotations from at least the minimum number; now is the time for any additional research that may be necessary. Also consider whether you have materials from the required *kinds* of sources. If you still need an audiovisual source, for example, now is the time to locate one.

Variety of Formats (Facts, Summaries, Paraphrases, and Quotations)

Consider the kinds of notes you have taken, remembering that an effective research paper incorporates information in a variety of forms: facts, summaries, paraphrases, and quotations. During this review, decide whether you can achieve an appropriate balance with the notes you have. If you cannot, now is the time to gather more kinds of notes from sources.

Information

Reviewing notes makes you aware of all the information you have gathered. Concentrating on only your notes (not on the vast amount of information that exists beyond them), you can rediscover important details, opinions, percentages, objections, statistics, and quotations that relate to your topic.

► COLLABORATION

Having divided the note-taking task to speed the research process or to use more sources than might be possible for one person, you and your collaborators each know only a portion of the information to be considered before planning the paper. To ensure that all collaborators actively contribute during planning stages, review the notes from all collaborators' research. How to do this varies from group to group: consider reading the notes aloud or combining the notes from all collaborators and having each person read the notes individually (which speeds the process).

Whether you use one of these two patterns or a variation, you and your collaborators should review all notes. Only then can all of you contribute during the planning stages.

Re-examining the requirements for the paper and rereading research notes requires a substantial amount of time, but it prepares you to revise the working thesis statement or the objective and to create an effective plan for the paper.

▶ EXERCISE 11.1   *A Review of Your Research*

List the source requirements (both number and kind) for your assignment. Then note whether you have matched or exceeded the requirements.

EXAMPLE

Required:
   3 books: I have 5.
   2 journal articles: I have 3.
   2 magazine articles: I have 2.
   1 newspaper article: I have 1.
   1 audiovisual source: I have 1.
   3 Internet sources: I have 7.   ▪▪

11b   Revise the working thesis statement or objective.

After rereading your notes, revise the working thesis statement or objective so that it accurately represents the paper you plan to write. Having recently reviewed the information gathered during research, test the validity of your working thesis statement:

- *Clarity.* Is the topic of the working thesis statement precise? If your focus has changed, revise the thesis statement.
- *Accuracy.* Does the working thesis statement accurately express your current view? If you have changed your views—based on your research—account for that in your revised thesis statement.
- *Balance.* Does the working thesis statement incorporate necessary qualifications and limitations? Having read a great deal about your topic, you should be aware of necessary qualifications and limitations. Add them to your revised thesis statement.
- *Style.* Is the working thesis statement worded effectively, establishing a tone appropriate for the paper as you conceive of it? If not, reword it.

If you cannot answer yes to these questions, revise the working thesis statement, knowing that at any time during the planning, drafting, and revising stages, you may need to modify the working thesis statement yet again. Once the revised thesis statement is clearly and effectively worded, print or type a clean copy to use while constructing an informal outline of the paper.

Jarah reviewed her working thesis statement:

> The Lincoln Memorial originally was built as an impressive monument to a
> beloved president, but it has since become a symbol of American protest.

At first, Jarah thought that her two-part sentence emphasized the original intent of the Memorial, as well as its shifting meaning. However, after some reconsideration, she concluded that the emphasis on *protest* alone was too narrow; after all, the Memorial had been used for other purposes as well. So she modified her working thesis statement in a small but significant way:

> The Lincoln Memorial originally was built as an impressive monument to a
> beloved president, but it has since become a symbol of American commemora-
> tion and demonstration.

Knowing that she could refine her thesis statement further, if necessary, Jarah decided she could move forward with organizing her paper.

COLLABORATION

Elissa and Jeremy disagreed on how effective their working thesis was. Elissa thought that it needed to be simplified, while Jeremy found its qualification useful. They made their respective cases, with Elissa arguing that their qualifications could be included in the preceding sentences, allowing them to sharpen the thesis itself. Jeremy found her argument convincing, and they agreed to present the general assumption—that birth order affects people's development—in several sentences that would be followed by this focused thesis statement:

> It is not surprising that a general theory about the effects of birth order has not
> emerged because many other variables besides birth order influence an individ-
> ual's personal, intellectual, and social development.

With this working thesis to guide them, Elissa and Jeremy began to organize their paper.

EXERCISE 11.2   *Working Thesis Statement*

Revise your working thesis statement so that it is clear, accurate, balanced, and well expressed. Have a peer from your class read it to make sure that it communicates the central idea of your paper effectively. ■■

11c   Develop an informal outline.

Outlines are structural plans, with headings and subdivisions to indicate the order in which materials will be presented and, to some extent, the amount of treatment each subtopic will receive. Informal outlines are flexible and relatively easy to complete, making them ideal for early stages of planning.

Strategies for Informal Outlines

An informal outline is intended for your use only and therefore does not need a great deal of development. Arrange information in lists marked with numbers, arrows, dots, dashes, or other convenient symbols to indicate the relative importance of ideas. However, be prepared to complete a formal outline when one is required (see section **11e**).

Organizing Principles

Decide whether a traditional organizational pattern—or a combination of patterns—would work best for your paper. A chronological pattern might work if your paper addresses issues affected by the passage of time. A topical, order-of-importance pattern might work if your paper addresses an issue whose ideas subdivide easily.

Also consider whether a traditional pattern of development or a combination of several patterns would work for your paper. *Description* (with emphasis on vivid detail) works well for informative reports. *Narration* (a chronological recounting of events) works well for biographical papers and historical accounts. *Illustration* (with emphasis on developed examples) succeeds when separate reasons are needed to support a point. *Problem and solution* (defining difficulties and explaining possible resolutions) is effective when a topic focuses on a troublesome issue. *Comparison and contrast* (with matched discussions of at least two subjects) works well when similarities and differences are important. *Process analysis* (a sequential explanation of how to do something) is appropriate for some reports or when an action is of primary importance. *Causation* (explaining how causes and effects are linked) is very useful when research leads you to connect events. *Classification* (a division of a topic into categories or subgroups) is particularly useful in analyses. *Definition* (explaining what something is) proves useful for establishing a context.

Most often, these organizing principles blend. For example, a research paper on the rising costs of prescription drugs might combine *definition* (to clarify the problem) and *classification* (to categorize the kinds of drugs or the people who use them). In another instance, a paper on Herman Melville might proceed chronologically in presenting background information, then follow a cause-and-effect pattern to discuss the effect Melville's father had on the writer's life and work.

Let the ideas from your research guide the organization of the paper. Be flexible, try different approaches, and remember that this is an *informal* outline for the paper. It can be revised easily at later stages of your work.

Allowing for an introduction and conclusion, Jarah created this rough outline to arrange the ideas in her paper:

Introduction (*Thesis statement:* The Lincoln Memorial originally was built as an impressive monument to a beloved president, but it has become a symbol of American commemoration and demonstration.)

- History of the Memorial
—Plans: Building, statue, murals
—Construction
—Completion and dedication
- The meaning of memorials and monuments
—Promote values and beliefs
—Symbolizes ideas
- Uses of the Memorial
—Yearly commemorative ceremonies
—Marian Anderson's concert (1939)
—NAACP Convention (1947)
—Civil Rights March (1963)
—Vietnam War protests (1967, 1969)
—Recent uses
Conclusion: The impact and future of the Memorial

COLLABORATION

As you plan a collaborative paper, discuss what elements should be included and where they should be placed in the paper. Drawing upon your collaborators' and your own individual experiences with organizing and writing papers, consider alternatives, always discussing why one strategy might work better than another. Take advantage of the fact that you have several individuals to contribute to the planning.

EXERCISE 11.3   *An Informal Outline*

Develop an informal outline that arranges the large elements from your research. Plan to add details and examples as you draft the paper.   ■■

11d Group your notes to follow your outline.

Using the major headings of the informal outline, sort your notes. First find a roomy place—a large table in the library, the floor of your family room, your bed. Then make label cards, using the major topics from your outline. Spread them out and then sort your notes.

If a note fits into more than one group, place it in the most appropriate group and place a cross-reference note (for example, "See Parker quotation, p. 219—in *Childhood*") in each of the other appropriate groups. Expect to have some notes that do not fit logically into any group. Label those notes *miscellaneous* and set them aside. You may see where they fit as you continue working; they may be useful in introductory or concluding sections; or they simply may not fit into the paper at all.

Use paper clips, binders' clips, rubber bands, or envelopes to keep groups of notes together. Keeping notes in separate groups by subtopic is important during the process of drafting the paper because it reduces clutter and allows you to focus on one section of the paper at a time.

Allow several hours for organizing your notes; rereading the notes takes time because it involves analyzing, reconsidering, and rearranging. Expect temporary chaos.

11e Prepare a formal outline, when needed.

After sorting notes into groups by major topics, decide how to arrange information within the sections of your paper. Organize notes from each group into a clear, logical sequence. Creating a formal outline is helpful, but revising the informal outline (with more detail) also works.

If you choose to develop a formal outline, adhere to the following conventions to establish divisions within the outline:

- *Major topics.* Use uppercase roman numerals (I, II, III) to indicate major topics.
- *Subdivisions.* Use uppercase letters (*A, B, C*) to indicate subdivisions of the major topics.
- *Clarifications.* Use arabic numerals (*1, 2, 3*) to indicate clarifications of subdivisions—usually examples, supporting facts, and so on.
- *Details.* Use lowercase letters (*a, b, c*) to indicate the details used to describe the examples.

In addition, observe the following conventions:

- Use parallel form throughout. Use words and phrases to develop a *topic outline* or use full sentences to develop a *sentence outline*. An outline may use sentences for major topics and use phrases in subdivisions of topics (a *mixed outline*), but should do so consistently.

- Include only one idea in each entry. Subdivide entries that contain two or more ideas.
- Include at least two entries at each sublevel.
- Indicate the inclusion of introductions and conclusions, but do not outline their content.
- Indent headings of the same level the same number of spaces from the margin.

Jarah evolved the structure of her paper by creating a formal outline, including chronological organization of material on the uses of the Lincoln Memorial. Her formal outline appears on pages 136–138.

Completing a formal outline requires attention to detail but helps you see how the specific elements of a paper work together. When submitting the final copy of your paper, consider including a revised formal outline; it can serve as the paper's "table of contents."

EXERCISE 11.4   *A Formal Outline*

Using the informal outline from Exercise 11.3 as a starting point, complete a formal outline, providing necessary elaboration. Create either a sentence, phrasal, or mixed outline, labeling it appropriately. ■■

Jarah Estes-Cooper

Dr. Robert Perrin

English 107

April 25, 2003

*Identifying
information*

Walking into History: The Legacy of the Lincoln Memorial

Title, centered

INTRODUCTION

*Introduction,
labeled but
unnumbered*

Thesis Statement: The Lincoln Memorial originally was built as an impressive monument to a beloved president, but it has become a symbol of American commemoration and demonstration.

*Thesis
statement in
full form*

I.   History of the Memorial

    A.   Preliminary work on the Memorial

        1.   Initial plans

            a.   Lincoln Monument Association (1867)

            b.   Site chosen (1901)

        2.   Architectural design

            a.   Henry Bacon, architect

            b.   Neoclassical design

            c.   Symbolic use of columns

        3.   Sculpture design

            a.   Daniel Chester French, sculptor

            b.   Symbolic representation

        4.   Mural design

            a.   Jules Guerin, painter

            b.   Symbolic representation

    B.   Construction

        1.   Start date: February 12, 1914

        2.   Stone used

        3.   Progress

        4.   Cost

    C.   Dedication

        1.   Convocation date: May 20, 1922

*Roman
numerals
indicate major
topics of
discussion.*

*Capital letters
indicate
subdivided
discussions.*

*Arabic
numerals
indicate
clarifications.*

    2.   Those in attendance
        a.   Warren G. Harding, U.S. President
        b.   Robert Morton, President of Tuskegee Institute
        c.   Robert Todd Lincoln, Lincoln's son

II. The meaning of memorials and monuments
  A. Promote values and beliefs
    1. Grandeur (the Memorial)
    2. Strength and understanding (the Lincoln statue)
  B. Symbolize ideas

III. Historical and political uses of the Memorial
  A. Yearly commemorative ceremonies
    1. February 12 (noon)
    2. Presidential speeches
    3. Wreath-laying ceremony
    4. Honor guard
  B. Marian Anderson's concert (Easter Sunday, 1939)
    1. Denied access to the DAR's Constitution Hall
    2. Arrangements with Secretary of Interior Harold Ickes
    3. 75,000 in attendance
  C. NAACP 38th Annual Convention (June 29, 1947)
    1. Closing session
    2. Walter White and Eleanor Roosevelt in attendance
    3. President Truman's address
  D. Civil Rights March on Washington (August 28, 1963)
    1. Culminating event of a multiday protest
    2. Thirteen civil rights leaders
        a. Spoke to some members of Congress
        b. Led the crowd to the Memorial
    3. Ten civil rights leaders
        a. Spoke with President Kennedy
        b. Gave speeches
    4. Martin Luther King, Jr.'s, now-famous "I Have a Dream" speech
        a. References to the Gettysburg Address
        b. Use of the Lincoln statue as backdrop
    5. More than 200,000 people

    E.   Vietnam War protest (October 21, 1967)

        1.   Peace activists, antiwar demonstrators

        2.   55,000 to 150,000 in attendance

        3.   Speech by Dr. Benjamin Spock

    F.   Vietnam War Moratorium (November 15, 1969)

        1.   Knowledge of the event

        2.   Known as the "March against Death"

        3.   600,000 in attendance

        4.   "Give Peace a Chance"

    G.   Other, more recent uses

        1.   AIDS quilt display (1987 to the present)

        2.   Million Man March (1995)

        3.   Promise Keepers (1997)

        4.   Million Mom March (2000)

        5.   Concerts (1999 and 2001)

CONCLUSION

Conclusion, labeled but unnumbered

12

Writing the Draft of the Paper

Allow ample time to write the draft of your paper because incorporating research materials and using in-text documentation extend the time it takes to compose.

▶ Remember that a researched paper, like all papers, develops in stages.

▶ Incorporate facts and statistics in your own sentences; always provide an in-text note to acknowledge the source.

▶ Acknowledge the author when paraphrasing information in your paper; always provide an in-text note to acknowledge the source.

▶ Introduce all quotations by mentioning the author (speaker) in your paper; always provide an in-text note to acknowledge the source.

▶ Place brief quotations in your paragraphs using quotation marks; set off long quotations ten spaces (without quotation marks); always provide an in-text note to acknowledge the source.

▶ Create a clear and interesting title for your research paper; use effective introductory and concluding strategies to begin and end the paper.

Expect the rough draft of a research paper, like all other rough drafts, to be messy and inconsistent, sketchy in some places and repetitive in others. To some extent, however, writing the rough draft of a research paper is more challenging than writing other papers because of its greater length and complexity. When drafting a research paper, remember the strategies that apply to any writing project, while also considering those that apply to research papers in particular.

12a   Remember general strategies for drafting papers.

Because the research paper is in many ways like all other papers, keep these overall writing strategies in mind:

- *Gather all materials together.* You can proceed with relatively few interruptions if your planning materials and writing supplies are nearby.
- *Work from the outline.* Write one paragraph or section at a time, in any order, postponing work on troublesome sections until you have gained momentum.
- *Remember the purpose of the paper.* Arrange and develop only the ideas presented in the outline—and closely related ideas that emerge as you write.
- *Use only ideas and details that support the thesis statement.* Resist tendencies to drift from your point or to provide interesting but extraneous details.
- *Remember readers' needs.* Include information and explanations that readers need in order to understand the discussion.
- *Do not worry yet about technical matters.* Concentrate on getting ideas down on paper; attend to punctuation, mechanics, and spelling later.
- *Rethink and modify troublesome sections.* If the outline creates problems, if an example seems weak, or if the order of the paragraphs no longer seems logical, change it.
- *Reread sections while writing.* Rereading earlier sections while writing helps you maintain a reasonably consistent tone.
- *Write alternative versions of troublesome sections.* Write multiple versions of troublesome sections; then choose the best one.
- *Periodically take a break from writing.* Interrupting your writing too often can cause inconsistencies in style and tone, but occasionally getting away from the work helps you maintain a fresh perspective and attain objectivity.

COLLABORATION

Because collaborative writing requires several people to compose together in order to achieve the best combined expression, expect some challenges.

Schedule a time when you and your collaborators can work for an extended period and decide on a method for writing. Consider having one person type or write, while others dictate phrases; this process, though slow, produces a draft that truly blends the work of all collaborators. Or consider dividing the writing, with each collaborator composing a portion of the paper or project; although this pattern of writing is efficient, it sometimes produces a paper whose tone and style shift from paragraph to paragraph, unless collaborators then revise heavily so that the individual styles merge into one style.

Think carefully about alternative composing patterns and choose the one that promises the most success for you and your collaborators.

12b   Consider strategies that apply principally to drafting research papers.

The research paper has its own peculiarities and demands. Consequently, keep these special strategies in mind:

- *Allow ample time.* Drafting a research paper requires more time than drafting other, briefer papers because of its length and complexity. Consequently, begin writing as soon as possible and write something each day.
- *Work on a section at a time.* Work steadily, section by section. When a section is difficult to write or when you need more information, leave that section for later and move to the next. Look for any needed new material as soon as possible.
- *Give special attention to technical language.* Define carefully any discipline-specific or other specialized language required in the paper. Writing thoughtful definitions of important technical terms clarifies ideas.
- *Think of the paper by section, not by paragraph.* Discussions of most sections require more than one paragraph, so use new paragraphs to present subsections of your discussion.
- *Use transitions to signal major shifts within the paper.* The multiparagraph explanations required for key points can make it difficult for readers to know when you shift from one major element of the paper to another. Consequently, emphasize transitions in the draft.
- *Incorporate research notes smoothly.* Materials from sources should support, not dominate, the paper. Incorporate source materials as needed to develop the thesis; do not simply string notes together with sentences. (For a complete discussion of incorporating research notes, see section **12c**.)

A research paper should present *your* views on a topic, views based on outside reading and interpretation; it should not merely compile what others have said about the subject. Consequently, contribute actively to the ideas in the paper: add comments on sources and disagree with them when necessary. Be a thinker, as well as a writer.

12c   Incorporate notes in the paper.

Incorporate information from note-taking in the research paper, providing clarifications, explanations, and illustrations of important ideas. Use information selectively to substantiate key points, not simply to show that you have gathered materials, and comment on the central ideas. Readers should know *why* you have included source material.

The following advice about the writing techniques for introducing quotations and clarifying discussions is appropriate for all documentary styles. Matters related to format (the use of parenthetical citations and spacing and indentation patterns) correspond to documentation patterns of the Modern

Language Association (MLA). If you are preparing the paper in American Psychological Association (APA), University of Chicago (Chicago or Turabian), or Council of Biology Editors (CBE) documentation patterns, check the documentation guidelines in Chapters 15–17.

Facts and Summaries

Incorporate facts and summaries in your own sentences. Sentences containing facts and summarized ideas require parenthetical notes (see section **12d**) to identify the sources of the information, as in this example:

> Unlike productions from earlier generations, current musicals are extravaganzas, developed by multinational groups and presented in multiple venues. *Les Misérables*—produced in France, England, and the United States in 1989—had eighteen companies touring worldwide, bringing in $450 million (Rosenberg and Harburg 65).
>
> > [Rosenberg, Bernard, and Ernest Harburg. *The Broadway Musical: Collaboration in Commerce and Art*. New York: New York UP, 1993.]

Commonly known information, however, does not require an identifying note; that *Les Misérables* is based on the novel of that name by Victor Hugo is generally known and consequently does not require a note (see section **10d** for a discussion of common knowledge).

Paraphrases

Include paraphrased materials wherever they fit into the paper. A one-sentence paraphrase should be followed immediately by a parenthetical note. Longer paraphrases, especially background information taken from a single source, should be placed in a separate paragraph with parenthetical documentation at the end; identify the author and source at the beginning of the paragraph. For example:

> In *School Choice: The Struggle for the Soul of American Education,* Peter W. Cookson, Jr., provides a useful summary of why people have come to question the government's monopoly of public education. According to Cookson, high dropout rates, in-school violence, disintegrating facilities, low educational standards, and cultural fragmentation have all contributed to education's decline. However, he contends that it was media attention to these troubles, coupled with the conservative backlash of the Reagan years, that gave the school choice movement its momentum (2–7).
>
> > [Cookson, Peter W., Jr. *School Choice: The Struggle for the Soul of American Education.* New Haven: Yale UP, 1994.]

Quotations

Use quotations selectively to add clarity, emphasis, or interest to a research paper, not to pad its length. Excessive quoting reduces the effectiveness of a paper because it suggests overdependence on other people's ideas.

Never include a quotation without introducing or commenting on it; readers cannot be expected to know why it is worth quoting. Instead, frame the quotation with your own ideas and provide evaluative comments, no matter how brief. A wide range of verbs may be used to introduce quotations, each creating its own kind of emphasis:

Some Verbs Used to Introduce Quotations

add	explain	reply
answer	mention	respond
claim	note	restate
comment	observe	say
conclude	offer	stress
declare	reiterate	suggest
emphasize	remark	summarize

The examples that follow (see also pages 143–147 and 150–151) demonstrate an effective pattern for introducing quotations: identify the author and source and explain the quotation's relevance to the discussion.

Quotations of prose or poetry can be either brief and included within the text, or long and set off from it.

Brief Prose Quotations

Include prose quotations of no more than four lines within the paragraph text. Enclose the words in quotation marks. For example:

> Awards shows are now being subsumed by the unsavory business of movie finance. In "Inside the Oscar Wars," Richard Corliss observes: "Movie studios love a good fight, and a bad one too. But the Oscar battles have become trench warfare and dirty tricks" (60). And the deeds are all done to increase studios' sales figures.
> [Corliss, Richard. "Inside the Oscar Wars." *Time* 25 Mar. 2002: 60–62.]

For variety, place identifying material at the end of the quoted material or, if it is not disruptive, in the middle of it. For example:

> Awards shows are now being subsumed by the unsavory business of movie finance. "Movie studios love a good fight, and a bad one too," observes Richard Corliss in "Inside the Oscar Wars." "But the Oscar battles have become trench warfare and dirty tricks" (60). And the deeds are all done to increase studios' sales figures.

To use only part of a sentence from a source, incorporate the material in your own sentence structure. Although based on the same passage as the preceding example, this passage uses only a small portion of the original:

> Awards shows are now being subsumed by the unsavory business of movie finance. In "Inside the Oscar Wars," Richard Corliss notes that "studios love a good fight, and a bad one too" (60). And the deeds are all done to increase studios' sales figures.

Punctuate such quotations according to the requirements of the entire sentence. Do not set them apart with commas unless the sentence structure requires commas.

Brief Verse Quotations

Incorporate verse quotations of one or two lines within the paragraph text. Use quotation marks, indicate line divisions with a slash (/) preceded and followed by one space, and retain the poem's capitalization. (Notations for poetry include line numbers, not pages.)

> In "Morning at the Window," T. S. Eliot offers a familiar, foggy image, the distant musings of a person who observes life but does not seem to live it: "The brown waves of fog toss up to me / Twisted faces from the bottom of the street" (5–6).
> [Eliot, T. S. "Morning at the Window." *The Complete Poems and Plays: 1909–1950*. New York: Harcourt, 1971. 16.]

Long Prose Quotations

Incorporate prose quotations of five or more typed lines by setting the quotation off from the body of the paragraph. Indent the quotation ten spaces from the left margin. Double-space the material but do not enclose it within quotation marks. If a clause introduces the quotation, follow it with a colon, as in this example:

> Anthropologists and social scientists are now realizing that a broader range of information must be collected in order for us to understand a broader range of ethnic and social groups. Rhoda H. Halperin offers this rationale in "Appalachians in Cities: Issues and Challenges for Research":
>
> > Family histories that reveal the dynamics of intergenerational relationships in all of their dimensions (education, economic, psychological)— the constant mentoring and tutoring, the patience of grandmothers with grandbabies—must be collected. We need as researchers to collect data

> that avoid the patronizing "we" (urban professionals) who know what is
> best for "you" or "them" (the poor people). (196)

Current studies, as a result, are developed in a multidimensional way.

> [Halperin, Rhoda H. "Appalachians in Cities: Issues and Challenges for Research."
> *From Mountains to Metropolis: Appalachian Migrants in American Cities.* Ed. Kathryn M.
> Borman and Phillip J. Obermiller. Westport: Bergin, 1994. 181–97.]

Long Verse Quotations

To quote three or more lines of poetry, follow the pattern for long prose
quotations: indent ten spaces, double-space the lines, and omit quotation
marks. Follow the poet's indentation patterns as closely as possible, as in
this example:

In "Poem [1]," Langston Hughes offers a spare, critical assessment of western culture:

> I am afraid of this civilization—
>
> So hard,
>
> So strong,
>
> So cold. (4–7)

In only twelve words, Hughes provides a sharp, insightful look at the world around him.

> [Hughes, Langston. "Poem [1]." *The Collected Poems of Langston Hughes.* Ed. Arnold
> Rampersad and David Roessel. New York: Knopf, 1994.]

Punctuation with Quotations

Single Quotation Marks. To indicate an author's use of quotations within a
passage, follow one of two patterns. In a brief passage, enclose the full
quotation in double quotation marks (" ") and change the source's punctuation to single quotation marks (' '), as in this example:

> In *Tribes: How Race, Religion, and Identity Determine Success in the*
> *New Global Economy,* Joel Kotkin emphasizes the influence of immigrants in
> American culture and business: "Even blue denim jeans, the 'uniform' of the gold
> rush—and indeed, the American West—owe their origination and popular name to
> Levi Strauss, a gold rush era immigrant to San Francisco" (57).
>
> > [Kotkin, Joel. *Tribes: How Race, Religion, and Identity Determine Success in the New*
> > *Global Economy.* New York: Random, 1993.]

In a long quotation—indented ten spaces and therefore not enclosed
within quotation marks—the author's quotation marks remain double, as
in this example:

James Sellers, in *Essays in American Ethics,* suggests that self-identity often is inextricably linked to one's nationality:

> National identity need not always be in the forefront of one's awareness of who he [or she] is. But in America, it is. The United States is the "oldest new nation," we are often told by political scientists; and the national heritage, while it has certainly not turned out to be a "melting pot," has become a powerful background influence upon the identity of Americans, reshaping even the ways in which they express their ethnicity or their religion. (97)

Whatever our race, religion, or ethnicity, we are, perhaps the most obviously, Americans.

> [Sellers, James. *Essays in American Ethics.* Ed. Barry Arnold. New York: Lang, 1991.]

Brackets. Use brackets to indicate that you have added words for clarity within a quotation. Most often, the words you add are specific nouns to substitute for a pronoun that is vague outside the context of the original work. However, you may also substitute a different tense of the same verb (*used* for *use*) so that the quotation blends effectively with your prose. For example, in the passage below, the bracketed phrase "value-destroying industries" (a commonly understood phrase in economic studies) substitutes for "one of these firms," which has no clear referent in the quotation or its introduction.

In "The Disintegration of the Russian Economy," Michael Spagat explains a major industrial dilemma: "Workers in these industries are receiving more wages than the wealth they are creating for society. So if [value-destroying industries] were closed down, money would be saved but the savings would not be enough to pay full unemployment compensation" (52).

> [Spagat, Michael. "The Disintegration of the Russian Economy." *Russia's Future: Consolidation or Disintegration?* Ed. Douglas W. Blum. Boulder: Westview, 1994. 47–67.]

Bracketed information can substitute for the original wording, as in the example above, or appear in addition to the original material: "she [Eleanor Roosevelt]." If a quotation requires extensive use of brackets, use another quotation or express the information in your own words.

Ellipses. Use ellipsis points (three spaced periods) to indicate that words are omitted from a quotation. Omissions from the middle of a sentence do not require any other punctuation. To indicate an omission from the end of a sentence, retain the sentence's end punctuation, followed by the ellipsis points.

> Robert I. Williams stresses the social dimensions of comedy in *Comic Practice: Comic Response:* "Humor is a guide. It is largely culture bound. Chinese Communist jokes do not do well here, just as ours tend to be duds in Beijing. . . . Yet there is a range of humor that works for a broad, variegated audience. The very existence of comic films is testimony" (56–57).
>
> [Williams, Robert I. *Comic Practice: Comic Response.* Newark: U of Delaware P, 1993.]

(Omitted: "The humor of a Chicago street gang will not work in a retirement home, even one in Chicago. Regional, age, gender, and social differences all enter in.")

When clarity is not compromised, ellipsis points are unnecessary at the beginning or end of a quotation because readers understand that quoted material comes from more complete sources.

Note: In some instances, authors use ellipsis points for stylistic effect. To distinguish your own use of ellipsis points to show omission from the author's use for effect, place *your* ellipsis points within brackets. Many instructors prefer the use of brackets with ellipsis points in all circumstances (even when none of your sources uses ellipsis points for effect); ask your instructor how to handle this matter.

12d Use parenthetical notes to document research.

Internal documentation identifies materials from sources and indicates where facts, quotations, or ideas appear in original sources. Chapters 15–17 discuss APA, Chicago, and CBE styles for attributing information; MLA style uses parentheses within the text to indicate the source of information and its location in the original.

Consistency of Reference

Parenthetical references must correspond to entries in the list of works cited. If a works-cited entry begins with an author's name, the parenthetical reference in the text must also cite the author's name—not the title, editor, translator, or other element. Readers then match the information within the parenthetical references with the information in works-cited entries.

Basic Forms of Parenthetical Notes

To avoid disrupting the text, parenthetical notes use the briefest possible form to identify the relevant source: the name of the author (or in some instances, the title) and for print sources, a page number (without a page abbreviation). For example:

Soon after Johnson was inaugurated in 1965, Operation Rolling Thunder began; ultimately American planes dropped 643,000 tons of explosives on North Vietnam (Brownmiller 20).

[Brownmiller, Susan. *Seeing Vietnam: Encounters of the Road and Heart.* New York: Harper, 1994.]

In the interests of clarity, you may incorporate the author's name in your sentences.

Brownmiller notes that soon after Johnson was inaugurated in 1965, Operation Rolling Thunder began; ultimately American planes dropped 643,000 tons of explosives on North Vietnam (20).

In special cases, however, the rule of using the author's last name and the page reference is superseded:

Special Circumstance	Rule and Sample
Two authors with the same last name	Include first and last name: (John Barratt 31), distinct from (Jessica Barratt 2–4).
Two works by the same author	Include the title or a shortened version of the title, separated from the author's name by a comma, maintaining the original punctuation for the shortened form: (Gould, *Mismeasure* 113), distinct from (Gould, "Wheel" 16).
Two authors	Include both last names: (Scott and Fuller 213–14).
Three authors	Include all last names, separated by commas: (Jarnow, Judelle, and Guerreiro 58).
Four or more authors	Include the first author's last name and *et al.* ("and others"), not italicized: (Gershey et al. 22).
Corporate author	Include the organization as the author: (AMA 117).
Multivolume works	Include the volume number after the author's name, followed by a colon: (Tebbel 4: 89–91).
Reference works	Include the author's name or a shortened form of the title, depending on how the work appears in the works-cited list; no page numbers are required for alphabetically arranged sources: (Angermüller) or ("Manhattan Project").
Poetry or verse drama	Include the author's name, a short title (if necessary), and line (not page) numbers: (Eliot, "Waste Land" 173–81).

Indirect Sources

Whenever possible, quote from an original source. However, in instances when the original source is unavailable to you, you can quote from an indirect source (the source where you found the quoted material).

Introduce the quotation by identifying the person you are quoting; then identify in the parenthetical note the source from which you have taken the quotation, introduced by the abbreviated phrase *qtd. in* ("quoted in"). For example:

> After a political blunder in which two of Truman's cabinet members issued simultaneous and contradictory statements about American-Russian relations, Truman asserted his share of the blame with typical candor: "Never was there such a mess and it is partly my making. But when I make a mistake it is a good one" (qtd. in Pemberton 69).
>
> > [Pemberton, William E. *Harry S. Truman: Fair Dealer and Cold Warrior* Boston: Twayne, 1989.]

Audiovisual Sources

Cite audiovisual sources, for which no page numbers can be given, by "author" (lecturer, director, writer, producer, performer, or interview respondent) or title, as they appear in the list of works cited. Such citations, however, are often clearer if incorporated in the text of the paper.

> The isolation and the despair of patients with AIDS are captured in these haunting images:
>
> > I walked the avenue till my legs felt like stone
> > I heard the voices of friends vanished and gone
> > At night I could hear the blood in my veins
> > Black and whispering as the rain. (Springsteen, "Streets")

Or

> The isolation and the despair of patients with AIDS are captured in these haunting images from Bruce Springsteen's "Streets of Philadelphia":
>
> > I walked the avenue till my legs felt like stone
> > I heard the voices of friends vanished and gone
> > At night I could hear the blood in my veins
> > Black and whispering as the rain.
>
> > [Springsteen, Bruce. "Streets of Philadelphia." *Philadelphia.* Soundtrack. Sony, 1993.]

Because audiovisual sources require limited information in parenthetical notes, incorporate all needed information in the written text when possible.

Electronic Sources

Cite electronic sources, for which no page can be given, by author or title, as they appear in your works-cited list. Of course, it is possible to include this information within your text, in which case there is no parenthetical note. To avoid the confusion of having no parenthetical reference— a reader may assume that you merely forgot to add your citation—you can provide brief, clarifying references to the electronic document in your sentences.

> The case for censorship often seems simple, but it seldom is. As Karla Peterson and Steve Harsin express in their Web site _Banned Books and Censorship: Information and Resources:_
>
>> Most would-be book banners act with what they consider to be the highest motives—protecting themselves, their families and communities from perceived injustices and evil and preserving the values and ideals they would have the entire society embrace. The result, however, is always and ever the denial of another's right to read.
>
> Such complexities and problems are what make censorship such a troubling issue.
> [Peterson, Karla, and Steve Harsin. _Banned Books and Censorship: Information and Resources._ 17 Oct. 2000. Loyola U Libraries. 9 Mar. 2003 <http://www.luc.edu/libraries/banned/>.]

Positioning Parenthetical Notes

Without disrupting the text, place parenthetical notes as close as possible to the material they identify—usually at the end of the sentence but before the end punctuation. Allow one space before the opening parenthesis.

Facts, Summaries, and Paraphrases

> Congressionally approved military assistance to foreign nations gradually increased from $2 billion per year during Kennedy's administration to $7 billion a year during the Reagan administration (Hinckley 122–23).
> [Hinckley, Barbara. _Less than Meets the Eye: Foreign Policy Making and the Myth of the Assertive Congress._ Chicago: Twentieth Century–U of Chicago P, 1994.]

Brief Quotations

For brief quotations, place the notes _outside_ the quotation marks but _before_ the end punctuation, a change in the usual pattern of placing end punctuation before closing quotation marks.

Economic and political power are intertwined because "together, the politically strong and our legislators devise measures to limit [economic] competition from those who are politically weaker" (Adams and Brock 118).

> [Adams, Walter, and James W. Brock. *Antitrust Economics on Trial: A Dialogue on the New Laissez-Faire.* Princeton: Princeton UP, 1991.]

Long Quotations

For long, set-off quotations (indented ten spaces and not enclosed with quotation marks), place a period at the end of the quotation. Then add the parenthetical note without additional punctuation.

Unlike the traditional "hard" sciences, the study of past cultures must, by nature, be somewhat intuitive. As Rachel Harry suggests in "Archaeology as Art":

> Objectivity in archaeology is at once both an easy and an impossible target to shoot down because it simply does not exist. Archaeologists can not *choose* objectivity. We will find what we look for, and are left with what by chance is revealed to us. (133)

Balance, then, must be achieved by reviewing a variety of archaeological studies, not just one.

> [Harry, Rachel. "Archaeology as Art." *Archaeological Theory: Progress or Posture?* Ed. Iain M. Mackenzie. Worldwide Archaeological Ser. Brookfield: Avebury, 1994. 131–39.]

EXERCISE 12.1 *Incorporating Research into Your Writing*

Write a series of paragraphs incorporating information, ideas, and quotations from the following five sources.

> **SOURCE 1:** Kane, Thomas J. *The Price of Admission: Rethinking How Americans Pay for College.* Washington: Brookings Institution, 1999. [The following paragraph appears on page 5; the following table is excerpted from Table 3-1, "Costs, Tuition, and State and Local Appropriations per Student, by Type of Institution, 1980–81, 1994–95," page 60.]

In the face of expanding public college enrollments, state governments have been unable to continue paying the same proportion of the cost for each student, and families have had to make up the difference with higher tuition. In 1980 state and local appropriations covered 83 percent of the educational cost per student at public two-year institutions and 76 percent at four-year institutions. Because parents were paying such a small share of the costs in 1980, even a modest shift of a few percentage points in the burden carried by students and their families meant a large percentage increase in tuition. Even though the share of costs covered by state appropriations fell by only 9 percentage points at public two-year colleges and 14 percentage points at public four-year institutions, the offsetting rise in the proportion covered by tuition revenues (that is, gross tuition less the value of scholarships and fellowships) meant that the share paid by students and families rose by nearly 60 percent.

Kind of School	Tuition: 1980–1981	Tuition: 1994–1995	Percent of Increase
Public two-year	$808	$1,693	110%
Public four-year	$1,840	$3,865	107%
Private four-year	$6,803	$13,099	92%

SOURCE 2: "Undergraduate Tuition and Fees, 1998." *Collegecosts.* 2000. 4 Feb. 2002 <http://www.collegecosts.org/cost2.txt>. [Information is excerpted from a listing of all four-year institutions in the United States, in order by tuition costs.]

Undergraduate Tuition and Fees, 1998

$26,500	Landmark College	VT
$24,630	Hampshire College	MA
$24,332	Brown University	RI
$24,152	Amherst College	MA
$24,144	Columbia College	NY
$24,066	Sarah Lawrence College	NY
$24,050	Wesleyan College	CT
$24,050	MIT	MA
$24,020	Brandeis University	MA
$23,974	Columbia University	NY

SOURCE 3: Bay, Mark. "Tuition Rising: Why College Costs So Much." Rev. of *Tuition Rising: Why College Costs So Much* by Ronald G. Ehrenberg. *Library Journal* 125.13 (2000): 122. [The following paragraph appears on page 122.]

Ehrenberg, a senior administrator and professor of economics at Cornell University, examines the factors influencing the spiraling tuition costs of the past decade: the need to spend money to have the best facilities, faculties, and learning tools in order to attract the best and brightest students, the need to spend for athletics and other programs to keep alumni support strong, the self-governing nature of university faculty, and the increasing pressure to spend in order to increase ratings in external publications.

SOURCE 4: "College Costs, Financial Aid Are Up . . ." *Journal of Financial Planning* 14.1 (2001): 29. [The following information appears on page 29.]

The Average Increase in Tuition for 2000–2001
   Private Four-Year: 5.2 percent (average: $16,332)
   Public Four-Year: 4.4 percent (average: $3,510)

Private Two-Year: 7.0 percent (average: $7,458)
Public Two-Year: 3.4 percent (average: $1,705)

Loans in 2000–2001 account for 59 percent of student aid; in 1980–1981 they accounted for 41 percent of financial aid.

> **SOURCE 5:** *Getting Ready for College Early: A Handbook for Parents of Students in the Middle and Junior High School Years.* Washington: Dept. of Education, 2000. 6 Feb. 2003 <http://www.ed.gov/pubs/ gettingreadycollegeearly/index.html>. [The following paragraphs are excerpted from an online government pamphlet.]

"We must make the thirteenth and fourteenth years of education—at least two years of college—just as universal in America by the 21st century as high school education is today, and we must open the doors of college to all Americans."
—*President Clinton,* State of the Union Address, February 4, 1997

Getting a college education is an investment that will pay back for a lifetime: people with college education have better job opportunities, earn more money, and develop skills and knowledge that can never be taken away.

■ ■

12e Plan your title and your introductory and concluding paragraphs.

The title and the beginning and ending paragraphs of a paper create important first and final impressions. These special sections of a paper can be developed, written, and rewritten at any time during planning, drafting, or revising.

Titles

A good title is descriptive, letting readers know what the paper is about. In nonscientific disciplines, readers expect titles to be imaginative, to spark their interest. To create an effective title, consider these strategies:

■ Use words or phrases that explicitly identify the topic. Search the draft of your paper for expressions that are clear and brief.
　　Charles A. O'Neill's "The Language of Advertising"
　　Judith Ortiz Cofer's "The Myth of the Latin Woman"

■ Play with language. Consider variations of well-known expressions. Try using alliteration (repetition of the initial—or other—consonant sounds) or assonance (repetition of vowel sounds).
　　Margaret Carlson's "The Boredom of Proof"
　　Shelby Steele's "Affirmative Action: The Price of Preference"

- Consider two-part titles, the first part imaginative, the second part descriptive. Separate the two parts with a colon.

    Holly Brubach's "Heroine Worship: The Age of the Female Icon"

    Susan Douglas's "Remote Control: How to Raise a Media Skeptic"

- Match the tone of the title to the tone of the paper. Use serious titles for serious papers, less formal titles for informal papers.

    Philip Wheelwright's "The Meaning of Ethics"

    Benjamin Demott's "Sure, We're All Just One Big Happy Family"

Keep an open mind as you write titles. Create several and select the one that best clarifies the paper's topic and—when appropriate—piques interest.

Jarah considered a variety of options for her title. She found through her research that the Lincoln Memorial is often referred to as the "Temple of Democracy" and thought she might include that phrase in her title. She also experimented with alliteration to produce the phrase "the Legacy of the Lincoln Memorial." In the process of writing her paper, she used a phrase that she liked and combined it with one of her other strategies to produce this two-part title: "Walking into History: The Legacy of the Lincoln Memorial."

Introductions

The introduction to a paper establishes a context for the discussion, clarifying the subject and your opinion. In addition, the introduction creates interest, drawing readers into the discussion. To achieve these goals, draft alternative introductions, keeping these general principles in mind:

- Adjust the length of the introduction to the length of the paper. A long paper needs a proportionately comprehensive introduction.
- Match the tone of the introduction to the tone of the paper. An informal paper needs an informal introduction, whereas a serious, academic paper requires a formal one.
- An introduction should suggest the focus of the paper, create interest, and perhaps indicate how the paper is developed.

Begin the introduction with one or more of the following general strategies and end it by presenting the thesis statement. The following strategies are well suited to researched papers:

- *Allusion.* Refer to a work of art, music, literature, or film—or to a mythical, religious, literary, or historical person or event.
- *Analogy.* Make a comparison that is relevant to the topic.
- *Anecdote.* Begin with a short description of a related incident.
- *Definition.* Define a term central to your topic. Avoid defining terms already understood, unless the definition serves a special purpose.

- *Description.* Use a description of a scene, person, or event to establish context or mood for your topic.
- *Facts and figures.* Begin with specific, interesting, useful information or statistics.
- *New discussion of an old subject.* Explain why a topic that may seem overly familiar is worth examining again.
- *Question.* Use a question or a series of questions to prompt readers to think about the topic.
- *Quotation.* Use what someone else has said or written in a poem, play, short story, book, article, essay, or interview.
- *Startling statement.* Use an arresting statement to get readers' attention and arouse their interest.

Conclusions

A conclusion re-emphasizes the point of a paper and provides an opportunity to create a desired final impression. Most conclusions begin with a brief but specific summary and then use a concluding strategy to present a general observation.

Some introductory strategies—such as allusion, analogy, anecdote, description, and quotation—also work well as concluding strategies. The following additional strategies are particularly appropriate for conclusions.

- *Challenge.* Ask readers to reconsider their current behavior or ideas or to consider new behavior and ideas.
- *Framing pattern.* Frame the paper by modifying some central words, phrases, or images from the introduction to reflect the progress of thought demonstrated in the paper. When appropriate, the introductory strategy may be repeated as the concluding strategy, intensifying the framing effect.
- *Summary.* Summarize, restate, or evaluate the major points of the paper. This strategy must be used carefully and thoughtfully to avoid mere repetition.
- *Visualization of the future.* Predict what the nature or condition of the topic will be in the near or distant future. Be realistic.

Jarah knew immediately that she wanted to open her paper with an anecdote, describing her early recollections of the Lincoln Memorial and her first visit; she thought it would create a degree of interest and allow readers to either envision what it was like to approach the Memorial if they had never visited the site or to remember their first visit. She then experimented with alternative ways to achieve her goals.

Jarah had more difficulty with her conclusion. She knew she did not want to repeat her introductory pattern but was uncertain about what concluding strategies to employ. So she experimented with several techniques. Finally, she decided to use a quotation about the symbolic meanings that monuments assume, to provide a very brief summary of the elements of her paper, and to incorporate the phrase "Temple of Democracy," which she had found in her reading.

EXERCISE 12.2   *Titles and Introductory and Concluding Paragraphs*

Write several titles for your paper. Then write two draft versions of the introduction and of the conclusion, using the guidelines given above. Make sure that your strategies both create interest and clearly and appropriately introduce your topic and conclude your discussion. Have a classmate review your titles and read your introductory and concluding paragraphs to help you select the most promising ones.   ■ ■

CHAPTER
13

Revising the Paper

QUICK REFERENCE

Revision provides a chance to improve the development and presentation of your draft. Though it can be challenging, it is time well spent.

▶ Set your draft aside for as long as possible so that you can reread it from a fresh perspective.

▶ Consider issues of content—title, thesis, organization, development, and balance.

▶ Consider issues of style—tone, sentences, diction, and variety.

▶ Consider issues of technical correctness—grammar, punctuation, mechanics, note style, citation style, and manuscript preparation.

▶ Have several people—ideally from your class—read and respond to your paper; direct their reading so that they respond to issues that concern you.

After writing the draft of the paper, set it aside for at least two or three days. Then reread it carefully. Consider the paper's organization, content, and style. Ideas should be logically organized, clearly expressed, and effectively supported with appropriate and illuminating facts, summaries, paraphrases, and quotations—all smoothly and accurately incorporated. Allow time for reworking the paper: strengthen underdeveloped sections by expanding them, clarify confusing sections by rewriting them, and tighten overly long sections by cutting unnecessary material.

13a   Reconsider content.

Examine the paper's content for clarity, coherence, and completeness. Consider these issues:

- *Effective title, introduction, and conclusion.* Is the title both interesting and clear? Do the introduction and the conclusion effectively lead into and out of the discussion? Are introductory and concluding strategies well matched to the paper's tone and purpose? Revise any ineffective elements.
- *Thesis matched to development.* Does the thesis accurately represent your opinion of the topic? Does the development of the paper support it? Revise the thesis to reflect the final version of the paper.
- *Sufficient support for your thesis.* Have you included enough ideas and information to support the thesis? Would additional facts, examples, or quotations strengthen the paper? If you discover underdeveloped areas, work on them.
- *Balance in cited materials.* Have you incorporated a variety of facts, summaries, paraphrases, and quotations to develop your ideas in a varied and interesting way? If you discover an over-reliance on one kind of material, consider using alternative patterns.
- *Appropriateness of organizational pattern.* Is the organization logical? Would another pattern work better? If you discover a flaw—large or small—in your organization, correct it now: rearrange paragraphs or move sections. Coherence is crucial, so make necessary adjustments.
- *Transitions between sections.* Have you led readers clearly from one part of the discussion to the next? If your connections are unclear, revise them.
- *Balance among sections.* Are the sections of the paper appropriately balanced in length and emphasis? If you discover inconsistencies, add or delete information as necessary.
- *Balance in the use of sources.* Have you used all sources well? You will, no doubt, find some sources more useful than others, but do not rely too heavily on any one view. Adjust the paper if it needs a more balanced use of sources.
- *Balance in kinds of sources.* Have you used all books or all journal articles or all Internet sources? This suggests a limited perspective on the topic. If you have not achieved balance in kinds of sources, rework the paper.

Consider your earlier written work in order to focus on troublesome areas. For example, if you frequently have trouble with conclusions, ask a classmate or your instructor to review only that element of your paper. Give attention to recurring writing problems so that they do not interfere with otherwise effective research work.

The revision stage is the time to reflect on the overall effectiveness of the paper's content. Assess all elements carefully and critically.

13b   Rework style.

Achieving coherent, balanced, well-developed content is one aspect of revision. Another is achieving a clear and compelling presentation of that content. Refine the paper's style, keeping these issues in mind:

- *Tone appropriate for subject and purpose.* Is the paper's tone suited to the topic and presentation? The paper should be fairly formal but not pretentious or artificial. It is important to maintain a uniform tone throughout: an amusing introduction followed by a serious presentation gives readers mixed signals.
- *Effective sentences.* Have you used a variety of sentence lengths and types? Have you used active, not passive, voice in most sentences?
- *Appropriate diction.* Are your word choices vivid, accurate, and suitable? Have you explained technical terms effectively?
- *Effective introduction of researched materials.* Have you introduced your researched materials with variety and clarity?
- *Effective transitions between sections.* Do your transitions effectively connect one main point to the next or one subpoint to the next?

From comments you have received on other papers, you know both the strengths and the weaknesses of your writing style. The research paper, because of its length and complexity, provides an opportunity to refine your style. Take the time to do so.

13c   Eliminate technical errors.

Technical revision focuses on grammar, punctuation, mechanics, spelling, and manuscript form. After revising content and style, consider technical revisions to make the presentation correct and precise. Give particular attention to issues related to documentation, remembering that different styles (MLA, APA, Chicago, CBE, and others) require different formats (see Chapters 14–17). Focus on the following issues, while watching for technical errors you make frequently:

- *Correct grammar used throughout.* Are your sentences complete? Do nouns agree with pronouns, and subjects with verbs, in number and gender as appropriate?
- *Punctuation and mechanics handled suitably.* Is all punctuation accurate? Are spelling, quotation marks, and the use of italics (or underlining) accurate?
- *Quotations suitably presented.* Have you introduced all quotations or merged them with your own sentences? Have you placed all brief quotations in quotation marks within your paragraphs? Have you set off long quotations ten spaces (and omitted the quotation marks)?
- *Paraphrases clearly incorporated.* Have you "translated" paraphrased ideas into your own words and selectively quoted phrases of special importance? Have you introduced long paraphrases?
- *Parenthetical notes correctly placed and punctuated.* Are parenthetical notes placed appropriately and punctuated accurately, according to the kind of information being cited and the required documentary style?

■ *Works-cited page prepared accurately.* Have you listed only those materials cited in the paper? Is your list appropriately arranged, according to the required documentary style? Is each citation complete and correct, depending on the required kind of information? Have you included all necessary citations?

■ *Manuscript guidelines used correctly.* Have you followed manuscript guidelines for the required documentary style? Are margins, line spacing, and paging accurate? Does your paper include all required elements? Review and follow manuscript guidelines carefully.

Make technical revisions slowly and carefully. If you are uncertain as to whether you have made an error, look up the applicable rule in this handbook or a grammatical handbook. Never ignore potential problems, hoping they may not be noticed.

COLLABORATION

Revising a collaborative paper or project is easy because you have already established a working relationship with your collaborators. In addition, because you have shared the responsibilities of planning and writing the paper, you have made many substantive changes during the process. To achieve some distance from your work, however, wait at least two or three days and then revise the paper, following these recommendations:

■ *Read the paper aloud.* Reading the work aloud allows you and your collaborators to respond simultaneously.

■ *Discuss troublesome elements as you read.* Stop whenever a collaborator feels something is not working well. Though somewhat slow, this process allows you to improve the paper in small stages.

■ *Make clear notations.* Make corrections and changes on the copy you read from. If a revision is too complex to complete during the reading, make notes in the margin and give the matter fuller attention later.

■ *Remember your separate strengths.* Each collaborator brings special expertise to the revision process. Use this fact to your advantage. If one collaborator is skilled with stylistic matters like transitions or word choice, give him or her special responsibility for those issues. If one is adept at technical issues of writing, depend on him or her in those instances. In areas where none of you feels especially skilled, consult textbooks or ask your instructor for advice.

13d Solicit responses from other readers.

After working on a research paper for weeks, quite naturally you lose your objectivity. That is normal. To get an unbiased response to the paper, consider working with a peer editor. Because a peer editor does not know the topic as well as you do, he or she can read and respond objectively and point out matters that require attention. Before asking someone to serve as your peer editor, however, consider the qualities of an effective peer editor and the strategies that make peer editing successful.

Qualities of a Peer Editor

- *Knowledgeable.* A good peer editor knows something, though not necessarily everything, about the research process. For this reason, someone in your class—with the same classroom experiences—is an excellent choice.
- *Thoughtful.* A good peer editor may know little about your topic, but he or she is a careful reader who gives attention to ideas and information.
- *Curious.* A good peer editor wants to know more about a subject, whatever it is. He or she poses questions, challenges assumptions, and requires thorough explanations.
- *Honest.* A good peer editor evaluates your work truthfully, recognizing that only honest criticism helps you improve your writing.
- *Flexible.* A good peer editor adapts to your needs, giving special attention to your concerns. He or she is flexible enough to realize that *you* must evaluate the comments and decide how to use them.
- *Collegial.* A good peer editor treats you with respect and is never overbearing; instead, he or she draws attention to specific concerns but leaves the method of addressing the problems up to you.
- *Thorough.* A good peer editor reviews writing comprehensively, looking at content, style, and technical matters, rather than focusing on isolated, specific elements out of context.

Issues to Remember for Peer Editing

- *Have a readable copy.* A "readable" paper does not have to be attractive, but it must be easy to work with: typed and double-spaced, with neat corrections, clear additions and deletions, and complete text (including work-cited entries).
- *Allow enough time.* Allow sufficient time for the peer editor to review the paper slowly and carefully. Do not expect him or her to read a ten-page paper carefully in ten minutes.
- *Ask specific questions.* Focus the peer editor's attention on specific elements: typical problems ("Look at my background paragraphs. . . . I always have trouble with those") or areas with which you experimented ("Also check whether I've varied the wording when I introduce quotes"). To get the best help, direct the peer editor's attention.

- *Consider every comment.* Once you have an editor's comments about features of the paper, consider each one carefully. Some notations are easy to respond to ("I can't believe I forgot to include the page!"), but others are troublesome because they challenge your writing on the topic ("What do you mean—my examples aren't convincing?"). Remember the spirit in which the comments are made and use them to improve the paper.

- *Remember that the paper is yours.* Strike a balance in the way you respond to a peer editor's notes. Some comments point out problems that are so self-evident that you should change your original immediately. At other times, you must think carefully about whether or not to make a proposed change. In the end, the paper is *yours,* so the difficult decisions are yours, too.

- *Decide whether to stay or to leave.* Decide whether or not to stay in the room with the peer editor. Staying has its advantage: you can provide brief explanations or clarifications. Leaving has its advantage, too: it replicates the experience that later readers will have (since you will not be standing nearby to explain unclear elements of the paper). Deciding whether to stay or to leave is a personal choice.

- *Wait before making changes.* Just as waiting between drafting and revising helps you achieve some critical distance, waiting between peer editing and another revision also makes sense. Take time to review the comments and suggestions thoughtfully. Hurrying never helps writing.

The peer-review process allows a representative reader to respond to your work: to discover where your paper succeeds and where it does not. After peer review, you can make necessary changes—this, of course, is important—before submitting a final copy.

COLLABORATION

Although collaboration includes multiple perspectives, your collaborative team has worked intensely on the paper or project. Collectively, you may still lack critical distance—the same problem that affects individual writers. For that reason, peer review remains an excellent strategy for getting another response to a paper, even one written collaboratively.

► EXERCISE 13.1   *Peer Evaluation of the Research Paper*

Have a peer editor review your reseasrch paper, using the following form.

RESEARCH PAPER EVALUATION

Course _____   Editor's Name _____

	Poor		*Excellent*		*Comments*
THESIS					
Topic Clarity	1	2	3	4	5
Clear Opinion	1	2	3	4	5
Tone and Style	1	2	3	4	5
CONTENT					
Use of Facts	1	2	3	4	5
Use of Ideas	1	2	3	4	5
Use of Quotations	1	2	3	4	5
Balanced Use of Sources	1	2	3	4	5
Use of Own Ideas	1	2	3	4	5
ORGANIZATION					
Logical Order	1	2	3	4	5
Balance of Sections	1	2	3	4	5
Use of Transitions	1	2	3	4	5
WORD CHOICE					
Vivid Word Choices	1	2	3	4	5
Varied Word Choices	1	2	3	4	5
Accurate Word Choices	1	2	3	4	5
SENTENCES AND STYLE					
Varied Sentences	1	2	3	4	5
Active Sentences	1	2	3	4	5
TECHNICAL MATTERS					
Grammatical Accuracy	1	2	3	4	5
Appropriate Usage	1	2	3	4	5
Correct Punctuation	1	2	3	4	5
Correct Spelling	1	2	3	4	5
In-Text Documentation	1	2	3	4	5
Works-Cited Page	1	2	3	4	5
Manuscript Form	1	2	3	4	5

SPECIAL CONCERNS

1. _____   2. _____

COMMENTS:

_____
_____
_____

Source Checklist

_____ books	_____ newspapers	_____ journals
_____ magazines	_____ audiovisual sources	_____ Internet sources

■■

CHAPTER

14

Using MLA Style
When Appropriate*

QUICK REFERENCE

Prepare MLA citations for sources, applying these general principles for formatting and incorporating required information.

▶ Begin the first line of each entry at the left margin but indent subsequent lines one-half inch.

▶ Arrange entries alphabetically using the first element, usually the author or title (omitting *a, an,* or *the*).

▶ Double-space entries; do not insert additional line spaces between entries.

▶ Provide full information (authors' complete names, titles with subtitles, complete electronic addresses), but shorten publishers' names (*Houghton,* not *Houghton Mifflin*) and abbreviate months (*Sept.,* not *September*).

▶ Invert the author's name when it begins an entry (*Perrin, Robert,* not *Robert Perrin*).

▶ When an element is missing, proceed to the next element: an article without a stated author begins with the article's title.

▶ Include electronic addresses in angle brackets <ncte.org> and divide these addresses after slashes when they extend beyond one line.

▶ Separate the major elements of an entry with periods and single spaces.

▶ Use the samples in this chapter as models when you prepare your own citations, combining information from several samples when a source has many features.

*The information in this chapter is based on Joseph Gibaldi's *MLA Handbook for Writers of Research Papers,* sixth edition (New York: Modern Language Association, 2003).

To acknowledge the use of other people's ideas, information, or exact words in a paper, include accurate citations: brief, technical descriptions of original sources, presented in very specific formats. Appearing at the end of a paper in a works-cited list, they provide basic information about sources so that interested readers may locate them for further study.

14a Prepare complete citations for the works-cited page.

Because works-cited entries direct readers to sources used in researched writing, these entries must be as complete as possible and presented in a consistent and recognizable format. As you review the following sample citations, give particular attention to the information describing the wide variety of potential sources.

To complete a citation for your paper, leaf through the sample citations until you find the one that most closely corresponds to your type of source. Remember that some citations combine information according to the guidelines noted below. Prepare your citations on 3" × 5" index cards (one citation per card), on sheets of paper, or in a computer file. If you prepare citations on a computer, use a separate file with an easily recognizable name (for example, *paper2.cit, research.cit,* or *aviation.cit*). Since a citation file will remain comparatively small, you can retrieve it quickly, add to or delete from it, and then copy and paste the complete works-cited file into the final draft of your paper.

Whichever method you choose—index cards, paper, or computer— record complete and accurate citations. Forgetting to record full information when you first use a source requires you to return to it at a later, possibly less convenient, time to supply remaining information.

Information for MLA Citations*

MLA (Modern Language Association) citations present information in an established order. When combining forms (to list a translation of a second edition, for example), follow these guidelines to determine the order of information:

1. *Author(s).* Use the name or names with the spelling and order shown on the title page of a book or on the first page of an article, without degrees, titles, or affiliations. If no author (individual or organization) is listed, note that fact to avoid confusion later on; an authorless work is listed by title in the works-cited entry.

---

*Electronic sources often require additional, specialized information. Full explanations of citations for electronic sources appear in section **14e.**

2. *Title.* List titles from part to whole. To cite part of a book (for example, a single essay in a collection), list the title of the essay (the part) before the book (the whole); list the title of an article before a periodical title, an episode before a program, or a song before an album. Use complete titles, including subtitles, no matter how long they are (using a colon and one space to separate the title from the subtitle).

3. *Additional information.* When a citation requires multiple elements, they are included in this order:

   - editor
   - translator
   - compiler
   - edition number
   - volume number
   - name of series

4. *Facts of publication.* For books, find the publisher's name and the place of publication on the title page, and the date of publication on the copyright page (immediately following the title page); use the publisher's name in abbreviated form (see samples in section **14b** and the list in Appendix B); use the first city listed if more than one is given; and use the most recent date shown. When the city is outside the United States, include an abbreviation for the country, if necessary for clarity. For periodicals, find the volume number, issue number, and date in the masthead (a listing of identifying information at the top of the first page of a newspaper or within the first few pages in a journal or magazine, often in combination with the table of contents).

5. *Page numbers.* When citing a part of a book or an article, provide inclusive page numbers without page abbreviations. Record inclusive page numbers from one to ninety-nine in full form (8–12, 33–39, 68–73); inclusive numbers of one hundred or higher require at least the last two digits and any other digits needed for clarity (100–02, 120–36, 193–206).

Format for MLA Citations

MLA citations follow general formatting guidelines, to ensure that they are consistent:

- Begin the first line of each entry at the left margin; indent subsequent lines five spaces (approximately one-half inch).
- Give the author's last name first (to alphabetize easily). If sources are co-authored, list additional authors' names in normal first-last order.
- Italicize or underline titles of full-length works; the meaning is the same. Be consistent throughout the paper.

- Separate major sections of entries (author, title, and publication information) with periods and one space, not two. When other forms of end punctuation are used (when titles end with question marks or exclamation points, for example), the period may be omitted.
- Double-space all entries; do not insert additional line spaces between entries.

Note that in sections **14b–14e**, sample works-cited entries are followed by corresponding sample parenthetical notes.

14b Follow the appropriate citation forms for books and other separately published material.

14b.1 A Book by One Author

Barr, Stephen M. *Modern Physics and Ancient Faith.* Notre Dame: U of Notre Dame P, 2003.
> **Parenthetical note** (Barr 216)

The letters *U* and *P,* without periods, abbreviate *University* and *Press.*

Gould, Eric. *The University in a Corporate Culture.* New Haven: Yale UP, 2003.
> **Parenthetical note** (Gould 17)

14b.2 A Book by Two or Three Authors

Authors' names appear in the order presented on the title page, which may or may not be alphabetical order. A comma follows the initial author's first name; second and third authors' names appear in normal order.

Fagan, Jay, and Glen Palm. *Fathers and Early Childhood Programs.* Clifton Park: Delmar, 2003.
> **Parenthetical note** (Fagan and Palm 66)

Kegley, Charles W., and Gregory A. Raymond. *How Nations Make Peace.* New York: St. Martin's, 1999.
> **Parenthetical note** (Kegley and Raymond 44)

The period following the first author's middle initial cannot substitute for the comma; both must be used.

MLA STYLE

14b.3 A Book by Four or More Authors

Include the first author's name in full form, but substitute _et al._ (meaning _et alii,_ Latin for "and others") for the names of additional authors. Note that _et al._ is not italicized in the citation and that its period substitutes for the one that normally follows the authors' names.

Gershey, Edward L., et al. _Low-Level Radioactive Waste: From Cradle to Grave._ New
York: Van Nostrand, 1990.

   **Parenthetical note**   (Gershey et al. 22)

Tucker, Susan Martin, et al. _Patient Care Standards: Collaborative Planning and Nursing
Interventions._ 7th ed. St. Louis: Mosby, 2000.

   **Parenthetical note**   (Tucker et al. 118)

14b.4 A Book with No Author Named

When no author or editor is named, list the work by title, or list an authorless book by editor to emphasize his or her work. To alphabetize books listed by title, use the first important word of the title, not the articles _a, an,_ or _the._

An Anglo-Saxon Chronicle. Ed. M. J. Swanton. Exeter, Eng.: U of Exeter P, 1990.

   **Parenthetical note**   (Anglo-Saxon Chronicle 23)

This citation emphasizes the work itself and is alphabetized by the first important word, _Anglo-Saxon,_ disregarding the article _An._ The name of the country is provided to clarify the city's location.

Swanton, M. J., ed. _An Anglo-Saxon Chronicle._ Exeter, Eng.: U of Exeter P, 1990.

   **Parenthetical note**   (Swanton 23)

This citation emphasizes the editor's work; notice that the abbreviation for _editor_ is not capitalized when it follows the person's name.

_United Press International Stylebook: The Authoritative Handbook for Writers, Editors,
and News Directors._ 3rd ed. Lincolnwood: Natl. Textbook, 1992.

   **Parenthetical note**   (_United Press International Stylebook_ 77)

Note that _national_ is abbreviated when it is part of a publisher's name.

14b.5 Multiple Works by the Same Author

When citing multiple works by the same author, present the first citation completely. Subsequent entries, alphabetized by title, are introduced by three hyphens and a period. Co-authored works require full names and are alphabetized after those with single authors.

Ehrenreich, Barbara. "Barefoot, Pregnant, and Ready to Fight." *Time* 8 May 2000: 62.

---. "Looking to Put Fatherhood in Its Proper Place." *New York Times* 20 June 1999, late ed.: L14.

---. "Who Needs Men? Addressing the Prospect of a Matrilinear Millennium." Interview. With Lionel Tiger. *Harper's* June 1999: 33–46.

Ehrenreich, Barbara, Elizabeth Hess, and Gloria Jacobs. *Re-Making Love: The Feminization of Sex*. Garden City: Anchor-Doubleday, 1986.

Alternative parenthetical notes
- *Time* article: (Ehrenreich, "Barefoot" 62)
- *New York Times* article: (Ehrenreich, "Looking to Put" L14)
- *Harper's* article: (Ehrenreich, "Who Needs Men?" 34)
- Multiple-author book: (Ehrenreich, Hess, and Jacobs 104)

14b.6 A Book by an Author Using a Pseudonym

Begin the entry with the pseudonym ("pen name"), the name that is associated with the book. After the name but before the period, place the author's true name in brackets.

Eliot, George [Mary Ann Evans]. *The Journals of George Eliot*. Ed. Margaret Harris and Judith Johnson. New York: Cambridge UP, 1998.

Parenthetical note   (Eliot 236)

Sand, George [Amatine-Aurore-Lucie Dupin]. *Lettres d'un voyageur*. Trans. Sacha Rabinovitch and Patricia Thomson. New York: Penguin, 1987.

Parenthetical note   (Sand 119)

Present an author's name exactly, including hyphens used in some multi-word names.

14b.7 A Book with an Organization as Author

When an organization is both the author and the publisher, present the name completely in the author position and use an abbreviation in the publisher position.

American Psychological Association. *Publication Manual of the American Psychological Association*. 5th ed. Washington: APA, 2001.

Parenthetical note   (American Psychological Association 323)

Gemological Institute of America. *The Diamond Dictionary.* Santa Monica: GIA, 1977.

    Parenthetical note   (Gemological Institute of America 29)

14b.8   An Edition Other than the First

The edition number, noted on the title page, usually follows the title of the book. However, when a book also has an editor, translator, or compiler, the edition number follows that information. Edition numbers are presented in numeral-abbreviation form (2nd, 3rd, 4th), not spelled out. *Edition* is abbreviated, with its period substituting for the end punctuation that separates elements of the citation.

Forging the American Character: Readings in United States History. Ed. John R. M. Wilson.
       4th ed. Upper Saddle River: Prentice, 2003.

    Parenthetical note   (*Forging* 83)

Editors' names, when they follow the title, are presented in normal order.

Griffin, James M., ed. *Global Climate Change: The Science, Economics, and Politics.*
       2nd ed. Northampton: Elgar, 2003.

    Parenthetical note   (Griffin 51)

14b.9   A Revised or Enlarged Edition

Indications of revised or enlarged editions appear on the title page; the abbreviation *Rev. ed.* or *Enlarged ed.,* not italicized, appears before the facts of publication.

Distance Learning Technologies: Issues, Trends, and Opportunities. Ed. Linda K. Lau.
       Rev. ed. Hershey: Idea Group, 2000.

    Parenthetical note   (*Distance Learning Technologies* 86)

Wattenburg, Martin P. *The Decline of American Political Parties: 1952–1996.* Enlarged
       ed. Cambridge: Harvard UP, 1998.

    Parenthetical note   (Wattenburg 211)

14b.10   A Reprint

A reprint, a newly printed but unaltered version of a book, is identified as such on the title page or copyright page. List the original publication date before the facts of publication and list the date of the reprinted edition after the publisher's name.

Beck, Theodric Romeyo. *Elements of Medical Jurisprudence.* 1823. Union: Lawbook Exchange, 1997.

    Parenthetical note   (Beck 426)

Loeb, Harold. *Life in a Technocracy: What It Might Be Like.* 1933. Syracuse: Syracuse
UP, 1996.
Parenthetical note   (Loeb 74)

14b.11   A Multivolume Work

A multivolume work may have one title, or it may have a comprehensive
title for the complete work and separate titles for each volume. When you
use the entire set of volumes, use the collective title and note the number of
volumes. In a corresponding parenthetical note, indicate the volume used,
followed by a colon, a space, and the page reference.

American Men and Women of Science. Ed. Pamela M. Kalte and Katherine H. Nenen.
21st ed. 8 vols. Detroit: Gale, 2003.
Parenthetical note   (*American Men and Women of Science* 1: 3)

Medal of Honor Recipients: 1863–1994. Ed. George Lang, Raymond L. Collins, and Ger-
ard F. White. 2 vols. New York: Facts on File, 1995.
Parenthetical note   (*Medal of Honor Recipients* 2: 6)

To emphasize a single volume, first cite the volume as a separate book.
Then add the volume number, the collection title, and the total number
of volumes.

Melville, Herman. *Moby-Dick or The Whale.* Ed. Harrison Hayford, Hershel Parker, and
G. Thomas Tanselle. Northwestern Newberry Ed. Evanston: Northwestern UP,
1988. Vol. 6 of *The Writings of Herman Melville.* 15 vols.
Parenthetical note   (Melville 482)

Northwestern-Newberry denotes a published series and consequently must
be included in the citation (see "A Work in a Series," section **14b.17**).

Roberts, J. M. *The Age of Revolution.* New York: Oxford UP, 1999. Vol. 7 of *The Illustrated
History of the World.* 10 vols.
Parenthetical note   (Roberts 66)

14b.12   An Edited Collection

When referring to an entire collection, not to selected parts, begin with its
title, adding other relevant information.

Nature, Nurture, and the Transition to Early Adolescence. Ed. Stephen A. Petrill. New
York: Oxford UP, 2003.
Parenthetical note   (*Nature* 93)

Space and Beyond: The Frontier Theme in Science Fiction. Ed. Gary Westfahl. Westport:
      Greenwood, 2000.

Parenthetical note   (*Space and Beyond* 39)

14b.13   A Work in a Collection

To cite a work in a collection, begin with the name of the selection's author.
Include the name of the specific selection (appropriately punctuated), collection title, publication facts, and the inclusive page numbers for the
selection. To cite more than one selection from the collection, prepare separate citations (see "Multiple Selections from the Same Collection," section **14b.15**).

Corrigan, Timothy. "Which Shakespeare to Love? Film, Fidelity, and the Performance of
      Literature." *High-Pop: Making Culture into Popular Entertainment.* Ed. Jim
      Collins. Malden: Blackwell, 2003. 155–81.

Parenthetical note   (Corrigan 157–58)

Melville, Herman. *Billy Budd, Sailor. The Complete Shorter Fiction.* Everyman's Library
      232. New York: Knopf, 1997. 403–77.

Parenthetical note   (Melville 465)

The title of the novel is italicized because *Billy Budd, Sailor* is a full-length
work.

Newsome, Chevelle. "Multiple Identities: The Case of Biracial Children." *Trans-Cultural
      Realities.* Ed. Virginia H. Milhous, Molefi Kete Asante, and Peter O. Nwosu.
      Thousand Oaks: Sage, 2001. 145–59.

Parenthetical note   (Newsome 150)

14b.14   A Previously Published Work in a Collection

To indicate that a selection has been previously published, begin the citation
with original facts of publication (most often information from publication in a journal). *Rpt.*, meaning "reprinted," begins the second part of the
citation, which includes information about the source you have used.

Bérubé, Michael. "Aesthetics and Literal Imagination." *Clio: A Journal of Literature, His-
      tory, and the Philosophy of History* 25.4 (1996): 439–46. Rpt. in *Falling into
      Theory: Conflicting Views of Reading Literature.* Ed. David H. Richter. 2nd ed.
      New York: Bedford, 2000. 391–97.

Parenthetical note   (Bérubé 394)

Wallace, Mike. "Mickey Mouse History: Portraying the Past at Disney World." *Radical History Review* 32 (1985): 33–55. Rpt. in *Customs in Conflict: The Anthology of a Changing World.* Ed. Frank Manning and Jean-Marc Philbert. Peterborough, ON: Broadview, 1990. 304–32.

    Parenthetical note   (Wallace 325–26)

Note that *Ontario,* abbreviated, clarifies the location of a city outside the United States.

14b.15   Multiple Selections from the Same Collection

To cite several selections from the same collection, prepare a citation for the complete work—beginning either with the editor's name or with the collection title. Additional references begin with the author of the selection and its title; however, instead of providing full publication information, include the editor's name (if that is how you began the full-source citation) or a shortened version of the title (if you began the full-source citation with the title); provide inclusive page numbers for the selection. Notice that all citations are alphabetized.

Edut, Ophira, ed. *Adiós Barbie: Young Women Write about Body Image and Identity.* Seattle: Seal, 1998.

Gilman, Susan Jane. "Klaus Barbie and Other Dolls I'd Like to See." Edut 14–21.

Heywood, Leslie. "All American Girls: Jock Chic, Body Image, and Sports." Edut 201–10.

    Alternative parenthetical notes
- (Edut iii)
- (Gilman 17)
- (Heywood 202)

Adiós Barbie: Young Women Write about Body Image and Identity. Ed. Ophira Edut. Seattle: Seal, 1998.

Gilman, Susan Jane. "Klaus Barbie and Other Dolls I'd Like to See." *Adiós* 14–21.

Heywood, Leslie. "All American Girls: Jock Chic, Body Image, and Sports." *Adiós* 201–10.

    Parenthetical note   (*Adiós* iii)

14b.16   An Article in an Encyclopedia or Other Reference Work

An author's name should be used when it is available. If only initials are listed with the article, match them with the name from the list of contributors, usually provided at the beginning or end of the reference work. Well-known reference books require no information other than the title, edition number (if any), and date. Citations for less well-known or recently published reference works include full publication information. Page numbers are not needed when a reference work is arranged alphabetically.

Abrams, Richard M. "Theodore Roosevelt." *The Presidents: A Reference History.* Ed.

    Henry F. Graff. 2nd ed. New York: Scribner's, 1996. 325–46.

  Parenthetical note   (Abrams 342)

Because the articles on the presidents are arranged chronologically, not alphabetically, page numbers are required.

Angermüller, Rudolph. "Salieri, Antonio." *The New Grove Dictionary of Music and Mu-*

    sicians. 2001 ed.

  Parenthetical note   (Angermüller)

This twenty-volume set is extremely well known and consequently needs no publication information. Note that the article title appears in the same form as it does in the reference book.

When no author's name (or related abbreviation) appears with an article, begin with the title, reproduced to match the pattern in the reference book. Other principles remain the same.

"Flatbed Scanner." *The GAFT [Graphic Arts Technology Foundation] Encyclopedia of*

    Graphic Communication. Ed. Frank J. Romano. Upper Saddle River: Prentice,

    1998.

  Parenthetical note   ("Flatbed Scanner")

Brackets are used to enclose the full name of the organization.

14b.17 A Work in a Series

Names of series (collections of books related to the same subject, genre, time period, and so on) are typically found on a book's title page and should be included just before the publishing information. Abbreviate the word *Series* if it is part of the series title.

Fogg, B. J. *Persuasive Technology: Using Computers to Change What We Think and Do.*

    Interactive Technology Ser. Boston: Kaufman, 2003.

  Parenthetical note   (Fogg 131)

Walker, Samuel, Cassia Spohn, and Miriam DeLone. *The Color of Justice: Race, Ethnicity,*
     and Crime in America. 3rd ed. Contemporary Issues in Crime and Justice Ser.
     Belmont: Wadsworth, 2003.
    Parenthetical note   (Walker, Spohn, and DeLone 37)

When volumes in a series are numbered, include both the series name
and the volume number, followed by a period.

Neumann, Erich. *The Origins and History of Consciousness.* Trans. R. F. C. Hull. Bollin-
     gen Ser. 42. Princeton: Princeton UP, 1973.
    Parenthetical note   (Neumann 55)

Waugh, Evelyn. *A Handful of Dust.* Everyman's Library 252. New York: Knopf, 2002.
    Parenthetical note   (Waugh 72)

14b.18   An Imprint

An imprint is a specialized division of a larger publishing company. When
an imprint name and a publisher name both appear on the title page, list
them together (imprint name first), separated by a hyphen and no additional spaces.

Coupland, Justine, and Richard Gwyn, eds. *Discourse, the Body, and Identity.* New York:
     Palgrave-Macmillan, 2003.
    Parenthetical note   (Coupland and Gwyn 128)

Palgrave is the imprint; Macmillan is the publisher.

Jardine, Lisa. *Ingenious Pursuits: Building the Scientific Revolution.* New York: Talese:
     Doubleday, 1999.
    Parenthetical note   (Jardine 39)

Nan A. Talese is the imprint, which is shortened to *Talese;* Doubleday is
the publisher.

14b.19   A Translation

A translator's name must always be included in a citation for a translated
work because he or she prepared the version that you read. To emphasize
the original work (the most common pattern), place the abbreviation
Trans. (for "translated by") and the translator's name after the title (but
following editors' names, if appropriate).

Agacinski, Sylvaine. *Time Passing: Modernity and Nostalgia.* Trans. Jody Gladding. New
York: Columbia UP, 2003.
   Parenthetical note   (Agacinski 84)

Beauvoir, Simone de. *The Ethics of Ambiguity.* Trans. Bernard Frechtman. New York:
Citadel, 1991.
   Parenthetical note   (Beauvoir 27)

If selections within a collection are translated by different people, then
the translator's name should follow the name of the selection. Placing the
translator's name after the book title indicates that he or she translated *all*
selections in the collection.

Foucault, Michel. "What Is an Author?" Trans. Josue V. Hatari. *Criticism: Major Statements.* Ed. Charles Kaplan. 4th ed. Bedford, 2000. 545–58.
   Parenthetical note   (Foucault 547–48)

Kiš, Danilo. "Dogs and Books." Trans. Duška Mikic-Mitchell. *The Oxford Book of Jewish
Stories.* Ed. Ilan Stavans. New York: Oxford UP, 1998. 325–35.
   Parenthetical note   (Kiš 330)

If you are discussing techniques of translation, place the translator's
name first, followed by a comma, the abbreviation *trans.,* and the title.
When appropriate, follow the title with the author's name, introduced
with *By.*

Thiébaux, Marcelle, trans. *The Writings of Medieval Women: An Anthology.* 2nd ed. New
York: Garland, 1994.
   Parenthetical note   (Thiébaux 64)

Wilbur, Richard, trans. *Tartuffe. The Misanthrope and Tartuffe.* By Molière. New York:
Harcourt, 1965. 165–326.
   Parenthetical note   (Wilbur 171)

14b.20   A Government Document—*Congressional Record*

Citations for *Congressional Record* are exceedingly brief: the italicized
and abbreviated title *Cong. Rec.,* the date (presented in day-month-year
order), and the page number. Page numbers used alone indicate Senate
records; page numbers preceded by an *H* indicate records from the House
of Representatives.

Cong. Rec. 18 May 1995: 6931.
   Parenthetical note   (*Cong. Rec.* 6931)

This simple citation for Senate records describes the introduction of the Telecommunication and Deregulation Act of 1995.

Cong. Rec. 7 Oct. 1994: H11251.
> **Parenthetical note**   (*Cong. Rec.* H11251)

Note the page reference, with the *H* indicating that the cited summary, titled "Appropriations for the Bureau of Land Management [State by State]," was part of House records.

14b.21   A Government Document—Committee, Commission, Department

Information that describes government documents is generally presented in this order: (1) country, state, province, or county; (2) government official, governing body, sponsoring department, commission, center, ministry, or agency; (3) office, bureau, or committee; (4) the title of the publication, italicized; (5) if appropriate, the author of the document, the number and session of Congress, the kind and number of the document; (6) the city of publication, the publisher, and the date.

United States. Cong. Budget Office. *Budget of the United States Government, Fiscal Year 2002.* Washington: GPO, 2001.
> **Parenthetical note**   (US, Cong., Budget Office, *Budget* 216)

The name of the Government Printing Office, the publisher of most federal documents, is abbreviated to save space.

United States. Commission on the Assassination of President Kennedy. *Investigation of the Assassination of President John F. Kennedy: Hearings before the President's Commission on the Assassination of President Kennedy.* 16 vols. Washington: GPO, 1964.
> **Parenthetical note**   (US, Commission on the Assassination 3: 68)

Note that multivolume government documents follow citation patterns like those of other multivolume collections.

United States. Cong. Senate. Subcommittee on Consumer Affairs of the Committee on Banking, Housing, and Urban Affairs. *Hearings on the "Fair Debt Collection Practices" Act.* 95th Cong., 1st sess. S 656, S 918, S 1130, HR 5294. Washington: GPO, 1990.
> **Parenthetical note**   (US, Cong., Subcommittee on Consumer Affairs 12)

The number and session of Congress are listed after the title of the document; the numbers of the related bills are also included with designations for Senate (*S*) and House of Representatives (*HR*).

When citing more than one work from the same government or agency, use three hyphens and a period, to substitute for identical elements.

United States. Cong. Senate. Committee on Aging. *Hearing*. 101st Cong., 1st sess. 1989.
Washington: GPO, 1990.

---. Dept. of Education. *Alcohol, Other Drugs, and College: A Parent's Guide*. Washington: GPO, 2000.

---. ---. *Families and Schools and Partners*. Washington: GPO, 2000.

---. ---. *School Involvement in Early Childhood*. By Donna Hinkle. Washington: GPO, 2000.

Parenthetical notes
(US, Cong., Senate, Committee on Aging 262)

(US, Dept. of Education, *Alcohol* 44)

(US, Dept. of Education, *Families* 31)

(US, Dept. of Education, *School Involvement* 9)

The use of sets of hyphens indicates when information corresponds to the preceding citation.

14b.22   A Government Document—Emphasis on Author

To emphasize the author of a government document, list his or her name first, name the document, provide supplementary information, and end with the facts of publication.

Rhoades, Stephen A. *Bank Mergers and Banking Structure in the United States, 1980–98*.
Federal Reserve Board of Governors. Washington: GPO, 2000.

Parenthetical note   (Rhoades 50)

14b.23   A Preface, Introduction, Foreword, Epilogue, or Afterword

To cite material that is separate from the primary text of a book, begin with the name of the person who wrote the separate material, an assigned title (if applicable) in quotation marks, a descriptive title for the part used (capitalized but not punctuated), the title of the book, the name of the book's author (introduced with *By*, not italicized), publication facts, and inclusive page numbers for the separate material. Note that most prefatory or introductory material is paged using lowercase roman numerals.

Danto, Arthur C. "Philosophical Autobiography." Foreword. *Genius—in Their Own Words: The Intellectual Journeys of Seven Great 20th-Century Thinkers.* Chicago: Open Court, 2002. vii–viii.
>   ***Parenthetical note***   (Danto vii)

Finnegan, William. Epilogue. *Crossing the Line: A Year in the Land of Apartheid.* New York: Harper, 1986. 401–09.
>   ***Parenthetical note***   (Finnegan 405)

Because no author is identified following the book's title, it is clear that William Finnegan wrote the book, as well as the epilogue.

14b.24   A Pamphlet

When pamphlets contain clear and complete information, they are cited like books.

Lyme Disease and Related Disorders. Groton: Pfizer, 2000.
>   ***Parenthetical note***   (*Lyme Disease* 4)

Wyatt, Mike. *Taking Off: A Guide to Backpacking Trails across North America.* Emmaus: Rodale, 1990.
>   ***Parenthetical note***   (Wyatt 7)

When information is missing, use these abbreviations: *N.p.* for "No place of publication," *n.p.* for "no publisher," and *n.d.* for "no date"; none of these abbreviations is italicized in the citation.

America's Cup? The Sober Truth about Alcohol and Boating. Alexandria: Boat/U. S., n.d.
>   ***Parenthetical note***   (*America's Cup?* 3)

Domestic Mistreatment of the Elderly: Towards Prevention. N.p.: American Assn. of Retired Persons, 1987.
>   ***Parenthetical note***   (*Domestic Mistreatment* 23)

14b.25   An Annual Report

Published for stockholders (in part as promotional material), annual reports do not follow traditional printing formats. Publication information often appears on the back cover, and the date often appears with the CEO's (Chief Executive Officer) letter to shareholders.

At Pfizer, Life Is Our Life's Work: 1998 Annual Report. New York: Pfizer, 1999.
    Parenthetical note   (At Pfizer 56)

The Document Company: 1993 Annual Report. Stamford: Xerox, 1994.
    Parenthetical note   (The Document Company 38)

14b.26   The Proceedings of a Conference

Print versions of speeches given at a conference, published proceedings can be useful sources of specialized information. To cite conference proceedings, include the author's (speaker's) name, the title of the speech or paper (in quotation marks), the title of the published work, the editor, the descriptive title *Proceedings* (not italicized) if not already clear, the title of the conference unless it is already clear from the title, the sponsoring organization or group, the date (presented in day-month-year order), the facts of publication, and inclusive page numbers.

Rich, John A. "The Health Crisis of Young Black Men in the Inner City." *The Crisis*
    of the Young African American Male in the Inner City. Proceedings. United
    States Commission on Civil Rights. 15–16 Apr. 1999. Washington: GPO, 2000.
    132–42.
    Parenthetical note   (Rich 139–40)

Woodford, Michael. "Optimal Monetary Policy Inertia." *Papers in Money, Macroeconom-*
    ics, and Finance: Proceedings of the Money, Macroeconomics, and Finance Re-
    search Group. Sept. 1997. New York: Blackwell, 1999. 1–35.
    Parenthetical note   (Woodford 20)

14b.27   A Dissertation

A citation for an unpublished dissertation begins with the author's name, the dissertation title in quotation marks, the abbreviation *Diss.* (not italicized), the name of the degree-granting school (with *University* abbreviated), and the date.

Lehner, Luis. "Gravitational Radiation from Black Hole Spacetimes." Diss. U. of Pitts-
    burgh, 1998.
    Parenthetical note   (Lehner 111)

Stevenson, David Stacey. "Heat Transfer in Active Volcanoes: Models of Crater Lake
    Systems." Diss. Open U, UK, 1994.
    Parenthetical note   (Stevenson 96)

When the university's location is unfamiliar, include the state, province, or country.

A published dissertation is a book and should be presented as such. However, include dissertation information between the title and the facts of publication.

Parnet, Harriet L. *The Terror of Our Days: Four American Poets Respond to the Holocaust.*
     Diss. Lehigh U, 2000. Bethlehem: Lehigh UP, 2001.
    Parenthetical note   (Parnet 204)

Salzman, Lisa. *Anselm Kiefer and Art after Auschwitz.* Diss. Harvard U, 1994. New York:
     Cambridge UP, 1999.
    Parenthetical note   (Salzman 85)

14b.28   A Book Written in a Language Other than English

The order of citation information does not change for a book written in a foreign language, but a number of matters require special attention. First, when listing the title, follow the capitalization patterns of the book's original language. Many languages capitalize only the first word and proper nouns and proper adjectives in titles. Second, include all accents and diacritical marks; if your computer or typewriter does not include such features, add them neatly by hand in black ink.

Brecht, Bertolt. *Mutter Courage und Ihre Kinder. Stücke: Aus dem Exil.* Berlin:
     Suhrkamp, 1962. 61–207. Vol. 7 of *Bertolt Brecht: Stücke.* 14 vols.
    Parenthetical note   (Brecht 7: 65–66)

This citation describes a play included in a collection that is itself part of a larger collection.

Genet, Jean. *Les bonnes. Oeuvres complètes.* Paris: Gallimard, 1968. 137–76.
    Parenthetical note   (Genet 138)

14b.29   Sacred Writings

Citations for sacred writings follow patterns similar to those for other books, with several notable variations. First, titles of sacred writings (the parts or the whole) are neither placed in quotation marks nor italicized; they are capitalized only. Second, full facts of publication are not required for traditional editions. When appropriate, include additional information according to the guidelines for the element.

The Bhagavad Gita. Trans. Juan Mascaró. New York: Penguin, 1962.
> *Parenthetical note* (Bhagavad Gita)

Include translators when appropriate.

The Holy Bible.
> *Parenthetical note* (Exod. 1.14–16)

This citation is for the King James version of the Bible, the traditional edition.

The Holy Bible. Ed. C. I. Scofield. New York: Oxford UP, 1945.
> *Parenthetical note* (Exod. 1.15–16)

This citation emphasizes the editorial work of C. I. Scofield; this, too, is a King James version.

The New Oxford Annotated Bible. Ed. Herbert G. May and Bruce M. Metzger. Rev. Standard Version. New York: Oxford UP, 1973.
> *Parenthetical note* (Exod. 1.15–16)

This citation provides full information, highlighting a version other than the King James and the editorial work that it includes.

14b.30 A Book Published before 1900

Because publication information was so erratically included in books published before 1900, include only the city (and country if the book was not published in the United States and the city is not easily recognized), followed by a comma (not a colon), and the publication date. Other information is presented in normal fashion.

Daniel, Samuel. *The Collection of the History of England*. 5th ed. London, 1685.
> *Parenthetical note* (Daniel 47)

Turner, J. A. *The Cotton Planter's Manual: Being a Compilation of Facts from the Best Authorities on the Culture of Cotton; Its Natural History, Chemical Analysis, Trade, and Consumption; and Embracing a History of Cotton and the Cotton Gin*. New York, 1857.
> *Parenthetical note* (Turner 55–58)

14c   Follow the appropriate citation forms for periodicals.

14c.1   An Article in a Monthly Magazine

To cite an article in a monthly magazine, include the author's name, the article's title in quotation marks, the magazine's name (italicized), the month (abbreviated) and year, and the inclusive pages of the article.

Furlow, Bryant. "The Uses of Crying and Begging." *Natural History* Oct. 2000: 62–67.
   Parenthetical note   (Furlow 62)

Note that the period comes before the closing quotation marks of the article's title, that one space (but no punctuation) separates the periodical title and the date, and that a colon and a space separates the date and the pages.

Warschauer, Mark. "Demystifying the Digital Divide." *Scientific American* Aug. 2003:
   42–47.
   Parenthetical note   (Warschauer 46)

14c.2   An Article in a Weekly Magazine

Citations for articles in weekly magazines are identical to those for monthly magazines, with one exception: the publication date is presented in more detailed form, in day-month-year order (with the month abbreviated). (See Appendix B.)

Gest, Ted. "Fixing Your School." *U.S. News and World Report* 9 Oct. 2000: 65–67.
   Parenthetical note   (Gest 65)

Even though magazines often use special typography, such as the ampersand in *U.S. News & World Report,* such material is standardized in citations.

Ordoñez, Jennifer. "Rap to the Rescue." *Newsweek* 4 Aug. 2003: 58.
   Parenthetical note   (Ordoñez 58)

14c.3   An Article in a Journal with Continuous Paging

Journals with continuous paging number issues sequentially for the entire year; when an entire issue is bound into a single numbered volume, the page numbers are sequential throughout. For this kind of journal, place the volume number after the journal title, identify the year in parentheses, follow it with a colon and a space, and then list page numbers.

Chiguluri, Rachel Roth. "The Politics of Discourse and the Discourse of Politics in _Tres Tristes Tigres._" _Revista de Estudios Hispánicos_ 37 (2003): 249–69.
Parenthetical note   (Chiguluri 250)

Sherman, Aurora, Brian de Vries, and Jennifer E. Lansford. "Friendship in Childhood and Adulthood: Lessons across the Life Span." _The International Journal of Aging and Human Development_ 51 (2000): 31–51.
Parenthetical note   (Sherman, de Vries, and Lansford 43)

14c.4   An Article in a Journal with Separate Paging

When journals page each issue separately, follow the volume number with a period and the issue number (without spaces).

Gumm, Alan J. "Musical and Technical Sources of Choral Dynamics." _Choral Journal_ 43.10 (2003): 27–39.
Parenthetical note   (Gumm 28–29)

Lewis, Jon. "'We Do Not Ask You to Condone This': How the Blacklist Saved Hollywood." _Cinema Journal_ 39.2 (2000): 3–30.
Parenthetical note   (Lewis 13)

14c.5   An Article in a Newspaper

Citations for newspapers resemble those for magazines: they include the author's name, article title (in quotation marks), newspaper title (italicized), the date (in day-month-year order, followed by a colon), and inclusive pages.

However, when newspapers have editions (_morning, evening, national_), they must be identified; after the year, place a comma and describe the edition, using abbreviations of common words.

When sections of newspapers are designated by letters, place the section letter with the page number, without a space (_A22, C3, F11_); if sections are indicated by numerals, place a comma after the date or edition (rather than a colon), include the abbreviation _sec._, the section number, a colon, a space, and the page number (_sec. 1: 22, sec. 3: 2, sec. 5: 17_).

When an article continues in a later part of the paper, indicate the initial page, followed by a plus sign (_22+, A17+, sec. 2: 9+_).

Weekly newspapers are cited just like daily newspapers.

Baard, Erik. "Cyborg Liberation Front: Inside the Movement for Posthuman Rights." _Village Voice_ 5 Aug. 2003: 38–41.
Parenthetical note   (Baard 40)

Bolado, Carolina. "Activists Push Affordable Housing." *Chicago Tribune* 1 Aug. 2003, sec. 2: 3.
    Parenthetical note   (Bolado 2: 3)

Heller, Scott. "What a Difference a Year Makes." *Chronicle of Higher Education* 5 Jan. 2001: A16+.
    Parenthetical note   (Heller A19)

Wilson, Scott. "A Hard New Life inside the Law." *Washington Post* 27 July 2003: A1.
    Parenthetical note   (Wilson A1)

14c.6   An Editorial

The citation for an editorial resembles that for a magazine or newspaper article, with one exception: the word *Editorial* (not italicized), with a period, follows the title of the essay.

Berkowitz, Bruce. "A Fresh Start against Terror." Editorial. *New York Times* 4 Aug. 2003, natl. ed.: A17.
    Parenthetical note   (Berkowitz A17)

Smalhout, James H. "Costly Safety Net." Editorial. *Barron's* 1 Jan. 2001: 41.
    Parenthetical note   (Smalhout 41)

14c.7   A Letter to the Editor

Letters to the editor follow a very simple format. Include the author's name, the word *Letter* (not italicized), the name of the publication (magazine, journal, or newspaper), and appropriate facts of publication. Do not record descriptive, attention-getting titles that the publications, not the authors, supply.

Davis, John Paul. Letter. *Harper's* Aug. 2003: 8.
    Parenthetical note   (Davis 8)

The quotation "The Difficult Reader" served as the functional title of this letter to the editor. It is not used in the citation.

Fecteau, J. Perry. Letter. *Business Week* 11 Aug. 2003: 12.
    Parenthetical note   (Fecteau 12)

The title that appeared with the letter—"African American Equality: Not a Black-and-White Issue"—is not included in the citation since it was created by the magazine's editorial staff.

MLA STYLE

14c.8 A Review

A citation for a review begins with the author's name and the title of the review (if one is provided). The abbreviation _Rev. of_ (not italicized) follows, with the name of the book, film, album, performance, product, or whatever else is being reviewed, followed by clarifying information. Publication information ends the citation, incorporating elements required for different kinds of sources.

Gleiberman, Owen. "The High Drama." Rev. of _Traffic_, dir. Steven Soderbergh. Perf. Benicio Del Toro, Catherine Zeta-Jones, Don Cheadle, and Michael Douglas. _Entertainment Weekly_ 5 Jan. 2001: 45–46.

   Parenthetical note   (Gleibermann 45)

Lacayo, Richard. "Total Eclipse of the Heart." Rev. of _A Ship Made of Paper_ by Scott Spender. _Time_ 17 Mar. 2003: 80.

   Parenthetical note   (Lacayo 80)

Sonnenfeld, Barry. "Gadget of the Month." Rev. of Sony Ericsson T610 [Combination cell phone and e-mail receiver]. _Esquire_ Sept. 2003: 118.

   Parenthetical note   (Sonnenfeld 118)

14c.9 An Abstract from _Dissertation Abstracts International_

This specialized citation requires the author's name, the title of the dissertation (in quotation marks), _DAI_ (the abbreviation for _Dissertation Abstracts International_) and the volume number, the year (in parentheses), a colon and space, and identification number. At the end of the citation, the degree-granting school is listed, with the word _university_ abbreviated.

Dikovitskaya, Margarita. "From Art to Visual Culture: The Study of the Visual after the Cultural Turn." _DAI_ 62 (2002): AAT3028516. Columbia U.

   Parenthetical note   (Dikovitskaya 165)

Williamson, Jo Ellen. "Teachers as Change Mediators in Educational Reform." _DAI_ 63 (2003): AAT3070477. U of Illinois, Urbana-Champaign.

   Parenthetical note   (Williamson 221)

When the school has several sites or when the location is unfamiliar, follow the school name with a comma and add the city and the country if it is not the United States.

14d   Follow the appropriate citation forms for audiovisual sources.

Finding documentation information for audiovisual sources is usually easy but sometimes requires ingenuity. CD cases provide copyright dates. Printed programs for speeches or syllabuses for course lectures provide names, titles, locations, and dates. Information about films or television programs can be obtained from their opening or closing credits or from media-related Internet sites. If you have difficulty finding the information to document audiovisual sources clearly, ask your instructor or a librarian for help.

14d.1   A Lecture

A citation for a formal lecture includes the speaker's name, the title of the lecture (in quotation marks), the name of the lecture series (if applicable), the location of the speech (university, library, meeting hall), the city, and the date in day-month year order.

Gould, Stephen Jay. "Interactions of Art and Science and the Largely Arbitrary Nature of
Academic Boundaries." Stanford Presidential Lectures in Humanities and Arts.
Stanford U. Stanford, 4 Nov. 1998.

    Parenthetical note   (Gould)

Johnson, Neil. "Living on the Edge of Chaos." Christmas Lectures. Royal Inst. London,
29 Dec. 1999.

    Parenthetical note   (Johnson)

For class lectures, provide as much of this information as possible: speaker, title of lecture (in quotation marks), a descriptive title, the school, the city, and the date.

Mitten, David M. "Greek Art and Architecture in the West: Southern Italy, Sicily, and
Campania." Class lecture. Harvard U. Cambridge, 15 May 1989.

    Parenthetical note   (Mitten)

14d.2   A Speech

A speech, unlike a lecture, is usually presented as part of a convention, meeting, ceremony, or other well-publicized event. A citation for a speech includes the speaker, the title of the speech (in quotation marks), the event at which the speech was presented, the city, and the date.

King, Martin Luther, Jr. "I Have a Dream." Lincoln Memorial. Washington, 28 Aug. 1963.

    Parenthetical note   (King)

Quayle, J. Danforth. "The Most Litigious Society in the World." American Bar Assn. Annual Meeting. Atlanta, 13 Aug. 1991.

    Parenthetical note   (Quayle)

The citation for an untitled speech provides the same basic information as the citation of a titled speech, with one exception: a descriptive title (without quotation marks) is used.

Nixon, Richard. Resignation Speech. White House. Washington, 8 Aug. 1974.

    Parenthetical note   (Nixon)

14d.3 A Work of Art

When artists title their own work, include this information: artist's name; the title (italicized); a brief description of the work; the museum, gallery, or collection where the work of art is housed; and the city and province or country, if needed for clarity.

Cézanne, Paul. *Houses along a Road*. Oil on canvas. The Hermitage, St. Petersburg.

    Parenthetical note   (Cézanne)

When works of art are known primarily by titles in foreign languages, provide a translated title within brackets; your translation follows the foreign-language title, is also italicized, and precedes the period.

Toulouse-Lautrec, Henri de. *La clownesse assise [The Seated Clown]*. Oil on canvas.
Marie Harriman Gallery, New York.

    Parenthetical note   (Toulouse-Lautrec)

When artists have not titled their work, use the title that art historians have given it (do not place it in quotation marks), followed by a brief description of the work. The rest of the citation is the same as that for other works of art.

Amateis, Edmond Romulus. Jonas Edward Salk. Sculpture in bronze. Natl. Portrait
Gallery, Washington.

    Parenthetical note   (Amateis)

Amateis, the sculptor, did not formally title this sculpture, a convention for statues of famous people. Consequently, "Jonas Edward Salk" is the attributed title of the statue of this scientist.

Madonna and Child with Cherubim. Bas relief in marble. Vatican Library, Vatican City.

    Parenthetical note   (Madonna and Child with Cherubim)

The citation for this anonymous work begins with the attributed title.

14d.4   A Map, Graph, Table, or Chart

Maps, graphs, tables, and charts are treated like books. Include the name (if known) of the author, artist, designer, scientist, or other person—or group—responsible for the map, graph, table, or chart. Then include the title (italicized), followed by a capitalized (but not italicized) descriptive title. Include other necessary information.

Phillips, Kevin L. *A Growing Income Disparity.* Chart. *Wealth and Democracy: A Political History of the American Rich.* New York: Broadway, 2002. 129.
   Parenthetical note   (Phillips 129)

This chart was developed by the author of the book in which it is included.

Pope, C. Arden. *Children's Respiratory Hospital Admissions.* Graph. "The Next Battle over Clean Air." By Hillary J. Johnson. *Rolling Stone* 18 Jan. 2001: 49.
   Parenthetical note   (Pope 49)

This graph is part of an article in a magazine.

14d.5   A Cartoon

Begin with the cartoonist's name, the title of the cartoon in quotation marks, and the word *Cartoon,* not italicized, followed by a period. Then include the citation information required for the source.

Bek. "I don't know if he's a great artist, but he's certainly annoying." Cartoon. *The New Yorker* 11 Aug. 2003: 60.
   Parenthetical note   (Bek 60)

For single-cell cartoons like this one, you may omit a title.

Davis, Jack, and Stan Hart. "Groan with the Wind." Cartoon. *Mad* Jan. 1991: 42–47.
   Parenthetical note   (Davis and Hart 43)

This cartoon appeared in a monthly magazine.

14d.6   A Film

To cite a film as a complete work, include the title (italicized), the director (noted by the abbreviation *Dir.,* not italicized), the studio, and the date of release. If you include other people's contributions, do so after the director's name, using brief phrases (*Screenplay by, Original score by*) or abbreviations (*Perf.* for "performed by," *Prod.* for "produced by") to clarify their roles.

Fight Club. Dir. David Fincher. Perf. Brad Pitt, Edward Norton, and Helena Bonham
Carter. Regency-20th Century Fox, 1999.

Parenthetical note   (_Fight Club_)

Note that dual-release films, like imprints, require the names of both the independent studio and the major distributor (the large film studio); the names are joined by a hyphen, without spaces.

Out of Africa. Dir. Sydney Pollack. Perf. Meryl Streep, Robert Redford, and Klaus Maria
Brandauer. Universal, 1985. Based on Isak Dinesen's _Out of Africa_, _Shadows on
the Grass_, and _Letters from Africa_.

Parenthetical note   (_Out of Africa_)

To emphasize the source of a film, include descriptive information at the end of the citation.

To emphasize the contribution of an individual (rather than the film as a whole), place the person's name first, followed by a comma and a descriptive title (beginning with a lowercase letter). The rest of the citation follows normal patterns.

Marshall, Rob, dir. _Chicago_. Perf. Renée Zellweger, Catherine Zeta-Jones, Richard Gere,
Queen Latifah, and John C. Reilly. Miramax, 2002.

Parenthetical note   (Marshall)

If your reference is to a VHS or DVD version of a film, include the format after the title or after the names of special contributors.

"Follow the White Rabbit and Take the Red Pills." _The Matrix_. Dir. Andy Wachowski and
Larry Wachowski. Perf. Keanu Reeves, Carrie-Anne Moss, and Lawrence Fish-
burne. DVD. Warner, 1999.

Parenthetical note   ("Follow the White Rabbit")

This citation refers to a special feature on the DVD; it follows the format of a selection within a collection.

Roman Holiday. Dir. William Wyler. Perf. Audrey Hepburn and Gregory Peck. VHS.
Paramount, 1992.

Parenthetical note   (_Roman Holiday_)

14d.7   A Filmstrip

Filmstrips are cited just as films are, with one exception: include the descriptive word _Filmstrip_ (not italicized) after the title. Add other information for clarity.

The Great American Deficit: Mortgaging the Future. Filmstrip. With audiotape. 76
  frames. Current Affairs Ser. Contemporary Media-New York Times, 1986.
  Parenthetical note   (*The Great American Deficit*)

Note that this filmstrip is part of a series and that it is co-published.

In Coal Country. Filmstrip. With audiotape. 73 frames. American School, 1990. Based on
  Judith Hendershot's *In Coal Country*.
  Parenthetical note   (*In Coal Country*)

To emphasize an original source, include descriptive information at the
end of the citation.

14d.8   A Television Broadcast

List regular programs by title (italicized), the network (CBS, CNN, FOX),
the local station when appropriate (including both the call letters and the
city, separated by a comma), and the broadcast date (in day-month-year
order). Include other people's contributions after the program title, using
brief phrases (*Written by, Hosted by*) or abbreviations (*Perf.* for "performed
by," *Prod.* for "produced by") to clarify their roles.

Curb Your Enthusiasm. Perf. Larry David, Cheryl Hines, Susie Essman, and Jeff Garlin.
  HBO. 6 Aug. 2003.
  Parenthetical note   (*Curb Your Enthusiasm*)

The Simpsons. With voices by Dan Castellaneta, Julie Kavner, Harry Shearer, Hank Azaria,
  Nancy Cartwright, and Yeardley Smith. FOX. WXIN, Indianapolis. 30 July 2002.
  Parenthetical note   (*The Simpsons*)

To cite a single episode of an ongoing program, include the name of the
episode, in quotation marks, before the program's title. Other elements are
presented in the same order used for a regular program.

"My Drama Queen." *Scrubs*. Perf. Zach Braff, Donald Faison, Sarah Chalke, and Judy
  Reyes. NBC. WTHR, Indianapolis. 14 Aug. 2003.
  Parenthetical note   ("My Drama Queen")

List special programs by title, followed by the name of the writer, director, producer, or performers. Include the name of the network, the local
station and city if appropriate, and the broadcast date (in day-month-year
order). If a special program is part of a series (for example, Hallmark Hall
of Fame, Great Performances, or American Playhouse), include the series
name, without quotation marks or italics, immediately preceding the name
of the network.

John Lennon: The Last Years. With Yoko Ono, Julian Lennon, and Jann Wenner. *Behind the Music.* VH1. 17 Jan. 2001.

   Parenthetical note   (*John Lennon*)

My House in Umbria. Dir. Richard Loncraine. Perf. Maggie Smith, Chris Cooper, and Giancarlo Gianni. HBO. 25 May 2003.

   Parenthetical note   (*My House in Umbria*)

14d.9   A Radio Broadcast

A citation for a radio broadcast follows the same guidelines as a television broadcast.

Murrow, Edward R. Report. CBS Radio. WCBS, New York. 13 Sept. 1940.

   Parenthetical note   (Murrow)

The War of the Worlds. CBS Radio. WCBS, New York. 30 Oct. 1938.

   Parenthetical note   (*The War of the Worlds*)

14d.10   A Recording

Citations for recordings usually begin with the performer or composer, followed by the title of the album (italicized except for titles using numbers for musical form, key, or number), the record company, and the copyright date.

List other contributors after the title, using brief phrases or abbreviations (*Cond.,* the abbreviation for conductor, *Perf.* for "performed by," *Composed by*) to clarify their roles. Orchestras (abbreviated *orch.*) and other large musical groups are listed without clarifying phrases, usually following the conductor's name.

When appropriate, include recording dates immediately following the title. Compact discs (CDs) are now the standard recording format; indicate other formats (audiotape, audiocassette, or LP, for long-playing record), when necessary, before the record company.

The notation for multidisc sets, similar to the pattern for multivolume books, appears immediately preceding the record company.

The Beatles. *Abbey Road.* Capital-EMI, 1969.

   Parenthetical note   (The Beatles)

Mahler, Gustav. Symphony no. 1 in D major. Cond. Georg Solti. Chicago Symphony Orch. LP. London, 1984.

   Parenthetical note   (Mahler)

Since this selection is titled by musical form and key, it is not italicized. As noted after the contributors, this is a long-playing record, not a CD.

To cite a single selection from a recording, include the selection title in quotation marks just before the title of the complete recording. All else remains the same.

Vivaldi, Antonio. Concerto in F major. *An Isaac Stern-Vivaldi Gala*. Perf. Isaac Stern,
>   Pinchas Zukerman, and Itzak Perlman. Cond. Zubin Mehta. New York Philhar-
>   monic Orch. Audiocassette. CBS, 1982.

   Parenthetical note   (Vivaldi)

Yoakam, Dwight. "An Exception to the Rule." *Population ME*. Audium, 2003.

   Parenthetical note   (Yoakam)

To emphasize the contribution of an individual (rather than the complete recording), place the person's name first, followed by a comma and a descriptive title (beginning with a lowercase letter). The rest of the citation follows normal patterns.

Fuentes, Ruben, and José Hernández, conds. *Canciones de mi padre*. By Linda Ronstadt.
>   Asylum, 1987.

   Parenthetical note   (Fuentes and Hernández)

Stansfield, Lisa. "They Can't Take That Away from Me." By George Gershwin. *The
>   Glory of Gershwin*. Polygram, 1994.

   Parenthetical note   (Stansfield)

To cite jacket notes, the print material that comes with many recordings, list the name of the writer and the description *Jacket notes* (not italicized), followed by a period. The rest of the citation follows normal patterns.

McClintick, David, and William Kennedy. Jacket notes. *Frank Sinatra: The Reprise Col-
>   lection*. 4 discs. Reprise, 1990.

   Parenthetical note   (McClintick and Kennedy)

14d.11   A Performance

A citation for a performance most often begins with the title of the work being performed, provides information about contributors, and ends with the facility (theater, center, auditorium, performance hall, or other venue), city, and performance date (in day-month-year order). To emphasize a particular contributor, begin the citation with his or her name.

When an untitled performance is cited, include the name of the performer or group and a descriptive title (*Concert, Recital*), not italicized. The rest of the citation follows normal patterns.

Boston Symphony Orchestra. "Four Last Songs." By Richard Strauss. Cond. Edo de
      Waart. Perf. Renée Fleming. Tanglewood Music Center, Lenox. 10 Aug. 2003.
    Parenthetical note   (Boston Symphony Orchestra)

Long Day's Journey into Night. By Eugene O'Neill. Perf. Vanessa Redgrave, Brian Den-
      nehy, Robert Sean Leonard, and Philip Seymour Hoffman. Plymouth Theatre,
      New York. 17 Aug. 2003.
    Parenthetical note   (*Long Day's Journey*)

Mo', Keb'. Concert. House of Blues, Orlando. 12 Jan. 2001.
    Parenthetical note   (Mo')

14d.12   An Exhibit

Citations for exhibits include the title, the word *Exhibit* (not italicized), the name of the museum or facility, the city, and the viewing date.

"Matisse and Beyond: The Painting and Sculpture Collection." Exhibit. San Francisco
      Museum of Modern Art, San Francisco. 1 Oct. 2003.
    Parenthetical note   ("Matisse and Beyond")

"Threads of Prosperity: American Domestic Textiles: 1750–1875." Exhibit. St. Louis Art
      Museum, St. Louis. Dec. 2003.
    Parenthetical note   ("Threads of Prosperity")

14d.13   An Interview

Citations for personally conducted interviews include the name of the person interviewed, the type of interview (personal or telephone), and the interview date.

Lindley, Richard. Telephone interview. 13 May 2003.
    Parenthetical note   (Lindley)

Otwell, Stephen. Personal interview. 11 Nov. 2002.
    Parenthetical note   (Otwell)

Citations for broadcast or printed interviews include the name of the person interviewed, the descriptive title *Interview* (not italicized), and necessary information to describe the source.

Caro, Niki. Interview. *Fresh Air*. Natl. Public Radio. WHYY, Philadelphia. 12 Aug. 2003.
Parenthetical note   (Caro)

Clinton, Hillary. Interview. *Larry King Live*. CNN. 11 Dec. 2000.
Parenthetical note   (Clinton)

14d.14   A Questionnaire or Survey

Citations for personally conducted questionnaires or surveys begin with your name since you are the author of the questionnaire or survey and the compiler of the results. Then include the word *Questionnaire* or *Survey* (not italicized) and the date (which may be inclusive) on which you gathered your information. You may include information about the location and conditions of your work if you feel such information provides additional clarity.

Beckford, Jon. Questionnaire. 15–17 Apr. 2003.
Parenthetical note   (Beckford)

Greene, Erika. Survey. Terre Haute: Indiana State U. 30 May 2003.
Parenthetical note   (Greene)

14d.15   A Transcript

Transcripts of programs are presented according to the source of the original broadcast, with clarifying information provided.

Block, Melissa, and Paul Dickson. "The Hidden Language of Baseball." *All Things Considered*. Natl. Public Radio. 7 Aug. 2003. Transcript.
Parenthetical note   (Block and Dickson)

Costello, Carol. "Eye on the Sky: Air Travel Delays." *Daybreak*. CNN. 11 Aug. 2003. Transcript.
Parenthetical note   (Costello)

14e   Follow appropriate citation forms for the Internet and other electronic sources.

The Internet provides an increasingly wide array of materials as businesses, organizations, government agencies, and publishers of all kinds transfer their print-based documents to the Web. This is a boon for researchers, making a wide range of sources available without the necessity of traveling to large research libraries or of using interlibrary loans. However, because of the variety of Internet sources, researchers face a considerable challenge when they try to provide clear documentation for the electronic sources they use. It is, nevertheless, a challenge worth facing.

As you gather citation information for Internet sources, be both resourceful and patient because the patterns of Internet publication are less consistent than those of traditional print publication. Whereas publishers of print texts usually place information in conventional locations—the publication date on the copyright page—Web designers seem less confined by such conventions. A Web site, for example, may place the publication or posting date at the top of the Web page (near the masthead), at the bottom of the home page, or elsewhere (for example, in the "About This Site" link). Further, because of the lack of standardization—or the creativity with which a site is designed—you may discover that some sources do not provide all the information that you need to complete a full citation. Therefore, you must be resourceful when trying to locate important information; your goal should be to provide the most complete information possible to describe each electronic source, following the patterns described in this section.

14e.1   An Online Scholarly Project or Information Database

To cite an entire online scholarly project or information database, present available information in this order: (1) the title of the project or database, italicized; (2) the editor or compiler, if identified, introduced with the abbreviation *Ed.* or *Comp.* (not italicized); (3) the version number, if applicable; (4) the date of electronic posting or the date of the most recent update; (5) the name of the sponsoring organization or institution; (6) the date you accessed the site; and (7) the electronic address (URL), placed in angle brackets.

Agroecosystems Research Group. Ed. L. T. Wilson. 18 Feb. 2003. College of Agriculture
       and Life Sciences. Texas A&M U. 18 Feb. 2003 <http://aesrg.tamu.edu/>.
   Parenthetical note   (*Agroecosystems Research Group*)

The On-line Books Page. Ed. John Mark Ockerbloom. 7 Aug. 2003. U Pennsylvania.
       11 July 2003 <http://digital.library.upenn.edu/books/>.
   Parenthetical note   (*The On-line Books Page*)

Project Gutenberg. Host Pietro Di Miceli. 5 Jan. 2003. U of Illinois. 6 Mar. 2003
       <http://promo.net/pg/>.
   Parenthetical note   (*Project Gutenberg*)

Thomas: Legislative Information on the Internet. 2003. Library of Congress. 1 Aug. 2003
       <http://thomas.loc.gov>.
   Parenthetical note   (*Thomas*)

The Victorian Web. Ed. George P. Landow. 21 Dec. 2002. Brown U. 3 Aug. 2003 <http://www.victorianweb.org/>.

    Parenthetical note   (*The Victorian Web*)

14e.2 A Source from an Online Scholarly Project or Information Database

To cite a selected source—article, illustration, map, and so on—from an online scholarly project or information database, begin with (1) the name of the author (or artist, compiler, or editor) of the individual source, if appropriate; (2) the title of the source, punctuated appropriately (quotation marks for articles, italics for charts, and so on); and (3) print information if the source reproduces a print version. Continue the citation with the name of the online project or database and other required information (see section **14e.1**). However, use the URL of the specific source, not the general address for the project or database, in angle brackets.

Austen, Jane. *Sense and Sensibility*. *Project Gutenberg*. Sept. 1994. U of Illinois. 20 July 2003 <http://www.ibiblio.org/gutenberg/etext94/sense11.txt>.

    Parenthetical note   (Austen)

Cody, David. "Queen Victoria." *The Victorian Web*. Ed. George P. Landow. 21 Dec. 2002. Brown U. 3 Aug. 2003 <http://www.victorianweb.org.vn/victor6.html>.

    Parenthetical note   (Cody)

Dickinson, Emily. "I felt a funeral in my brain." *Emily Dickinson: Poems. Bartleby.com*. Columbia U. 6 Aug. 2003 <http://www.bartleby.com/113/4112.html>.

    Parenthetical note   (Dickinson)

"Electricity per 500 KWH: Average Price Data." *Bureau of Labor Statistics*. June 2003. Bureau of Labor Statistics. 11 Aug. 2003 <http://data.bls.gov/cgi-bin/surveymost>.

    Parenthetical note   ("Electricity per 500 KWH")

Rooney, Megan. "Sense and Censorship." *Chronicle of Higher Education* 49.40 (2003): 6. *ProQuest*. 2003. Bell and Howell. 11 Aug. 2003 <http://proquest.umi.com/pqdwed/>.

    Parenthetical note   (Rooney)

14e.3 A Professional Web Site

To cite a professional Web site, provide (1) the name of the author, editor, or host, if any; (2) the title of the site, italicized; (3) the date of electronic posting or the date of the most recent update; (4) the name of the organization or institution, if any, affiliated with the site; (5) the date you accessed the site; and (6) the URL, placed in angle brackets.

ABA Law Student Division. 2003. American Bar Association. 21 July 2003
<http://www.abanet.org/lsd/home.html>.
   Parenthetical note   (*ABA Law Student Division*)

National Rifle Association. 2003. NRA. 11 June 2003 <http://www.nra.org/>.
   Parenthetical note   (*National Rifle Association*)

UNICEF. 10 Aug. 2003. United Nations. 11 Aug. 2003 <http://www.unicef.org/>.
   Parenthetical note   (*UNICEF*)

14e.4   A Corporate Web Site

To cite a corporate Web site, provide (1) the name of the author, editor, or host, if any; (2) the title of the site, italicized; (3) the date of electronic posting or the date of the most recent update; (4) the name of the corporation sponsoring the site; (5) the date you accessed the site; and (6) the URL, placed in angle brackets.

General Motors. 2003. GM. 2 Aug. 2003 <http://www.gm.com/flash_homepage/>.
   Parenthetical note   (*General Motors*)

Lilly. 2000. Eli Lilly. 14 Mar. 2003 <http://www.lilly.com/>.
   Parenthetical note   (*Lilly*)

14e.5   An Online Book

Online books exist in two forms: those previously published and now available electronically and those available only in electronic form.

   To cite an online book that has a corresponding print version, first prepare a standard citation describing the print version (see section **14b**). Then provide additional electronic information: (1) information required for a scholarly project or information database, including the date of electronic posting or the date of the most recent update (see section **14e.1**); (2) the date you accessed the site; and (3) the specific URL of the book, not the general project or database, placed in angle brackets.

Lofting, Hugh. *The Voyages of Doctor Dolittle.* Philadelphia: Lippincott, 1922. *Project Gutenberg.* Jan. 1998. U of Illinois. 2 Feb. 2003 <ftp://ibiblio.org/pub/docs/books/gutenberg/etext98/vdrdl10.text>.
   Parenthetical note   (Lofting)

Witemeyer, Hugh. *George Eliot and the Visual Arts*. New Haven: Yale UP, 1979. *The Vic-*
>   *torian Web*. Ed. George P. Landow. 20 Sept. 2000. Brown U. 15 Jan. 2003
>   <http://www.victorianweb.org/authors/>.
>   ***Parenthetical note***   (Witemeyer)

To cite an online book that is available only in electronic form, provide (1) the name of the author or editor; (2) the title, italicized; (3) the date of electronic posting or the date of the most recent update; (4) the name of the sponsoring organization or institution; (5) the date you accessed the site; and (6) the URL of the book, not the database or project, placed in angle brackets.

Buxhoeveden, Sophie. *The Life and Tragedy of Alexandra Feodorvna, Empress of Russia*.
>   1999. *Russian History Website*. 15 Jan. 2001 <http://www.alexanderpalace.org/
>   alexandra/>.
>   ***Parenthetical note***   (Buxhoeveden)

To cite a selection from an online book—a chapter from a book, an essay or poem from a collection, and so on—provide this information: (1) the author of the selection and (2) the title of the selection, in quotation marks or italicized, as appropriate. Then continue the citation with the book title, providing necessary facts of electronic publication (see samples above).

Housman, A. E. "To an Athlete Dying Young." *A Shropshire Lad*. London:
>   Paul, 1896. *Bartleby.com*. 2003. Verse Collection. 22 Apr. 2003
>   <http://www.bartleby.com/123/19.html>.
>   ***Parenthetical note***   (Housman)

14e.6   An Article in an Online Encyclopedia or Reference Source

To cite an article from an online encyclopedia or reference source, provide (1) the author of the entry, if there is one; (2) the title of the entry exactly as it appears in the source ("Paige, Satchel"); (3) the name of the reference work, italicized; (4) the date of electronic posting or the date of the most recent update; (5) the date you accessed the site; and (6) the URL for the specific article, not the general reference, in angle brackets.

"Carnegie, Andrew." *The New Dictionary of Cultural Literacy*. 3rd ed. 2002.
>   *Bartleby.com*. 10 Aug. 2002 <http://www.bartleby.com/59/18/
>   carnegieandr.html>.
>   ***Parenthetical note***   ("Carnegie")

Children in Foster Care. Chart. _Infoplease Almanac_. Mar. 2003. 13 Apr. 2003 <http://
     www.infoplease.com/ipa/A0778809.html>.

    Parenthetical note   (_Children in Foster Care_)

"Machismo." _Yourdictionary_. 2000. 27 Mar. 2003 <http://www.yourdictionary.com/
     ahd/m/m0009000.html>.

    Parenthetical note   ("Machismo")

14e.7 An Online Government Document— _Congressional Record_

To cite the online version of _Congressional Record_, first provide the information required for the print source (see section **14b.20**). Then continue
the citation with (1) the date of electronic posting or date of the most recent update; (2) the phrase _United States Cong._, not italicized; (3) the date
you accessed the site; and (4) the URL, in angle brackets, for your specific
reference within the general, online version of _Congressional Record_.

Cong. Record. 13 Mar. 2003. S3761-62. 2003. United States Cong. 15 July 2003 <http://
     frwebgate.access.gpo.gov/cgi-in/waisgate.cgi?/WAISdocID=63241510424>.

    Parenthetical note   (_Cong. Rec._, 13 Mar. 2003)

Cong. Record. 22 May 2003. H4625-706. 2003. United States Cong. 1 Aug. 2003
     <http://frwebgate.access.gpo.gov/cgi-in/waisgate.cgi?/ WAISdocID=63266420>.

    Parenthetical note   (_Cong. Rec._, 22 Mar. 2003)

14e.8 An Online Government Document

To cite an online version of a government document—book, report, proceedings, brochure, and so on—first provide the information required for
the print source (see section **14b.21**). Then continue the citation with the
information appropriate to the electronic source, whether it is a scholarly
project or an information database (see section **14e.1**) or a Web site (see
section **14e.3** or **14e.4**).

United States. Cong. Budget Office. _Budgeting for Naval Forces: Structuring Tomorrow's
     Navy at Today's Funding Level_. By Eric J. Labs. Washington: GPO, 2000. _Bud-
     get Statistics_. Oct. 2000. Cong. Budget Office. 6 May 2003 <http://www.cbo.gov/
     showdoc.cfm?index=2603&sequence=0&form=1>.

    Parenthetical note   (US., Cong. Budget Office)

---. Dept. of Education. Natl. Inst. on Early Childhood Development. _Helping Your Child
     through Early Adolescence_. 12 Nov. 2002. Dept. of Education. 9 Aug. 2003
     <http://www.ed.gov/pubs/parents/adolescence/part1.html>.

    Parenthetical note   (US., Dept. of Education)

14e.9   An Online Pamphlet

To cite an online pamphlet, first provide the information required for a printed pamphlet (see section **14b.24**). Then continue the citation with the information appropriate to the electronic source, whether it is a scholarly project or an information database (see section **14e.1**) or a Web site (see **14e.3** or **14e.4**).

Students' Right to Read. Rev. ed. Urbana: NCTE, 1982. *NCTE.* 2000. Natl. Council of
       Teachers of English. 10 June 2003 <http://www.ncte.org/positions/
       right-to-read.shtml>.
       Parenthetical note   (*Students' Right*)

Your Family Disaster Plan. Jessup: FEMA, 1991. *FEMA.* 11 Feb. 2003. Federal
       Emergency Management Administration. 4 Mar. 2003 <http://www.fema.gov/rrr/
       famplan.shtm>.
       Parenthetical note   (*Your Family Disaster Plan*)

14e.10   An Online Annual Report

To cite an online annual report, provide (1) the title of the report, italicized; (2) the date of electronic posting or date of the most recent update; (3) the name of the corporation, organization, or agency; (4) the date on which you accessed the report; and (5) the URL for the report, not the general Web site address, in angle brackets.

Alcoa 2002 Annual Report. 20 Feb. 2003. Alcoa Aluminum. 24 July 2003 <http://
       www.alcoa.com/global/en/investment/pdf/Alcoa02AR.pdf>.
       Parenthetical note   (*Alcoa 2002 Annual Report*)

Global Presence: Ispat International Annual Report. 2002. Ispat International. 11 May
       2003 <http://www.inland.com/download/en/ispat_ann_rep_02.pdf>.
       Parenthetical note   (*Global Presence*)

"The Table Is Set": Tyson Foods, Inc., 2002 Annual Report. 2002. Tyson Foods. 3 May
       2003 <http://www.tysonfoodsinc.com/IR/publications/annualreport/pdf>.
       Parenthetical note   (*"The Table Is Set"*)

14e.11   An Article in an Online Magazine

To cite an article in an online magazine, provide (1) the name of the author, if appropriate; (2) the title of the article, in quotation marks; (3) the name of the magazine, italicized; (4) the date of electronic publication or the date of the most recent update; (5) the date on which you accessed the article; and (6) the URL of the specific article, not the general magazine site, in angle brackets.

Hoffman, Paul. "Chess Queen." *Smithsonian* Aug. 2003. 11 Aug. 2003 <http://
www.smithsonianmag.si.edu/smithsonian/issues03/aug03/pdf/
smithsonian_august_03_chess_queen.pdf>.
  Parenthetical note   (Hoffman)

Ramer, Sarah. "It's More than the Economy, Stupid." *Newsweek* 18 Aug. 2003. 20 Aug.
2003 <http://www.msnbc.com/news/950350.asp?ob1=0#BODY>
  Parenthetical note   (Ramer)

Wauder, Jonathan. "Time to Play Doctor: A Step-by-Step Game Plan for Choosing the
Most Qualified and Convenient Doctor for You." *Menshealth.com.* 2003. 6 Aug.
2003 <http://www.menshealth.com/cda/article/0.6916.SI-3-67-0-118.00.html>.
  Parenthetical note   (Wauder)

Note that a magazine article that is retrieved through a periodical database, rather than directly from an online publication, is cited as a source
from an information database (see section **14e.2**).

14e.12   An Article in an Online Journal

To cite an article in an online journal, provide (1) the name of the author, if
appropriate; (2) the title of the article, in quotation marks; (3) the name of the
journal, italicized; (4) the volume and issue number; (5) the year of publication, in parentheses; (6) the date on which you accessed the article; and (7)
the URL of the specific article, not the general journal site, in angle brackets.

Hopcroft, Rosemary. "Is Gender Still a Status Characteristic?" *Current Research in
Social Psychology* 7.20 (2002). 26 Apr. 2003 <http://www.uiowa.edu/~grpproc/
crisp/crisp.7.20.html>.
  Parenthetical note   (Hopcroft)

Jabbour, Nicholas. "Syphilis from 1880 to 1920: A Public Health Nightmare and the First
Challenge to Medical Ethics." *Essays in History* 42 (2000). 26 Mar. 2003 <http://
www.etext.lib.virginia.edu/journals/eh/eh42/jabbour42>.
  Parenthetical note   (Jabbour)

Note that a journal article that is retrieved through a periodical database,
rather than directly from an online publication, is cited as a source from an
information database (see section **14e.2**).

14e.13   An Article in an Online Newspaper

To cite an article in an online newspaper, provide (1) the name of the author, if appropriate; (2) the title of the article, in quotation marks; (3) the

name of the newspaper, italicized; (4) the date of electronic publication or the date of the most recent update; (5) the date on which you accessed the article; and (6) the URL of the specific article, not the general newspaper site, in angle brackets.

Foreman, Judy. "The Health and Harm of New Cancer Drugs." *Boston Globe* 12 Aug. 2003.
12 Aug. 2003 <http://www.boston.com/yourlife/health/diseases/ articles/
2003/08/12/the_help_and_harm_in_new_cancer_drugs>.

Parenthetical note (Foreman)

Strauss, Joe. "Going Back to Basics." *St. Louis Post Dispatch* 11 Aug. 2003. 12 Aug.
2003 <http://www.stltoday.com/stltoday/sports/stories.nsf/sports/Cardinals>.

Parenthetical note (Strauss)

Note that a newspaper article that is retrieved through a periodical database, rather than directly from an online publication, is cited as a source from an information database (see section **14e.2**).

14e.14 An Online Transcript of a Lecture or Speech

To cite an online transcript of a speech or lecture, first provide the information required for a lecture (see section **14d.1**) or a speech (see section **14d.2**). Then include (1) the word *Transcript,* not italicized; (2) the date of electronic publication or the date of the most recent update; (3) the date on which you accessed the transcript; and (4) the URL of the specific transcript, not the general site.

Faulkner, William. Nobel Prize in Literature Acceptance Speech, Nobel Prize Ceremony,
Stockholm. 10 Dec. 1950. Transcript. 12 Aug. 2003 <http://www.pbs.org/
greatspeeches/timeline/index.html>.

Parenthetical note (Faulkner)

Havel, Vaclav. "The Need for Transcendence in the Postmodern World." Independence
Hall, Philadelphia. 4 July 1994. Transcript. 6 May 2003 <http://
www.worldtrans.org/whole/havelspeech.html>

Parenthetical note (Havel)

14e.15 A Work of Art Online

To cite a work of art online, provide (1) the name of the artist, if known; (2) the assigned title of the work of art, italicized, or the common name of the work of art, not italicized; (3) a phrase describing the artistic medium; (4) the museum, gallery, or collection where the work is housed; (5) the city; (6) the date on which you accessed the work of art; and (7) the URL of the specific work of art, not the general site on which you found it, in an-gle brackets.

Picasso, Pablo. _Les Demoiselles d'Avignon._ Oil on canvas. Museum of Modern Art. New
York. 21 Aug. 2003 <http://www.moma.org/collections/depts/paint_sculpt/
blowups/paint_sculpt_006.html>.

Parenthetical note   (Picasso)

Wood, Grant. _American Gothic._ Oil of beaverboard. Art Inst. of Chicago. Chicago.
16 Sept. 2003 <http://www.artic.edu/aic/collections/modern/73c_wood.html>.

Parenthetical note   (Wood)

14e.16   An Online Map, Graph, Table, or Chart

To cite a map, graph, table, or chart online, first provide the information required for the kind of visual element (see section **14d.4**). Then continue the citation with the information appropriate to the electronic source, whether it is a scholarly project or an information database (see section **14e.1**) or a Web site (see section **14e.3** or **14e.4**).

The Billboard 200. Chart. 8 Aug. 2003. 10 Aug. 2003 <http://www.billboard.com/bb/
charts/bb200.jsp>.

Parenthetical note   (_The Billboard 200_)

Experimental Poverty Measures by Selective Characteristics: 2001. Table. _Current Population Survey, 2002 Annual Demographic Supplement._ 2002. U.S. Census Bureau.
18 Aug. 2003 <http://www.census.gov/hhes/poverty/poverty01/table9.pdf>.

Parenthetical note   (_Experimental Poverty Measures_)

New York City Subway Route Map. Map. 15 Sept. 2002. New York City Subway Resources. 9 Jan. 2003 <http://www.nycsubway.org/maps/route/>.

Parenthetical note   (_New York City Subway_)

14e.17   An Online Cartoon

To cite a cartoon online, provide (1) the name of the cartoonist, if known; (2) the assigned title of the cartoon, in quotation marks; (3) the word _Cartoon,_ not italicized; (4) the source, italicized; (5) the date of electronic publication or the date of the most recent update; (5) the date on which you accessed the cartoon; and (6) the URL of the cartoon, not the general site on which you found it, in angle brackets.

Byrnes, Pat. "Just remember, son, that it doesn't matter whether you win or lose—unless
you want Daddy's love." Cartoon. *Cartoonbank*. 23 June 2001. 1 Aug. 2003
<http://www.cartoonbank.com/cartoon_closeup.asp?pf>.

> ***Parenthetical note***   (Byrnes)

Gorrell, Bob. "The Mother of All Targets." Cartoon. *Creators.com*. 1 Aug. 2003
<http://www.creators.com/editorial_show.cfm?comicname+bg>.

> ***Parenthetical note***   (Gorrell)

14e.18   An Online Film or Filmclip

To cite an online film or filmclip, first provide the information required for
a film (see section **14d.6**). Then include (1) the name of your electronic
source, italicized; (2) the date of electronic publication or the date of the
most recent update; (3) the date on which you accessed the film or filmclip; and (4) the URL of the film or filmclip, not the general site on which
you found it, in angle brackets.

"The First Lunar Landing." Video clip. With Buzz Aldrin. 1999. *Apollo Lunar Surface
Journal*. 4 Mar. 2003. NASA. 30 July 2003 <http://www.hq.nasa.gov/alsj/
BuzzinEagle.html>.

> ***Parenthetical note***   ("The First Lunar Landing")

14e.19   An Online Transcript of a Television or Radio Broadcast

To cite an online transcript of a television or radio broadcast, first provide the information required for a television or radio broadcast (see
sections **14d.8** and **14d.9**). Then include (1) the word *Transcript*, not italicized; (2) the date on which you accessed the transcript; and (3) the URL
of the transcript, not the general site on which you found it, in angle
brackets.

"Amid the Tall Trees: Planting the Seed of Empathy." *Nightline*. With Joe O'Connor.
ABC, New York. 2 Aug. 2003. Transcript. 12 Aug. 2003 <http://abcnews.go.com/
sections/nightline/living/ntl_oconnortrees_030802.html>.

> ***Parenthetical note***   ("Amid the Tall Trees")

"Incitements to Violence in the Mideast." *All Things Considered*. With Melissa Block and
Peter Kenyon. NPR, Washington. 25 July 2003. Transcript. 19 Aug. 2003 <http://
www.npr.org/programs/atc/transcripts/2003/jul/030725.kenyon.html>.

> ***Parenthetical note***   ("Incitements to Violence")

14e.20   An Online Recording

To cite an online recording of previously released material, first provide the information required for a traditional recording (see section **14d.10**). Then include (1) the date of electronic publication or the date of the most recent update; (2) the date on which you accessed the recording; and (3) the URL of the recording, not the general site on which you found it, in angle brackets.

To cite an online recording that has not been previously released, provide (1) the name of the recording artist; (2) the title of the selection; and (3) performance information like concert locations and dates, recording studios, locations, and other relevant information. Then provide information about your source for the recording, whether a database (see section **14e.1**) or a Web site (see section **14e.3** or **14e.4**).

Dylan, Bob. "Buckets of Rain." *Blood on the Tracks*. Columbia, 1975. *Bobdylan.com*.

> 2003. 2 Aug. 2003 <http://www.bobdylan.com/songs/buckets.html>.
>
> ***Parenthetical note***   (Dylan)

Jones, Norah. "Feelin' the Same Way." House of Blues. Chicago. 16 Apr. 2002. *Norah*

> *Jones*. 2003. 25 July 2003 <http://www.norahjones.com/av/default.htm>.
>
> ***Parenthetical note***   (Jones)

14e.21   An Online Exhibit

To cite an online exhibit, first provide the information required for a traditional exhibit (see section **14d.12**); however, use the descriptive phrase *Online exhibit*, not italicized. Then include (1) the date on which you accessed the exhibit and (2) the URL of the exhibit, not the general site on which you found it, in angle brackets.

"Celebrity Caricature in America." Online exhibit. National Portrait Gallery, Washington.

> 23 Aug. 1993. 11 Aug. 2003 <http://www.npg.si.edu/exh/caricatures/index.htm>.
>
> ***Parenthetical note***   ("Celebrity Caricature")

"Genetics: Decoding Life." Online exhibit. Museum of Science and Industry, Chicago. 2003.

> 16 Apr. 2003 <http://www.msichicago.org/exhibit/genetics/t_tourstart.html>.
>
> ***Parenthetical note***   ("Genetics: Decoding Life")

14e.22   An Online Transcript of an Interview

To cite an online transcript of an interview, first provide the information required for an interview, either television, radio, or print (see section

14d.13). Then include the word *Transcript,* not italicized, and continue the citation with the information appropriate to the electronic source, whether it is a scholarly project or an information database (see section **14e.1**) or a Web site (see section **14e.3** or **14e.4**), including the URL of the transcript, not the general site on which you found it, in angle brackets.

Polanski, Roman. Press Conference. Interview. Cannes Film Festival. Cannes. 2002.

> Transcript. *Filmscouts.* 2003. 14 Aug. 2003 <http://www.filmscouts.com/scripts/
>
> interview.cfm?File=3012>.

Parenthetical note   (Polanski)

Powell, Colin L. Press Briefing. Interview. Washington Foreign Press Center. Washington,

> 7 Aug. 2003. Transcript. *U.S. Dept. of State.* 2003. U.S. Dept. of State. 31 Aug.
>
> 2003 <http://www.state.gov/secretary/rm/2003/2311.htm>.

Parenthetical note   (Powell)

14e.23   CD-ROM Sources

If a CD-ROM source reproduces material available in print form, begin the citation with full print information: author (or editor), title, and facts of publication (see sections **14b.1–14c.8** for complete citation patterns). If the material is not available in print form, begin the citation with identifying information: (1) author, if given; (2) title, italicized; and (3) the date of the material, if appropriate. Citations for both kinds of materials then include (1) the title of the publication, italicized; (2) the description *CD-ROM,* not italicized; (3) the city, if known, and name of the company that produced the CD-ROM; and (4) the date of electronic publication.

The Baseball Encyclopedia: The Complete and Definitive Record of Major League Base-

> *ball.* CD-ROM. New York: Macmillan, 1996.

Parenthetical note   (*The Baseball Encyclopedia*)

Chen, Jim X. *Guide to Graphics Software Tools.* CD-ROM. New York: Springer, 2003.

> **Parenthetical note**   (Chen)

Earthquakes and Eruptions. CD-ROM. Washington: Smithsonian, 2000.

> **Parenthetical note**   (*Earthquakes and Eruptions*)

Welmers, William E. "African Languages." *The New Grolier Multimedia Encyclopedia.*

> 1994 ed. CD-ROM. New York: Grolier, 1994.

Parenthetical note   (Welmers)

14e.24   An E-mail Interview

To cite an e-mail interview, include (1) the name of the person you interviewed, (2) the phrase *E-mail interview,* not italicized, and (3) the date of
the e-mail posting.

Washburne-Freise, Marla. E-mail interview. 14 May 2003.
   Parenthetical note   (Washburne-Freise)

14e.25   An Online Posting

To cite an online posting to a forum or discussion group, provide (1) the
name of the author, if known; (2) the official title of the posting, in quotation
marks, or a descriptive title, without quotation marks; (3) the phrase *Online
posting,* not italicized; (4) the date of electronic publication or the date of the
most recent update; (5) the name of the forum or discussion group; (6) the
date on which you accessed the posting; and (7) the URL of the posting, not
the general forum or discussion site on which you found it, in angle brackets.

Waitt, D. "Native Plant Information Network." Online posting. 4 June 2003. Native Plants
      Forum. 13 Aug. 2003 <http://forums.gardenweb.com/forums/load/natives/
      msg062359004143.html?8>.
   Parenthetical note   (Waitt)

Whinney, Kathryn. "Disturbing Vision." Discussion of *A Clockwork Orange.*
      Online posting. 11 Jan. 2001. Book Lover's Discussion. 15 Jan. 2001
      <http://www.whatamigoingtoread.com/book.asp?bookid=6395>.
   Parenthetical note   (Whinney)

EXERCISE 14.1   *A Sample Works-Cited Page*

From the following sets of information on sources related to Toni Morrison's
novel *Beloved,* produce sample works-cited entries and arrange them alphabetically to produce a sample works-cited page. *Note:* Some information is included
for the sake of clarity only; it should not be incorporated into the citations.

1. Produced by Harpo Productions; released in 1998; the movie *Beloved;* directed by Jonathan Demme; distributed by Touchstone Pictures; starring
   Oprah Winfrey and Danny Glover.
2. Published by Alfred A. Knopf, Incorporated; written by Toni Morrison;
   published in 1987; the novel *Beloved;* winner of the Pulitzer Prize for fiction; New York, New York.
3. Published in 1998; written by Missy Dehn Kubitschek; published by
   Greenwood Press; the book *Toni Morrison: A Critical Companion;* 224 pages
   long; Westport, Connecticut; part of the Critical Companions to Popular
   Contemporary Writers Series.

4. Directed by Jonathan Demme; a review written by Richard Corliss; the review "Bewitching *Beloved*"; published in *Time* magazine; a review of the film *Beloved;* with performances by Oprah Winfrey and Danny Glover; appearing on pages 74, 75, 76, and 77; published on October 5, 1998.

5. Written by Dinita Smith; the article "Toni Morrison's Mix of Tragedy, Domesticity and Folklore"; appearing in section E; published in the *New York Times;* appearing on page 1 and four more separated pages; published January 8, 1998; appearing in a late edition.

6. A collected set of information titled "Historical Events Affecting Characters in *Beloved*"; appearing in a Web site titled *Toni Morrison's Beloved;* posted from the University of Texas; first posted on October 30, 1998; retrieved February 12, 2001; compiled by Ali Lakhia, Glenn Schuetz, Katie Gilette, and Scott Lloyd; available at <http://www.cs.berkeley.edu/~lakhia/morrison/history.html>.

7. Appearing on pages 92–110; in a collection edited by Donna Bassin; published by Yale University Press in New Haven; written by Marianne Hirsch; a chapter titled "Maternity and Rememory: Toni Morrison's *Beloved*"; part of a book titled *Representations of Motherhood;* published in 1991.

8. Published in 1991; appearing on pages 153–169; published in the journal *Journal of Narrative Technique,* which uses continuous pages throughout a volume; written by Eusebio L. Rodrigues; an article titled "The Telling of *Beloved*"; appearing in volume 21.

9. Published in the journal *Religion and Literature,* which uses separate pages with each issue; appearing on pages 119–129; appearing in issue 1 of volume 27; an article titled "Who Are the Beloved? Old and New Testaments, Old and New Communities of Faith"; written by Danille Taylor-Guthrie; published in 1995.

10. Published by Gale Publishers, Incorporated; the 9th edition; an entry titled "Morrison, Toni"; published in 1999; published in *Who's Who among African Americans.*

11. Appearing on page 14 and five additional, separated pages; published December 1987; an article titled "Telling How It Was"; written by Geoffrey C. Ward; published in *American Heritage.*

12. A book titled *Conversations with Toni Morrison;* published in 1991; edited by Danille Taylor-Guthrie; published in Jackson, Mississippi; published by the University Press of Mississippi.

13. An essay titled "'Postmodern Blackness': Toni Morrison's *Beloved* and the End of History"; written by Kimberly Chabot Davis, a doctoral student at the University of Virginia; posted February 11, 2002; written in 1998; retrieved February 17, 2003; appearing in a Web site called *Beloved;* available at <http://thecriticalvoice.com/postmodern_beloved.html>.

14f   When appropriate, follow MLA guidelines to prepare your manuscript.

Writers in language-related disciplines follow these guidelines—based on the principles adopted by the MLA—for preparing and presenting manuscripts. If a paper or project provides you with special challenges or if you are required to follow other style guidelines, consult your instructor.

Paper

Use white, medium-weight, 8½" × 11" paper. Avoid unusual paper—such as onion-skin or colored paper—for most projects.

Printing Formats

Use the best printer available. Laser or inkjet printers are preferred.

Use a standard, nondecorative font (Courier, Times Roman, Helvetica, Palatino, or some other) in a conventional size (12 point is standard, but easily readable fonts may be as small as 11 point or as large as 14 point). Avoid unusual fonts (script, for example) for most academic writing.

Do not justify the right margins of your papers. Such justification creates unusual spaces between words and after punctuation and, consequently, can distort the look of your prose and create inaccuracies in the internal spacing of the works-cited entries of a research paper.

Take advantage of the italics feature of your word processor to set titles, foreign words, and words for emphasis in slanted type when possible. However, since underlining creates the same meaning as italics, you may choose instead to use the underlining feature. Whichever form you choose, be consistent throughout the paper.

Spacing

Double-space everything: the heading, the title (if it requires more than one line), the text, set-in quotations, notes, the works-cited page, and any appended material.

Margins

Leave one-inch margins on the left, right, and bottom of the page; the page header (which appears at the top) determines the top margin (see the sample paper that follows). Most word processing programs have default margins of one inch; if yours does not, reset the margins.

Indent paragraphs five spaces using the "Tab" feature. To indent the second and subsequent lines of works-cited entries, use the "Indent" feature of your word processor; this feature holds the five-space indentation until you enter a hard return.

Indent set-in quotations ten spaces, using the "Indent" feature; if the indent feature of your word processor works in five-space increments, click it twice to achieve the ten spaces. This feature holds the ten-space indentation until you enter a hard return.

Paging

In the upper-right corner of each page (flush right), one-half inch from the top, type your last name, a space, and the page number. Two spaces below, the text of the paper continues (whether it is the heading on the first page or the text on subsequent pages). Word processing programs provide easy-to-set options for creating these headers; check under "*Insert*" or "Format" on the tool bar.

Headings and Title

A paper in MLA style has no separate title page. Instead, in the upper left-hand corner of the first page, two spaces below the header, type on separate lines your name, your instructor's name, the course number, and the date. Two lines below the date, center the paper's title. Capitalize all important words in the title but do not italicize it, place it in quotation marks, or follow it with a period. Two lines below the title, begin the first paragraph of the paper.

Tables, Graphs, Charts, Maps, and Illustrations

Graphic materials—tables, charts, maps, and other illustrations—should be placed in your paper as close as possible to the discussion they illustrate, not at the end of the paper.

A table—a visual presentation of statistical data, generally in columns—is labeled by the word *Table* (not italicized), numbered, and titled. This identifying information appears above the table and is typed flush with the left margin; the table should also be typed flush with the left margin and should use horizontal lines, as necessary, to provide clarity. Below the table, the source of the data is introduced by the word *Source* (not italicized) and a colon, as in the sample below.

Table 1

Poverty Thresholds in 1998 by Family Size and Number of Children

Size of Family Unit	0 Children	1 Child	2 Children	3 Children
One person	8,480			
Two persons	10,915	11,235		
Three persons	12,750	13,120	13,133	
Four persons	16,813	17,088	16,530	16,588
Five persons	20,275	20,570	19,940	19,453
Six persons	23,320	23,413	22,930	22,468
Seven persons	26,833	27,000	26,423	26,020
Eight persons	30,010	30,275	29,730	29,253

Source: United States. Bureau of the Census. 1999. 3 Mar. 2003
<http:// www.census.gov/hhes/poverty/threshld/thresh98.html>.

Other illustrations—graphs, charts, maps, line drawings, photographs, and so on—are placed in the paper with descriptive material below the illustration. The abbreviation *Fig.* (short for *figure,* not italicized) appears under the illustration with a number and descriptive title or caption, as in the sample on the next page.

Times Roman	COPPERPLATE GOTHIC
Arial	Courier
Abadi MT Condensed	FC-Kristi (Handwriting)
Arrus BT	Tempus Sans ITC
Book Antiqua	Verdana
Century Gothic	OCR-A

Fig. 1. Alternative Fonts

Most word processing programs now include features to create tables, charts, and graphs in a uniform and efficient way. If you are preparing a paper that requires a variety of these illustrations, experiment with these options.

Submitting the Paper

Submit manuscripts according to your instructor's guidelines. If you receive no specific directions, secure the pages with a paper clip in the upper-left corner. Place lengthy papers in a 9" × 12" manila envelope with your name and course information typed or written on the outside. Always keep a photocopy—or another printed copy—of your paper.

Be aware that instructors may ask for a disk copy of the paper. In that case, submit a copy of the paper on a separate disk, clearly labeled with your name and course information, as well as a note about your word processing program (Microsoft Word 2000, WordPerfect 10). Keep a disk version for yourself.

Estes-Cooper 1

Jarah Estes-Cooper

Dr. Robert Perrin

English 107

April 25, 2003

Walking into History: The Legacy
of the Lincoln Memorial

I had seen it before, but only in pictures. It was in our history book. It was on a poster in Mr. McFarlan's government classroom. It was in a video I had watched in American history. It was in the books I had skimmed before the trip. But nothing prepared me for the feeling I got as I approached it with my fellow band members. We walked west along the reflecting pool, and it got larger and larger until we were standing at the foot of the steps, the steps that led to the Lincoln Memorial.

As I looked up the steps at the front of the Memorial, I realized that I was, in a sense, walking into the pictures, the posters, and the videos. Like thousands of people before me, I was walking into history. After all, the Lincoln Memorial is more than an impressive stone monument. Instead, it has become a symbol of American commemoration and demonstration.

Plans to construct a memorial to Abraham Lincoln began in March 1867, when the United States Congress established the Lincoln Monument Association; however, the current site for the memorial was not chosen until 1901 (US, National Park Service, "Lincoln: The Memorial"). Designed by Henry Bacon to resemble a Greek temple, the rectangular memorial's flat roof is supported by thirty-six columns, one for each state in the Union at the time of Lincoln's death, and texts of Lincoln's Gettysburg Address and second inaugural address are included on the south and north interior walls (US, National Park Service, "Lincoln: The Memorial"). The nineteen-

---

Margin notes:

Last name and page number appear on every page, ½ inch from top.

Identification information, 1 inch from top of page

2 spaces above and below the centered title

Left and right margins of 1 inch

A lead-in to the thesis statement

The thesis statement

Jarah begins with background information.

Both the "author" and a brief title are required when an author has two works.

Estes-Cooper 2

foot statue of Lincoln within the memorial was designed by Daniel
Chester French, who later observed, "The memorial tells you what
manner of man you are coming to pay homage to: his simplicity, his
grandeur, and his power" (US, National Archives and Records Administration, "Unfinished"). Jules Guerin, who had done other commissioned work for the government, planned two murals: above the
Gettysburg address, a mural was to "[depict] the angel of truth free-
ing a slave," while above the inaugural speech another mural would
represent the unity of the North and South (US, National Park Service, "Lincoln: The Memorial").

 With designs complete, construction began on February 12,
1914, forty-nine years after Lincoln's assassination. The exterior
was constructed of Colorado Yule marble and Tripods Pink
Tennessee marble, while the interior used Indiana limestone and
marble from Alabama, Georgia, and Tennessee (US, National Park
Service, "Stones and Mortar"). Progress was slow, and the memorial
was not completed until early 1922, at a cost of nearly three-million
dollars ("Lincoln Memorial," *Encarta*). On May 20, 1922, President
Warren G. Harding presided over the Memorial's dedication,
which included a speech by Robert Morton, President of Tuskegee
Institute; in attendance was Robert Todd Lincoln, President
Lincoln's son (US, National Park Service, "Lincoln: The Memorial").

 In the years that followed, thousands of visitors to the Capital
climbed the vast staircase and walked within the Memorial, looking
at the mammoth statue of the seated president, reading the carved
speeches, and examining the murals. The responses were consistently
positive, and the Lincoln Memorial became one of the most popular
sites in Washington.

 Surely part of the Memorial's appeal is its beauty, but another
facet of its appeal rests in the ideals that it represents. Leland M.
Roth, in *Understanding Architecture: Its Elements, History, and
Meaning*, asserts that the symbolic function of architecture "is

*Information
from a Web
site generally
does not
include a page
number.*

*Brackets are
used to
substitute
depict for
depicts.*

*Information
that appears
in many
sources—the
date
construction
began—is
common
knowledge
and requires
no citation.*

*Jarah
provides a
useful
transition.*

*The quotation
is introduced
with the
author's name
and the
source's title.*

Estes-Cooper 3

most easily perceived in religious and public buildings where the
principal intent is to make a broad and emphatic proclamation of
communal values and beliefs" (5). In many ways, the Lincoln
Memorial does proclaim "values and beliefs." Its size—99 feet
high, 188 feet wide, and 118 feet deep—and simple design
suggest grandeur and importance (US, National Park Service,
"Stones and Mortar"). Its imposing statue of Lincoln shows a man
who was, like the country, strong yet understanding: "One of the
president's hands is clenched, representing his strength and
determination to see the war to a successful conclusion. The
other hand is an open, much more relaxed hand representing his
compassionate[,] warm nature" (US, National Park Service,
"Lincoln: The Memorial"). Charles L. Griswold, a professor of
philosophy at Boston University, comments on symbolic architecture
in this way:

> [T]he architecture by which a people memorializes
> itself is a species of pedagogy. It therefore seeks to
> instruct posterity about the past and, in doing so, nec-
> essarily reaches a decision about what is worth re-
> covering. . . . We must understand the monument's
> symbolism, social context, and the effects its archi-
> tecture works on those who participate in it. (71, 73)

Writing specifically about the Lincoln Memorial, Griswold observes
that "Lincoln's temple is, then, a monument to national unity
achieved by the martyrdom of Lincoln himself" (80).

Over the years, the Memorial has served a variety of specific
ceremonial functions. For example, at noon on February 12 of each
year, the current president places a wreath at the side of Lincoln's
statue. While most presidents make only brief comments, some see
the ceremony as an opportunity to illustrate the symbolic principles
of honoring Lincoln, as Harry Truman did in 1947, when the traditional military color guard was made nontraditional and highly sym-

*Quotations
that function
as
independent
sentences are
often
introduced
with a colon.*

*Long
quotations are
set in 10
spaces and do
not use
quotataion
marks; note
that the
period
precedes the
parenthetical
note.*

*First example
of the
activities at
the Memorial*

Estes-Cooper 4

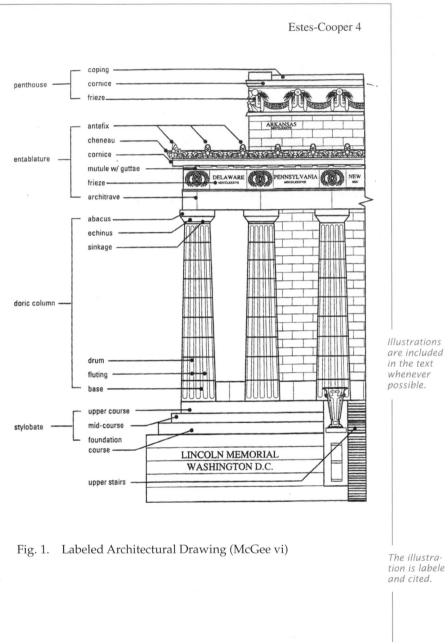

penthouse
- coping
- cornice
- frieze

entablature
- antefix
- cheneau
- cornice
- mutule w/ guttae
- frieze
- architrave

ARKANSAS

DELAWARE   PENNSYLVANIA   NEW

doric column
- abacus
- echinus
- sinkage
- drum
- fluting
- base

stylobate
- upper course
- mid-course
- foundation course
- upper stairs

LINCOLN MEMORIAL
WASHINGTON D.C.

Fig. 1. Labeled Architectural Drawing (McGee vi)

Illustrations are included in the text whenever possible.

The illustration is labeled and cited.

Estes-Cooper 5

bolic: it was composed of young black children (US, *National Archives and Records Administration*).

The commemorative nature of the Memorial has been over-shadowed on numerous occasions, however, by the use of the monument as a location for demonstrations—both subtle and obvious. The earliest of these "demonstrations" was on Easter Sunday, 1939. Marian Anderson, recognized throughout the world as one of opera's greatest contraltos, was scheduled to perform in Washington, DC, but the Daughters of the American Revolution (DAR), an all-white organization, denied her access to Constitution Hall. Eleanor Roosevelt protested this action by resigning her membership in the DAR, and within days the Department of the Interior granted Anderson the right to perform her concert on the steps of the Lincoln Memorial (Allen). Attended by 75,000 people, the concert received extensive press coverage. Scott A. Sandage notes in "A Marble House Divided: The Lincoln Memorial, the Civil Rights Movement, and the Politics of Memory: 1939–1963" that the concert was the first large-scale gathering at the Memorial "to evoke laudatory national publicity and earn a positive place in American public memory." In subsequent years, other protests drew upon the impact of Anderson's performance, for it had "set the stage for future rallies and protests" ("Lincoln Memorial," *The Mall*).

Almost a decade later, the National Association for the Advancement of Colored People (NAACP) held the closing session of its thirty-eighth convention on the steps of the Lincoln Memorial (US, *National Archives and Record Administration*). Walter White, the NAACP president, and Eleanor Roosevelt sat in clear view as President Harry Truman delivered the closing address before 10,000 people (US, *National Archives and Record Administration*). Though the crowd was far smaller than that at the Anderson concert, the location of the address, with all of its symbolic associations, further

Jarah's treatment of Marian Anderson's concert is detailed, using specific facts.

A portion of Sandage's work is merged with Jarah's own sentence.

A chronological transition leads to the next example.

Estes-Cooper 6

helped to emphasize the role that the Memorial was to play in the
civil rights movement.

Perhaps the most-recognized event held at the Lincoln
Memorial was the Civil Rights March on Washington in August
1963. The now-famous gathering was the closing event of a full
day of activity. The demonstrators in the "March on Washington
for Jobs and Freedom" began to gather at the Washington Monument
in the morning while thirteen of their leaders spoke with Congressional leaders; following these conversations, the leaders led the
crowd westward through the National Mall toward the Lincoln
Memorial ("Civil Rights"). Later in the day, ten of the leaders—
representing religious, labor, and social- and political-action
groups—spoke with President Kennedy while the crowd continued
to grow ("Civil Rights").

Jarah's word choices—most-recognized and now-famous—acknowledge her readers' familiarity with the event.

But what Americans know best is that Martin Luther King,
Jr.—the last of ten speakers—mesmerized the crowd, the nation, and
the world while standing before the Lincoln Memorial ("Civil
Rights"). King began his speech with a sentence that would stir
memories and make clear his purpose: "Five score years ago, a
great American, in whose symbolic shadow we stand today, signed
the Emancipation Proclamation" (qtd. in Sandage). The famous
speech continued with other now-quotable lines, while the statue of
"Lincoln brooded over his shoulder—the statue bathed in special
lights to enhance its visibility on television and in news photographs"
(Sandage). The crowd was enormous—estimates range from 250,000
to 400,000 people—and the setting was ideal. For where else other
than the Lincoln Memorial could King's point have been so powerfully made?

Jarah quotes a portion of King's speech that relates to her topic.

In less than a decade, the Lincoln Memorial became the
backdrop for further protests, this time against US involvement in the
Vietnamese War. On October 21, 1967, between 55,000 and 150,000
people (the numbers are highly disputed) attended a rally organized

Another time-related transition links the discussion.

Estes-Cooper 7

Another illustration allows readers to see what the Memorial looked like with the crowd assembled.

Fig. 2. Marchers at the Lincoln Memorial (US, *National Archives and Records Administration,* "Civil Rights")

Estes-Cooper 8

by the National Mobilization Committee to End the War in Vietnam ("Vietnamese"). The rally, which included a speech by Dr. Benjamin Spock (the famous pediatrician and author), was only the beginning of the protest; after the speeches, approximately 35,000 of the people marched to the Pentagon where approximately 600 were arrested for disorderly behavior ("Vietnamese").

Two years later—on November 15, 1969—another antiwar protest was held at the Lincoln Memorial. Plans were in place by late August; even the South Vietnamese ambassador Bui Diem knew of the upcoming demonstration and cabled South Vietnam's President Thieu this simple statement: "On November 15 they propose a great march, the 'March Against Death'" (268). Also known as the Vietnam War Moratorium, it drew approximately 600,000 people, making it the largest gathering of people in the history of the city (Hall). The symbolism of hundreds of thousands of protestors singing "Give Peace a Chance" in front of the Lincoln Memorial was evident because by 1969, the Lincoln Memorial was clearly associated with American protests (Wiener).

The quotation is introduced by the author's name and position (an alternative to the title of the selection).

In the following decades, the Lincoln Memorial—and the area of the National Mall that spreads before it—has served as the location for many other protests and rallies: the AIDS quilt has been displayed each year since 1987, the Million Man March convened there in 1995, the Promise Keepers gathered there in 1997, and the Million Mom March protested against gun violence in 2000 (Wiener). In addition, the Memorial has served as the location for a variety of recent public celebrations. It was the site of a 1999 New Year's concert that included a speech by President Clinton ("2000 Washington"). And in 2002, a two-and-a-half hour concert on the steps of the Memorial celebrated the inauguration of President Bush (Halladay and Morrison).

Jarah includes a brief catalog of other events to suggest that the Memorial's use continues.

In an article titled "Monuments in an Age without Heroes," Nathan Glazer reminds us that a "successful monument incorporates

Estes-Cooper 9

Ellipsis points indicate that material was omitted from quotation.

Jarah revisits the images of her introduction.

A title is quoted and then modified as Jarah's closing strategy.

symbolic meanings . . . and can carry new meanings attributed to it over time without any necessary diminishment." The Lincoln Memorial surely has done that. It remains a beautiful piece of architecture, one easily recognized in its hundreds of images in history and travel books, in film references, and even on the reverse side of the $5 bill. Yet because of its associations with commemorations, celebrations, and, most importantly, major demonstrations throughout the twentieth century, the Lincoln Memorial has assumed a symbolic role that few other national landmarks have achieved. Once, the Memorial was known as "The Temple of Democracy" (US, National Park Service, "Lincoln: The Memorial"). Through its varied use by the American people, it has become "The Temple of Our Democracy in Action."

Estes-Cooper 10

Page numbering is sequential.

Works Cited

Heading, centered, 1 inch from the top of page.

Allen, Jenny. "Righteous Song in the Open Air." *Life* (1998). *ProQuest.*
　　2002. Bell and Howell. 19 Feb. 2003. <http://
　　proquest.umi.com/pqdweb/>.

"Civil Rights: March on Washington." *Facts.com.* 2003. 22 Feb. 2003
　　<http://www.2facts.com/stories/index/h006707.asp>.

The entire list is alphabetized.

Diem, Bui. *In the Jaws of History.* With David Chanoff. Boston:
　　Houghton, 1987.

Glazer, Nathan. "Monuments in an Age without Heroes." *Public Inter-*
　　est 123 (1996). *ProQuest.* 2002. Bell and Howell. 18 Feb. 2003
　　<http://proquest.umi.com/pqdweb/>.

Note: First lines begin at the regular margin; subsequent lines are indented.

Griswold, Charles L. "The Vietnam Veterans Memorial and the Wash-
　　ington Mall: Philosophical Thoughts on Political Iconogra-
　　phy." *Critical Issues in Public Art: Content, Context, and*
　　Controversy. Ed. Harriet F. Senie and Sally Webster. Washing-
　　ton: Smithsonian Inst., 1992. 71–100.

Hall, Cindy. "Washington's Great Gatherings." *USA Today* 2000.
　　16 Mar. 2003 <http://www.usatoday.com/news/index/
　　mman006.htm>.

Halladay, Jessie, and Blake Morrison. "Martin Kicks Off Inaugural
　　Festivities: Bush Shares Stage with Pop Sensation." *USA To-*
　　day 19 Jan. 2001. *ProQuest.* 2001. Bell and Howell. 18 Feb.
　　2003 <http://proquest.umi.com/pqdweb/>.

"Lincoln Memorial." *Encarta Reference.* 2003. MSN. 1 Mar. 2003
　　<http://encarta.msn.com/encnet/refpages/
　　RefArticle.apx?refid+761578453>.

When two citations begin with the same title, alphabetize according to the next element: *Encarta* precedes *Mall*.

"Lincoln Memorial." *The Mall.* 2000. 19 Feb. 2003 <http://
　　library.thinkquest.org/2813/mall/lincoln.html>.

McGee, Elaine S. *Colorado Yule Marble: Building Stone of the Lincoln*
　　Memorial. US Geological Survey. Dept. of the Interior. Wash-
　　ington: GPO, 1999.

Roth, Leland M. *Understanding Architecture: Its Elements, History,*
　　and Meaning. New York: Icon-Harper, 1993.

Estes-Cooper 11

Sandage, Scott A. "A Marble House Divided: The Lincoln Memorial,
    the Civil Rights Movement, and the Politics of Memory,
    1939–1963." *Journal of American History* 80 (1993).
    ProQuest. 2002. Bell and Howell. 18 Feb. 2003
    <http://proquest.umi.com/ pqdwcb/>.

"2000 Washington, DC: Capital Thrills." *People* 17 Jan. 2000. *Pro-
    Quest*. 2002. Bell and Howell. 19 Feb. 2003 <http://
    proquest.umi.com/pqdweb/>.

United States. *National Archives and Records Administration*. 13 May
    1998. College Park. 12 Mar. 2003 <http://www.nara.gov/
    cgi-bin/starfinder/>.

---. ---. "Civil Rights March on Washington, DC." Photograph. *Na-
    tional Archives and Records Administration*. 13 May 1998.
    College Park. 11 Mar. 2003 <http://www.nara.gov/cgi-bin/
    starfinder/17260/ standards.txt>.

---. ---. "The Unfinished Lincoln Memorial." *National Archives and
    Records Administration*. 13 May 1998. College Park. 11 Mar.
    2003 <http://www.nara.gov/education/teaching/memorial/
    memhome.html>.

---. National Park Service. "Lincoln: The Memorial." *Lincoln Memorial*.
    8 July 2002. NPS. 5 Feb. 2003 <http://www.nps.gov/linc/
    memorial/>.

---. ---. "Lincoln Memorial." *Monuments and Memorials*. 1999. 7 Feb.
    2003 <http://www.kreative.net/ cooper/tourofdc/
    monuments/lincoln-memorial/>.

---. ---. "Stones and Mortar: The Statistics of the Monuments and
    Memorials on the National Mall." 8 Aug. 2002. NPS. 5 Feb.
    2003 <http://www.nps.gov/nama/mortar/mortar.htm#linc>.

"Vietnamese War Protests: Washington Demonstrations." *Facts.com*.
    2000. 22 Feb. 2003 <http://www.2facts.com/stories/index/
    h01825.asp>.

Wiener, Jon. "Save the Mall." *Nation* 13 Nov. 2000. *ProQuest*. 2002. Bell
    and Howell. 18 Feb. 2003 <http://proquest.umi.com/ pqdweb/>.

Numbers are alphabetized as if they were spelled out.

Indicate the repetition of an element with three hyphens and a period.

Though repeating the element United States, this citation introduces a new department in the second position.

Using APA Style When Appropriate*

QUICK REFERENCE

Prepare APA citations for sources, applying these general principles for formatting and incorporating required information.

▶ Begin the first line of each entry at the left margin; indent subsequent lines six spaces (a five-space "Tab" is acceptable).

▶ Arrange entries alphabetically using the first element, usually the author or title (omitting *a*, *an*, or *the*).

▶ Double-space entries; do not insert additional line spaces between entries.

▶ Provide some information in abbreviated form: authors' initials and last names (R. Perrin, not Robert Perrin) and publishers' names (*Houghton*, not *Houghton Mifflin*).

▶ Include some information in full form: university presses (Oxford University Press) and months (*September*, not *Sept.*).

▶ Invert the author's name when it begins an entry (*Perrin, R.*, not *Robert Perrin*) and follow it with the year in parentheses [(2004)].

▶ When an element is missing, proceed to the next element: an article without a stated author begins with the article's title.

▶ Use an ampersand (&), not the word *and*, to join the names of multiple authors.

▶ Capitalize only the first word and proper nouns and proper adjectives in book titles and use italics, not underlining (*Moving beyond the American experience*).

▶ Capitalize all major words in periodical titles and italicize the title *and* volume number (*Journal of Educational Research, 66*).

*The information in this chapter is based on the *Publication Manual of the American Psychological Association*, fifth edition (Washington: APA, 2001). While the chapter describes APA style and the sample materials illustrate APA citations, the primary text follows the conventions of MLA.

▶ Separate the major elements of an entry with periods and single spaces.

▶ Use the samples in this chapter as models when you prepare your own reference-list entries, combining information from several samples when a source has many features.

To acknowledge the use of other people's ideas, information, or exact words in a paper, include accurate in-text citations in the paper and entries in the reference list. These elements provide basic information about sources so that interested readers may locate them for further study.

15a   Recognize the distinct documentation patterns of APA style.

APA (American Psychological Association) documentation has two areas of emphasis: (1) the authors of source materials and (2) the dates on which sources were published or presented. This pattern is commonly described as the author-date style.

When incorporating information from a source, use an in-text citation that includes, at minimum, the author's last name and the year of publication or presentation; however, the complexity of some sources requires the inclusion of additional information.

15b   Consider patterns for in-text citations.

An in-text citation corresponds to an entry in the reference list at the end of the paper. The information in an entry for the reference list determines what information appears in the in-text citation. For example, if the reference-list entry for a book begins with the author's name, the author's name appears in the in-text citation; however, if an entry for a book begins with the title, the title (or a shortened version of it) appears in the in-text citation. In-text citations must correspond to entries in the reference list.

Basic Forms of In-Text Citations

To avoid disrupting the text, in-text citations briefly identify only the name of the author or the title under which the source appears in the reference list and give the appropriate date. For the sake of clarity and smoothness, you may incorporate some of the necessary information in your sentences. For example:

APA STYLE

Survivors have a higher than normal chance of also dying. For example, widows and widowers have a forty percent higher chance of death during the first six months after losing a spouse than other people their age (Backer, Hannon, & Gregg, 1994).

Or

Survivors have a higher than normal chance of also dying. Backer, Hannon, and Gregg (1994) explain that widows and widowers have a forty percent higher chance of death during the first six months after losing a spouse than other people their age.

[Backer, Barbara, Natalie Hannon, and Joan Young Gregg. *To Listen, to Comfort, to Care: Reflections on Death and Dying.* Albany: Delmar, 1994.]

In special cases, the rule of using the author's name and the date is superseded:

Special Circumstance	Rule and Sample
Two authors with the same last name	Include initials and last name: (Barratt, J., 2002), distinct from (Barratt, L., 2003).
Multiple works by the same author (same year)	Use letters to distinguish the sources: (Morrison, 2003a), distinct from (Morrison, 2003b); the letters indicate the alphabetical order of the titles.
Two authors	Use both last names, joined by an ampersand: (Scott & Fuller, 2001).
Three, four, or five authors	The *first* notation includes all names (Jarnow, Judelle, & Guerriro, 2003). *Subsequent* citations, except as noted, use the first author's name and *et al.* ("and others"), not italicized: (Jarnow et al., 2003). Further references within a single paragraph omit the date: (Jarnow et al.).
Six or more authors	Use the first author's name and *et al.,* not italicized: (Gershey et al., 2002).
Organization as author	When confusion is possible, present the organization name in full (Iowa State University, 2003) or provide clarifying information in the first notation (National Council of Teachers of English [NCTE], 2001) and use the shortened form in subsequent notations (NCTE, 2001).
Multiple publication dates	Include both dates, separated by a slash: (Jagger & Richards, 1994/2001).
Reference works	List by author if applicable (Angermüller, 2003) or by a shortened form of the title ("Manhattan Project," 2003).

Two or more works by the same author (same note)	To note several works by the same author (all included in the reference list), include the author's name and all dates in chronological order, separated by commas: (Vidich, 2000, 2001, 2004).
Two or more works by different authors (same note)	To note several works by different authors in the same note, list each author (in alphabetical order) and date, separated by semicolons: (Bennet, 2002; Greene, 2000; Swift, 2003).
Parts of sources	To note only a portion of a source, include author or title as appropriate, the date, and clarifying information: (Thomas, 2003, p. 451) or (Spindrell, 2002, chaps. 2–3).

15c   Prepare complete entries for the reference list.

The reference list, the alphabetically arranged sources used in a paper, follows the text. Reference-list entries follow the formats described below. (See page 262 for a sample reference page.)

Information for Reference-List Entries

Reference-list entries vary because of the different information they include, but all must follow an established order for presenting information:

1. *Author(s).* Take the name or names from the first page of an article or from the title page of a book. Authors' names are listed in the order in which they appear (not alphabetical order), and initials are used instead of first or middle names.
2. *Publication date.* For professional journals and books, include the publication year in parentheses. For popular magazines and newspapers, include the year and the month or the year, month, and day in parentheses.
3. *Title.* List titles completely, taking information from the first page of an article or the title page of a book. Include both titles and subtitles, no matter how long they are.
4. *Additional information.* Include any of the following information *in the order presented here* if it is listed on the first page of an article, the title page of the book, or the first page of the essay, chapter, or other subsection:
   - translator
   - edition number
   - volume number
   - issue number (if the journal is paginated by issue)
   - inclusive pages

5. *Facts of publication.* For periodicals, take the volume number, issue number (if needed), and date from the masthead (listing of information at the top of the first page of newspapers or within the first few pages in journals and magazines, often in combination with the table of contents). For books, take the publisher's name from the title page and the date from the copyright page (immediately following the title page); use the publisher's name in abbreviated form (see samples in section **15e** and Appendix B), the first city listed if more than one is given (and an abbreviation for the state, province, or country if the city is not well known), and the most recent date.

Note: In sections **15e–15g**, sample reference-list entries are followed by corresponding in-text citations.

Format for Reference-List Entries

To ensure easy reading, entries for the reference list must follow this format consistently.

- Begin the first line of each entry at the left margin; indent subsequent lines (six spaces is preferred, but a five-space "Tab" is generally acceptable).
- Identify authors by last names and first and middle initials. Give the author's last name first (to make the citation easy to alphabetize). If sources are co-authored, invert the names of all authors, and use an ampersand (&), not the word *and,* to join the names of multiple authors.
- When no author is identified, list the source by title.
- For periodicals, include the full title with all major words capitalized, a comma, and the volume number. Italicize the title or the title and volume number, including the separating comma and the period that follows the volume number. For books, capitalize only the first word of titles and subtitles and proper nouns and proper adjectives; all other words are lowercase; the title is italicized.
- Shorten the names of commercial publishers by using only main elements of their names (*Harcourt,* not *Harcourt Brace*) and by dropping descriptive titles (*Publishers, Company*). However, list university presses, organizations, and corporations that serve as publishers completely, using the words *Books* and *Press* whenever they are part of an academic publisher's name.
- Separate major sections of entries (author, title, and publication information) with periods, including elements enclosed in parentheses or brackets. However, separate the place of publication from the publisher's name by a colon and one space.
- Only one space separates elements in APA entries.
- Page numbers are listed completely (176–179, not 176–9 or 176–79) and introduced by the abbreviations *p.* (for page) or *pp.* (for pages). No commas are used to separate digits of numbers one thousand or larger when citing pages (pp. 1295–1298).
- Double-space entries.

Some of the entries included below—for example, annual reports, interviews, works of art, and cartoons—are not included in the *Manual*. They have been included, however, because they can be worthwhile sources in student research papers. APA principles for supplying information and formatting are used in these entry forms.

15d Follow the appropriate reference-list entry forms for periodicals.

15d.1 An Article in a Journal with Continuous Paging

When an article comes from a journal with continuous paging, list authors first, followed by the year of publication and the title of the article. Include next the title of the journal (with all major words capitalized), a comma, the volume number, and another comma (all italicized). Finish the citation by including the inclusive page numbers, without a page abbreviation.

Chiguluri, R. R. (2003). The politics of discourse and the discourse of politics in *Tres*
       Tristes Tigres. Revista de Estudious Hispánicos, 37, 249–269.
    In-text citation   (Chiguluri, 2003)

Nussbaum, J. F., & Bettini, L. M. (1994). Shared stories of the grandparent-grandchild
       relationship. *The International Journal of Aging and Human Development, 39,*
       67–80.
    In-text citation   (Nussbaum & Bettini, 1994)

15d.2 An Article in a Journal with Separate Paging

When a journal has separate paging for each issue, follow the volume number with the issue number, in parentheses; no space separates the volume from the issue, and the issue number is not italicized. All other information in the citation is the same as in a citation for a journal with continuous paging.

Gumm, A. J. (2003). Musical and technical sources of choral dynamics. *Choral Journal,*
       43(10), 27–39.
    In-text citation   (Gumm, 2003)

Lewis, J. (2000). "We do not ask you to condone this": How the blacklist saved Holly-
       wood. *Cinema Journal, 39*(2), 3–30.
    In-text citation   (Lewis, 2000)

APA STYLE

15d.3   An Article in a Monthly Magazine

Articles from monthly magazines are listed by author; the date is listed by year *and* month, separated by a comma, in parentheses. The article title appears without special punctuation. The title of the magazine, however, is presented with all major words capitalized, followed by a comma and the volume number and another comma (all italicized). The entry ends with inclusive page numbers listed without page abbreviations.

If no author is listed with the article, begin with the article's title, followed by the date and magazine title.

Furlow, B. (2000, October). The uses of crying and begging. *Natural History, 109,* 62–67.
   In-text citation   (Furlow, 2000)

Warschauer, M. (2003, August). Demystifying the digital divide. *Scientific American, 289,* 42–47.
   In-text citation   (Warschauer, 2003)

15d.4   An Article in a Weekly Magazine

Weekly magazines are presented just as monthly magazines are, with one important difference: the day (along with the year and month) is included in parentheses.

Gest, T. (2000, October 9). Fixing your school. *U.S. News and World Report, 129,* 65–67.
   In-text citation   (Gest, 2000)

Ordoñez, J. (2003, August 4). Rap to the rescue. *Newsweek, 142,* 58.
   In-text citation   (Ordoñez, 2003)

15d.5   An Article in a Newspaper

Citations for newspapers resemble those for magazines, except that paging is indicated with a page abbreviation (*p.* or *pp.*, not italicized), and section numbers or letters are included. The page abbreviation precedes the page and section numbers.

Bolado, C. (2003, August 1). Activists push affordable housing. *Chicago Tribune,* p. 2:3.
   In-text citation   (Bolado, 2003)

When newspaper sections are numbered, a colon with no space is used to separate the section (section 2, in the sample above) from the page number (page 3 of section 2, in the sample above).

Wilson, S. (2003, July 27). A hard new life inside the law. *The Washington Post,* p. A1.
   In-text citation   (Wilson, 2003)

When sections are indicated by letters, they are presented along with the page numbers, with no intervening punctuation or space.

15d.6   An Editorial

The entry for an editorial, an opinion-based essay, resembles that for a magazine or newspaper article, with one exception: the word *Editorial* (not italicized), placed within brackets and followed by a period, comes after the title of the essay, if there is one.

Berkowitz B. (2003, August 4). A fresh start against terror [Editorial]. *The New York Times*, p. A17.

In-text citation   (Berkowitz, 2003)

Herbert B. (2001, January 1). Addicted to guns [Editorial]. *The New York Times*, p. A17.

In-text citation   (Herbert, 2001)

15d.7   A Letter to the Editor

Following the author's name and the publication date, include the phrase *Letter to the editor* (not italicized) in brackets, followed by a period. The rest of the entry follows the pattern appropriate for the periodical.

Davis, J. P. (2003, August). [Letter to the editor]. *Harper's, 307,* 8.

In-text citation   (Davis, 2003)

Fecteau, J. P. (2003, August 11). [Letter to the editor]. *Business Week,* 12.

In-text citation   (Fecteau, 2003)

Business Week does not use volume numbers, so none can be listed.

15d.8   A Review

After the author, date, and review title (if there is one), include a descriptive phrase that begins "Review of the book (film, record, car, computer game)" and ends with the specific product name; enclose this information in brackets, followed by a period. Then continue the entry as is appropriate for the source.

Lacayo, R. (2003, March 17). Total eclipse of the heart [Review of *A ship made of paper* by Scott Spender]. *Time, 161,* 80.

In-text citation   (Lacayo, 2003)

Sonnenfeld, B. (2003, September). Gadget of the month [Review of Sony Ericsson T610 combination cell phone and e-mail receiver]. *Esquire, 140,* 118.

In-text citation   (Sonnenfeld, 2003)

15d.9   An Abstract from *Dissertation Abstracts International*

This specialized entry requires the author's name, the year in parentheses, and the title of the dissertation (without any special punctuation). In parentheses, include the phrase *Doctoral dissertation* (not italicized), the degree-granting university, and the year of completion—all separated with commas; follow the parenthesis with a period. Close the entry by identifying *Dissertation Abstracts International* (italicized), followed by the volume number and a comma (also italicized), and the dissertation's identification number.

Dikovitskaya, M. (2002). From art to visual culture: The study of the visual after the cultural turn. (Doctoral dissertation, Columbia University, 2002). *Dissertation Abstracts International, 62,* AAT3028516.

   In-text citation   (Dikovitskaya, 2002)

Williamson, J. E. (2003). Teachers as change mediators in educational reform. (Doctoral dissertation, University of Illinois, Urbana-Champaign, 2003). *Dissertation Abstracts International, 63,* AAT3070477.

   In-text citation   (Williamson, 2003)

15e   Follow the appropriate reference-list entry forms for books and other separately published materials.

15e.1   A Book by One Author

Barr, S. M. (2003). *Modern physics and ancient faith.* Notre Dame, IN: University of Notre Dame Press.

   In-text citation   (Barr, 2003)

University and *Press* are spelled out because the publisher has a university affiliation.

Gould, E. (2003). *The university in a corporate culture.* New Haven, CT: Yale University Press.

   In-text citation   (Gould, 2003)

15e.2   A Book by Two or More Authors

Authors' names appear in the order presented on the title page, not alphabetical order. All authors are listed, no matter how many, and all of their names are inverted. An ampersand (&) joins the last two names in the series.

Fagan, J., & Palm, G. (2003). *Fathers and early childhood programs.* Clifton Park, NY:
   Delmar.
   In-text citation   (Fagan & Palm, 2003)

Kegley, C. W., & Raymond, G. A. (1999). *How nations make peace.* New York: St. Martin's.
   In-text citation   (Kegley & Raymond, 1999)

15e.3   A Book with No Author Named

When no author or editor is named, list the book by title. When an editor is listed, begin the entry with the editor's name.

*United Press International stylebook: The authoritative handbook for writers, editors,
   and news directors* (3rd ed.). (1992). Lincolnwood, IL: National.
   In-text citation   (United Press International, 1992)

This source is listed by title. *United Press International* has each word capitalized since it is an organization. With an authorless book, the edition number follows the title, in parentheses; notice that the number is not italicized and that the period that normally would follow the title follows the closing parenthesis instead. The year follows the edition number. See sections **15e.6** and **15e.7** for the common patterns for presenting editions.

Swanton, M. J. (Ed.). (1990). *An Anglo-Saxon chronicle.* Exeter, England: University of
   Exeter Press.
   In-text citation   (Swanton, 1990)

This source is listed by editor. As in this sample, the country can also be listed when confusion is possible.

15e.4   Multiple Works by the Same Author

When citing several sources by the same author, repeat the name completely each time. Alphabetical order takes precedence, with single authors listed before multiple authors. List works by single authors or by the same multiple authors chronologically; if several works were published in the same year, arrange them alphabetically by title.

Ehrenreich, B. (1999, June 20). Looking to put fatherhood in its proper place. *The New
   York Times,* p. L14.

Ehrenreich, B. (1999, June). Who needs men? Addressing the prospect of a matrilinear
   millennium. [Interview]. *Harper's, 298,* 33–46.

Ehrenreich, B. (2000, May 8). Barefoot, pregnant, and ready to fight. _Time, 156,_ 62.

Ehrenreich, B., Hess, E., & Jacobs, G. (1986). _Re-making love: The feminization of sex._
Garden City, NY: Anchor-Doubleday.

Alternative in-text citations

- The _Times_ article: (Ehrenreich, 1999a)
- The _Harper's_ article: (Ehrenreich, 1999b)
- All three single-author works in the same citation: (Ehrenreich, 1999a, 1999b, 2000)
- The multiple-author book: (Ehrenreich, Hess, & Jacobs, 1986)

Ehrenreich's three separately written works appear first, arranged in chronological order. The Ehrenreich, Hess, and Jacobs book follows.

15e.5   A Book with an Organization as Author

When an organization is listed as the author, spell out the name completely in the author position. When the organization is also the publisher, use the referent _Author,_ not italicized, in the publisher position.

American Medical Association. (1989). _Manual of style_ (8th ed.). Baltimore: Williams.
   First in-text citation   (American Medical Association [AMA], 1989)
   Second in-text citation   (AMA, 1989)

American Psychological Association. (2001). _Publication manual of the American Psy-
chological Association_ (5th ed.). Washington, DC: Author.
   First in-text citation   (American Psychological Association [APA], 2001)
   Second in-text citation   (APA, 2001)

15e.6   An Edition Other than the First

The edition number, which appears on the title page, follows the title of the book, in parentheses, but it is not italicized.

Griffin, J M. (2003). _Global climate change: The science, economics, and politics_ (2nd
ed.). Northhampton, MA: Elgar.
   In-text citation   (Griffin, 2003)

Wilson, J. R. M (Ed.). (2003). _Forging the American character: Readings in United
States history_ (4th ed.). Upper Saddle River, NJ: Prentice.
   In-text citation   (Wilson, 2003)

15e.7   A Revised or Enlarged Edition

Descriptions of revised or enlarged editions are enclosed in parentheses following the title. As with other editions, the parenthetical information precedes the period that follows the title, and this information is not italicized.

Hiltz, S. R., & Turoff, M. (1993). *The network nation: Human communication via computer* (Rev. ed.). Cambridge: Massachusetts Institute of Technology Press.

In-text citation   (Hiltz & Turoff, 1993)

Lau, L. K. (Ed.). (2000). *Distance learning technologies: Issues, trends, and opportunities* (Rev. ed.). Hershey, PA: Idea Group.

In-text citation   (Lau, 2000)

15e.8   A Multivolume Work

Volume information appears in parentheses following the title but before the period. When citing a separately titled volume of a multivolume work, list the single volume number with the individual title.

Packard, F. R. (1973). *History of medicine in the United States* (Vols. 1–2). New York: Hafner.

In-text citation   (Packard, 1973)

This citation refers to a complete two-volume work.

Roberts, J. M. (1999). *The age of revolution: Vol. 7. The illustrated history of the world.* New York: Oxford University Press.

In-text citation   (Roberts, 1999)

This citation refers to a single volume of a ten-volume collection.

15e.9   An Edited Collection

Present an entire edited collection like a traditional book, with the editor's name in the author position.

Petrill, S. A. (Ed.). (2003). *Nature, nuture, and the transition to early adolescence.* New York: Oxford University Press.

In-text citation   (Petrill, 2003)

To cite a single selection, begin with the name of the author of the selection, followed by the date in parentheses. The title of the individual selection follows the publication date; no special punctuation is used.

Introduced by the word _In_ (not italicized), the collection editor is listed next (his or her name is in normal order, followed by the abbreviation _Ed._ in parentheses), followed by a comma and the title of the collection, italicized. Inclusive page numbers appear in parentheses. Page numbers are listed completely and are followed by the city and publisher.

Corrigan, T. (2003). Which Shakespeare to love? Film, fidelity, and the performance of
literature. In J. Collins (Ed.), _High-pop: Making culture into popular entertain-
ment_ (pp. 155–181). Malden, MA: Blackwell.

    In-text citation   (Corrigan, 2003)

15e.10   A Previously Published Work in a Collection

When selections have been reprinted from works published earlier, provide identifying information in parentheses at the end of the entry. Follow the order appropriate for the original source, although page numbers appear with the abbreviation for pages. Note that the closing parenthesis is _not_ followed by a period.

Bérubé, M. (2000). Aesthetics and literal imagination. In D. H. Richter (Ed.), _Falling into
theory: Conflicting views of reading literature_ (2nd ed., pp. 391–397). New York:
Bedford. (Reprinted from _Clio: A Journal of Literature, History, and the Philosophy of History, 24_(4), pp. 439–446, 1996)

    In-text citation   (Bérubé, 2000)

Wallace, M. (1990). Mickey Mouse history: Portraying the past at Disney World. In F.
Manning & J.-M. Philbert (Eds.), _Customs in conflict: The anthology of a changing world_ (pp. 304–332). Peterborough, ON: Broadview. (Reprinted from _Radi-
cal History Review, 32,_ pp. 33–55, 1985)

    In-text citation   (Wallace, 1990)

15e.11   An Article in an Encyclopedia or Other Reference Work

Begin with the author's name, when it is available, followed by the date in parentheses. Then list the subject heading under which the material appears, without special punctuation; follow it with the title of the reference work. In parentheses, but before the period that follows the title, include the volume number and inclusive pages. End the reference-list entry with the city and publisher.

Angermüller, R. (2001). Salieri, Antonio. In _The new Grove dictionary of music and
musicians_ (Vol. 16, pp. 415–421). New York: Grove.

    In-text citation   (Angermüller, 2001)

If an article in a reference source has no author, begin with the subject title, followed by the date in parentheses. The rest of the entry follows a normal pattern.

Fluoxetine Hydrochloride [Prozac]. (1995). In *Nursing 96 drug handbook* (pp. 383–384). Springhouse, PA: Springhouse.

    In-text citation   (Fluoxetine Hydrochloride, 1995)

15e.12   A Work in a Series

When books are part of a series, that fact will be stated on the title page. The entry follows the pattern for a similar book, except that the series title (capitalized and italicized) appears in a phrase that immediately precedes the city and publisher.

Fogg, B. J. (2003). *Persuasive technology: Using computers to change what we think and do.* In *Interactive Technology Series.* Boston: Kaufman.

    In-text citation   (Fogg, 2003)

When volumes in a series are numbered, include that information along with the series title.

Waugh, E. (2002). *A handful of dust.* In *Everyman's Library: Vol. 252.* New York: Knopf.

    In-text citation   (Waugh, 2002)

15e.13   A Translation

Under most circumstances, the translator of a text is cited in parentheses immediately after the title of the selection (whether it is an essay or chapter or a complete text) but before the closing period for that element. To emphasize the translator's work, however, you can begin the entry with his or her name.

Agacinski, S. (2003). *Time passing: Modernitey and nostalgia* (J. Gladding, Trans.). New York: Columbia University Press.

    In-text citation   (Agacinski, 2003)

This sample indicates that Gladding translated the entire book.

Foucault, M. (2000). What is an author? (J. V. Hatari, Trans.). In C. Kaplan (Ed.), *Criticism: Major statements* (4th ed, pp. 545–558). Boston: Bedford.

    In-text citation   (Foucault, 2000)

This sample indicates that Hatari translated only the selection presented in this entry; had he translated the entire collection, his name would have appeared after the anthology title.

15e.14   A Government Document—Committee, Commission, Department

Entries for government documents follow the patterns used for other similar sources. Since many government documents are book-length, that pattern most often applies. It is important, however, to note that APA style requires publication numbers for government documents, if available (check on the title page or back cover), presented in parentheses after the title; also note that *Government Printing Office* is spelled out, not abbreviated.

Commission on Migrant Education. (1992). *Invisible children: A portrait of migrant education in the United States* (92-0607-P). Washington, DC: Government Printing Office.

> **In-text citation**   (Commission on Migrant Education, 1992)

Commission on the Assassination of President Kennedy. (1964). *Investigation of the assassination of President John F. Kennedy: Hearings before the president's commission on the assassination of President Kennedy* (Vols. 1–16). Washington, DC: Government Printing Office.

> **In-text citation**   (Commission on the Assassination of President Kennedy, 1964)

15e.15   A Preface, Introduction, Foreword, Epilogue, or Afterword

Untitled materials that are included before the primary text begins (preface, introduction, or foreword) or after it (epilogue or afterword) are cited separately by providing a descriptive title (within brackets), followed by complete citation information.

Danto, A. C. (2002). Philosophical autobiography. [Foreword]. *Genius—in their own words: The intellectual journeys of seven great 20th-century thinkers* (pp. vii–viii). Chicago: Open Court.

> **In-text citation**   (Danto, 2002)

Notice that the page numbers are indicated in lowercase roman numerals, as is often the case with introductory material.

Walburg, Rivka. (1992). [Epilogue]. *A child like that* (pp. 170–177). New York: Feldheim.

> **In-text citation**   (Walburg, 1992)

15e.16   A Pamphlet or Brochure

When pamphlets or brochures contain clearly presented information, they are cited like books, with a descriptive title enclosed in brackets. When information is missing, use these abbreviations: *N.p.* for "No place of publication," *n.p.* for "no publisher," *n.d.* for "no date," and *n.p.* for "no page." None of these abbreviations is italicized in an entry.

Adams, A. B. (1984). *Hospice care* [Pamphlet]. New York: American Cancer Society.
   In-text citation   (Adams, 1984)

Lyme disease and related disorders [Brochure]. (2000). Groton, NY: Pfizer Company.
   In-text citation   (*Lyme disease*, 2000)

15e.17   An Annual Report

Annual reports are normally presented like unauthored books.

Alcan. (2000). *Paving the way to a bright future: Annual report 1999.* New York: Author.
   In-text citation   (Alcan, 2000)

Xerox. (1994). *The document company: 1993 annual report.* Stamford, CT: Author.
   In-text citation   (Xerox, 1994)

15e.18   An Unpublished Dissertation

The entry for an unpublished dissertation begins with the author's name, the date, and the title, presented in the pattern used for a book. However, the phrase *Unpublished doctoral dissertation* (not italicized) follows, with the degree-granting university and city (and state, province, or country, if needed for clarity) completing the entry. Published dissertations are books and should be cited accordingly.

Lehner, L. (1998). *Gravitational radiation from black hole spacetimes.* Unpublished
      doctoral dissertation. University of Pittsburgh.
   In-text citation   (Lehner, 1998)

Because the city is included in the university name, none is required in the closing of the citation.

Straw, W. O. (1990). *Popular music as a cultural commodity: The American recorded
      music industries, 1976–1985.* Unpublished doctoral dissertation. McGill University, Montreal, Quebec.
   In-text citation   (Straw, 1990)

APA STYLE

Follow the appropriate reference-list entry forms
for audiovisual sources.

15f.1   A Lecture or Speech

The entry for a lecture or speech generally includes the speaker's name, the
date of the speech, the title of the speech (italicized) or a description of
the speech (in brackets), a series title or a description of the speechmaking
context, and the location (most often, only the city).

Gould, S. J. (1998, November 4). *Interactions of art and science and the largely arbitrary*
nature of academic boundaries. Lecture presented for the Stanford Presidential
Lectures in Humanities and Arts, Stanford University, Stanford.

   In-text citation   (Gould, 1998)

Nixon, R. (1974, August 8). [Resignation speech]. Speech presented at the White House,
Washington, DC.

   In-text citation   (Nixon, 1974)

Note that *Resignation speech,* the descriptive title of the speech, is given
within brackets and is not italicized.

15f.2   A Work of Art

Entries for works of art include the name of the artist when known, the
completion date, the title of the work (either assigned by the artist or attributed to the work), a description of the medium (enclosed in brackets),
the museum or collection name, and the city (and state, province, or country, when necessary to avoid confusion).

Gauguin, P. (1891). *The brooding woman* [Painting in oil]. Worcester Art Museum,
Worcester, MA.

   In-text citation   (Gauguin, 1891)

Toulouse-Lautrec, H. de. (1895). *La clownesse assise [The seated clown]* [Painting in
oil]. Marie Harriman Gallery, New York.

   In-text citation   (Toulouse-Lautrec, 1895)

When works of art are known primarily by titles in foreign languages, provide a translated title within brackets for clarity; the translation follows the
foreign-language title, is also italicized, and precedes the description.

Amateis, E. R. (1958). Jonas Edward Salk [Sculpture in bronze]. National Portrait
Gallery, Washington, DC.

   In-text citation   (Amateis, 1958)

Amateis, the sculptor, did not formally title this sculpture, a convention when artists create statues of famous people. Consequently, "Jonas Edward Salk" is the attributed title of the statue of this distinguished scientist and therefore is not italicized.

15f.3   A Map, Graph, Table, or Chart

Maps, graphs, tables, and charts are treated like books. Include the name of the author (if known), artist, designer, scientist, or other person—or group—responsible for the map, graph, table, or chart. The name is followed by the publication date, in parentheses. Include the title as it is presented in the source, but without special punctuation such as quotation marks; follow the title with a descriptive label in brackets, followed by a period. Then include whatever citation information is required for the source.

Kane, T. J. (1999). Distribution of federal loans to college undergraduates [Chart]. In T. J. Kane, *The price of admission: Rethinking how Americans pay for college* (p. 94). Washington, DC: Brookings Institute.

In-text citation   (Kane, 1999)

Phillips, K. L. (2002). A growing income disparity [Chart]. In K. L. Phillips, *Wealth and democracy: A political history of the American rich* (p. 129). New York: Broadway.

In-text citation   (Phillips, 2002)

15f.4   A Cartoon

Begin with the cartoonist's name, the date on which the cartoon appeared, the title of the cartoon, if there is one, and the word *Cartoon* in brackets, but not italicized. Then include other information required for the source.

Bek. (2003, August 11). I don't know if he's a great artist, but he's certainly annoying [Cartoon]. *The New Yorker, 79,* 60.

In-text citation   (Bek, 2003)

Davis, J., & Hart, S. (1991, January). Groan with the wind [Cartoon]. *Mad, 42–47.*

In-text citation   (Davis & Hart, 1991)

Mad magazine does not use volume numbers, so none is included in the entry.

15f.5   A Film

Entries for films begin with the producer's or director's name (with the description *Producer* or *Director* in parentheses but not italicized), followed by the year of release, the film title (italicized), and descriptive title (in brackets). The entry ends with the country of origin and the company.

Fincher, D. (Director). (1999). *Fight club* [Film]. United States: Regency-20th Century Fox.
  In-text citation   (Fincher, 1999)

Note that dual-release films require the names of both the independent studio and the major distributor (the large film studio); the names are joined by a hyphen, without spaces.

Marshall, R. (Director). (2002). *Chicago* [Film]. [With Renée Zellweger, Catherine Zeta-
    Jones, Richard Gere, Queen Latifah, & John C. Reilly]. United States: Miramax.
  In-text citation   (Marshall, 2002)

15f.6   A Filmstrip

Filmstrips are cited just as films are, with one exception: include the descriptive title *Filmstrip* in brackets (but not italicized) after the title.

In coal country [Filmstrip with audiotape]. (1990). United States: American School.
  In-text citation   (*In coal country*, 1990)

Songs of the Civil War [Filmstrip with audiotape]. (1965). In *Our heritage of American
    music* (Filmstrip 6). United States: Society for Visual Education.
  In-text citation   (*Songs of the Civil War*, 1965)

Note that one filmstrip from a multi-item set is presented in the same pattern as one book from a multivolume collection.

15f.7   A Television Broadcast

Regular programs are listed by producer or director, broadcast date when appropriate, the title (italicized), a descriptive phrase (in brackets), the city (and state or country, if necessary), and the network (spelled out completely). If you include other people's contributions, do so after the program title (in brackets), using brief phrases (*Narr. by, With, Written by*—not italicized) to clarify their roles.

Charles, L., Gordon, B., Weide, R. B., & Steinberg, D. (Directors). (2003). *Curb your en-
    thusiasm* [Television series]. [With Larry David, Cheryl Hines, Susie Essman, &
    Jeff Garlin]. New York: Home Box Office.
  In-text citation   (Charles, Gordon, Weide, & Steinberg, 2003)

This entry emphasizes the program as a whole, without specifying any particular episode or broadcast date.

Winston, R. (Producer). (2003, August 14). My drama queen [Television series episode].

    In *Scrubs.* [With Zach Braff, Donald Faison, Sarah Chalke, & Judy Reyes]. New

    York: National Broadcasting Company.

    In-text citation   (Winston, 2003)

This more traditional entry refers to a specific episode, broadcast on a specific date. Note the use of *In* (not italicized) to introduce the program title.

15f.8 A Radio Broadcast

An entry for a radio broadcast follows the guidelines for a television broadcast.

Murrow, E. R. (1940, September 13). [Radio broadcast]. New York: WCBS.

    In-text citation   (Murrow, 1940)

15f.9 A Recording

Entries for recordings begin with the writer-composer's name, the date of the recording, and the selection title. If the recording artist is not the writer-composer, place his or her name in brackets, using the phrase *Recorded by* (not italicized). Then include the album title (introduced by the word *On*), the recording format (in brackets), the city (and perhaps state or country), and company.

    If the recording contains previously recorded material, include information about original recordings in parentheses at the end.

The Beatles. (1969). *Abbey road* [CD]. Hollywood-London: Capital-EMI.

    In-text citation   (The Beatles, 1969)

To emphasize a single selection on a recording, include the title of the brief work (without special punctuation), followed by the title of the complete recording and other production information.

Yoakam, Dwight. (2003). An exception to the rule. On *Population ME* [CD]. Nashville, TN:

    Audium.

    In-text citation   (Yoakam, 2003)

15f.10 An Interview

Although APA style has no entry format for interviews, the following recommendations maintain APA principles. If you need to document such a source, include the name of the person interviewed, the interview date, the type of interview (personal or telephone) enclosed in brackets, and the context for the interview (city and state when applicable).

Otwell, S. (2002, November 14). [Personal interview]. Terre Haute, IN.
   In-text citation   (Otwell, 2002)

If the interview is part of a broadcast, include appropriate entry information.

Clinton, H. (2000, December 11). [Interview]. *Larry King live* [Television broadcast]. Atlanta, GA: Cable News Network.
   In-text citation   (Clinton, 2000)

15f.11 A Transcript

Transcripts of programs are presented according to the source of the original broadcast, with clarifying information provided in brackets. The entry ends with information about availability.

Block, M., & Dickson, P. (2003, August 7). The hidden language of baseball. *All things considered* [Radio broadcast]. [Transcript]. Washington, DC: National Public Radio. Available: Journal Graphics On-line.
   In-text citation   (Block & Dickson, 2003)

Costello, C. (2003, August 11). Eye on the sky: Air travel delays. *Daybreak* [Television broadcast]. [Transcript]. Atlanta, GA: Cable News Network. Available: Journal Graphics On-line.
   In-text citation   (Costello, 2003)

15g Follow the appropriate reference-list entry forms for electronic sources.

Electronic sources exist in many formats—online databases, electronic publications of traditional print sources, organizational Web sites, CD-ROMs, e-mail-based discussion groups, and others. To allow researchers to cite these sources, APA has developed the relatively simple and flexible strategy of, first, following patterns that exist for comparable print sources and, second, adding information about electronic access. With this system, the entry ends with what APA calls a "retrieval statement." For online sources, today's most common source, the retrieval statement follows this pattern:

Retrieved *Month, day, year,* from *electronic address*

Notice that the retrieval statement has no end punctuation, since a closing period might be misconstrued as part of the electronic address.

    As you gather information for electronic sources, be resourceful in finding important information; your goal should be to provide the most complete set of information possible for each electronic source, following the patterns described in this section.

15g.1 An Online Scholarly Project, Information Database, or Professional Web Site

If you refer to an entire online scholarly project, information database, or professional Web site, you do not need to include an entry in your reference list. However, you must identify the title of the source clearly in the text of your paper (capitalized but without special punctuation) and provide a very basic in-text citation (the electronic address), as in these samples:

> The Victorian Web presents a wide range of information on the period, ranging from discussions of art to important people, from the history of ideas to the elements of popular culture (http://www.victorianweb.org/).

> The Web site UNICEF provides links to a variety of useful sources that discuss the welfare of children around the world (http://www.unicef.org/).

15g.2 A Source from an Online Scholarly Project, Information Database, or Professional Web Site

To cite a source—article, illustration, map, and so on—from an online scholarly project, information database, or professional Web site, include (1) the name of the author (or artist, compiler, or editor) of the individual source, if available; (2) the date; (3) the title of the source, without special punctuation; (4) the name of the project, database, or Web site; and (5) the retrieval statement.

Cody, D. (2002, December 21). Queen Victoria. The Victorian Web. Retrieved May 31, 2003, from http://www.victorianweb.org.vn/victor6.html

In-text citation (Cody, 2002)

Electricity per 500 KWH: Average price data. (2003, June). Washington, DC: Bureau of Labor Statistics. Retrieved August 11, 2003, from http://data.bls.gov/cgi-bin/surveymost

In-text citation (Electricity per 500 KWH, 2003)

15g.3 An Article in an Online Journal

To cite an article in an online journal, provide (1) the name of the author, if appropriate; (2) the date in parentheses; (3) the title of the article; (4) the name of the journal and the volume number, italicized, and the issue number, not italicized; and (5) the retrieval statement.

Hopcroft, R. (2002). Is gender still a status characteristic? *Current Research in Social Psychology 7*(20). Retrieved April 26, 2003, from http://www.uiowa.edu/~grpproc/crisp/crisp.7.20.html

In-text citation   (Hopcroft, 2002)

Jabbour, N. (2000). Syphilis from 1880 to 1920: A public health nightmare and the first challenge to medical ethics. *Essays in History, 42.* Retrieved March 26, 2003, from http://www.etext.lib.virginia.edu/journals/eh/eh42/jabbour42.html

In-text citation   (Jabbour, 2000)

15g.4   An Article in an Online Magazine

To cite an article in an online magazine, provide (1) the name of the author, if appropriate; (2) the date in parentheses; (3) the title of the article; (4) the name of the magazine and volume number, italicized; and (5) the retrieval statement.

Hoffman, P. (2003, August). Chess queen. *Smithsonian, 34.* Retrieved August 11, 2003, from http://www.smithsonianmag.si.edu/smithsonian/issues03/aug03/pdf/smithsonian_august_03_chess_queen.pdf

In-text citation   (Hoffman, 2003)

Ramer, S. (2003, August18). It's more than the economy, stupid. *Newsweek, 142.* Retrieved August 20, 2003, from http://www.msnbc.com/news/950350.asp?ob1=0#BODY

In-text citation   (Ramer, 2003)

15g.5   An Article in an Online Newspaper

To cite an article in an online newspaper, provide (1) the name of the author, if appropriate; (2) the date of publication in parentheses; (3) the title of the article; (4) the name of the newspaper, italicized; and (5) the retrieval statement.

Foreman, J. (2003, August 12). The health and harm of new cancer drugs. *Boston Globe.* Retrieved August 12, 2003, from http://www.boston.com/yourlife/health/diseases/articles/2003/08/12/the_help_and_harm_in_new_cancer_drugs

In-text citation   (Foreman, 2003)

Strauss, J. (2003, August 11). Going back to basics. *St. Louis Post Dispatch.* Retrieved August 12, 2003, from http://www.stltoday.com/stltoday/sports/stories.nsf/sports/Cardinals

In-text citation   (Strauss, 2003)

15g.6   An Online Book

Online books exist in two forms: those previously published and now available electronically and those available only in electronic form.

To cite an online book that has a corresponding print version, first prepare a standard entry describing the print version (see section **15e**). Then provide the retrieval statement, which includes (1) the date you accessed the site; (2) the name of the source, whether online project, database, or Web site; and (3) the general electronic address of the site where the book can be retrieved, not the specific electronic address for the book.

Lofting, H. (1922). *The voyages of Doctor Dolittle.* Philadelphia: Lippincott. Retrieved
February 2, 2003, from the Project Gutenberg: ftp://ibiblio.org/pub/docs/
books/gutenberg/

In-text citation   (Lofting, 1922)

To cite an online book that is available only in electronic form, provide (1) the name of the author or editor; (2) the title, italicized; and (3) the retrieval statement.

Buxhoeveden, S. (n.d.). *The life and tragedy of Alexandra Feodorvna, empress of
Russia.* Retrieved January 15, 2003, from the Russian History Web site: http://
www.alexanderpalace.org

In-text citation   (Buxhoeveden, n.d.)

15g.7   An Article in an Online Encyclopedia
or Reference Source

To cite an article from an online encyclopedia or reference source, provide (1) the author of the entry, if there is one; (2) the date, in parentheses; (3) the title of the entry exactly as it appears in the source, without special punctuation; (4) the name of the reference work, italicized; (5) facts of publication, if the source first existed in print form; and (6) the retrieval statement.

Children in foster care. (2003, March). [Chart]. *Infoplease almanac.* Retrieved
April 13, 2003, from http://www.infoplease.com/

In-text citation   (Children in foster care, 2003)

Machismo. (2000). *Yourdictionary.* Retrieved March 27, 2003, from
http://www.yourdictionary.com/

In-text citation   (Machismo, 2000)

15g.8   An Online Government Document

To cite an online version of a government document—book, report, proceedings, brochure, and so on—first provide the information required for the print source (see section **15e.14**). Then continue the citation with the retrieval statement.

Congressional Budget Office. (2000, October). *Budgeting for naval forces: Structuring
    tomorrow's Navy at today's funding level.* By E. J. Labs. Washington: Government
    Printing Office. Retrieved May 6, 2003, from http://www.cbo.gov/
In-text citation   (Congressional Budget Office, 2000)

National Institute on Early Childhood Development. (2002, November 12). *Helping
    your child through early adolescence.* Retrieved August 9, 2003, from
    http://www.ed.gov/pubs/
In-text citation   (National Institute on Early Childhood Development, 2002)

15g.9   An Online Transcript of a Lecture or Speech

To cite an online transcript of a speech or lecture, first provide the information required for a lecture or a speech (see section **15f.1**). Then include (1) the word *Transcript,* not italicized and in brackets, and (2) the retrieval statement.

Faulkner, W. (1950, December 10). Nobel Prize in Literature acceptance speech. Nobel
    Prize Ceremony, Stockholm. [Transcript]. Retrieved August 12, 2003, from
    http://www.pbs.org/greatspeeches/timeline/index.html
In-text citation   (Faulkner, 1950)

Havel, V. (1994, July 4). The need for transcendence in the postmodern world [Address].
    Independence Hall, Philadelphia. [Transcript]. Retrieved May 6, 2003, from
    http://www.worldtrans.org/whole/havelspeech.html
In-text citation   (Havel, 1994)

15g.10   An Online Map, Graph, Table, or Chart

To cite a map, graph, table, or chart online, first provide the information required for the kind of visual element (see section **15f.3**). Then provide the retrieval statement.

The Billboard 200 [Chart]. (2003, August 8). Billboard.com. Retrieved August 10, 2003,
    from http://www.billboard.com/bb/charts/bb200.jsp
In-text citation   (The Billboard 200, 2003)

Experimental poverty measures by selective characteristics: 2001 [Table]. (2002).
> *Current population survey, 2002 annual demographic supplement.*
> United States Census Bureau. Retrieved August 18, 2003, from
> http://www.census.gov/hhes/poverty/poverty01/table9.pdf

In-text citation   (Experimental poverty measures, 2002)

15g.11   An Online Transcript of a Television or Radio Broadcast

To cite an online transcript of a television or radio broadcast, first provide the information required for audiovisual entries (see section **15f.7** or **15f.8**). Then include (1) the word *Transcript,* not italicized and in brackets, and (2) the retrieval statement.

Amid the tall trees: Planting the seed of empathy. (2003, August 2.) *Nightline* [Television
> broadcast]. [With Joe O'Connor]. New York: American Broadcasting Company.
> [Transcript]. Retrieved August 12, 2003, from http://abcnews.go.com/sections/
> nightline/living/ntl_oconnortrees_030802.html

In-text citation   (Amid the tall trees, 2003)

Incitements to violence in the Mideast. (2003, July 25). *All Things Considered* [Radio
> Broadcast]. [With Melissa Block & Peter Kenyon]. Washington, DC: National
> Public Radio. [Transcript]. Retrieved August 19, 2003, from http://www.npr.org/
> programs/atc/transcripts/2003/jul/030725.kenyon.html

In-text citation   (Incitements to violence, 2003)

15g.12   An Online Transcript of an Interview

To cite an online transcript of an interview, first provide the information required for an interview, either television, radio, or print (see section **15f.10**). Then include (1) the word *Transcript,* not italicized and in brackets, and (2) the retrieval statement.

Polanski, R. (2002, May 24). [Interview]. Press Conference. Cannes Film Festival. Cannes.
> [Transcript]. Retrieved August 14, 2003, from http://www.filmscouts.com/scripts/
> interview.cfm?File=3012

In-text citation   (Polanski, 2002)

Powell, C. L. (2003, August 7). [Interview]. Press Briefing. Washington Foreign Press
> Center, Washington, DC. [Transcript]. Retrieved August 31, 2003, from
> http://www.state.gov/secretary/rm/2003/2311.htm

In-text citation   (Powell, 2003)

APA STYLE

15g.13   CD-ROM Sources

If a CD-ROM source reproduces material available in print form, begin the
entry with full print information: author (or editor), date, title, and facts of
publication (see sections **15d.1–15f.11** for complete patterns); then add a
retrieval statement. If the material is not available in print form, begin the
entry with identifying information: (1) author, if given; (2) date; (3) title,
italicized; and (4) the retrieval statement.

The retrieval statement for CD-ROM sources includes (1) the title of the
source, without special punctuation; and (2), in parentheses, the name of
the database; the description _CD-ROM,_ not italicized; the release date; and
an item number, if applicable.

Chen, J. X. (2003). _Guide to graphics software tools._ (Springer, CD-ROM, 2003 release).
   In-text citation   (Chen, 2003)

Welmers, W. E. (1994). African languages. _The New Grolier Multimedia Encyclopedia._
        Retrieved from Grolier database (Grolier, CD-ROM, 1994 release).
   In-text citation   (Welmers, 1994)

15g.14   An E-mail Interview

Interviews conducted through e-mail correspondence are considered personal communication. As such, they are not included in an APA reference
list. However, they are cited in the text of the paper by enclosing the
phrase _personal communication_ (not italicized) and the date of the e-mail
in parentheses.

H. S. Davis (personal communication, March 13, 2003) noted that classroom technology
        is only as good as the people who use it.

15g.15   An Online Posting

To cite an online posting to a forum or discussion group, provide (1) the
name of the author, if known; (2) the official or descriptive title of the posting; (3) the phrase _Message posted to,_ not italicized; (4) the name of the forum or discussion group followed by a comma; (5) the phrase _archived at,_
not italicized; and (6) the URL.

Waitt, D. (2003, June 4). Native plant information network. Message posted to Native
        Plants Forum, archived at http://forums.gardenweb.com/forums/load/natives/
        msg062359004143.html?8
   In-text citation   (Waitt, 2003)

15h   When appropriate, follow APA guidelines to prepare your manuscript.

Writers in psychology, education, and related fields follow these guidelines to ensure that manuscripts are prepared in a uniform and generally understood way.

Paper

Use heavy-weight, white bond 8½" × 11" paper. Avoid onionskin and colored paper.

Printing Formats

Use a clear, easy-to-read, standard print font or typeface; styles with serifs (cross lines on individual letters) like Times Roman and Courier are preferred, while sans serif styles like Helvetica should be reserved for the lettering of figures and illustrations. Work should be prepared in twelve-point fonts.

Use italics (*slanted type*) to identify titles of complete works.

Spacing

Double-space everything: the elements of the title page, the abstract, the text, the references, and any supplementary material. For visual clarity, you may triple- or quadruple-space between elements of the paper; however, never use less than double-spacing.

Margins

Leave one-inch margins at the left, right, top, and bottom of each page. (See below.) If the "default" margins for your word processing program are not one inch, reset them. Do not justify the right margin; instead leave the right text edge irregular. Indent paragraphs five to seven spaces (a "Tab" setting is acceptable); use the same indentation throughout the paper. Indent long quotations five spaces.

Paging

In the upper right corner of each page, one-half inch from the top, type the first two or three words of the paper's title, followed by five spaces and the page number (without an abbreviation for *page*). Two spaces below, the text begins.

Word processing programs usually have default patterns for placing page numbers (often centered at the bottom of the page). In that case, change the page numbering format. Search the "Insert" or "Format" commands for "Headers," lines that will run at the top of every page in the manuscript. Set the header at the beginning of the document, make sure that it is flush with the right margin, and include the short title, five spaces, and the code to number pages automatically.

Number Style

Express numbers one through nine (and zero) in words and all other numbers in numeral form (10; 237; 1,400). When numbers are used for comparison, all appear in numeral form (3 of 16 children).

Under special circumstances, numbers appear in written form: when they begin sentences, titles, or headings; when they present common fractions (one third, three fourths); and when a written form might be less confusing than a numeral form (zero-percent increase).

Title Page

Prepare a separate title page. The top line of the title page is the header. The first page-specific element, however, is the running head, a short version of the article's title; typing from the left margin, include the words *Running head* (not italicized, but followed by a colon), and the running head (no more than fifty characters) in all uppercase letters.

Center the title below the running head and capitalize all major words. If the title is too long to fit on one line, divide it logically and center all lines. Two lines below, center your name (capitalized normally). On the line below your name, type your affiliation—typically, your school—or substitute the course title.

After typing your title, name, and other identifying information, center this information on the page vertically. This key information, as a result, is centered from top to bottom and from left to right.

Abstract

The abstract, a brief paragraph describing the major ideas in the paper, appears on the page following the title page; it can be no more than 120 words. Underneath the header, type the descriptive title *Abstract,* centered but not italicized; two spaces below, type the abstract as a single, unindented paragraph. In the abstract only, use digits for all numbers except those that begin sentences.

The Text

The text of the paper begins on the third page. The header, as always, appears on the top line of the page. Two spaces below, the title is centered, with all important words capitalized. Two spaces below the title, the text begins.

Headings for Sections

Use headings to divide and subdivide the paper into logical, and sometimes sequential, sections. Level-1 headings are centered, with all major words capitalized; level-2 headings are centered and italicized, with all major words capitalized; level-3 headings are flush left and italicized, with all major words capitalized.

Level-1 Heading

Level-2 Heading

Level-3 Heading

Papers that require only one level of division would use level-1 headings; papers that require two levels of division use a combination of level-1 and level-3 headings; papers that require three levels of division, use level-1, level-2, and level-3 headings. When new headings are required, do not begin new pages. Simply continue two lines below. If a paper requires four or more levels of headings, consult the APA *Publication Manual.*

Tables, Graphs, Charts, Maps, and Illustrations

Place tables, graphs, charts, maps, and illustrations in one of two places: at the end of the text (the pattern required for professionals) or near the discussion in the text (the pattern common for student papers). If placed at the end of the paper, these materials should be located according to the guidelines noted in "Order of the Manuscript." (See below.) If placed in the text, they should be included on separate pages following the textual discussion; these pages are also numbered. Very small graphics may appear on the page with written material.

Order of the Manuscript

Place your manuscript pages in this order: title page (page 1), abstract (page 2), text (begin on page 3), and reference list (start on a new page and number sequentially). If you include any of these optional sections, place them after the reference list in this order: appendixes (new page), author's note (new page), footnotes (new page), tables (new pages, each one separate), figure captions (new page, listed together), and figures (new pages, each one separate).

Submitting the Paper

Submit manuscripts according to your instructor's guidelines. If you receive no specific guidelines, secure the pages with a paper clip in the upper left corner and place them in a manila envelope with your name and course information typed or written on the outside. Always keep a photocopy—or another printed copy—of the paper.

APA STYLE

Be aware that instructors may ask for a disk copy of the paper. In that case, submit a copy of the final paper on a separate disk, clearly labeled with your name and course information, as well as a note about your word processing program (Microsoft Word 2000, WordPerfect 10). Keep a disk version for yourself.

APA STYLE

Beyond Birth Order   1

Running head: BEYOND BIRTH ORDER

Beyond Birth Order:

Recognizing Other Variables

Elissa Allen and Jeremy Reynolds

Psychology 256

A working title, followed by 5 spaces and the page number, appears ½ inch from the top of every page.

The running head, labeled, is in all capitals; it is flush with the left margin.

Identifying information is centered from top to bottom and from left to right.

½ inch from
top of page

The label uses
normal
capitalization.

1-inch side
margins

The abstract
(no more
than 120
words)
describes the
paper.

Abstract

Although scholars continue to make a case for birth-order effects
in children's development, exclusive reliance on this useful but one-
dimensional criterion ignores other variables that affect children's
personal, intellectual, and social development. The sex of other siblings,
the time between births, the size of the family, the age of the mother,
the physiological condition of the children, the absence of a parent, and
the birth order of the parents also influence a child's development.

Beyond Birth Order   3

Beyond Birth Order:

Recognizing Other Variables

Sigmund Freud, Queen Elizabeth II, Albert Einstein, William Shakespeare, George Washington, Jacqueline Kennedy, John Milton, Julius Caesar, Leontyne Price, and Winston Churchill. What do these famous people have in common? They were all first-born children. The fact that so many important people in all spheres of influence have been first-born children has lent credence to the notion that birth order helps determine the kind of people we become.

Scientific studies over the years have, in fact, suggested that birth order affects an individual's development. For example, recent studies (Pine, 1995) have suggested that first-born children acquire language skills sooner than later-born children. The Parent and Child Guidance Center (2001) explains this premise very simply: "Because they spend so much time with adults, [first-born children] talk in more of an adult way." Further, Ernst and Angst (1983) explained the underlying premise of birth order effects this way: "Everybody agrees that birth order differences must arise from differential socialization by the parents. There is, however, no general theory on how this differential socialization actually works" (p. x). Stein (2001) adds that birth-order effects are more pronounced in families that are competitive and autocratic and are less obvious in families that are cooperative and democratic. It is not surprising, then, that a general theory has not emerged because many other variables besides birth order influence an individual's personal, intellectual, and social development.

Sex of the Siblings

While acknowledging that birth order plays a part in an individual's development, scholars have begun to recognize that it is only one variable. For example, Sutton-Smith and Rosenberg (1970) observed that even in two-child families there are four possible variations

The title, centered, uses normal capitalization.

Introductory strategy (allusions) creates interest.

Historical context established

Note the use of past tense to discuss past scholarship.

General references cite author and date.

Specific references cite author and date, as well as specific page.

Thesis statement

Heading, with spaces above and below

Beyond Birth Order   4

*Note the use
of a list with
numbered
elements.*

*Common
knowledge
suggests that
the number
increases to
24.*

for sibling relationships based on gender: (1) first-born female, second-born female; (2) first-born female, second-born male; (3) first-born male, second-born male; (4) first-born male, second-born female. In families with three children, the variations increase to 24. To suggest that being the first-born child is the same in all of these contexts ignores too many variables.

The Time between Births

*A summary
presents
Forer's ideas
clearly.*

Forer (1976) suggested that when the births of children are separated by five or more years, the effects of birth order are changed. For example, in a family with four children (with children aged 12, 6, 4, and 2 years old), the second child would be more likely to exhibit the characteristics of an oldest child because of his or her nearness in age to the younger children and the six-year separation in age from the oldest child. This pattern would differ from that of a sibling in a four-child family if the children were spaced by fewer than three years (for example, if the children were 10, 8, 5, 3 years old); this second child would exhibit the characteristics typical of a second-middle child.

*Numbers
used in
comparisons
must all
appear in the
same form.*

*Elissa and
Jeremy provide
their own
example; it
does not
require
documentation.*

Size of Family

*Scholars are
always
referred to by
last names
only.*

Studies have also suggested that the size of the family modifies the effects of birth order. Whereas in moderate-sized families (two to four children) the first-born child usually achieves the highest level of education, Forer (1969) observed that the "a first-born child from a large family has often been found to obtain less education than a last-born child from such a family" (p. 24). Whether this occurs because large families tend to have lower socioeconomic status or whether it is the result of varied family dynamics, the overall size of the family seems to alter the preconceived notions of birth order and its influence on a child's development.

Beyond Birth Order   5

Age of the Mother

Studies have suggested that a mother's age has a strong bearing on the child's learned behavior, regardless of birth order. Sutton-Smith and Rosenberg (1970) offered this perspective:

> On a more obvious level, younger mothers have more stamina and vigor than older mothers. One speculation in the literature is that they are also more anxious and uncertain about their child-training procedures, and that this has an effect of inducing anxiety in their offspring. (p. 138)

It seems safe to assume, then, that the third child of a woman of 28 will have a different experience growing up than the third child of a woman of 39. They may share the same relational patterns with their siblings, but they do not share the same patterns with their mothers.

Physiological Factors

Early studies on birth order failed to account for physiological differences among children, even among those who shared the same birth status. Forer (1969) asserted, however, that "special conditions involving a child in a family may change the birth-order effect both for him and for his siblings" (p. 19). Such conditions as a child's mental retardation, severe hearing loss, blindness, disabling handicaps—or even extreme beauty, exceptional intelligence, or great physical skill—can alter the dynamics of the family and consequently affect the traditionally described effects of birth order. In short, a middle child whose physiological conditions are outside the normal spectrum—because of different potential and opportunity—does not have the same life experiences as a middle child who is considered average.

Absence of a Parent

Parents may be absent from family units for a variety of reasons: A parent may die, creating a permanent void in a family unit; a

Long quotations are indented 5 spaces and double-spaced.

The in-text citation follows the closing period of the quotation.

A summary usefully connects ideas.

parent may be gone to war or be hospitalized for an extended period,
creating a temporary but notable disruption in the family; or a parent
may travel for business or be gone for brief periods to attend school,
creating a brief but obvious interruption in the family's normal work-
ings. These conditions affect a child's experiences and can, under certain circumstances, mitigate the effects of birth order. Toman (1993)
explained that the effects are greater

A long quoted list must represent the original source as accurately as possible.

    a. the more recently they have occurred,

    b. the earlier in a person's life they have occurred,

    c. the older the person lost is (in relation to the oldest family
       member)

    d. the longer the person has lived together with the lost
       person,

    e the smaller the family,

    f. the greater the imbalance of sexes in the family resulting
       from the loss,

    g. the longer it takes the family to find a replacement for the
       lost person,

    h. the greater the number of losses, and the graver the losses,
       that have occurred before. (pp. 41–42)

Such disruptions—whether major or minor—alter the family unit and
often have a greater influence on the child than the traditional effects of
birth order.

Birth Order of Parents

    A number of scholars have asserted that the birth order of par-
ents influences to a high degree their interrelationships with their children and, consequently, creates an impact that extends beyond the
simple birth order of the children. Toman (1993) described the family
relationships, based on birth order, that promise the least conflict and,
hence, best situation for children's development:

> If the mother is the youngest sister of a brother and has an
> older son and a younger daughter, she can identify with her
> daughter and the daughter with the mother. The daughter, too,
> is the younger sister of a brother. Moreover, the mother has no
> trouble dealing with her son, for she had an older brother in
> her original family and her son, too, is an older brother of a
> sister. (p. 199)

Toman's assumption that parents relate better to their children when
they have shared similar sibling-related experiences leads to this assumption: when parents can create a positive and productive home
environment (because of familiar familial relationships), the children
benefit. When conflict occurs because sibling relations are unfamiliar,
everyone suffers. Parent-child relationships—determined, at least in
part, by the parents' own birth orders—would consequently vary from
family to family, even when children of those families share the same
birth order.

Conclusion

According to U.S. census information, collected from 92,119
randomly selected mothers, 28% of children are first born, 28% second
born, 20% middle born, and 18% youngest born (Simpson, Bloom,
Newlon, & Arminio, 1994). As long as census takers, scholars, family
members, parents, and children think in terms of birth order, we will
have an oversimplified perspective of why children develop as they do.
Yet recent studies (Parish, 1990) have suggested that adolescents recognize that family structure and personal interaction have a stronger
bearing on their perceptions of themselves, other family members, and
their families than do birth order or even gender. And, importantly, Web
sites like Matthias Romppel's Birth Order Research approach the issue
cautiously, suggesting that birth-order effects on children are change-
able (http://www.romppel.de/birth-order/). Perhaps we should take our
cues from these young people and current scholars and recognize that
birth order is but one interesting variable in personality development.

Percentages are represented in numeral-symbol form.

Multiple authors are all listed, with an ampersand between the last two names.

A reference to a complete Web site occurs in the paper, but an entry is not included in the reference list.

References

Page numbers continue sequentially.

The descriptive title is centered.

Birth order and your child. (2001). Parent and Child Guidance Center.
Retrieved March 11, 2003, from http://trfn.clpgh.org/pcgc/
birthorder.html

Note that italics are used, not underlining.

Ernst, C., & Angst, J. (1983). *Birth order: Its influence on personality.*
Berlin: Springer.

Forer, L. K. (1969). *Birth order and life roles.* Springfield, IL: Thomas.

Names are repeated in subsequent citations.

Forer, L. K. (1976). *The birth order factor: How your personality is
influenced by your place in the family.* New York: McKay.

Parish, T. S. (1990). Evaluations of family by youth: Do they vary as a
function of family structure, gender, and birth order? *Adolescence, 25,* 353–356.

Pine, J. M. (1995). Variations in vocabulary development as a function
of birth order. *Child Development, 66,* 272–281.

Simpson, P. W., Bloom, J. W., Newlon, B. J., & Arminio, L. (1994).
Birth-order proportions of the general population in the United
States. *Individual Psychology: Journal of Adlerian Theory, 50,*
173–182.

Note: First lines are not indented; subsequent lines are.

Stein, H. T. (2001). Alderian overview of birth order characteristics. Alfred Alder Institute of San Francisco. Retrieved March 6, 2003,
from http://ourworld.compuserve.com/homepages/hstein/
birthord.htm

Sutton-Smith, B., & Rosenberg, B. G. (1970). *The sibling.* New York:
Holt.

Toman, W. (1993). *Family constellation: Its effects on personality and
social behavior.* New York: Springer.

CHAPTER

16

Using Chicago Style When Appropriate*

QUICK REFERENCE

Prepare Chicago-style notes for sources, applying these general principles for formatting and incorporating required information.

▶ Indent the first line of each note five spaces but begin subsequent lines at the normal left margin.

▶ Number notes in the order in which they appear in the text; use superscript numbers (one-half space above the line) and leave no space before the first element ([1]*Robert Perrin*). As an option, the numbers may appear on the same line, followed by a period and one space (1. *Robert Perrin*). Either style is acceptable, but they should not be mixed.

▶ Single-space notes; double-space between notes.

▶ Provide full information (authors' complete names, titles with subtitles, months) but shorten publishers' names by omitting corporate designations (*Houghton Mifflin,* not *Houghton Mifflin Company*).

▶ Present the authors' names in normal order and complete form.

▶ When an element is missing, proceed to the next element: an article without a stated author begins with the article's title.

▶ Separate the major elements of a note with commas.

▶ Use the samples in this chapter as models to prepare your own notes, combining information from several samples when a source has many features.

CHICAGO STYLE

---

*The information in this chapter is based on *The Chicago Manual of Style,* fifteenth edition (Chicago: U of Chicago P, 2003), and Kate L. Turabian's *A Manual for Writers of Term Papers, Theses, and Dissertations,* sixth edition (Chicago: U of Chicago P, 1996). While the chapter describes Chicago style and the sample materials illustrate Chicago notes and citations, the primary text of this chapter follows the conventions of MLA.

To acknowledge the use of other people's ideas, information, or exact words in a paper, include accurate footnotes or endnotes. These elements provide basic information about sources so that interested readers may locate them for further study.

16a   Recognize the distinct documentation patterns in Chicago style.

Requiring footnotes (placed at the "foot" or bottom of pages) or endnotes (listed at the end of the paper), University of Chicago style provides full publication information within each notation. Because notes in Chicago style are thorough, you can frequently omit a bibliography; at other times, instructors require one.

16b   Consider patterns for footnotes and endnotes.

At the end of a phrase, sentence, paragraph, or other element containing or referring to information from a source, place a note number one-half space (not a full space) above the line; most word processing programs call this a superscript number and have commands to place the numbers automatically. Each reference receives a numbered notation (numbered sequentially throughout the paper), even when it refers to a previously acknowledged source. (See the sample paper for examples.) When a note corresponds to a quotation, the note number follows the closing quotation mark. The sample below illustrates both patterns.

> Marketers of products for women must begin to acknowledge that the collective marketing group "women" is no longer accurate. In 1985, for example, thirty-six percent of women were single with no children, nine percent were single parents, twenty-eight percent were married with no children, and twenty-seven percent were married with children.[1] Multiple marketing strategies, consequently, must address the diverse needs and interests of women. As Gerry Myers observes in *Targeting the New Professional Woman*, "Old questions and outdated premises just won't work anymore. Marketers need a fresh approach and a comprehensive look at the woman's market."[2]

> [1]Gerry Myers, *Targeting the New Professional Woman: How to Market and Sell to Today's 57 Million Working Women* (Chicago: Probus, 1994), 174.

> [2]Ibid., 188.

Under most circumstances, use only one note per sentence because combining several references in a single sentence makes it difficult for readers to determine which information corresponds to which note.

Information for Chicago Notes

Footnotes or endnotes vary in the information they include (and the location of the notes), but all must follow an established order for presenting information. To combine forms (to list a translation of a second edition, for example), use these guidelines to determine the order in which to include information.

1. *Author(s).* Take the name or names from the title page of a book or the first page of an article. Authors' names are listed in the order in which they appear, which may or may not be alphabetical. If no author (individual or or ganization) is listed, make a note of that for yourself.
2. *Title.* List titles from part to whole. When citing part of a book (for example, a single essay in a collection), list the title of the essay (the part) before the title of the book (the whole); list the title of an article before a periodical title, an episode title before a program title, a song title before the title of an album. Take the title of a book from the title page; take the title of an article, essay, or chapter from the first page of the subsection. Use complete titles, including subtitles, no matter how long they are.
3. *Additional Information.* Include any of the following information *in the order presented here* if it is listed on the title page of the book or on the first page of an article, essay, chapter, or other subsection:

   - editor
   - compiler
   - translator
   - edition number
   - volume number
   - name of series

4. *Facts of Publication.* For books, take the publisher's name and the place of publication from the title page and the date of publication from the copyright page (immediately following the title page). Use the publisher's name in full, excluding the article *The* and corporate designations (Company, Limited, Incorporated); however, retain the word *Press*. When *University* is part of the publisher's name, it may be abbreviated if the pattern is applied consistently in all notes and citations. List the first city (place of publication) if more than one is given (and an abbreviation for the state, province, or country, if needed for clarity, using either Chicago-style abbreviations or two-letter postal abbreviations; see Appendix B) and the most recent publication date shown. For periodicals, take the volume number, issue number,

and date from the masthead (the listing of information found at the top of the first page of a newspaper or within the first few pages of a journal or magazine, often in combination with the table of contents).

5. *Page Numbers.* Include the page number or numbers from which you gathered ideas, information, or quotations. Present inclusive numbers from one to ninety-nine in full form (1–14, 23–28, 72–99); for 101–109 (201–209 and so on), include only the changed number (101–3, 405–8); for 110–199 (210–299 and so on), include two or more digits as appropriate (115–17, 325–53, 597–601).

Format for Chicago Footnotes and Endnotes

To ensure easy reading, notes must follow this format consistently:

- Indent the first line of each note five spaces (one "Tab"). Begin the note with a superscript note number (one-half space above the line), followed by the first element of the note; no space should separate the note number from the first letter of the first word; an alternative format presents note numbers on the same line, followed by a period and one space. In both formats, subsequent lines begin at the normal left margin.

- List all authors' names in complete form and normal order (do not invert the order within a name).

- When no author is named, begin the note with the source's title.

- Use the complete title, no matter how long; a colon and a space separate the title from the subtitle.

- Separate major sections of entries (author, title, publication information, and pages) with commas. When end punctuation is used (that is, when a title ends with a question mark or an exclamation point, for example), retain the comma. Enclose facts of publication in parentheses, followed by a comma and page reference.

- Single-space the notes themselves, but double-space between them.

Some of the entries included below—for example, letters to the editor and many electronic sources—are not included in either the Chicago or the Turabian manual. They have been included, however, because they can be worthwhile sources in student research papers. The principles of Chicago style are used for supplying information and formatting notes.

Positioning Footnotes and Endnotes

Footnotes and endnotes both identify the sources used in a paper. Use whichever form your instructor prefers.

Footnotes

Footnotes provide information at the "foot" or bottom of the page on which a reference occurs. Most word processing programs have a footnoting feature that automatically places notes at the bottom of the page and formats the notes according to generally accepted patterns. Two lines below the body of the paper, a two-inch line separates the text from the footnotes. Two lines below this separation line, begin the single-spaced footnote (following the guidelines noted above). When more than one note appears at the bottom of the page, separate the notes with two spaces. (See page 304.)

Endnotes

Endnotes provide information at the end of the paper. Beginning on a new page (with the page number centered at the bottom), center the word *NOTES* (two inches from the top of the page, not italicized). Following the order in which note numbers appear in the paper, provide a corresponding list of notes. Single-space the notes themselves but double-space between them. If notes continue on additional pages, do not repeat the heading; subsequent page numbers are positioned in the upper right corner, within the normal margin. (See the sample paper.)

Multiple References to the Same Source

Once a complete note for a source has appeared, subsequent references to that source may be shortened, as long as clarity is maintained.

Same Source, Same Page (Consecutive Notes)

If two references to the same source and page appear consecutively, without an intervening note, the abbreviation *Ibid.* (Latin for "in the same place") may be used; it is not italicized:

[2]Ibid.

Same Source, Different Page (Consecutive Notes)

If different page references from the same source appear consecutively, without an intervening note, *Ibid* may be used. However, provide the new page number. Notice that the period for the abbreviation *Ibid.* precedes the comma.

[3]Ibid., 203.

Same Source (Nonconsecutive Notes)

When subsequent but nonconsecutive references appear, *Ibid.* is not used. However, it is unnecessary to repeat full publication information. Instead, provide the author's last name and page information; to distinguish between two sources by the same author, include a shortened form of the title; to distinguish between two authors with the same last name, include first names as well.

[4]Thomas, 17.
[5]Thomas, *Myths*, 78.
[6]Clayton Thomas, 135.

16c   Follow the appropriate note forms for books
and other separately published materials.

16c.1   A Book by One Author

[1]Stephen M. Barr, _Modern Physics and Ancient Faith_ (Notre Dame, Ind.: University of Notre Dame Press, 2003), 216.

[2]Eric Gould, _The University in a Corporate Culture_ (New Haven, Conn.: Yale University Press, 2003), 17.

16c.2   A Book by Two or Three Authors

Authors' names appear in the order presented on the title page, which may or may not be alphabetical order.

[1]Charles W. Kegley and Gregory A. Raymond, _How Nations Make Peace_ (New York: St. Martin's Press, 1999), 7.

[2]Jay Fagan and Glen Palm, _Fathers and Early Childhood Programs_ (Clifton Park, N.Y.: Delmar, 2003), 66.

16c.3   A Book by Four or More Authors

Using the descriptive phrase _and others_ (not italicized) saves space when a work has four or more authors; however, when you are required to include a separate bibliography with your paper, those citations must include all names. (See page 288.)

[1]Susan Martin Tucker and others, _Patient Care Standards: Collaborative Planning and Nursing Interventions,_ 7th ed. (St. Louis: Mosby-Yearbook, 2000), 448.

[2]Edward L. Gershey and others, _Low-Level Radioactive Waste: From Cradle to Grave_ (New York: Van Nostrand Reinhold, 1990), 174.

16c.4   A Book with No Author Named

When no author or editor is named, list the work by title. If an "authorless" book has been edited, list the work by title or by editor to emphasize his or her work. Use the same emphasis both in notes and in corresponding citations.

[1]_An Anglo-Saxon Chronicle,_ ed. M. J. Swanton (Exeter, England: University of Exeter Press, 1990), 34.

This note emphasizes the work itself.

List the editor before the title to emphasize his or her work with the text.

[2]M. J. Swanton, ed., _An Anglo-Saxon Chronicle_ (Exeter, England: University of Exeter Press, 1990), 34.

[3]_United Press International Stylebook: The Authoritative Handbook for Writers, Editors, and News Directors,_ 3rd ed. (Lincolnwood, Ill.: National Textbook, 1992), 41.

16c.5   A Book by an Author Using a Pseudonym

Use the pseudonym only; if a bibliography is included with the paper, that citation includes the author's real name within brackets. (See page 288.)

[1]George Eliot, *The Journals of George Eliot,* ed. Margaret Harris and Judith Johnson (New York: Cambridge University Press, 1998), 118–21.

[2]Dr. Seuss, *Horton Hears a Who!* (New York: Random House, 1954), 16–17.

16c.6   A Book with an Organization as Author

When an organization is both the author and the publisher, spell out the name completely in both the author and publisher position.

[1]American Psychological Association, *Publication Manual of the American Psychological Association,* 5th ed. (Washington: American Psychological Association, 2001), 15–22.

16c.7   An Edition Other than the First

The edition number, noted on the title page, follows the title of the book. When a book also has an editor, translator, or compiler, the edition number follows that information. Edition numbers are presented in abbreviated form (2nd, 3rd, 4th), not spelled out. *Edition* (not italicized) is abbreviated.

[1]*Forging the American Character: Readings in United States History,* ed. John R. M. Wilson, 4th ed. (Upper Saddle River, N.J.: Prentice, 2003), 83.

[2]James M. Griffin, ed., *Global Climate Change: The Science, Economics, and Politics,* 2nd ed. (Northampton, Mass.: Elgar, 2003), 51.

16c.8   A Revised or Enlarged Edition

Place abbreviated information about revised or enlarged editions after the title.

[1]Martin P. Wattenburg, *The Decline of American Political Parties: 1952–1996,* enlarged ed. (Cambridge: Harvard University Press, 1998), 83.

16c.9   A Reprint

To refer to a reprint, a newly printed but unaltered version of a book, list original facts of publication first, followed by the information about the reprint. Add a note to clarify your use of page references.

[1]John Palmer, *The Comedy of Manners* (London: Bell, 1913; repr., New York: Russell and Russell, 1962), 288–89. Citations are to the reprinted edition.

16c.10   A Multivolume Work

To refer to an entire multivolume set, present the collection by its complete title, followed by the total number of volumes and the facts of publication.

> ²*American Men and Women of Science,* ed. Pamela M. Kalte and Katherine H. Nenen, 21st ed., 8 vols. (Detroit: Gale, 2003), 37.

To emphasize a single volume, begin by citing the volume as a single book. Then add the volume number, the collection title, the total number of volumes, and the facts of publication.

> ²J. M. Roberts, *The Age of Revolution,* vol. 7, *The Illustrated History of the World,* 10 vols. (New York: Oxford University Press, 1999), 23–24.

16c.11   A Work in a Collection

Author, selection, and collection title are followed by the editor's name, if applicable. Facts of publication and page references end the note.

> ¹Timothy Corrigan, "Which Shakespeare to Love? Film, Fidelity, and the Performance of Literature," in *High-Pop: Making Culture into Popular Entertainment,* ed. Jim Collins (Malden, Mass.: Blackwell, 2003), 157–58.

Inclusive pages for the selection or chapter may be listed in the note immediately preceding the facts of publication but are required for a citation in a bibliography.

> ²Chevelle Newsome, "Multiple Identities: The Case of Biracial Children," in *Trans-Cultural Realities,* ed. Virginia H. Milhous, Molefi Kete Asante, and Peter O. Nwosu (Thousand Oaks, Calif.: Sage, 2001), 150.

16c.12   An Article in an Encyclopedia or Other Reference Work

Well-known reference books require no publication information other than the title and edition number. Less familiar reference works or recently published ones require full publication information. Include (1) the name of the reference work, (2) the edition, (3) the abbreviation *s.v.* (for *sub verso,* meaning "under the word"), and (4) the term as it appears in the reference work, in quotation marks. To emphasize the writer of the entry, include his or her name in parentheses at the end of the note.

> ¹*The New Grove Dictionary of Music and Musicians,* 2001 ed., s.v. "Salieri, Antonio" (by Rudolph Angermüller).

> ²Richard M. Abrams, "Theodore Roosevelt," in *The Presidents: A Reference History,* ed. Henry F. Graff, 2nd ed. (New York: Charles Scribner's Sons, 1996), 331.

The long article in this reference source is treated like a chapter from a book, and a page number is required because the articles on presidents are arranged chronologically, not alphabetically.

16c.13   A Work in a Series

Names of series (collections of books related to the same subject, genre, or time period) are typically found on the title page and should be included just before the publishing information. If series titles have been assigned numbers, include them after the series title, using the abbreviation *no.* (not italicized) for number.

[1]B. J. Fogg, *Persuasive Technology: Using Computers to Change What We Think and Do,* Interactive Technology Series (Boston: Kaufman, 2003), 131.

[2]Evelyn Waugh, *A Handful of Dust,* Everyman's Library, no. 252 (New York: Knopf, 2002), 72.

16c.14   An Imprint

An imprint is a specialized division of a larger publishing company. When an imprint name and a publisher's name both appear on the title page, list them together (imprint second), separated by a comma.

[1]Justine Coupland and Richard Gwyn, ed., *Discourse, the Body, and Identity* (New York: Macmillan, Palgrave, 2003), 128.

Macmillan is the publisher; Palgrave is the imprint.

16c.15   A Translation

A translator's name must always be included in a citation because he or she prepared the version of the work that you read. To emphasize the original work (the most common pattern), place the abbreviation *trans.* (for "translated by," not italicized) and the translator's name after the title (but following editors' names, if appropriate).

[1]Sylvaine Agacinski, *Time Passing: Modernity and Nostalgia,* trans. Jody Gladding (New York: Columbia University Press, 2003), 84.

If selections within a collection are translated by different people, the translator's name follows the selection. Placing the translator's name after the book title signals that he or she translated *all* selections in the collection.

[2]Danilo Kiš, "Dogs and Books," trans. Duška Mikic-Mitchell, in *The Oxford Book of Jewish Stories,* ed. Ilan Stavans (New York: Oxford University Press, 1998), 325.

If you discuss techniques of translation, place the translator's name first, followed by a comma, the abbreviation *trans.,* and the title of the work. If appropriate, follow the title with the author's or editor's name, introduced with *by* (not italicized).

[3]Marcelle Thiébaux, trans., *The Writings of Medieval Women: An Anthology,* 2nd ed. (New York: Garland Publishers, 1994), xi–xii.

16c.16 A Government Document—*Congressional Record*

Notes for *Congressional Record* include the title of the selection or section, the title *Congressional Record* spelled out in full (not abbreviated) and italicized, the volume number, the date in parentheses, a colon, and the page number. Page numbers used alone indicate Senate records; page numbers preceded by an *H* indicate records from the House of Representatives.

¹Introduction of the Campaign Spending Limit and Election Reform Act of 1993, *Congressional Record* 139 (June 15, 1993): 7276.

²"Public School Statistics of the United States in 1880," table, *Congressional Record* 13 (June 13, 1882): H4825.

16c.17 A Government Document—Committee, Commission, Department

Information to describe government documents is generally presented in this order in citations: (1) country, state, province, or county (when necessary to avoid confusion); (2) governing body, sponsoring department, commission, center, ministry, or agency; (3) office, bureau, or committee; (4) the title of the publication, italicized; (5) if appropriate, the author of the document, the number and session of Congress, the kind and number of the document; (6) the city of publication, the publisher, and the date; and (7) the appropriate page or pages.

¹U.S. Congress, Budget Office, *Budget of the United States Government, Fiscal Year 2002* (Washington, D.C.: GPO, 2003), 13.

The Government Printing Office, the publisher of most federal documents, may be abbreviated to save space.

²Commission on the Assassination of President Kennedy, *Investigation of the Assassination of President John F. Kennedy: Hearings before the President's Commission on the Assassination of President Kennedy,* vol. 3 (Washington, D.C.: GPO, 1964), 177–78.

Multivolume government documents (like this sixteen-volume collection) follow note patterns like those of other multivolume collections.

³Federal Reserve Board of Governors, *Bank Mergers and Banking Structure in the United States, 1980–98,* by Stephen A. Rhoades (Washington, D.C.: GPO, 2000), 55–56.

16c.18 A Preface, Introduction, Foreword, Epilogue, or Afterword

To document material separate from the primary text, begin with the author's name, followed by a descriptive phrase like *introduction to* (not italicized), the title of the book, the name of the author of the book (introduced with *by,* also not italicized), publication facts, and appropriate page numbers. Note that the page numbers for most prefatory or introductory material are lowercase roman numerals.

> [1]Arthur C. Danto, "Philosophical Autobiography," foreword to *Genius—in Their Own Words: The Intellectual Journeys of Seven Great 20th-Century Thinkers* (Chicago: Open Court, 2002), vii.

This introduction has a formal title, which is included within quotation marks, followed by the descriptive title.

> [2]R. Buckminster Fuller, introduction to *Design for the Real World,* by Victor Papanek (New York: Pantheon Books, 1971), ix.

16c.19 A Pamphlet

When pamphlets contain clear and complete information, they are presented the way books are. When information is missing, use these abbreviations: *n.p.* for "no place of publication," "no publisher," or "no page"; use *n.d.* for "no date." These abbreviations are not italicized in notes.

> [1]Mike Wyatt, *Taking Off: A Guide to Backpacking Trails across North America* (Emmaus, Pa.: Rodale Press, 1990), 3.

> [2]*Lyme Disease and Related Disorders* (Groton, N.Y.: Pfizer, 2000), 3.

16c.20 An Annual Report

Because they are published for stockholders and are, to an extent, promotional materials, annual reports do not follow traditional printing formats. Publication information often appears on the back cover, and the date often appears with the CEO's letter to shareholders.

> [1]*At Pfizer, Life Is Our Life's Work: 1998 Annual Report* (New York: Pfizer, 1999), 66.

> [2]*The Document Company: 1993 Annual Report* (Stamford, Conn.: Xerox, 1994), 12.

16c.21 The Proceedings of a Conference

Begin a note for conference proceedings with the author's name, the title of the speech or paper (in quotation marks), a descriptive title if the speech had a special conference role (for example, *keynote address,* not italicized), and the facts of publication.

> [1]John A. Rich, "The Health Crisis of Young Black Men in the Inner City," in *The Crisis of the Young African American Male in the Inner City,* United States Commission on Civil Rights, April 15–16, 1999 (Washington, D.C.: GPO, 2000), 136–37.

> [2]*Proceedings: The First National Conference on Visual Literacy,* ed. Clarence M. Williams and John L. Debes III (New York: Pitman, 1970).

This note refers to the entire collected proceedings.

CHICAGO STYLE

16c.22   **A Dissertation**

Begin a note for an unpublished dissertation with the author's name and the title, in quotation marks. In parentheses, include the description *Ph.D. diss.* (not italicized), a comma, the degree-granting university, and the date. The note ends with the page reference, outside the closing parenthesis.

> [1]Harriet L. Parnet, "The Terror of Our Days: Four American Poets Respond to the Holocaust" (Ph.D. diss., Lehigh University, 2000), 111.

A published dissertation is presented like a book (See **16.c.1**).

16c.23   **A Book Written in a Language Other than English**

A note for a book written in a foreign language varies from normal patterns in several ways. When listing the title, follow the capitalization patterns of the book's original language. Many foreign languages capitalize only the first word and proper nouns and proper adjectives in titles. Second, include all accents and diacritical marks; if your printer does not offer such options, add them neatly by hand in black ink.

To include an English translation of the title, use parentheses following the foreign-language title. The English version of the title, neither italicized nor placed in quotation marks, is capitalized as if it were a sentence.

> [1]Jean Genet, *Les bonnes*, in *Oeuvres complètes* (Paris: Gallimard, 1968), 175–76.

> [2]Manuel Puig, *El beso de la mujer araña* (The kiss of the spider woman) (Barcelona: Seix Barral, 1976), 22.

16c.24   **Sacred Writings**

Notes for sacred writings follow patterns similar to those for other books, with several notable variations. First, titles of sacred writings (the parts or the whole) are neither placed in quotation marks nor italicized; they are simply capitalized in the normal way. Second, full facts of publication are not required for traditional editions. When appropriate, include additional information according to the guidelines for the element.

> [1]The Bhagavad Gita, trans. Juan Mascaró (New York: Penguin Books, 1962), 2:13.

> [2]Psalm 23:3–6.

This note is for the King James version of the Bible, the traditional English-language edition; other editions are indicated in parentheses after the line numbers but before the closing period, as in the sample below.

> [3]Psalm 23:3–6 (New English Bible).

16d Follow the appropriate note forms for periodicals.

16d.1 An Article in a Monthly Magazine

The note for a monthly magazine requires the author's name, the article's title in quotation marks, the name of the magazine (italicized), the month (either spelled out or abbreviated, as long as the pattern is used consistently in both notes and bibliographic citations) and year, and appropriate pages.

> [1]Bryant Furlow, "The Uses of Crying and Begging," *Natural History,* October 2000, 65.

> [2]Mark Warschauer, "Demystifying the Digital Divide," *Scientific American,* August 2003, 46.

16d.2 An Article in a Weekly Magazine

Notes for articles in weekly magazines are identical to those for monthly magazines, with one exception: the publication date is presented in more detailed form.

> [1]Ted Gest, "Fixing Your School," *U.S. News and World Report,* October 9, 2000, 66.

> [2]Jennifer Ordoñez, "Rap to the Rescue," *Newsweek,* August 4, 2003, 58.

16d.3 An Article in a Journal with Continuous Paging

Journals with continuous paging number the issues sequentially for the entire year. Place the volume number one space after the journal title (with no punctuation), identify the year (or month or season and year) in parentheses, follow it with a colon, and then list page numbers.

> [1]Rachel Roth Chiguluri, "The Politics of Discourse and the Discourse of Politics in *Tres Tristes Tigres*," *Revista de Estudios Hispánicos* 37 (2003): 250.

> [2]Aurora Sherman, Brian de Vries, and Jennifer E. Lansford, "Friendship in Childhood and Adulthood: Lessons across the Life Span," *The International Journal of Aging and Human Development* 51 (2000): 50.

16d.4 An Article in a Journal with Separate Paging

When journals page each issue separately, follow the volume number with a comma and the issue number, identified with the abbreviation *no.* (not italicized).

> [1]Alan J. Gumm, "Musical and Technical Sources of Choral Dynamics," *Choral Journal* 43, no. 10 (2003): 28–29.

> [2]Jon Lewis, "We Do Not Ask You to Condone This: How the Blacklist Saved Hollywood," *Cinema Journal* 39, no. 2 (2000): 4.

CHICAGO STYLE

16d.5   An Article in a Newspaper

Notes for newspapers resemble those for magazines: they include the author's name, article title (in quotation marks), newspaper title (italicized), the date, and pages (including sections, when appropriate). If information is taken from nonsequential pages, separate the page numbers with commas.

When newspapers are divided into sections, provide clarifying information. For sections identified by letters, place the section letter with the page number, without a space (A22, C3, F11); for sections identified by numerals, include the abbreviation *sec.* (not italicized) and the section number after the newspaper title.

[1]Erik Baard, "Cyborg Liberation Front: Inside the Movement for Posthuman Rights," *Village Voice*, August 5, 2003, 40.

[2]Carolina Bolado, "Activists Push Affordable Housing," *Chicago Tribune*, sec. 2, August 1, 2003, 3.

[3]Scott Wilson, "A Hard New Life inside the Law," *Washington Post*, July 27, 2003, A1.

16d.6   An Editorial or a Letter to the Editor

The note for an editorial is presented like one for a magazine or newspaper article, as is a note for a letter to the editor; for clarity, the word *editorial* or phrase *letter to the editor* (neither one italicized), with commas before and after, follows the title.

[1]Bruce Berkowitz, "A Fresh Start against Terror," editorial, *New York Times*, August 4, 2003, A17.

[2]John Paul Davis, letter to the editor, *Harper's*, August 2003, 8.

16d.7   A Review

Reviews begin with the author's name and the title of the review, if any. The phrase *review of* (not italicized) follows, with the name of the book, film, album, performance, product, or whatever else is being reviewed. Publication information ends the note, incorporating elements required for different kinds of sources.

[1]Richard Lacayo, "Total Eclipse of the Heart," review of *A Ship Made of Paper*, by Scott Spender, *Time*, March 17, 2003, 80.

[2]Owen Gleiberman, "The High Drama," review of *Traffic*, dir. by Steven Soderbergh, *Entertainment Weekly*, January 5, 2001, 45.

16d.8 An Abstract from *Dissertation Abstracts International*

Include the author's name, the title of the dissertation (in quotation marks); the degree and degree-granting university, in parentheses; the title *Dissertation Abstracts International* and the volume number; the year, in parentheses; and the identification number.

> [1]Margarita Dikovitskaya, "From Art to Visual Culture: The Study of the Visual after the Cultural Turn" (Ph.D. diss., Columbia University), *Dissertation Abstracts International* 62 (2002), AAT3028516.

16e Follow the appropriate note forms for audiovisual sources.

Finding the documentation information for audovisual sources is usually easy but sometimes requires ingenuity. CD cases provide the manufacturers' catalog numbers and copyright dates. Both printed programs for speeches and syllabuses for course lectures provide names, titles, locations, and dates. Information about films or television programs can be obtained from their opening or closing credits, from reference books, or from a variety of online sources. If you have difficulty in finding the information to document audiovisual sources clearly, ask your instructor or a librarian for help.

16e.1 A Lecture or Speech

A note for a lecture includes the speaker's name and the title of the lecture (in quotation marks). In parentheses, place the name of the lecture series or context for the speech (if applicable), the location of the speech (university, library, meeting hall), the city (and state, if necessary), and the date.

> [1]Neil Johnson, "Living on the Edge of Chaos" (lecture, Royal Institution, London, December 29, 1999).

> [2]Richard Nixon, Resignation Speech (speech, White House, Washington, D.C., August 8, 1974).

Notice that the description of the speech begins with a capital letter, even though it follows a comma.

16e.2 A Work of Art

When artists' names are known and the artists have titled their own work, include this information: artist's name; the title (italicized); a description of the work; the date of the work; the museum, gallery, or collection where the work of art is housed; and the city (and state, province, or country, if needed for clarity).

¹Paul Gauguin, *The Brooding Woman,* oil on canvas, 1891, Worcester Art Museum, Worcester, Mass.

²Henri de Toulouse-Lautrec, *La clownesse assise* (The seated clown), oil on canvas, 1895, Marie Harriman Gallery, New York.

When works of art are known primarily by titles in foreign languages, provide a translated title within parentheses; the translation follows the foreign-language title, is not italicized, and precedes the comma.

16e.3 A Map, Graph, Table, or Chart

Maps, graphs, tables, and charts are treated like books. If known, include the name of the author, artist, designer, scientist, or other person—or group—responsible for the map, graph, table, or chart. Include the title as it appears in the source, italicized, followed by a descriptive title. Then include the information required for your source.

¹C. Arden Pope, *Children's Respiratory Hospital Admissions,* graph, "The Next Battle over Clean Air," by Hillary J. Johnson, *Rolling Stone,* January 18, 2001, 49.

This chart is part of an article in a magazine.

²Kevin L. Phillips, *A Growing Income Disparity,* chart, *Wealth and Democracy: A Political History of the American Rich* (New York: Broadway, 2002), 129.

16e.4 A Cartoon

Begin with the cartoonist's name; the title of the cartoon, in quotation marks; and the word *cartoon,* not italicized, followed by a comma. Then include the publication information required for the source.

¹Bek, "I don't know if he's a great artist, but he's certainly annoying," cartoon, *The New Yorker,* August 11, 2003, 60.

²Jack Davis and Stan Hart, "Groan with the Wind," cartoon, *Mad,* January 1991, 42.

16e.5 A Film

When referring to a film as a complete work, include the title (italicized), the director, the studio, the date of release, and the format—film, VHS, or DVD. If you include other people's contributions, do so after the director's name, using brief phrases (*produced by, with, original score by, edited by*—not italicized) to clarify their roles.

If you begin the citation with the director's name, follow it with the abbreviation *dir.* (also not italicized).

¹David Fincher, dir., *Fight Club,* with Brad Pitt, Edward Norton, and Helena Bonham Carter, 20th Century Fox, Regency, 1999, film.

When a film has a dual release, include the names of both studios separated by commas.

    [2]Rob Marshall, dir., *Chicago,* with Renée Zellweger, Catherine Zeta-Jones, Richard Gere, Queen Latifah, and John C. Reilly, Miramax, 2002, film.

16e.6   A Filmstrip

Filmstrips are identified as films are, with one exception: include a descriptive title (*filmstrip,* not italicized) at the end of the note.

    [1]*The Great American Deficit: Mortgaging the Future,* Current Affairs Series, Contemporary Media, New York Times, 1986, filmstrip.

This filmstrip is part of a series; it is also co-produced.

16e.7   A Television Broadcast

Regular programs are listed by title (italicized), the network (CBS, CNN, FOX), and the local station (including both the call letters and the city—and state if required for clarity—separated by a comma); following a comma, include the broadcast date. List other contributors after the program title, using brief phrases (*narrated by, with, written by*—not italicized) to clarify their roles.

To cite an episode of a program, include the episode's name in quotation marks before the program's title. Other elements are presented in the same order as is used for a regular program.

    [1]"My Drama Queen," *Scrubs,* with Zach Braff, Donald Faison, Sarah Chalke, and Judy Reyes, NBC, WTHR, Indianapolis, August 14, 2003.

    [2]*My House in Umbria,* with Maggie Smith, Chris Cooper, and Giancarlo Gianni, HBO, New York, May 25, 2003.

16e.8   A Radio Broadcast

A note for a radio broadcast follows the guidelines for a television broadcast.

    [1]"The War of the Worlds," with Orson Welles, WCBS, New York, October 30, 1938.

16e.9   A Recording

Notes for recordings usually begin with the performer or composer, followed by the title of the album (italicized except for titles using numbers for musical form, key, or number), the recording format, the record company and catalog number, and the copyright date. List other contributors after the title, using brief phrases (*conducted by, with, composed by*—not italicized) to clarify their roles; orchestras and other large musical groups are listed without clarifying phrases and usually follow the conductor's name.

Compact discs (CDs) are now the standard recording format; indicate other formats, when necessary, preceding the catalog number. The information about multidisc sets, similar to the pattern for multivolume books, appears immediately preceding the catalog number.

A note for a single selection from a recording includes the selection title in quotation marks just before the title of the complete recording, introduced by the word *on* (not italicized). All else remains the same.

[1]The Beatles, *Abbey Road*, Capital-EMI CDp7-46446-2, 1969.

[2]Gustav Mahler, Symphony no. 1 in D major, conducted by Georg Solti, Chicago Symphony Orchestra, record, London 411731-2, 1984.

[3]Dwight Yoakam, "An Exception to the Rule," *Population ME*, Audium 8-81762-7, 2003.

16e.10   A Performance

A note for a performance usually begins with the title of the work being performed, provides information about contributors, and ends with the facility (theater, center, auditorium, performance hall, or other venue), city (and state, if needed for clarity), and performance date. To create other emphasis, the note can begin with the name of a contributor.

[1]*Long Day's Journey into Night*, written by Eugene O'Neill, with Vanessa Redgrave, Brian Dennehy, Robert Sean Leonard, and Philip Seymour Hoffman, Plymouth Theatre, New York, August 17, 2003.

[2]Boston Symphony Orchestra, "Four Last Songs," by Richard Strauss, conducted by Edo de Waart, with Renée Fleming, Tanglewood Music Center, Lenox, Mass., August 10, 2003.

16e.11   An Exhibit

Notes for exhibits include the title, the word *exhibit* set off by commas but neither italicized nor placed in quotation marks, the name of the museum or facility, the city, and the viewing date.

[1]"Threads of Prosperity: American Domestic Textiles: 1750–1875," exhibit, St. Louis Art Museum, December 2003.

16e.12   An Interview

Notes for personally conducted interviews include the name of the person interviewed, the phrase *interview by author* (not italicized), and the interview date and place, when applicable. Clarifying information may be added when appropriate.

¹Stephen Otwell, interview by author, November 11, 2002, Chicago, tape recording, Cook County Library.

²Richard Lindley, telephone interview by author, May 13, 2003.

Notes for broadcast or printed interviews begin with the name of the person who was interviewed, followed by the program title, if applicable. The remaining portion of the note should follow the pattern required for the source.

³Hillary Clinton, interview, *Larry King Live*, CNN, Atlanta, December 11, 2000.

16e.13   A Transcript

Transcripts of programs are presented according to the source of the original broadcast, with clarifying information provided. The entry ends with information about availability.

¹Carol Costello, "Eye on the Sky: Air Travel Delays," transcript, *Daybreak*, CNN, Atlanta, August 11, 2003. Available: Journal Graphics Online.

16f   Follow the appropriate note forms for electronic sources.

Electronic sources exist in many formats—online databases, electronic publications of traditional print sources, organizational Web sites, CD-ROMs, e-mail-based discussion groups, and others. To allow researchers to cite these sources, Chicago has adopted the relatively straightforward strategy of, first, following citations patterns that exist for comparable print sources and, second, adding information about electronic access.

As you gather citation information for electronic sources, you must be resourceful in finding important information; your goal should be to provide the most complete set of information possible for each electronic source, following the patterns described in this section.

If a source URL extends beyond one line, break it after a slash (/) or a double slash (//); before a period, a hyphen, an underline, a question mark, or a tilde (~); or either before or after an equals sign or an ampersand (&).

16f.1   An Online Scholarly Project, Information Database, or Professional Web Site

To create a note for an entire online scholarly project, information database, or Web site, present available information in this order: (1) the title of the project, database, or Web site, not italicized; (2) the editor or compiler, if identified, introduced with the abbreviation *ed.* or *comp.* and not italicized; (3) the city, "publishers" (sponsor, affiliated institution, or corporation), and publication or posting date—all in parentheses; (4) the electronic address (URL); and (5) an access note in parentheses.

[1]The On-line Books Page, ed. John Mark Ockerbloom (Philadelphia: University of Pennsylvania, 2003), http://digital.library.upenn.edu/books (accessed July 11, 2003).

[2]Thomas: Legislative Information on the Internet (Washington, D.C.: Library of Congress, 2001), http://thomas.oc.gov (accessed January 10, 2003).

16f.2   A Source from an Online Scholarly Project, Information Database, or Professional Web Site

To create a note for a selected source—article, illustration, map, and so on—from an online scholarly project, information database, or Web site, begin with (1) the name of the author (or artist, compiler, or editor) of the individual source, if appropriate, and (2) the title of the source, punctuated accordingly (quotation marks for articles, italics for charts, and so on). Continue the note with the name of the online project, database, or Web site and other required information (see **16f.1**).

[1]Jane Austen, *Sense and Sensibility,* Project Gutenberg (Urbana: University of Illinois, 1994), http://www.ibiblio.org/gutenberg/etext94/sense11.txt (accessed July 20, 2003).

[2]David Cody, "Queen Victoria," The Victorian Web, ed. George P. Landow (Providence, R.I.: Brown University, December 12, 2002), http://www.victorianweb.org.vn/victor6.html (accessed August 3, 2003).

16f.3   An Online Book

Online books exist in two forms: those previously published and now available electronically and those available only in electronic form.

To prepare a note for an online book that has a corresponding print version, first complete a standard note describing the print version (see section **16c**). Then provide additional electronic information required for a scholarly project, information database, or Web site, as appropriate (see section **16f.1**).

[1]Hugh Lofting, *The Voyages of Doctor Dolittle* (Philadelphia: Lippincott, 1922), Project Gutenberg (Urbana: University of Illinois, 1998), ftp://ibiblio.org/pub/docs/books/gutenberg/etext98/vdrdl10.txt (accessed February 2, 2003).

[2]Hugh Witemeyer, *George Eliot and the Visual Arts* (New Haven, Conn.: Yale University Press, 1979), The Victorian Web, ed. George P. Landow (Providence, R.I.: Brown University, 2000), http://www.victorianweb.org/authors/eliot/nw/contents.html (accessed January 15, 2003).

A note for an online book that is available only in electronic form includes (1) the name of the author or editor; (2) the title, italicized; and (3) the information required for the scholarly project, information database, or Web site.

[1]Sophie Buxhoeveden, *The Life and Tragedy of Alexandra Feodorvna, Empress of Russia* [book on-line], Russian History Website (1999), http://www. alexanderpalace.org/alexandra/ (accessed January 11, 2003).

A note for a selection from an online book—a chapter from a book, an essay or poem from a collection, and so on—provides this information: (1) the author of the selection and (2) the title of the selection, in quotation marks or italicized, as appropriate. The note then continues with the information required for the scholarly project, information database, or Web site (see section **16f.1**).

[1]A. E. Housman, "To an Athlete Dying Young," in *A Shropshire Lad* (London: Paul, 1896), Bartleby.com (2003), http://www.bartleby.com/123/19.html (accessed April 22, 2003).

16f.4 An Article in an Online Encyclopedia or Reference Source

A note for an article from an online encyclopedia or reference source supplies (1) the title of the electronic source, italicized; (2) the posting date; (3) the abbreviation *s.v.* (for *sub verso,* meaning "under the word"); (4) the term as it appears in the reference work, in quotation marks; (5) the URL; and (6) an access note in parentheses. (See also **16f.1**).

[1]*Infoplease Almanac* (2003), s.v. "Children in Foster Care," http://www. infoplease.com/ipa/A0778809.html (accessed January 13, 2003).

[2]*The New Dictionary of Cultural Literacy,* 3rd ed., s.v. "Carnegie, Andrew," Bartleby.com (2002), http://www.bartleby.com/59/8/carnegieandr.html (accessed August 10, 2003).

16f.5 An Online Government Document

A note for an online version of a government document—book, report, proceedings, brochure, and so on—first provides the information required for the print source (see sections **16c.16** and **16c.17**). It then continues with the information appropriate to the electronic source, whether it is a scholarly project, information database, or Web site (see section **16f.1**).

[1]U.S. Congress, Budget Office, *Budgeting for Naval Forces: Structuring Tomorrow's Navy at Today's Funding Level,* by Eric J. Labs, Congressional Budget Office (Washington, D.C.: GPO, 2000), http://www.cbo.gov/showdoc.cfm?index=2603& sequence=0&form=1 (accessed May 6, 2003).

[2]Department of Education, National Institute on Early Childhood Development, *Helping Your Child through Early Adolescence,* Department of Education (Washington, D.C.: Department of Education, November 12, 2002), http://www.ed.gov/pubs/ parents/adolescence/part1.html (accessed August 9, 2003).

CHICAGO STYLE

16f.6 An Article in an Online Magazine

A note for an article in an online magazine includes (1) the name of the author, if appropriate; (2) the title of the article, in quotation marks; (3) the name of the magazine, italicized; (4) the date of electronic publication or the date of the most recent update; (5) the URL; and (6) an access note in parentheses.

[1]Paul Hoffman, "Chess Queen," *Smithsonian,* August 2003, http://www. smithsonianmag.si.edu/smithsonian/issues03/aug03/pdf/smithsonian_august_03 _chess_queen.pdf (accessed August 11, 2003).

[2]Sarah Ramer, "It's More than the Economy, Stupid," *Newsweek,* August 18, 2003, http://www.msnbc.com/news/950350.asp?ob1=0#BODY (accessed August 20, 2003).

16f.7 An Article in an Online Journal

To present a note for an article in an online journal, supply (1) the name of the author, if appropriate; (2) the title of the article, in quotation marks; (3) the name of the journal, italicized, and the volume and issue number, as needed; (4) the year of electronic publication or of the most recent update, in parentheses; (5) the URL; and (6) an access note in parentheses.

[1]Rosemary Hopcroft, "Is Gender Still a Status Characteristic?" *Current Research in Social Psychology* 7, no. 20 (2002), http://www.uiowa.edu/~grpproc/ crisp/crisp.7.20.html (accessed April 26, 2003).

[2]Nicholas Jabbour, "Syphilis from 1880 to 1920: A Public Health Nightmare and the First Challenge to Medical Ethics," *Essays in History* 42 (2000), http://www. etext.lib.virginia.edu/journals/eh/eh42/jabbour42.html; (accessed March 26, 2003).

16f.8 An Article in an Online Newspaper

A note for an article in an online newspaper includes (1) the name of the author, if appropriate; (2) the title of the article, in quotation marks; (3) the name of the newspaper, italicized; (4) the date of electronic publication or the date of the most recent update; (5) the URL; and (6) an access note in parentheses.

[1]Judy Foreman, "The Health and Harm of New Cancer Drugs," *Boston Globe,* August 12, 2003, http://www.boston.com/yourlife/health/diseases/articles/2003/ 08/12/the_help_and_harm_in_new_cancer_drugs (accessed August 12, 2003).

[2]Joe Strauss, "Going Back to Basics," *St. Louis Post Dispatch,* August 11, 2003, http://www.stltoday.com/stltoday/sports/stories.nsf/sports/Cardinals (accessed August 11, 2003).

16f.9 An Online Transcript of a Lecture or Speech

To prepare a note for a transcript of a speech or lecture, first provide the information required for a lecture or speech (see section **16e.1**). Then include (1) the URL and (2) an access note in parentheses.

[1]William Faulkner, Nobel Prize in Literature Acceptance Speech (speech, Nobel Prize Ceremony, Stockholm, December 10, 1950), http://www.pbs.org/greatspeeches/timeline/index.html (accessed August 12, 2003).

[2]Vaclav Havel, "The Need for Transcendence in the Postmodern World" (speech, Independence Hall, Philadelphia, July 4, 1994), http://www.worldtrans.org/whole/havelspeech.html (accessed May 6, 2003).

16f.10　A Work of Art Online

To prepare a note for a work of art online, first provide information required for a work of art (see section **16e.2**). Then include (1) the URL and (2) an access note in parentheses.

[1]Grant Wood, *American Gothic,* oil on beaverboard, 1930, Art Institute of Chicago, Chicago, http://www.artic.edu/aic/collections/modern/73c_wood.html (accessed September 16, 2003).

[2]Pablo Picasso, *Les Demoiselles d'Avignon,* oil on canvas, 1907, Museum of Modern Art, New York, http://www.moma.org/collections/depts/paint sculpt/blowups/paint_sculpt_006.html (accessed August 21,2003).

16f.11　An Online Map, Graph, Table, or Chart

To prepare a note for a map, graph, table, or chart online, first provide the information required for the kind of visual element (see section **16e.3**). Then continue the note with the information appropriate to the electronic source, whether it is a scholarly project, information database, or Web site (see section **16f.1**).

[1]*Experimental Poverty Measures by Selective Characteristics: 2001,* table, Current Population Survey, 2002 Annual Demographic Supplement (Washington, D.C.: U.S. Census Bureau, 2002), http://www.census.gov/hhes/poverty/poverty01/table9.pdf (accessed August 18, 2003).

[2]*New York City Subway Route Map,* map, New York City Subway Resources (New York: New York City Subway, 2002), http://www.nycsubway.org/maps/route/ (accessed September 11, 2003).

16f.12　An Online Transcript of a Television or Radio Broadcast

A note for an online transcript of a television or radio broadcast includes (1) the title of the episode, if appropriate, in quotation marks; (2) the title of the program, italicized; (3) the city, the broadcast company, and the date of the original broadcast in parentheses; (4) the URL; and (5) an access note in parentheses.

[1]"Amid the Tall Trees: Planting the Seed of Empathy," *Nightline,* with Joe O'Connor (New York: ABC, August 2, 2003), http://abcnews.go.com/sections/nightline/living/ntl_oconnortrees_030802.html (accessed August 12, 2003).

[2]"Incitements to Violence in the Mideast," *All Things Considered,* with Melissa Block and Peter Kenyon (Washington, D.C.: NPR, July 25, 2003), http://www.npr.org/programs/atc/transcripts/2003/jul/030725.kenyon.html (accessed August 19, 2003).

16f.13 An Online Exhibit

A note for an online exhibit begins with the information required for a traditional exhibit (see section **16e.11**). Next, include (1) the URL and (2) an access note in parentheses.

[1]"Celebrity Caricature in America," exhibit, National Portrait Gallery, Washington, D.C., August 23, 1993, http://www.npg.si.edu/exh/caricatures/index.htm (accessed August 11, 2003).

[2]"Genetics: Decoding Life," exhibit, Museum of Science and Industry, Chicago, 2003, http://www.msichicago.org/exhibit/genetics/t_tourstart.html (accessed April 16, 2003).

16f.14 CD-ROM Sources

If a CD-ROM source reproduces material available in print form, begin the citation with full print information: author (or editor), title, and facts of publication (see sections **16c–16d**). If the material is not available in print form, provide (1) the author, if given; (2) the title, italicized; (3) the phrase *CD-ROM,* not italicized; and (4) the city, electronic publisher, and release date—all in parentheses.

[1]*The Baseball Encyclopedia: The Complete and Definitive Record of Major League Baseball,* CD-ROM (New York: Macmillan, 1996).

[2]*Earthquakes and Eruptions,* CD-ROM (Washington, D.C.: Smithsonian, 2000).

[3]Jim X. Chen, *Guide to Graphics Software Tools,* CD-ROM (New York: Springer, 2003).

16f.15 An E-mail Interview

A note for an e-mail interview follows the pattern of a traditional interview, with the word *E-mail* added (not italicized) for clarity.

[1]Marla Washburne-Freise, E-mail interview by author, May 14, 2003.

16f.16 An Online Posting

To prepare a note for an online posting to a forum or discussion group, supply (1) the name of the author, if known; (2) the official title of the posting, in quotation marks; (3) the name of the forum or discussion group; (4) the date of electronic publication or the date of the most recent update; (5) the URL; and (6) an access note in parentheses.

[1]D. Waitt, "Native Plant Information Network," Native Plants Forum, June 4, 2003, http://forums.gardenweb.com/forums/load/natives/msg062359004143.html?8 (accessed August 13, 2003).

[2]Kathryn Whinney, "Disturbing Vision," Discussion of *A Clockwork Orange*, Book Lover's Discussion, January 11, 2001, http://www.whatamigoingtoread.com/book.asp?bookid=6395 (accessed January 15, 2003).

16g When required, prepare a bibliography.

When instructors require a bibliography, arrange in alphabetical order all sources for the paper (described in your footnotes or endnotes). Citations in a bibliography include the same information that is contained in notes, but the format for each entry varies.

Formatting the Bibliography Page

Begin the first page of a bibliography with a heading presented in all capital letters; you may use *BIBLIOGRAPHY,* or you may title this section *SELECTED BIBLIOGRAPHY, WORKS CITED,* or *WORKS CONSULTED,* as suits your needs; these headings are not italicized in the paper. The heading is centered, two inches from the top of the page. The page number is centered at the bottom of the first page of the bibliography; on subsequent pages, no heading is required, and page numbers appear in the upper right corner (within the regular margin). (See pages 302–303 for a sample.)

Format for Bibliography Entries

To ensure easy reading, entries for a bibliography must consistently follow this format:

- Begin the first line of each entry at the left margin and indent all subsequent lines five spaces.
- Put the author's last name first (to make it easy to alphabetize and locate in the bibliography). If sources are co-authored, list additional authors' names in normal, first-last order.
- When no author is named, list the source by the title.
- Cite the complete title; use a colon and a single space to separate the title from the subtitle.
- Separate major sections of entries (author, title, and facts of publication) with periods. When other forms of end punctuation are used (when a title ends with a question mark, for example), the period may be omitted.
- Entries are single-spaced, with double-spacing between entries.

Sample Entries from a Bibliography

The following entries illustrate how to convert information found in footnotes or endnotes into bibliographic style.

Books

Barr, Stephen M. *Modern Physics and Ancient Faith.* Notre Dame: University of Notre Dame Press, 2003.

Tucker, Susan Martin, Mary M. Canobbio, Eleanor Vargo Paquette, and Marjorie Fyfe Wells. *Patient Care Standards: Collaborative Planning and Nursing Interventions,* 7th ed. St. Louis: Mosby-Yearbook, 2000.

All authors are listed in the entry for a bibliography list, but only the first author's names are inverted.

Seuss, Dr. [Theodore Seuss Geisel]. *Horton Hears a Who!* New York: Random House, 1954.

In addition to the pseudonym, the author's real name is required (in brackets) in a bibliographic entry.

Roberts, J. M. *The Age of Revolution.* Vol. 7, *The Illustrated History of the World.* 10 vols. New York: Oxford University Press, 1999.

Elements that follow periods are capitalized, as with *Vol.* in this example.

Agacinski, Sylvaine. *Time Passing: Modernity and Nostalgia.* Translated by Jody Gladding. New York: Columbia University Press, 2003.

The simple notation *trans.* (as used in the note) requires full explanation in a citation.

Danto, Arthur C. "Philosophical Autobiography." Foreword to *Genius—In Their Own Words: The Intellectual Journeys of Seven Great 20th-Century Thinkers,* vii–viii. Chicago: Open Court, 2002.

Inclusive pages are required for a work in a collection. Notice the use of lowercase roman numerals for this introductory material.

Periodicals

Furlow, Bryant. "The Uses of Crying and Begging." *Natural History,* October 2000, 62–67.

Although periods separate the author, article title, and periodical title in an entry, commas still divide the periodical title and the publication information. Notice that inclusive pages are required.

Chiguluri, Rachel Roth. "The Politics of Discourse and the Discourse of Politics in *Tres Tristes Tigres.*" *Revista de Estudios Hispánicos* 37 (2003): 249–69.

Parentheses enclose the year, and a colon introduces the page numbers for journal articles.

Baard, Erik. "Cyborg Liberation Front: Inside the Movement for Posthuman Rights." *Village Voice,* August 5, 2003, 38–41.

Berkowitz, Bruce. "A Fresh Start against Terror." Editorial. *New York Times,* August 4, 2003, A17.

Audiovisual Sources

Johnson, Neil. "Living on the Edge of Chaos." Lecture presented at the Royal Institution. London, December 29, 1999.

Gauguin, Paul. *The Brooding Woman.* Oil on canvas. 1891. Worcester Art Museum, Worcester, Mass.

Fincher, David, dir. *Fight Club.* With Brad Pitt, Edward Norton, and Helena Bonham Carter. 20th Century Fox, Regency, 1999, film.

Otwell, Stephen. Interview by author, November 11, 2002, Chicago. Tape recording, Cook County Library.

Electronic Sources

The On-line Books Page. Ed. John Mark Ockerbloom. Philadelphia: University of Pennsylvania, 2003, http://digital.library.upenn.edu/books (accessed January 16, 2003).

Austen, Jane. *Sense and Sensibility.* Project Gutenberg. Urbana: University of Illinois, September 1994. http://www.ibiblio.org/gutenberg/etext94/sense11.txt (accessed July 20, 2003).

Ramer, Sarah. "It's More than the Economy, Stupid." *Newsweek,* August 18, 2003. http://www.msnbc.com/news/950350.asp?ob1=0#BODY (accessed August 20, 2003).

Waitt, D. "Native Plant Information Network." Native Plants Forum, June 4, 2003. http://forums.gardenweb.com/forums/load/natives/msg062359004143.html?8 (accessed August 13, 2003).

Multiple Works by the Same Author

When citing multiple works by the same author, cite the first work completely. Subsequent entries, alphabetized by title, are introduced by three hyphens and a period. Subsequent references that are co-authored require the use of the author's full name.

Ehrenreich, Barbara. "Barefoot, Pregnant, and Ready to Fight." *Time,* May 8, 2000, 62.

———. "Looking to Put Fatherhood in Its Proper Place." *New York Times,* June 20, 1999, late ed., L14.

———. "Who Needs Men? Addressing the Prospect of a Matrilinear Millennium." Interview. With Lionel Tiger. *Harper's,* June 1999, 33–46.

Ehrenreich, Barbara, Elizabeth Hess, and Gloria Jacobs. *Re-Making Love: The Feminization of Sex.* Garden City, N.Y.: Doubleday, Anchor, 1986.

16h   When appropriate, follow Chicago guidelines to prepare your manuscript.

Writers using Chicago style must follow these guidelines for preparing a manuscript.

Paper

Use heavy-weight white bond 8½" × 11" paper. Acid-free paper is preferable.

Printing Formats

Use a clear, easy-to-read standard print font; styles with serifs, such as Times Roman and Courier, are preferred in pica (12-point, a large print size) or elite (10-point, a smaller print size). Laser or ink-jet printers are preferred.

Use italics *or* underlining consistently within your manuscripts to identify the titles of books, periodicals, albums, paintings, and so on.

Spacing

Double-spacing is used for the majority of the paper, but selected elements are single-spaced: footnotes, endnotes, indented quotations, sources included in the bibliography, and visual elements like tables and charts. When elements are single-spaced, double-spacing should separate them.

Margins

A one-inch margin on the left side is required; a one-and-one-half-inch margin on the left is preferred; a one-inch margin is required for the bottom and the right side of the page. On the first page of a paper (or section), the top margin must be two inches; on subsequent pages, a one-inch margin is required.

Indent paragraphs and notes six to eight spaces (a traditional five-space "Tab" may be acceptable, but ask your instructor); indent long quotations four spaces (a five-space "Tab" may be acceptable).

Paging

Either of two paging styles is acceptable. One style centers page numbers at the top of each page, and the other places page numbers in the upper right corner of each page. The numbers in either style are placed within the normal one-inch margins.

With both styles, the first page of a section—such as the first page of the text or endnotes or the bibliography—has the page number placed at the bottom, centered and within the normal margin. Most word processing programs allow you to change the position of the page numbering easily, a page at a time, to accommodate this style.

Title Page

Prepare a separate title page. If your instructor does not provide a sample, include the name of your school (centered), the title of the paper, the course (identified by department and number, not by its descriptive title), your name, and the date of submission.

Information on the title page is centered between the right and left margins and the top and bottom margins. Additionally, the amount of space between the school and title should be the same as the space between your name and the date; the space between the title and the course should be the same as the space between the course and your name. Visual symmetry is the goal. The title page is not counted in the page numbering. Paging instead begins with the text. (See the sample on page 293.)

A blank page follows the title page, so that the print from the first page of the text does not show through to the title page. Neither page is numbered.

The Text

The text of the paper begins on the page after the unnumbered blank page. Two inches from the top, center the title of the paper (presented in all uppercase letters); three spaces below, the text begins. This first textual page is considered page 1 in the numbering of the pages; the number appears at the bottom of the page, centered.

Headings for Sections

When headings are required, to divide and subdivide a discussion into logical sections, follow these patterns: first-level headings are centered, in italics or bold, with important words capitalized; second-level headings are centered with important words capitalized (but without any distinguishing print features); third-level headings begin at the left margin, in italics or bold, with important words capitalized.

This Is a First-Level Heading

This Is a Second-Level Heading

This Is a Third-Level Heading

When new headings are required, do not begin new pages. Simply leave a four-line space and type the heading. The text begins two spaces below the heading.

Tables, Graphs, Charts, Maps, and Illustrations

Place tables, graphs, charts, maps, and illustrations in the text whenever possible (separated from the discussion by three spaces above and below). Each kind of visual element is numbered sequentially (Table 1, Table 2, Graph 1, Graph 2), titled (Frequency of Requests), and referred to in the paper by number ("See Figure 1," not "in the next figure"). If a table, graph, chart, map, or illustration appears on a separate page, that page is numbered with the paper.

Order of the Manuscript

Place your manuscript pages in this order: title page (unnumbered), blank page (unnumbered), text (begin on page 1, numbered at the bottom of the page), appendix (new page, optional), endnotes (new page, an alternative to footnotes), and bibliography (new page, may or may not be required).

Submitting the Paper

Submit manuscripts according to your instructor's guidelines. If you receive no specific guidelines, secure the pages with a paper clip in the upper left corner and place them in a manila envelope with your name and identifying information about the paper typed or written on the outside. Always keep a photocopy—or another printed copy—of the paper.

Be aware that instructors may ask for a disk copy of the paper. In that case, submit a copy of the final paper on a separate disk, clearly labeled with your name and course information, as well as a note about your word processing program (Microsoft Word 2000, Word Perfect 10). Keep a backup disk version for yourself.

At least 1-inch margin

Matched spacing below first line and above last line

Centered top to bottom

INDIANA STATE UNIVERSITY

MUSIC THERAPY: AN ART OF COMMUNICATION

MUSIC 235

BY
SHINGO ENDO

APRIL 11, 2003

The cover page is followed by a blank page.

MUSIC THERAPY: AN ART OF COMMUNICATION

For many people, listening to their favorite music at the end of a busy day or going to a concert on a weekend is an essential aspect of their lives. Most people know that being involved with music, either playing or listening, is a rewarding and pleasurable experience because music relieves stress effectively.

However, it is often forgotten, or not known, that beyond its entertainment value music has a salutary effect on people with illness and distress, a fact once underestimated by mainstream medicine.[1] In the United States, so many people think of music as a mood modifier that this view overshadows the medical effects of music.[2] Yet because music possesses a power to reach a level of awareness that goes beyond verbal and physical communication, it offers important treatment for mentally or physically impaired people.

Music therapy, though itself a rather new medical discipline, can be traced back to 1500 B.C. in Egypt, where magicians used sound and music to communicate directly with what they believed to be the evil spirits in a patient's body.[3] Later, the Greeks developed a systematic use of music to alleviate disorder, and now they are most often regarded as the founders of music therapy.[4] However, it was not until after World War II that doctors began sustained and rigorous experimentation in music therapy.[5]

Two early, successful examples of music therapy in the United States are worth noting. One is the result of concerts by community music groups. When groups performed in hospitals for injured veterans of World War II, staff noted that many patients responded to the music and "perked up and got better."[6] And in 1959, dentists first used music as a way to minimize pain during surgery—a technique which allowed them to use lower dosages of nitrous oxide when treating their

2 inches to top of page, 1-inch right margin

Title in all capitals, centered

3 spaces

1 to 1½-inch left margin

The general introduction begins.

Position of note number

Shingo's thesis statement

Historical context for the discussion

The first extended example

A quotation incorporated in a sentence

Page number for first text page of paper

1

2

patients.[7] Since then, hundreds of research studies have demonstrated the positive effects of music on a wider range of symptoms, and research has helped to establish music therapy as a behavioral science.[8]

A transitional paragraph to introduce methods of treatment

Yet a central question remains: What, then, is music therapy? It is self-explanatory that therapists use music to heal people—but how? In what situations? And how effective is it? These factors are less known.

An example using a popular film

Awakenings, a popular film based on the writings of neurologist Oliver Sacks, presents the lives of post-encephalitic patients, who were catatonic, as well as partially paralyzed, in a mental ward in the 1960s.

An extended description to clarify the example from a film

In one scene, an elderly female patient, who is otherwise immobile, reacts to a recording of an aria from *La Bohème*. At first, her eyes are unfocused, but gradually they narrow, and as the melody reaches its familiar climax, the patient appears to be in a state of catharsis. As a further experiment with music therapy, a male nurse plays big-band music for elderly patients as an accompaniment to their meals. The music provides a stimulus for the patients and somehow prompts them to begin eating on their own. The charge nurse later reports to the doctor: "It's not just any music; it has to be music that's right for them."[9] These examples from a well-known film only hint at the uses of music therapy.

A summary of ideas, in Shingo's own words

Juliette Alvin, a renowned British music therapist, explains that severely regressed patients, with whom contact is difficult, sometimes react when they hear music that was recorded when they were young.[10] And Florence Tyson, in *Psychiatric Music Therapy: Origins and Development,* says that music is "especially effective as a psychological stimulus in a total hospital environment when used as an accompaniment to meals, calisthenics, and remedial exercises."[11]

Another incorporated quotation

During the years from 1950 to 1970, many state mental hospitals had full-scale music programs, incorporating activities such as these:

A long quotation, single-spaced and indented 5 spaces

> small orchestra, band, chamber music, chorus; music-listening appreciation; ward and auditorium concerts; musical quiz, variety and talent shows; staging of Broadway-type musicals; individual music study, including creative musical writing; folk and square dancing, religious choir, holiday pageants; maintenance

3

of muscal instruments, construction of simple instruments; maintenance of representative library records.[12]

Larol Merle-Fishman, a New York music therapist, states in *The Music within You,* that "either playing an instrument or joining a singing group builds confidence, nurtures creative self-expression, and helps you to understand who you are."[13] Tyson describes a range of patients' responses to those activities: "clapping hands, sudden smiling, humming, singing or dancing, which often provided the opening toward contact with reality and resocialization."[14]

Early activities in music therapy, with their considerable emphasis on the pleasurable and recreational aspects of music, were mainly conducted by large institutions for mentally ill people. However, they have virtually disappeared today, partly because of increasing costs, and have been replaced by music therapy with more focus on the cognitive, emotional, and spiritual areas of patients' lives.[15] These new areas of treatment are compatible with the community-based day centers, small hospital units, and hostels where treatment usually occurs.[16] Now music therapists have to work outside of the security of a hospital department because the way society deals with people with serious illness or disabilities has changed.

In these new settings, the practices and techniques used in music therapy change according to the individual needs of patients. As Donald E. Michel points out in *Music Therapy*, therapy is about bringing "changed behavior," and it is also an "individualized procedure."[17] Music can be used in various ways to accomplish these goals.

One of the important new developments in music therapy is the use of improvisation. This spontaneous activity can be done by using any instruments—from African percussion to the grand piano. With their instruments, patients can develop feelings of self-identification through music-making; they may express their feelings through the instruments instead of through speech. Many music therapists employ improvisation to initiate a non-verbal conversation with patients. The goal is not to achieve musical perfection, but to express the self, and it

Introduction of quotation by using author's name and title

Second references to authors use last name only.

Discussion of treatment that has been replaced

Quoting isolated phrases

Discussion of a therapy that is common knowledge

4

often evokes feelings patients have not even recognized. Improvisation is a widely used procedure today for treating schizophrenic, as well as brain-injured, patients.

An example related to autistic children

Music is no less effective for helping children with disabilities or behavior disorders. The treatment of autistic children is perhaps the best known among them, providing many successful cases. Through frequent music sessions, autistic children often show responses and curiosity in recorded or improvised music or simple rhythm instruments, and the interest in music can often be used to draw these children into contact with their therapists.[18] Through active associations with music—improvising and singing, for example—autistic children improve responsiveness and behavior.[19]

An example related to Alzheimer patients

Music is often the last thing that is destroyed from memories in people with Alzheimer's disease and other forms of dementia. These older adults often remember the words to songs, even when they cannot remember whether they've eaten lunch.[20] And what's even more striking is that music, at least for a short time, often helps patients to stay organized for a time afterward.[21] Rosemary Bakker, a gerontologist, re-emphasizes that the music must be matched to the patient's life experiences. For an elderly patient

> [some] good old fashioned swing music [is] wonderful. For a 50-year-old patient, R&B might do the trick. Soft, or "elevator music" is never inappropriate. Most older patients . . . respond well to instrumental hymns and spirituals.[22]

Although the scientific reason why individually selected music brings a brief lucidity to Alzheimer's patients is not yet known, it certainly reveals the power of music to evoke deep-seated memories.

Discussion of music's appeal

What parts of music do these patients react to? Music has many elements such as tone, color, loudness, duration, rhythm, pitch, melody, and so on. Each element seems to have its own therapeutic power. For example, Natasha Spender observes that rhythm has "a

5

power to focus energy and to bring structure into the perception of temporal order."[23] In addition, Juliette Alvin notes that rhythm "expresses an alternation of tension and relaxation through stresses, accentuation, breathing spaces, strong and weak beats."[24]

Pitch and the melodic interval between notes certainly evokes emotional responses in people. Much of the folk music from America, Scotland, and Ireland is based on the _pentatonic scale_, which consists of C,D,E,G,A—a melodic scale popular in music therapy group work because of its pleasing non-western sound.[25]

Technical information summarized from a source

Harmony may also appeal to emotions. The proportionally spaced harmonies of major chords soothe, strengthen, and regularize while minor chords may ease sorrow or yearning.[26]

Yet, we usually do not separate these elements when we listen to music. Music provokes feelings, but as we all know, these feelings cannot always be translated into words. Indeed that is what makes music so unique and effective when used in therapeutic ways; music does not fall into the trap of intrusive language. Philosopher Suzanne Langer elaborates this:

> The real power of music lies in the fact that it can be "true" to the life of feeling in a way that language cannot, for its significant forms have the _ambivalence_ of content which words cannot have.[27]

Quotation marks used within an indented quotation

Music also helps to assist inmates of correctional institutions, who need to learn skills to be adapted to society. Jeff Mayors, who teaches music therapy at a correctional facility in Washington, DC, uses harp music to relieve inmates' stress. Some of the inmates say their bodies, minds, and souls are in balance after listening to Mayors' harp sound, and it even causes a desire in them to reach out and help others.[28]

An example about inmates

Music therapy is itself very versatile because of its variety and accessibility. As a greater number of health-care professionals have realized the value of music therapy, they have begun to coordinate their efforts. Founded in 1998, the American Music Therapy Association now has 3,800 board-certified members who forward "the progressive development of the therapeutic use of music in rehabilitation, special education, and

The conclusion, which visualizes the future

6

community settings."[29] It is certain, as a result, that medical research, along with psychological and biological study, will continue to explore the effects of music therapy, and new clinical uses of music therapy will expand its potential in the future. And through these advancements, we will be reminded of something we often forget in the flow of commercial music—the indispensable power and the humanizing quality of music.

NOTES

2 inches from
top of page

Heading in all
capitals,
centered

[1]Rick Weiss, "Music Therapy: Doctors Explore the Healing Potential of Rhythm and Song," *Washington Post*, July 5, 1994, WH11–12.

[2]Ibid.

Same source,
same page

[3]Juliette Alvin, *Music Therapy* (New York: Basic Books, 1966), 21–23.

[4]Leslie Bunt, *Music Therapy: An Art beyond Words* (London: Routledge and Kegan Paul, 1994), 10.

[5]Ibid., 11.

Same source,
new page
Shortened
reference

[6]Weiss, 11.

[7]Michael Scofield and Mark Teich, "Mind-Bending Music," *Health* 19 (1987): 70.

[8]Bunt, 11.

[9]*Awakenings*, directed by Penny Marshall, with Robin Williams and Robert De Niro, Columbia, 1990, film.

Single-spaced
with double-
spacing
between notes

[10]Juliette Alvin, *Introduction to Music Therapy: Papers Read at the Two Day Course Given at the University of London Institute of Education April 13th–14th, 1961* (London: The Society for Music and Remedial Music, 1961), 7.

[11]Florence Tyson, *Psychiatric Music Therapy: Origins and Development* (New York: Creative Arts Rehabilitation Center, 1981), 8.

[12]Ibid., 12.

[13]Scofield and Teich, 76.

[14]Tyson, 9.

[15]Bunt, 160–61.

[16]Ibid.

[17]Donald E. Michel, *Music Therapy: An Introduction to Therapy and Special Education through Music* (Springfield, Ill.: Thomas, 1976), 6.

Numbered
sequentially,
but centered
at bottom to
start a new
section

Subsequent pages

No heading is required on subsequent note pages.

[18]Ibid., 49.

[19]Paul Nordoff and Clive Robbins, "Improvised Music as Therapy for Autistic Children," in *Music Therapy*, ed. E. Thayer Gaston (New York: Macmillan, 1968), 192–93.

Note: First lines indented; subsequent lines at the regular margin

[20]Ann Hardie, "Old Songs Strike Right Note," *Atlanta Journal and Atlanta Constitution*, 12 March 1994, El.

[21]Weiss, WH12.

[22]Music Therapy for Parkinson's and Dementia (2002), http://caregiver.on.ca/cgihmmt.html (accessed January 15, 2003).

[23]*The New Grove Dictionary of Music and Musicians*, ed. Stanley Sadie, 2001 ed., s.v. "Music Therapy" (by Natasha Spender).

A short title distinguishes Alvin's two sources.

[24]Alvin, *Music Therapy*, 67.

[25]Bunt, 67.

[26]Mary Priestley, *Music Therapy in Action* (New York: St. Martin's Press, 1975), 214.

[27]Bunt, 73.

[28]Courtland Milloy, "A Healing Force in London Prison," *Washington Post*, February 9, 1992, C3.

[29]"About the American Music Therapy Association," American Music Therapy Association (Silver Spring, Md.: American Music Therapy Association, 2002), http://www.musictherapy.org/about.html (accessed January 13, 2003).

*2 inches from
top of page*

WORKS CITED

*Heading in all
capitals,
centered*

"About the American Music Therapy Association." American Music
      Therapy Association. Silver Spring, Md.: American Music
      Therapy Association, 2002. http://www.musictherapy.org/
      about.html (accessed January 13, 2003).

Alvin, Juliette. *Music Therapy*. New York: Basic Books, 1966.

---. *Introduction to Music Therapy: Papers Read at the Two Day
      Course Given at the University of London Institute of Educa-
      tion April 13th–14th, 1961*. London: The Society for Music
      and Remedial Music, 1961.

*Second source
by the same
author*

Awakenings. Directed by Penny Marshall. With Robin Williams and
      Robert De Niro. Columbia, 1990.

Bunt, Leslie. *Music Therapy: An Art beyond Words*. London: Routledge
      and Kegan Paul, 1994.

Hardie, Ann. "Old Songs Strike Right Note." *Atlanta Journal and At-
      lanta Constitution*, March 12, 1994, El.

Michel, Donald E. *Music Therapy: An Introduction to Therapy and
      Special Education Through Music*. Springfield, Ill.: Thomas,
      1976.

*Single-spaced,
with double-
spacing
between
citations*

Milloy, Courtland. "A Healing Force in London Prison." *Washington
      Post*, 9 February 1992, C3.

*Note: First
lines at the
regular
margin;
subsequent
lines indented*

Music Therapy for Parkinson's and Dementia. 2002. http://
      caregiver.on.ca/cgihmmt.html (accessed January 15, 2003).

The New Grove Dictionary of Music and Musicians. Ed. Stanley Sadie.
      2001 ed. s.v. "Music Therapy" (by Natasha Spender).

Nordoff, Paul, and Clive Robbins. "Improvised Music as Therapy for
      Autistic Children." In *Music Therapy*. Ed. E. Thayer Gaston.
      New York: Macmillan, 1968. 191–93.

*Numbered
sequentially,
but centered
at bottom to
start a new
section*

10

Subsequent
pages

No heading is
required on
subsequent
citation pages.

Priestley, Mary. *Music Therapy in Action*. New York: St. Martin's
     Press, 1975.

Scofield, Michael, and Mark Teich. "Mind-Bending Music." *Health* 19
     (1987): 69–76.

Tyson, Florence. *Psychiatric Music Therapy: Origins and
     Development*. New York: Creative Arts Rehabilitation Center,
     1981.

Weiss, Rick. "Music Therapy: Doctors Explore the Healing Potential of
     Rhythm and Song." *Washington Post*, July 5, 1994, WH11–12.

MUSIC THERAPY: AN ART OF COMMUNICATION

For many people, listening to their favorite music at the end of
a busy day or going to a concert on a weekend is an essential aspect of
their lives. Most people know that being involved with music, either
playing or listening, is a rewarding and pleasurable experience because
music relieves stress effectively.

However, it is often forgotten, or not known, that beyond its
entertainment value music has a salutary effect on people with illness
and distress, a fact once underestimated by mainstream medicine.[1] In
the United States, so many people think of music as a mood modifier
that this view overshadows the medical effects of music.[2] Yet because
music possesses a power to reach a level of awareness that goes beyond
verbal and physical communication, it offers important treatment for
mentally or physically impaired people.

Music therapy, though itself a rather new medical discipline,
can be traced back to 1500 B.C. in Egypt, where magicians used sound
and music to communicate directly with what they believed to be the
evil spirits in a patient's body.[3] Later, the Greeks developed a systematic use of music to alleviate disorder, and now they are most often regarded as the founders of music therapy.[4]

---

[1]Rick Weiss, "Music Therapy: Doctors Explore the Healing
Potential of Rhythm and Song," *Washington Post*, 5 July 1994, WH11.

[2]Ibid.

[3]Juliette Alvin, *Music Therapy* (New York: Basic Books,
1966), 21–23.

[4]Leslie Bunt, *Music Therapy: An Art beyond Words* (London:
Routledge and Kegan Paul, 1994), 10.

Footnotes appear after a separation line; they are single-spaced, with double-spacing between notes.

1

CHAPTER

17

Using CBE Style
When Appropriate*

QUICK REFERENCE

Prepare CBE citations for sources, applying these general principles for formatting and incorporating required information.

▶ Begin the first line of each entry with a citation number at the left margin, but indent subsequent lines so they align with the first word on the first line.

▶ Arrange entries in the order in which they appear in the paper; repeat the number for a source if it is used again.

▶ Double-space entries; do not insert additional line spaces between entries.

▶ Provide comprehensive information (authors' names, titles with subtitles, complete electronic addresses), but shorten publishers' names (*Houghton,* not *Houghton Mifflin*) and abbreviate months without periods (*Sept,* not *September*).

▶ Invert the author's name, without a comma, when it begins an entry and use first initials with no periods (*Perrin R,* not *Robert Perrin*).

▶ Do not use quotation marks or italics to signify titles; capitalize only the first words and proper nouns and proper adjectives of book and article titles; however, capitalize all words in journal titles.

▶ Separate the major elements of an entry with periods and single spaces.

▶ Use the samples in this chapter as models to prepare your own citations, combining information from several samples when a source has many features.

*The information in this chapter is based on *Scientific Style and Format: The CBE [Council of Biology Editors] Manual for Authors, Editors, and Publishers,* sixth edition (Chicago: Cambridge UP, 1994); the information on manuscript preparation is derived from the *CBE Style Manual,* fifth edition (Bethesda: CBE, 1983). While the chapter describes CBE style and the sample materials illustrate CBE citations, the primary text follows the conventions of MLA.

CBE STYLE

305

To acknowledge the use of other people's ideas, information, or exact words in a paper, include accurate in-text documentation and citations in the list of literature cited. These elements provide basic information about sources so that interested readers may locate them for further study.

17a   Recognize the distinct documentation patterns of CBE style.

CBE (Council of Biology Editors) style presents information in the biological, physical, and mathematical sciences, disciplines for which reproducible results are especially important. Although CBE style emphasizes periodicals and books, it provides additional information on alternative sources, including maps, audiovisual materials, government documents, and electronic sources.

17b   Consider patterns for in-text documentation.

CBE recommends two general systems for citing documents: (1) the citation-sequence system and (2) the name-year system. This chapter presents the citation-sequence system.

When using citation-sequence documentation, list and number references in the sequence cited in the paper, with separately numbered lists for information included in tables and for explanatory information that accompanies figures (graphs, tables, illustrations, maps). List the paper's first reference with the numeral *1* on the "Literature Cited" page, the second with the numeral *2,* and so on. In subsequent references to a source, it is important to use the same numeral. Therefore, nine uses of the first source—anywhere in the paper—produce nine references to source 1.

In-Text Citations

Include reference numbers in the paper to identify information from a source, whether in the middle of a sentence or at the end. Using superscript numbers (one-half space above the line, in a slightly smaller font size) is the preferred style, as in this example:

> Between 1993 and 1996, a number of studies[1,2,4] linked muscle degeneration and joint pain with the residual effects of poliomyelitis.

However, in another, alternative, style, numbers are included in parentheses. (The styles, of course, should not be mixed within a paper.) Because it allows for page references, parenthetical style is most useful for papers that cite specific information (rather than make general references to sources) and quote from sources. To follow parenthetical style, include in parentheses the number of the source, a comma, and, if necessary, the page or pages (introduced with the abbreviation *p*, without a period and not italicized). For example:

> Between 1993 and 1996, a number of studies (1,2,4) linked muscle degeneration and joint pain with the residual effects of poliomyelitis.

> Dr. Ronald Talbert observed that "patients' new-found symptoms are, it seems, the results of past medical problems" (3, p 751).

When multiple citations are listed in the same location in a sentence, indicate sequential citations by using a hyphen (*1-4* indicates sources 1, 2, 3, and 4), but nonsequential numbers are separated with commas and no spaces (*1,3,6* refers only to the three sources noted).

17c Complete citations for the reference page.

Information for CBE Citations

Citations vary because of the different information they include, but all must follow an established order for presenting information:

1. *Author(s) or Editor(s).* Take the name or names from the title page of a book or from the first page of an article. Authors' or editors' names are listed in the order in which they appear (not alphabetical order), and initials (without periods) are used in place of first and middle names. Up to ten authors or editors are listed individually; additional contributors are then indicated by the phrase *and others* (not italicized). If no author or editor is listed, make a note of that for yourself; the entry begins with the word *Anonymous* (not italicized), in brackets.

2. *Title.* Include full titles and subtitles, no matter how long. One-word titles of scientific journals are presented in complete form, although multiword titles of scientific journals are abbreviated (without periods) when possible (see the citations below and Appendix B for examples). Capitalize the first word and proper nouns and proper adjectives in book and article titles.

3. *Additional information.* Include second and subsequent edition numbers following the book's title. Include this information in numeral-abbreviation form (*2nd, 3rd, 4th*), with *edition* abbreviated (*ed*) without a period and not italicized. Include the names of editors, translators, and other contributors, followed by a comma and an abbreviated description of their roles (*ed, trans*).

4. *Facts of Publication.* For books, include the place of publication, an abbreviated name of the publisher (see Appendix B for samples), the date of publication, and the total number of pages (followed by the abbreviation *p*); the period that follows ends the citation. When the city of publication is unfamiliar or when several cities share the same name, include the state, province, or country in parentheses: Springfield (IL) or Cambridge (Eng). If the book is part of a multivolume series, include the volume number after

the title. Follow the journal title with the year, a three-letter abbreviation for the month (without a period), and day, as appropriate (without intervening punctuation); follow the month or day with a semicolon (and no space), the volume number, the issue number in parentheses, a colon (without a space following), and the inclusive page numbers.

5. *Page Numbers.* When citing only part of a source (for example, a chapter from a book or an article from a journal), provide inclusive page numbers. Include only those digits required for clarity, without commas in numbers of one thousand or larger (12–5, 137–42, 1883–1901). When pages for articles are nonsequential, separate the pages with commas and spaces (23–4, 26, 28–31). Look up page numbers yourself; do not rely on the table of contents.

Format for CBE Citations

References presented in CBE style follow this format:

- Begin the first line of each entry at the left margin. Type the reference number and a period, followed by one space, and begin the entry. Subsequent lines should align with the first letter of the first word of the entry. With computers, use the "Indent" feature; you may have to adjust Tab placement for proper alignment.

- Begin each entry with the author's or editor's last name, followed by one space, the initials for his or her first and middle names, and a period. No periods are used with the initials, and no space appears between them. If sources are produced collaboratively, up to ten authors' or editors' names are listed (all inverted), separated by commas.

- Cite the complete title; use a colon and one space to separate the title from the subtitle. For books and articles, capitalize only the first word of the title (but not the subtitle) and capitalize proper nouns and proper adjectives. In the name of a journal, all words (including abbreviations) are capitalized; the articles *a, an,* and *the,* conjunctions, and prepositions are omitted. Titles are neither italicized nor underlined.

- Separate major sections of entries (author, title, publication information, and paging) with periods and single spaces.

- For books, separate the place of publication from the publisher by a colon and a space; the publisher is separated from the year by a semicolon and a space; end with the total number of pages. For periodicals, separate the year, month, or day from the volume by a semicolon, without a space; enclose the issue number, when appropriate, in parentheses, without spaces before or after; follow the volume number or issue number, as applicable, with a colon and no space, followed by the inclusive page numbers.

- Double-space all entries.

17d   Follow the appropriate citation forms for books and other separately published materials.

17d.1   A Book by One Author

1. Tate RL. Soil microbiology. New York: J Wiley; 2000. 508 p.

Only the first word in the title is capitalized; the publisher's name is presented in abbreviated form.

2. Cloudsley-Thompson JL. The diversity of amphibians and reptiles: an introduction. New York: Springer; 1999. 254 p.

17d.2   A Book by Two or More Authors

Authors' names are listed in the order in which they appear on the title page, not in alphabetical order.

1. Wingender J, Neu TR, Fleming HC. Microbial extracellular polymeric substances: characterization, structure, and function. New York: Springer; 1999. 258 p.

2. Dey PM, Harborne JB. Plant biochemistry. San Diego: Academic Pr; 1997. 554 p.

17d.3   A Book with No Author Named

When a book has no known author, use the word *Anonymous* (not italicized) in brackets in the author position. Present other information required for the source.

1. [Anonymous]. The medical advisor: the complete guide to alternative and conventional treatments. Alexandria (VA): Time-Life; 1996. 1152 p.

Note that the two-letter state abbreviation is provided in parentheses for clarity.

17d.4   A Book with an Organization as Author

When organizations that serve as authors are not clearly identified in the title, list them in the author position. Note that in the "author" position, no abbreviations are used, whereas in the "publisher" position, abbreviations are acceptable.

1. American Medical Association manual of style: a guide for authors and editors. 9th ed. Baltimore: Williams & Wilkins; 1998. 660 p.

The organization title is capitalized, but the other words of the title are not.

Note as well that the ampersand (&) is retained in the publisher's name; however, it should not be used in titles of papers or in the text of scientific writing.

2. National Academy of Sciences. Capitalizing on investments in science and technology. Washington: Nat Academic Pr; 1999. 118 p.

17d.5 A Book with an Editor or Compiler as Author

When the editor or editors are listed first in the citation, the word *editor* or *editors* (not italicized) appears in full form.

1. Juo PS, editor. Concise dictionary of biomedicine and molecular biology. Boca Raton (FL): CRC Pr; 1996. 983 p.

17d.6 An Edition Other than the First

The edition number follows the title in numeral-abbreviation form (*2nd*, not *second*), along with the abbreviation *ed* (not italicized). The period after *ed* in a citation is not part of the abbreviation; rather, it marks the end of the element.

1. Roberts C, Manchester K. The archeology of disease. 2nd ed. Ithaca (NY): Cornell Univ Pr; 1999. 243 p.

2. Norris DO. Vertebrate endocrinology. 3rd ed. San Diego: Academic Pr; 1997. 634 p.

17d.7 A Volume of a Multivolume Work

Cite the particular volume used, even when a work includes multiple volumes, using the word *Volume* (not italicized) and an arabic numeral, not a roman numeral or a letter.

1. Drauz K, Waldman H, editors. Enzyme catalysis in organic synthesis: a comprehensive handbook. Volume 2. New York: VCH; 1995. 544 p.

2. Farmer DS, King JR, Parkes KC, editors. Avian biology. Volume 4. London: Academic Pr; 1993. 504 p.

17d.8 A Work in a Collection

When citing a single selection from a collection (for example, an essay from a book), begin with the name of the author of the individual selection, followed by the title of the selection. Using the word *In* (not italicized), followed by a colon and a space, list the editor or editors, the title of the collection, and the facts of publication. Follow the date of publication with a period and one space; then list the inclusive pages of the selection, using the abbreviation *p* without a period.

1. Norris PR, Johnson DB. Acidophilic microorganisms. In: Horikoshi K, Grant WD, editors. Extremophiles: microbial life in extreme environments. New York: Wiley-Liss; 1998. p 133–53.

Notice that other rules (about multiple authors and multiple editors, for example) remain the same as for other sources.

2. Fentress JC, Bolivar VJ. Developmental aspects of movement sequences in mammals. In: Ossenkopp KP, Kavaliers M, Sanberg PR, editors. Measuring movement and locomotion: from invertebrates to humans. New York: Chapman & Hall; 1996. p 95–114.

17d.9   A Translation

When a work has been translated, the translator's name is listed after the title of the work, followed by the word *translator* (not italicized).

1. Concise encyclopedia: biology. Scott TA, translator. New York: WD Gruyter; 1996. 1287 p.

2. Rensch B. Biophilosophy. Sym Cam, translator. New York: Columbia Univ Pr; 1971. 377 p. Translation of: Biophilosophie auf erkenntnistheoretischer grundlage.

When a translator's title tells less than original author's, provide the full title of the original, introduced by the phrase *Translation of* (not italicized) and a colon.

17d.10   A Government Document

Begin a citation with an abbreviated title for the sponsoring group (if known), a brief description of the legislative session, and the date, all separated by commas.

1. Regulation of recombinant DNA research, Hearings before the Subcommittee on Science, Technology, and Space, 95th Cong, 1st Sess (November 2,8,10, 1977).

17d.11   A Report

Reports are presented in a format that resembles that for a book. When no author is noted, begin the citation with the name of the organization. Following the date of publication, identify as many of these elements as possible, separated by periods: report number, contract number, total number of pages, and availability.

1. National Institute on Drug Abuse. Recovery training and self-help: relapse prevention and aftercare for drug addicts. Rockville (MD): Nat Inst on Drug Abuse; 1993. Report 93-3521. 250 p. Available from: Nat Inst of Health.

17d.12   The Proceedings of a Conference

A citation for conference proceedings follows the pattern used for books, with several exceptions. Following the title of the publication, include the name of the conference (if it is not already clear from the title), the inclusive dates of the conference, and the place of the conference—all separated by semicolons. Then include the facts of publication, a period, and the total number of pages, followed by the abbreviation *p*; the period that follows the page abbreviation ends the citation.

1. Clark JW, Lindenau T, Ristig ML, editors. Scientific applications of neural nets. WE Heraeus Seminar; 1998 May 11–13; Bad Honnef, Ger. New York: Springer. 288 p.

2. Hildebrand LP, Magoon OT, editors. Coastlines of Canada. 8th symposium on coastal and ocean management. 1993 Jul 19–23; New Orleans. New York: Am Soc of Civil Engineers. 224 p.

17d.13   A Dissertation

After the author's name and the title, include the word *dissertation* (not italicized) in brackets, followed by a period. Include the city (and state or country, if necessary for clarity), a colon and one space, and the degree-granting university (without abbreviations). Follow the name of the university with a semicolon, one space, the year of the degree, the total number of pages, and a period. Close the citation with the phrase *Available from* (not italicized), a colon (and one space), the source, and an identifying number when available.

1. Dhabhar FS. Stress-induced enhancement of antigen-specific, cell-mediated immunity: the role of hormones and leukocyte trafficking [dissertation]. New York: Rockefeller University; 1996. 350 p. Available from: University Microfilms, Ann Arbor, MI; AAT9708514.

2. Fan W. Discovering, mapping and characterization of 39 new genes in human MHC class I region by CDNA selection [dissertation]. New Haven (CT): Yale University; 1994. 249 p. Available from: University Microfilms, Ann Arbor, MI; AAC9432138.

17e Follow the appropriate citation forms for periodicals and audiovisual sources.

17e.1 An Article in a Journal with Continuous Paging

To present information from a journal with continuous paging, include the volume number and inclusive page numbers, separated by a colon and no space.

1. Mulleners WM, Palmer JE, Koehler PJ, Vredeveld JW. Suppression of perception in migraine: evidence for reduced inhibition in the visual cortex. Neurology 2001 Jan;56:178–83.

2. Chesson P. General theory of competitive coexistence in spatially-varying environments. Theor Population Biol 2000 Nov;58:211–37.

Note that all major words in the journal's title are capitalized and that all articles and prepositions are omitted.

17e.2 An Article in a Journal with Separate Paging

To present information from a journal with separate paging, include issue numbers in parentheses after the volume number, without spaces.

1. Buttner JK. Photosynthesis and respiration in a jar. Sci Activ: Classroom Projects and Curriculum Ideas 2000 Summer;37(2):10–15.

2. MacKenzie AH. Planimal house. Sci Teacher 2001;68(1):40–1.

17e.3 An Article with Author Affiliation

To identify the affiliations of the authors, include appropriate information in parentheses after each author's name. Include department or division, if known; university, corporation, or funding group; and the city and state, when necessary. Full forms, not abbreviations, are required when listing affiliations.

1. Kaetzel CS (Department of Pathology and Microbiology/Immunology, University of Kentucky, Lexington). Polymeric Ig receptor: defender of the fort or Trojan horse? Curr Biol 2001 Jan;11(1):R35–8.

2. Leise EM (Kewalo Marine Lab, University of Hawaii, Honolulu), Hadfield MG (Department of Biology, University of North Carolina, Greensboro). An inducer of mulluscan metamorphosis transforms activity patterns in a larval nervous system. Biol Bull 2000 Dec;199:241–50.

CBE STYLE

17e.4　A Single Page of an Article

To cite a single page of an article—perhaps in referring to a diagram, table, or chart—present clarifying facts in parentheses at the end of the citation.

1. Halford MH, Stacker SA. Revelations of RYK receptor. BioEssays 2001 Jan;23:34–45. (p 42, figure: Speculative model of RYK function).

Note that one-word journal titles are not abbreviated.

17e.5　An Entire Issue of a Journal

Because journals in the sciences often present complete issues that address a single theme, you may refer to an entire issue. When appropriate, a descriptive title of the issue's theme precedes the title of the journal. All else remains the same.

1. Sato S, Lansksy P, Rospars JP, editors. Neural Coding. BioSystems 2000 Oct–Dec;58(1–3).

17e.6　An Article in a Newspaper

When newspapers are divided into sections, follow the date with a semicolon, no space, the abbreviation *Sect* (not italicized) and a colon (without a period or space), the section's letter or number, a colon, the page number, and (in parentheses) the column number where the article begins. When newspapers are paged sequentially (without section numbers or letters), separate the date from the page number by a colon and no space.

1. Regalado A. Molecule able to block HIV's entrance into a cell is found by MIT scientist. Wall Street J 2001 Jan 12;Sect B:6(col 2).

2. Grady D. As polio fades, Dr. Salk's vaccine re-emerges. New York Times 1999 Dec 14;Sect F:1(col 2).

17e.7　A Map

Begin by identifying the area represented by the map. Then add a formal or descriptive title and, in brackets, name the type of map. Next, include the title of the source (book or periodical) introduced by the word *In* (not italicized) and a colon. Identify the place of publication, the publisher, and the date of publication. End the citation with a physical description of the map, if necessary.

1. Islands. Geographical comparison by continent [topographical map]. In: The Times atlas of the world. 9th ed. London: Time Books; 1994. p xv. 2-color.

17e.8 Audiovisual Materials

Information to clarify the kind of audiovisual material—*film, filmstrip, audiotape* (not italicized)—appears in brackets following the title. When appropriate, list authors, editors, or producers. Next, identify the place of publication, publisher, and date. Following the date, include a physical description of the materials if necessary. If appropriate, the citation ends with a series title in parentheses, a listing of accompanying materials, and an availability statement.

1. Rachel Carson's silent spring [videotape]. Boston: WGBH Ed Foundation; 1993. (American experience series).

2. Biological clocks [filmstrip]. Washington: Nat Geographic Soc; 1984. 2-color filmstrips. Accompanied by: 2 audiotapes. (Educational filmstrips series).

17e.9 An Electronic Source

Citations for electronic sources follow patterns similar to those of other sources: begin with the author's name (when known), followed by the title; then include the electronic source and its distributor. Information about accessibility should be included at the end of the citation, introduced by the word *Accessed* (not italicized) and the date. End the citation with the electronic address for retrieving the information, but do not follow it with a period.

An Online Book

To cite an online book, provide information parallel to that required for a traditional print source. Then add information that clarifies the way in which you accessed the electronic source. Notice that *World Wide Web* is spelled out and that a period does not follow the electronic address.

1. Limb C, Rodal A, Willis L. MIT biology hypertextbook. Cambridge (MA): MIT; 1998. Online. World Wide Web. Accessed 2002 Jan 23. http://esg-www.mit.edu.8001/esgbio/ 7001main.html

A Web Site

A citation for a Web site—or an article, chart, image, or other element from a Web site—includes (1) the author, editor, compiler, artist, or other person who created the material; (2) the name of the element, if appropriate; (3) the name of the Web site; (4) the institution, school, or corporation that sponsors or is affiliated with the site; and (5) information about electronic access.

CBE STYLE

2. Sulik KK, Bream PR, Poe T, Bindra K. Limb development. 26 images. Embryo im-
    ages: normal and abnormal mammalian development. Greenwood Genetic Center and
    University of North Carolina, Chapel Hill. Online. World Wide Web. Accessed 2003
    Feb 2. http://www.med.unc.edu/embryo_images/unit-mslimb/mslimb-htms

An Online Report

A citation for an online report includes (1) the author or group that produced the document; (2) the title of the document; and (3) information
about electronic access.

3. Centers for Disease Control. A public health action plan to combat antimicrobial resis-
    tance. Online. World Wide Web. Accessed 2003 Jan 20. http://www.eoenabled.com/
    bioresearchonline/out.asp?n=33563695&tid=2&r=33563687

An Article in an Online Journal

To cite an article in an online journal, include (1) the name of the author or
authors; (2) the title of the article; (3) the name of the journal, with appropriate information about date, volume, and number, as applicable; and
(4) information about electronic access.

4. Walters L (Kennedy Institute of Ethics, Georgetown University, Washington). Ethical
    issues in human gene therapy. Human genome news 1999 Feb;10(1). Online. World
    Wide Web. Accessed 2002 Dec 29. http://www.ornl.gov/hgmis/publicat/hgn/v10nl/
    16walter.html

Note that this citation also provides the author's affiliation for additional
clarity.

A CD-ROM Source

A citation for a CD-ROM source includes (1) the author or company, as appropriate; (2) the title of the source; (3) the city and publisher; (4) the word
CD-ROM, not italicized; and (5) the year of release.

5. Deaton ML, Winebrake JJ. Dynamic modeling of environmental systems. New York:
    Springer. CD-ROM; 2000.

6. Hartwell L. Genetics: from genes to genomes. Boston: McGraw. CD-ROM; 2000.

CBE STYLE

17f When appropriate, follow CBE guidelines to prepare your manuscript.

Writers in biological, physical, and mathematical sciences adhere to the following guidelines to ensure that manuscripts are prepared in a uniform fashion. Use these guidelines unless your instructor advises you to follow a different pattern.

Paper

Use white bond 8½″ × 11″ paper.

Printing Formats

Use a clear, easy-to-read, standard print font; script style is unacceptable. Do not attempt to create visual interest in a manuscript by using unusual fonts, enlarged font sizes, or all capital letters for titles or headings. Instead, present the entire manuscript in a conventional style, preferably using Courier or Times Roman.

Spacing

Double-space everything: text, quotations, footnotes, tabular material, and references. However, for clarity, triple- or quadruple-space before and after equations included within the text.

Margins

Leave one- to one-and-a-half-inch margins on the left, right, top, and bottom of each page. Reset the "default" margins on a computer if they are not sufficiently wide. Indent paragraphs five spaces. Indent long quotations either five or ten spaces; use the same indentation for all long quotations within a paper.

Paging

In the upper right corner of every page, within the standard margin, include a brief version of the paper's title, followed by the page number. When using a word processing program, set a header at the beginning of a document, making sure that it is flush with the right margin.

Title Page

Prepare a separate title page. The title should be either indicative (describing in a straightforward fashion the topic addressed in the paper) or informative (presenting the conclusion of the paper). Below the title, list your name in full. Below that, list your affiliation (your school or the title of your course).

CBE STYLE

Abstract

An abstract of approximately 250 words appears on a separate page following the title page. This brief, paragraph-length description of the paper includes as much of the following information as is appropriate: the goal of the study; the methodology used for the study; clear identification of organisms, drugs, and so on used as part of the study; definitions of key words; and the results of the study, succinctly stated.

Because of the length limits of abstracts, they should not include tabular material, details from the study, or references to other people's work.

The Text

The primary text begins on a new page and follows the abstract. Beneath the page header, list the title again or simply begin the paper.

Because CBE style is most often used for papers describing scientific experimentation, as well as traditional library research, the body of the paper is often presented in a fairly regularized five-element sequence.

The paper begins with an introductory section, frequently set off with the heading *Introduction* (not italicized). This opening section identifies the specific subject; presents the scientific, scholarly, or social context for the work; and articulates the hypothesis (thesis) or states the problem.

The paper continues with an extended, but not overly detailed, description of how the study was completed. Most often, such descriptions explain the design of the experiment; the subjects, materials, and procedures used; and techniques for evaluating the work. Anything out of the ordinary should be explained with care.

The third section of the paper describes the outcome of the study. It provides illustrative material—tables, graphs, illustrations—and comments briefly on comparative findings.

The fourth section, the discussion of results, includes interpretations of any findings. Has the work been sufficiently illuminating? Must further work be done? How do these findings compare with other research? What conclusions are logical? This section allows for interpretation and speculation.

The fifth section, literature cited, is a full bibliographic listing of sources used in the paper. As with all other documentary forms, it includes key information to help readers locate the sources used in the paper.

Headings for Sections

In the interest of clarity and readability, use headings to divide lengthy papers into sections and subsections. Well-worded, consistently placed headings guide readers through the manuscript, identifying the major divisions of the discussion and drawing attention to the most important subordinate elements. Headings of the same importance must be presented in consistent grammatical form—most often, simple phrases.

Level-1 headings are centered, with extra space (triple or quadruple) above and below. Level-2 headings are placed at the left margin, with text continuing on the next line. Level-3 headings begin a paragraph and are separated from the first sentence by only a period and a space.

Level-1 Heading

Level-2 Heading

    Level-3 Heading. The text continues on the same line.

All important words are capitalized in each kind of heading.

Tables, Graphs, Charts, Maps, and Illustrations

Visual material—tables, graphs, charts, maps, illustrations, formulas, and equations—should be presented as clearly and concisely as possible. Complex or large materials should be presented on separate pages, usually at the end of the paper, but smaller visual elements may be presented in the text, as close as possible to the appropriate discussion.

Order of the Manuscript

Although a paper may not contain all of these elements, arrange the sections in this order, with each new section beginning on a new page: (1) title page, (2) abstract, (3) the paper, (4) acknowledgments, (5) literature cited, (6) explanatory footnotes, (7) tables, and (8) descriptive titles for tables, charts, and graphs.

Submitting the Paper

Submit manuscripts according to your instructor's guidelines. If you receive no specific guidelines, secure the pages with a paper clip in the upper left corner and place them in a manila envelope with your name and identifying information about the paper typed or written on the outside. Always keep a photocopy—or another printed copy—of the paper before submitting it.

Be aware that instructors may ask for a disk copy of the paper. In that case, submit a copy of the final paper on a separate disk, clearly labeled with your name and course information, as well as a note about your word processing program (Microsoft Word 2000, Word Perfect 10). Keep a disk version for yourself.

Polio 1

Polio: The Great Crippler

Kristin Garfield

Biology 242

Polio 2

Abstract

Poliomyelitis, a virus that attacks the neural-muscular system, has plagued humans for thousands of years. First described by ancient Egyptians, the disease gained medical prominence in the twentieth century, as scientists identified the virus, developed vaccines, and launched immunization programs to eradicate the disease. Although efforts to eliminate the disease have proved increasingly successful, Post Polio Syndrome, which affects a high percentage of polio survivors, continues to pose new problems for the medical community.

The paging continues sequentially.

A descriptive title

An abstract of no more than 250 words describes the paper; it should include no technical information.

The paper begins on page 3.

Polio 3

The centered title has normal capitalization.

Polio: The Great Crippler

In the preface to *Polio and Its Problems*, published in 1948, Roland H. Berg observes that

Long quotations, double-spaced, are indented ten spaces.

> *polio is an uncontrolled disease*. Nothing that medical
> science can yet do can prevent one case or one epidemic
> from occurring; nor can health officials foretell where
> or when polio will make its next visitation (1, p ix).

Parenthetical notes identify the source number and, when necessary, the page.

Berg's ominous tone was sadly appropriate at a time when poliomyelitis crippled 20,000 people a year (2, p 42). In the years since, the disease has been, to a great extent, understood and controlled.

The research objective

However, an understanding of the disease is best achieved by reviewing its history and examining its lingering effects.

Headings divide the paper, with 4 spaces above and below.

The Identification of Polio

A historical summary establishes a context for the paper.

Although the earliest representations of polio-like symptoms appear in Egyptian murals, the first medical description of polio occurred in 1784 (1, p 8). However, it was not until 1908 that Karl Landsteiner, an Austrian physician, identified the small spherical virus, composed of protein and RNA, that produces polio (2, p 42). Even after the virus had been identified, medical responses to the disease were inexact and sometimes misleading. The American epidemic of 1916, for example, did not match the "poor sanitation" model that scientists

Brief quotations are incorporated within the paper.

believed at the time caused most diseases. As Alan R. Hinman notes: "the characteristics of epidemic polio in 1916 did not jibe with the dominant view of public health sanitation (since cases occurred in af-

Note how quotation marks are presented within quoted material.

fluent, educated, 'sanitary' households as well as in slums and among immigrants)" (3, p 793). Such confusion about the cause of the disease, along with the severity of the symptoms, made polio a difficult disease to treat.

Polio 4

The Nature of the Disease

The polio virus, in one of its three strains, enters the body
through ingestion or breathing and multiplies in the throat or intestines;
within ten days, if the infected individual does not produce sufficient
antibodies, the virus enters the central nervous system where it resides
(4, p 187). Ninety percent of infected individuals have mild cases, but
the other ten percent develop high fevers, have swelling of the mem-
branes surrounding the brain and spinal cord (meningitis), and experience extreme neck and back pain (5, p 32–33). One to two percent
(included in the ten percent with severe symptoms) develop paralysis,
from which many seem to recover (4, p 187).

*Physiological
conditions and
symptoms
ground the
discussion.*

Medical Treatments

In the early- and mid-twentieth century, victims of polio who
survived the initial stages of the disease were helped by a variety of
means: "iron lungs," wheelchairs, leg braces, canes, medication for pain,
and sometimes surgery. However, on April 12, 1955, Jonas Salk announced that his research efforts at the University of Pittsburgh (first
described in 1953) had been successful: an injectable vaccine could
protect individuals from polio (5, p 30). An oral polio vaccine—first developed by H. Koprowski, G. A. Jervis, and T. W. Norton in 1952—was
then introduced for mass distribution by Albert Sabin in 1956 (4, p 30).

*Treatments
illustrate the
history of the
disease.*

Efforts to Eradicate Polio

With vaccines available, health officials in the United States
began a serious campaign to eliminate polio, as they had smallpox.
Through massive immunization programs—many paid for with government monies—polio has been effectively eliminated in the United
States; the last recorded case of polio in the United States was in 1979
(6, p 1857). The efforts of the Pan-American Health Organization, a
sub-group of the World Health Organization (WHO), helped reduce the

*Information
that is
common
knowledge
does not
require
documentation.*

*Technical
information,
however,
requires
documentation.*

Polio 5

*Statistical
information
strengthens
the discussion.*

number of cases in the western hemisphere from 2,300 in 1977 to 489 in 1984 (7, p 363). The on-going efforts, with a total cost of $500 million, have made it possible to report the last case in the western hemisphere in 1991 (8, p 6, col 1). But the battle is not over. Although world-wide polio cases decreased by seventy percent between 1988 and 1993, 9,714 cases were still reported in 1993 (9, p A8, col 3).

Residual Effects

*Discussion of
manifestations
creates a
context for
this section of
the paper.*

Approximately 500,000 survivors of polio live in the United States (10, p 23), including 132,000 who survived the 1952–1954 epidemic (11, p 23). Decades after they suffered from the disease—and after many were able to resume full lives—roughly twenty-five percent experience recurrent, polio-like symptoms (12, p 1397). Described as Post-Polio Syndrome (PPS), this range of problems includes loss of muscle strength, severe joint pain, difficulty in breathing, and extreme fatigue (11, p 23).

The cause of PPS is still under investigation. Many scientists feared that the virus had inexplicably reactivated after being dormant for so long, but studies to isolate poliovirus antibodies in victims' spinal fluids have produced negative results (5, 10–11, 13). Most scientists

*General
references to
multiple
sources
require only
the citation
numbers.*

believe that these problems are the result of survivors' overuse of other muscles to compensate for muscles damaged by initial bouts of polio (5, 10–14). As Neil Cashman, Director of the Postpolio Clinic of the University of Chicago, explains, "The musculoskeletal syndrome of postpolio patients is just the long-term effect of working in an unusual fashion. Tendons, muscles, and joints become more painful due to chronic strain" (12, p 1398).

In addition to musculoskeletal problems, PPS sufferers experience a range of new symptoms, including pulmonary dysfunction, sleep disorders, dysphagia, cold intolerance, degenerative arthritis, and social and psychological problems (15). Medical staff have become increasingly aware that they must address the psychological problems

Polio 6

that occur because of recurrent symptoms (11). As Richard Bruno, chairperson of the International Post-Polio Task Force, observes:

> The most difficult aspect of treating PPS is not decid-
> ing whether a short- or long-leg brace will be most
> helpful. The challenge is helping polio survivors face
> the pain of their abusive pasts and accept appearing
> more disabled now—by slowing down, asking for
> help, and using new adaptive equipment—so they
> won't become more disabled later in life (16).

These are, surely, great challenges for both polio survivors and medical professionals.

Conclusion

Our understanding of polio enables us to control its spread, although until it is eradicated worldwide, the threat will continue. Yet medical men and women around the globe must continue their efforts to bring under control the disease that has killed or disabled more than ten million people throughout history (8, p 6, col 4).

A brief summary closes the discussion.

Literature Cited

1. Berg RH. Polio and its problems. Philadelphia: Lippincott; 1948. 174 p.

2. Hogle JM, Chow M, Filman DJ. The structure of poliovirus. Sci Am 1987 Mar;256(3):42–9.

3. Hinman AR. Review of: Dirt and disease: polio before FDR. J Am Med Assoc 1994 Mar;271:792–3.

4. Stratton KR, Howe CJ, Johnston RB, editors. Adverse events associated with childhood vaccines: evidence bearing on causality. Washington (DC): Nat Acad Pr; 1994. 464 p.

5. Dalakas MC, Bartfeld H, Kurland LT. Polio redux. Sciences 1995 Jul/Aug;35(4):30–5.

6. Robbins FC. Eradication of polio in the Americas. J Am Med Assoc 1993 Oct;270:1857–8.

7. Beardsley T. Polio eradication. Nature 1985 May;315(5):363.

8. [Anonymous]. Polio is reported conquered in the Americas. NY Times 1994 Oct 2:6(col 1).

9. Rochell A. WHO nears goal of eliminating polio from earth. Atlanta Constitution 1994 Jul 15;Sect A:8(col 3).

10. [Anonymous]. Polio throws up a second phase. New Sci 1986 Jun;110(6):23.

11. Backman ME. The post-polio patient: psychological issues. J Rehabilitation 1987 Oct/Dec;53(4):23–6.

12. Raymond CA. Decades after polio epidemic, survivors report new symptoms. J Am Med Assoc 1986 Mar;255:1397–1404.

13. Sharief MK, Hentges R, Ciardi M. Intrathecal immune response in patients with post-polio syndrome. N Eng J Med 1991 Sep;325:749–55.

14. Stone R. Post-polio syndrome: remembrance of viruses past. Science 1994 May;264:909.

15. Anderson W. An approach to the patient with suspected post polio syndrome. Polio Survivors' Guide. Polio Outreach Advisory Council, Washington. Online. World Wide Web. Accessed 2001 Jan 14. http://www.eskimo.com/~dempt/ppspamph.htm

Polio 8

Subsequent pages do not require a heading.

16. Bruno RL (Post-Polio Institute, Englewood Hospital and Medical Center, Englewood, New Jersey). Post-polio research: the state of the art, 1998. New Mobility. Online. World Wide Web. Accessed 2001 Feb 1. http://newmobility.com/review_article.cfm?id=93&action=browse

Note: Source numbers align with the left margin. Descriptive material appears after a space, with subsequent lines under the author's name.

A

Document Design and Manuscript Preparation

Although research papers in MLA, APA, Chicago, and CBE styles have distinct requirements (for headings, set-in quotations, and so on), they may also benefit from additional document design. Consequently, you should take advantage of the full range of features that current word processing programs provide so that your final paper is presented in the most effective way.

Before devoting time to document design for a research paper, decide what degree of design is necessary or appropriate for achieving your goals. Consider these questions:

- Does convention dictate the document's design? If so, have you followed guidelines carefully?
- Will design elements enhance or detract from the document's purpose?
- Will the time spent on document design create proportional benefits?
- Are design elements matched to the expectations of prospective readers?
- Do you have the expertise to use specific design features? If not, do you have time to learn?

Basic Printing Features

Today's word processing programs provide a tremendous range of basic features—those available from the toolbar—that can be manipulated to create effective documents. These features, if used selectively, can enhance the readability of all types of documents, including the research paper.

Margins and White Space

Each documenation style (MLA, APA, Chicago, and CBE) establishes a minimum margin width, usually from one to one and one-half inches; however, you can widen margins slightly to position text on the page more attractively. Be advised, however, that too much white space makes a document look "airy."

Line Spacing and Readability

Research papers in all disciplines use double spacing, but in preparing supporting materials, explore line-spacing options. Remember, however, that lines typed with less than single spacing are generally too cramped (and elements of letters sometimes touch) and that anything greater than triple spacing appears too open.

Justification

Justification, adjusting the spacing between words and letters in a typed or printed line, detemines the appearance of a document's right and left text edges. Left justification (preferred for most academic writing) creates a straight vertical line on the left side and leaves the right edge irregular or "ragged." Full justification (used in printed texts or documents designed to look like printed texts) creates straight text edges on both the left and the right.

Justification Patterns

Left justification is the standard pattern for academic papers. It creates a ragged right edge because it maintains equal spacing between words.

Full justification creates straight text edges on both sides of the page. Used to create the look of printed documents, full justification uses unequal spacing between words to achieve its effect.

The visual appeal of different justification patterns depends in part on the font size you use. Small fonts produce enough characters per line (words, numbers) that the adjusted spacing for full justification looks good; however, with large fonts, the unequal spacing between words can be visually distracting.

For academic papers (essays and research papers), generally use left justification.

Font Selection

Fonts (different designed versions of letters, numbers, and symbols) allow you to create different "looks" for your manuscripts. Fonts with serifs (small cross marks on letters) like Times New Roman replicate the look of traditional printed materials, while sans-serif fonts (those without cross marks) like Arial create the look of technical materials.

For most academic writing (essays and research papers), select an attractive font that is not too unusual. As a general rule, do not mix fonts within an academic paper.

Representative Fonts	
Serif	Sans Serif
Arrus BT	Abadi MT
New Baskerville	Arial
Book Antiqua	Century Gothic
Palatino	Eurostile
Times New Roman	Lucinda Sans

Font Size

Fonts are measured in points, ranging from extremely small (4 points) to extremely large (70 points or larger). For most academic writing, select a 10- to 14-point font, with the understanding that 12 point is the most commonly used size.

Boldface

Boldface—sometimes referred to simply as *bold*—is an enhanced version of a font, with thicker and darker letters. It can be used effectively to create visual emphasis for headings and labels. In academic writing, boldface should be used very selectively.

Italics

In research papers, use italics in conventional ways: to indicate the titles of full-length works, to identify foreign words and phrases, and so on. In instances when the italicized version of a font is not sufficiently distinct, use underlining instead; it has the same meaning, even though its look is different.

Underlining

Used for the same purposes as italics, underlining (also called underscoring) places a line beneath a letter, number, word, phrase, or title. It can appear in either of two forms: continuous underline (a solid line under all words and the spaces between them) or broken underline (under only each separate word). Since underlining uses the base font, it works particularly well with fonts whose italics are not very distinct.

Bullets

Bullets are visual elements used to draw attention to listed items that are not numbered (because numbers establish an order of importance). Bullets are generally filled circles of different sizes (from small to large), but they can have other shapes, including triangles, diamonds, and squares.

Styles of Bullets

- The most conventional style is the small filled circle. It provides emphasis without seeming intrusive.

- For stronger visual emphasis, use a large filled circle. It will stand out more.

▼ A triangle is a typical alternative. Like the small circle, it is not intrusive.

■ A large filled square is another alternative. It creates a bold, simple look.

Horizontal and Vertical Lines

Using the graphics features of most word processing programs, you can insert a horizontal or vertical line to divide text. Lines create visual separation of elements within your document and, if used selectively, can create simple visual interest.

Lines created using the graphics feature (as opposed to those produced by a series of individual underlines from the keypad) extend automatically between margins and adjust if you change margins or fonts at a later time. Further, you can choose from a wide range of line styles: single, double, thin, thick, and so on.

Visual Elements

Beyond the print-related features of document design are elements that can add visual interest and create clarity: headings, textboxes, tables, charts, and illustrations. In addition to providing useful information, these elements enhance the look of documents and provide visual breaks in otherwise uninterrupted text. However, the visual elements must relate to, illustrate, clarify, or in some way enhance the document, or they will seem extraneous.

When needed for clarity, provide a label, number, and brief description of visual elements like tables, charts, and illustrations. MLA style requires that the word *Table* (not italicized), the table number, and a descriptive title appear above the table, flush with the left margin. For other visual elements—graphs, charts, or illustrations—the abbreviation *Fig.* (short for *figure,* not italicized), a number, and a descriptive title or caption are placed below the element. Unless a visual element is of your design and contains your own information, acknowledge your source. Below the element, use the word *Source* (not italicized), a colon, and a complete citation.

Experiment with the use of visual elements: expand or reduce their size, position them in different ways, and create alternative versions. Preview materials as you work, either by printing individual pages or by using the "View," "Zoom," or "Print Preview" option on the toolbar.

Headings

A brief document generally does not need headings. Long documents are made more readable by breaking the text into divisions with headings, appropriately worded and positioned. A heading—a brief description of the text that follows—can be presented as a word (Design), phrase (Document Design), or brief sentence (Design Documents with Care.). When a text is complex, sections may be further subdivided by using subheadings; in such instances, follow these general guidelines: A-level headings are generally centered; B-level headings are frequently flush left; C-level headings are positioned at the start of a paragraph, followed by a period, and placed in italics.

Headings: Positioning Three Levels (MLA Style)

This Is an A-Level Heading

The paragraph continues following a line space; the space can be increased for additional visual emphasis.

This is a B-Level Heading

The paragraph continues following a line space; the space can be increased for additional visual emphasis

　　This is a C-Level Heading. The paragraph continues on the same line.

Other documentation styles (APA, Chicago, CBE, and others) have very specific guidelines for the preparation of headings. If you use one of those styles, follow guidelines carefully.

Textboxes

A textbox is what its name suggests: a box that contains text of some kind. A textbox is often used to emphasize a selected quotation or other material.

Most word processing programs have toolbar features for creating a textbox, with a pleasing array of options so that you can create the visual effects that you want. The textbox below provides a listing of some typical options.

Textbox Options	
Captions:	You can position captions automatically.
Content:	You can create the content within the text-box, or you can copy it from another file.
Position:	You can position the textbox on the page, or you can position the textbox within a paragraph.
Border Style:	You can select the style for the border: single, double, thick, shadowed, and so on.
Fill Style:	You can shade the interior of the box if you wish or select special-effects back-grounds.

Tables

To present information (numerical comparisons, statistics, and so on) for easy interpretation, consider incorporating a table in your document. Because a table organizes information within a grid, it is especially helpful when information needs to be correlated in a number of ways.

Word processing programs now provide easy-to-use drop-down menus for creating tables, allowing you to select the numbers of columns (the vertical separations) and rows (the horizontal separations) that form the table. Further, you can select the look of the table from a wide range of options: single line, double line, no line, and others.

Before creating a table, make a quick sketch so that you can determine the number of necessary elements. You can, of course, add or delete columns or rows at a later stage, but the process is easier if you plan before developing the table.

Table 1

Population Change in Four Midwestern States: 2000–2001

Population Change in Four Midwestern States: 2000–2001					
State	Births	Deaths	International Migration	Domestic Migration	Population Change
Illinois	231,194	134,303	75,160	−100,286	63,008
Indiana	107,126	69,179	9,344	−12,522	34,260
Kansas	48,712	31,045	7,927	−19,306	6,223
Missouri	94,677	68,762	8,151	887	34,496

Source: United States. Bureau of the Census <http://eire.census.gov/popest/data/state/
populartables/table02.php>.

Charts and Graphs

When a visual representation of comparative information communicates
more effectively than the use of numbers, prepare a chart or graph. A pie
chart divides a circle (the "pie") into "slices" that represent proportional
divisions: 25% shows as a quarter of the pie, 50% as one-half. A bar chart
uses vertical columns of varying widths to represent each element, in a
sense showing how elements "stack up" against each other. You can also
create an area chart to show volume. A graph—the most common is the
line graph—shows the degree of change in an element, so a graph is ideal
for showing increases and decreases over time.

Most word processing programs have chart- and graphmaking features, although they are considerably more complicated to use than features for making tables or textboxes. However, when proportions are
dramatically different, charts and graphs are more helpful than number-
focused information alone.

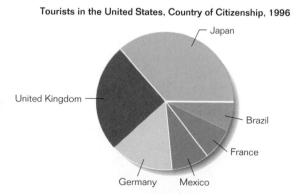

Tourists in the United States, Country of Citizenship, 1996

Fig. 1. Tourists in the United States, 1996: Country of Citizenship
Source: United States. Immigration and Naturalization Service. Department of Justice
<http://www.ins.usdoj.gov/graphics/aboutins/statistics/299.htm>.

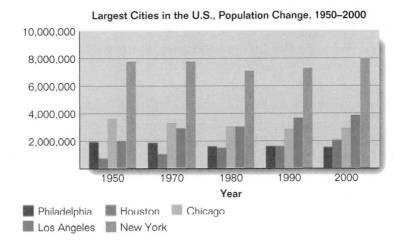

Fig. 2. Largest Cities in the U.S.: Population Change, 1950–2000
Source: United States. Bureau of the Census <http://eire.census.gov/popest/data/state/populartables>.

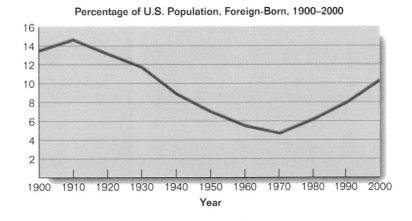

Fig. 3: Percentage of U.S. Population: Foreign-Born, 1900–2000
Source: United States. Bureau of the Census <http://eire.census.gov/popest/data/populartables>.

Illustrations

In many writing contexts, illustrations can enhance the effectiveness of a document. When possible, include illustrations within the text, instead of appending them at the end of the document.

Special Illustrations

Illustrations can be scanned into the document, imported from other files, or downloaded from the Internet. It is important to provide full attribution for the source of the illustration, position the illustration as close as possible to the discussion it supports, and refer to the illustration as appropriate.

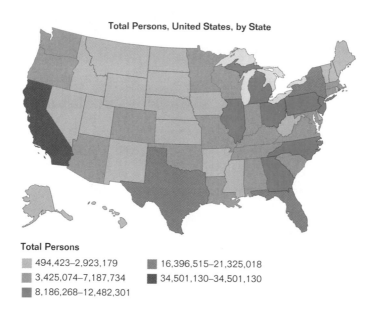

Fig. 4. U.S. Population Distribution: 2001
Source: United States. Bureau of the Census <http://factfinder.census.gov/home/en/pep.html>.

Paper

For research papers, use white, medium-weight, 8½-by-11-inch paper; avoid unusual paper such as onionskin or colored paper.

Designing documents is an interesting and sometimes challenging process, but it is worth the effort. The printing and visual options that are available can strengthen the presentation of your ideas.

1/2" Fairbanks 1

1"

Nakia Fairbanks

1" Dr. P. Slagle

English 236

10 September 2003

Title of the Paper

1"

1"

1/2" Fairbanks 2

1"

1"

MLA Manuscript Guidelines

Writers in language-related disciplines should follow these guidelines, based on the principles adopted by the Modern Language Association, for preparing and presenting manuscripts. If a paper or project poses special challenges, or if you are required to follow other style guidelines, consult with your instructor.

Paper. Use white, medium-weight, 8½"-by-11" paper. Avoid unusual paper.

Printing Formats. Use the best printer available. Laser or inkjet printers produce the highest-quality printing, but dot-matrix printers are acceptable if set in the correspondence-quality (double-strike) mode.

Use a nondecorative, 10–14 point font, justify only the left margin, and use either italics or underlining consistently.

Spacing. Double-space everything: the heading, the title (if it requires more than one line), the text, set-in quotations, notes, the works-cited page, and any appended material.

Margins and Indentations. Leave one-inch margins on the left, right, and bottom of the main text; paging (which appears at the top) determines the top margin.

Indent paragraphs one-half inch (five spaces) using the "Tab" feature. Also indent second and subsequent lines of works-cited entries one-half inch. Indent set-in quotations one inch (ten spaces) using the "Indent" feature.

Paging. In the upper right corner of each page, one-half inch from the top, type your last name, a space, and the page number (without a page abbreviation). Two spaces below, the text of the paper begins. For convenience and consistency, set these options using the "Header" feature of your word processing program.

Heading and Title. A paper in MLA style has no separate title page. Instead, in the upper left corner of the first page, two spaces below the header, type on separate lines (1) your name, (2) your instructor's name, (3) the course name and number, and (4) the date.

Two lines below the date, center the paper's title. Capitalize all important words but do not use italics, boldface, or quotation marks for special effect. Two lines below the title, begin the paper.

Visual Elements. Incorporate a visual element—textbox, table, chart, illustration—within the text, as close as possible to the discussion it supports; cite the source when appropriate.

Abbreviations and Shortened Forms of Publishers' Names

Modern Language Association (MLA)

Time

AD	*anno Domini*, "in the year of the Lord"
a.m.	*ante meridiem*, "before noon"
BC	"before Christ"
BCE	before common era
CE	common era
cent., cents.	century, centuries
hr., hrs.	hour, hours
min., mins.	minute, minutes
mo., mos.	month, months
p.m.	*post meridiem*, "after noon"
sec., secs.	second, seconds
wk., wks.	week, weeks
yr., yrs.	year, years

Months

Jan.	January	July	July
Feb.	February	Aug.	August
Mar.	March	Sept.	September
Apr.	April	Oct.	October
May	May	Nov.	November
June	June	Dec.	December

Days

Mon.	Monday	Fri.	Friday
Tues.	Tuesday	Sat.	Saturday
Wed.	Wednesday	Sun.	Sunday
Thurs.	Thursday		

States and Territories

AK	Alaska	MT	Montana
AL	Alabama	NC	North Carolina
AR	Arkansas	ND	North Dakota
AS	American Samoa	NE	Nebraska
AZ	Arizona	NH	New Hampshire
CA	California	NJ	New Jersey
CO	Colorado	NM	New Mexico
CT	Connecticut	NV	Nevada
DE	Delaware	NY	New York
DC	District of Columbia	OH	Ohio
FL	Florida	OK	Oklahoma
GA	Georgia	OR	Oregon
GU	Guam	PA	Pennsylvania
HI	Hawaii	PR	Puerto Rico
IA	Iowa	RI	Rhode Island
ID	Idaho	SC	South Carolina
IL	Illinois	SD	South Dakota
IN	Indiana	TN	Tennessee
KS	Kansas	TX	Texas
KY	Kentucky	UT	Utah
LA	Louisiana	VA	Virginia
MA	Massachusetts	VI	Virgin Islands
MD	Maryland	VT	Vermont
ME	Maine	WA	Washington
MI	Michigan	WI	Wisconsin
MN	Minnesota	WV	West Virginia
MO	Missouri	WY	Wyoming
MS	Mississippi		

Geographical Names

AB	Alberta	Fr.	France
Afr.	Africa	Ger.	Germany
Alb.	Albania	Gr.	Greece
Ant.	Antarctica	Gt. Brit.	Great Britain
Arg.	Argentina	Hung.	Hungary
Arm.	Armenia	Ire.	Ireland
Aus.	Austria	Isr.	Israel
Austral.	Australia	It.	Italy
BC	British Columbia	Jap.	Japan
Belg.	Belgium	LB	Labrador
Braz.	Brazil	Leb.	Lebanon
Bulg.	Bulgaria	MB	Manitoba
Can.	Canada	Mex.	Mexico
Den.	Denmark	NB	New Brunswick
Ecua.	Ecuador	Neth.	Netherlands
Eng.	England	NF	Newfoundland
Eur.	Europe	No. Amer.	North America

Norw.	Norway	SK	Saskatchewan
NS	Nova Scotia	So. Amer.	South America
NT	Northwest Territories	Sp.	Spain
NZ	New Zealand	Swed.	Sweden
ON	Ontario	Switz.	Switzerland
Pan.	Panama	Turk.	Turkey
PE	Prince Edward Island	UK	United Kingdom
Pol.	Poland	US, USA	United States, United
Port.	Portugal		States of America
PQ	Province de Québec	USSR	Union of Soviet Socialist
PRC	People's Republic of China		Republics
Russ.	Russia	YT	Yukon Territory
Scot.	Scotland		

General Abbreviations and Reference Words

abbr.	abbreviation, abbreviated
abr.	abridged, abridgment
acad.	academy
adapt.	adapted by, adaption
app.	appendix
arch.	archaic
art.	article
assn.	association
assoc.	associated, associate
attrib.	attributed to
aux.	auxiliary
b.	born
BA	Bachelor of Arts
bib.	biblical
bibliog.	bibliography, bibliographer, bibliographic
biog.	biography, biographer, biographical
bk.	book
BM	British Museum, London (now British Library)
BS	Bachelor of Science
bull.	bulletin
©	copyright
c. (ca.)	*circa,* "about" (used with approximate dates: c. 1500)
cf.	*confer,* "compare"
ch., chs.	
(chap., chaps.)	chapter, chapters
chor.	choreographed by, choreographer
col.	column
coll.	college
colloq.	colloquial
comp.	compiled by, compiler
cond.	conducted by, conductor
Cong.	Congress
Cong. Rec.	*Congressional Record*

Const.	Constitution
cont.	contents; continued
(contd.)	continued
d.	died
DA	Doctor of Arts
DA, DAI	*Dissertation Abstracts, Dissertation Abstracts International*
DAB	*Dictionary of American Biography*
dept.	department
dev.	developed by, developer, development
dir.	directed by, director
diss.	dissertation
dist.	district
distr.	distributed by, distributor
div.	division
DNB	*Dictionary of National Biography*
doc.	document
ed.	edited by, editor, edition
EdD	Doctor of Education
eds.	editors, editions
educ.	education, educational
e.g.	*exempli gratia,* "for example"
et al.	*et alii, et aliae,* "and others"
etc.	*et cetera,* "and so forth"
fig.	figure
front.	frontispiece
fwd.	foreword, foreword by
govt.	government
GPO	Government Printing Office, Washington, DC
H. Doc.	House Document
hist.	history, historian, historical
HMSO	Her (His) Majesty's Stationery Office
HR	House of Representatives
H. Rept.	House [of Representatives] Report
H. Res.	House [of Representatives] Resolution
i.e.	*id est,* "that is"
illus.	illustrated by, illustrator, illustration
inc.	incorporated; including
inst.	institute, institution
intl.	international
introd.	introduced by, author of introduction, introduction
irreg.	irregular
JD	*Juris Doctor,* Doctor of Law
jour.	journal
l., ll.	line, lines
lang.	language
LC	Library of Congress
leg.	legal
legis.	legislation, legislative, legislature, legislator
lit.	literally, literary, literature

LLB	*Legum Baccalaureus,* Bachelor of Law
LLD	*Legum Doctor,* Doctor of Law
ltd.	limited
MA	Master of Arts
mag.	magazine
MD	*Medicinae Doctor,* Doctor of Medicine
misc.	miscellaneous
MS	Master of Science
ms., mss.	manuscript, manuscripts
n, nn	note, notes
narr.	narrated by, narrator
natl.	national
n.d.	no date of publication
NED	*New English Dictionary*
no.	number
nonstand.	nonstandard
n.p.	no place of publication
n. pag.	no pagination
ns	new series
numb.	numbered (as is a series)
obs.	obsolete
OED	*Oxford English Dictionary*
op.	opus (work)
orch.	orchestra, orchestrated by
orig.	original, originally
os	old series; original series
P	Press, when used citing university presses
p., pp.	pages, pages (required only for clarification)
par.	paragraph
perf.	performed by, performer
PhD	*Philosophiae Doctor,* Doctor of Philosophy
philol.	philological
philos.	philosophical
pl.	plate; plural
pref.	preface, preface by
proc.	proceedings
prod.	produced by, producer
PS	postscript
pseud.	pseudonym
pt.	part
pub., publ.	published by, publisher, publication
qtd.	quoted
r.	reigned
rec.	recorded, record
reg.	registered; regular
rept.	reported by, report
res.	resolution
resp.	respectively

rev.	revised by, revision; review, reviewed by (write *review,* in full, when confusion seems likely)
rpm	revolutions per minutes (with recordings)
rpt.	reprinted by, reprint
S	Senate
sc.	scene
S. Doc.	Senate Document
sec. (sect.)	section
ser.	series
sess.	session
sic	"thus so" (used in brackets to identify an error in the original)
sing.	singular
soc.	society
S. Rept.	Senate Report
S. Res.	Senate Resolution
st.	stanza
St., Sts.	Saint, Saints
substand.	substandard
supp.	supplement
syn.	synonym
trans. (tr.)	translated by, translator, translation
ts., tss.	typescript, typescripts
U	University, when used citing university presses
UP	University Press
usu.	usually
var.	variant
vers.	version
vol., vols.	volume, volumes
vs. (v.)	versus, "against"; *v.* preferred in legal titles
writ.	written by, writer

Shortened Forms of Publishers' Names

Abrams	Harry N. Abrams, Inc.
Acad. for Ed. Dev.	Academy for Educational Development, Inc.
ALA	American Library Association
Allen	George Allen and Unwin Publishers, Inc.
Allyn	Allyn and Bacon, Inc.
Appleton	Appleton-Century-Crofts
Ballantine	Ballantine Books, Inc.
Bantam	Bantam Books, Inc.
Barnes	Barnes and Noble Books
Basic	Basic Books
Beacon	Beacon Press
Benn	Ernest Benn, Ltd.
Bobbs	Bobbs-Merrill Company
Bowker	R. R. Bowker Co.
CAL	Center for Applied Linguistics
Clarendon	Clarendon Press

Dell	Dell Publishing Co., Inc.
Dodd	Dodd, Mead, and Co.
Doubleday	Doubleday and Co., Inc.
Dover	Dover Publications, Inc.
Dutton	E. P. Dutton, Inc.
Einaudi	Giulio Einaudi Editore
Farrar	Farrar, Straus, and Giroux, Inc.
Feminist	The Feminist Press at the City University of New York
Free	The Free Press
Funk	Funk and Wagnalls, Inc.
Gale	Gale Research, Inc.
Gerig	Gerig Verlag
GPO	Government Printing Office
Harcourt	Harcourt Brace and Company
Harper	HarperCollins Publishers, Inc.
Harvard Law Rev. Assn.	Harvard Law Review Association
Heath	D. C. Heath and Co.
HMSO	Her (His) Majesty's Stationery Office
Holt	Holt, Rinehart, and Winston, Inc.
Houghton	Houghton Mifflin Company
Humanities	Humanities Press International, Inc.
Knopf	Alfred A. Knopf, Inc.
Larousse	Librairie Larousse
Lippincott	J. B. Lippincott Co.
Little	Little, Brown, and Co.
Macmillan	Macmillan Publishing Co., Inc.
McGraw	McGraw-Hill Book Co.
MLA	The Modern Language Association of America
NAL	The New American Library, Inc.
NCTE	The National Council of Teachers of English
NEA	The National Education Association
New York Graphic Soc.	New York Graphic Society
Norton	W. W. Norton and Co., Inc.
Penguin	Penguin Books
Pocket	Pocket Books
Popular	The Popular Press
Prentice	Prentice-Hall, Inc.
PUF	Presses universitaires de France
Putnam's	G. P. Putnam's Sons
Rand	Rand McNally and Co.
Random	Random House, Inc.
Rizzoli	Rizzoli Editore
St. Martin's	St. Martin's Press, Inc.
Scott	Scott, Foresman, and Co.
Scribner's	Charles Scribner's Sons
Simon	Simon and Schuster, Inc.
UMI	University Microfilms International
Viking	The Viking Press, Inc.

University Presses maintain all distinguishing words but use the abbreviations *U* and *P*, without periods. When the abbreviations appear together, no space separates them. The following samples represent the shortened forms: Harvard UP, UP of Kansas, U of Chicago P.

University of Chicago (Chicago)
States and Territories

Ala.	Alabama	Mo.	Missouri
Alaska	Alaska	Mont.	Montana
Amer.Samoa	American Samoa	Nebr.	Nebraska
Ariz.	Arizona	Nev.	Nevada
Ark.	Arkansas	N.H.	New Hampshire
Calif.	California	N.J.	New Jersey
C.Z.	Canal Zone	N.Mex.	New Mexico
Colo.	Colorado	N.Y.	New York
Conn.	Connecticut	N.C.	North Carolina
Del.	Delaware	N.Dak.	North Dakota
D.C.	District of Columbia	Ohio	Ohio
Fla.	Florida	Okla.	Oklahoma
Ga.	Georgia	Oreg. (Ore.)	Oregon
Guam	Guam	Pa.	Pennsylvania
Hawaii	Hawaii	P.R.	Puerto Rico
Idaho	Idaho	R.I.	Rhode Island
Ill.	Illinois	S.C.	South Carolina
Ind.	Indiana	S.Dak.	South Dakota
Iowa	Iowa	Tenn.	Tennessee
Kans.	Kansas	Tex.	Texas
Ky.	Kentucky	Utah	Utah
La.	Louisiana	Vt.	Vermont
Maine	Maine	Va.	Virginia
Md.	Maryland	V.I.	Virgin Islands
Mass.	Massachusetts	Wash.	Washington
Mich.	Michigan	W.Va.	West Virginia
Minn.	Minnesota	Wis. (Wisc.)	Wisconsin
Miss.	Mississippi	Wyo.	Wyoming

Council of Biology Editors (CBE)
Words Frequently Used in Journal Titles

Abstr	Abstracts	Arch	Archives
Acad	Academy	Assoc	Association
Adv	Advances	Biochem	Biochemistry
Agric	Agricultural, Agriculture	Bot	Botanical, Botany
Am	American	Bull	Bulletin
Ann	Annals	Bur	Bureau
Annu	Annual	Chem	Chemistry

Coll	College	Monogr	Monographs
Commun	Communication	Mus	Museum
Curr	Current	Nat	National
Dev	Development	Nat	Natural
Entomol	Entomology	Newsl	Newsletter
Environ	Environment,	Nucl	Nuclear
	Environmental	Org	Organic
Eur	European	Organ	Organization
Genet	Genetics	Palaeontol	Paleontology
Geol	Geological, Geology	Phy	Physics
Immunol	Immunology	Proc	Proceedings
Inst	Institute, Institution	Psychol	Psychology
Int	International	Publ	Publications
J	Journal	Rev	Review
Lab	Laboratory	Sci	Science
Mar	Marine	Soc Sci	Social Science
Math	Mathematical,	Soc	Society
	Mathematics	Stud	Studies
Mem	Memoirs	Symp	Symposium
Meteorol	Meteorology	Univ	University
Microbiol	Microbiology	Zool	Zoological, Zoology

Shortened Forms of Publishers' Names

AA Balkama	A. A. Balkama
Addison-Wesley	Addison-Wesley Publishing Company
American Inst of Physics	American Institute of Physics
American Mathematical Soc	American Mathematical Society
Analytic Pr	The Analytic Press, Inc.
Atheneum	Atheneum Publishers
Blackwell Scientific	Blackwell Scientific Publications, Inc.
Cambridge Univ Pr	Cambridge University Press
CRC Pr	CRC Press, Inc.
DR Godine	David R. Godine, Publisher
Dover	Dover Publications, Inc.
Elsevier Science	Elsevier Science Publishing Co., Inc.
Futura	Futura Publishing Co., Inc.
Galileo	The Galileo Press
Geological Soc of America	Geological Society of America
Graphics Pr	Graphics Press
Harper & Row	Harper & Row, Publishers, Inc.
Harvard Univ Pr	Harvard University Press
Henry Holt	Henry Holt & Co., Inc.
J Wiley	John Wiley & Sons
Keynes	The Keynes Press
Longman	Longman Group
Macmillan	Macmillan Publishing Co., Inc.
McGraw-Hill	McGraw-Hill, Inc.

Merck	Merck & Co., Inc.
NY Acad of Sciences	New York Academy of Sciences
Sage	Sage Publications, Inc.
Shoe String	The Shoe String Press, Inc.
Smithsonian Inst Pr	Smithsonian Institution Press
Van Nostrand Reinhold	Van Nostrand Reinhold Company

Glossary of Computer Terms

ASCII (American Standard Code for Information Interchange) An unformatted, universally readable version of a document.

Bit (Binary Digit) The smallest unit of computer data, represented in 0s or 1s.

Bookmark An electronic selection or listing of a URL so that it can be automatically recalled at a later time.

Boolean Search A process that allows for combinations of search terms using *and*, *or*, or *not*.

Browser A software system that allows users to gain access to the Internet. Examples: Microsoft Internet Explorer and Netscape Navigator.

Bug A recurring problem caused by an error in computer code or logic.

Byte (Binary Term) A combination of 8 (but up to 10) bits of data that represent a letter, number, or punctuation mark.

CD-ROM (Compact Disc—Read-Only Memory) A compact disc that stores encoded files to be read (but not added to or modified) using laser optics.

Chip An integrated circuit produced on a small piece of silicon.

CPU (Central Processing Unit) The central system of a computer that controls its functions.

Database A file containing data records that can be configured and interpreted in a variety of ways.

Desktop Publishing The use of computer software that combines text and graphics (usually printed on laser printers) to reproduce the look of typeset materials.

Disk A magnetized round plastic (floppy) or metal (hard) devise that stores digital information in the form of files.

Domain Words or abbreviations that, as part of an Internet address, describe the kind of source. Examples: *.com* for a "commercial" site, *.edu* for an "educational" site, or *.gov* for a "government" site.

DOS (Disk Operating System) A disk-based system that controls a computer's functions.

Download To copy a file from a remote computer or site through a modem or on the Internet.

Drop-Down Menu A list of preset options from which to select a function or feature. Example: After clicking on *font* (or on the icon), a list of available fonts appears.

E-mail (Electronic Mail) Electronic correspondence and materials sent on the Internet.

Encryption Encoding information so that unauthorized users cannot gain access to it.

FAQ (Frequently Asked Questions) A document providing answers to often-asked questions about a topic or Internet site.

File A document that contains stored information. Examples: A computer program, a graphic element, or a personally created document.

Flame An insulting or derogatory message, often on listservs or newsgroups.

Free-Text Field A window, within a program or database, that allows users to insert their own terms and information before initiating a search.

FTP (File Transfer Protocol) A method for transferring files on the Internet.

Gigabyte (GB) Equal to 1,024 megabytes. (*See* Megabytes.)

Graphic User Interface (GUI) A graphically oriented operating system that uses icons and menus that users select with a clickable mouse. Example: Microsoft Windows.

Hard copy A printed copy of a document or file.

Hardware The mechanical equipment of a computer system. Examples: computer, monitor, disk drive, printer, modem, scanner.

Home Page The initial page (or link) to a site on the Internet, providing additional links to material within the site, as well as possible links to other sites.

HTML (Hypertext Markup Language) A coding language that incorporates directions that allow movements between elements of Internet sites.

HTTP (Hypertext Transport Protocol) The primary protocol that allows users to connect with Web sites on the Internet.

Hypertext A complex system (using nonsequential connections) for creating links among elements (pages, features within pages, images, videos, other sites, and so on) on the Internet.

Icon A small, symbolic image used in GUIs to represent a function or feature. Example: A magnifying glass to represent the "enlarge image" function.

Internet A complex, high-speed network of computers that allows users to send and collect electronic information (in its many forms) around the world.

JPEG (Joint Photographic Experts Group) A file format for encoding graphics, usually on the Internet.

Keyword Search A process (using a search engine) for locating information using key words.

Kilobytes (K) Equal to 1,024 bytes.

Link A connection among elements of a site and among different sites.

Megabyte (MB) Equal to 1,048,576 bytes.

Menu A list of options from which to choose a function, select a format, or designate a file.

Modem (Modulator-Demodulator) A device that allows computers to send and receive electronic information over telephone lines.

Network A connected group of computers that shares resources.

Peripheral A supplemental devise—printer, modem, joystick, speakers—linked to and controlled by a computer.

Protocol A code that allows computers to connect with appropriate sources. Example: HTTP, FTP. (*See* URL.)

Search Engine An Internet program that locates sites using keyword searching. Examples: *AltaVista, Excite, Google, HotBot, Lycos, Yahoo.*

Server Software that runs programs (within networks) or allows information to be transferred (on the Internet).

Software The computer programs that make computers (hardware) operate.

Toolbar A bar, at the top or bottom of the computer screen, that incorporates icons and menus to allow users to select functions and drop-down features.

Upload To send a file to a remote computer or site through a modem or on the Internet.

URL (Uniform Resource Locator) An electronic Internet address, composed of sequenced elements (protocol//domain name.directory path.file name.domain). Example: <http://www.whitehouse.gov>.

Usenet A network of worldwide Internet discussion groups.

Virus An invasive program that "infects" computer files, thereby making them inoperable.

Web Site A site on the Internet identified by a URL, reached through a search or link from another site. (*See* URL.)

World Wide Web (WWW) The interlinked, hypertext-based network of electronic materials that are available around the world.

Index

Abbreviations
    CBE style for, 346–347
    Chicago style for, 346
    MLA style for, 339–394
    and note-taking, 114
Abstracts
    and APA papers, 252, 256
    and CBE papers, 318, 321
    See also Citation/Abstract and
      Dissertation Abstracts International
Academic Guide to the Internet, 2
Academic subjects, topics from, 2
Accent marks, and foreign languages, 181,
    274
Accuracy
    in note-taking, 115
    of working thesis statement, 130
Active voice, 159
Activities, choosing subject from, 2
Ad hominem, 108
Aesthetic perspective, obtaining from
    audiovisual sources, 62
.aero, 81
Affiliations of Web sites, 73, 82
Afterwords
    APA entry form for, 238
    Chicago note form for, 272–273
    MLA citation form for, 178–179
Alliteration, using in titles, 153
Allusion, in introduction, 154
AltaVista, 65, 70
American College of Sports Medicine, 3
American Psychological Association
    (APA) style, 3, 224–262
    and audiovisual sources, 240–244
    and book sources, 232–239
    and citations, 225–250
    and electronic sources, 244–250
    format for reference-list entries,
      228–229
    information for reference-list entries,
      227–228
    and manuscript preparation, 251–254

    and patterns for in-text citations,
      225–227
    and periodical sources, 229–232
    sample paper, 255–262
Ampersand (&)
    and APA entry form, 224, 228
    and MLA citation form, 183
Analogy
    false, 108
    in introduction, 154
Anecdote, in introduction, 154
Annual reports
    APA entry form for, 239
    Chicago note form for, 273
    MLA citation form for, 179–180
Annual reports (Online), MLA citation
    form for, 201
Anonymous artwork, MLA citation form
    for, 188
Anonymous author, CBE citation form for,
    309
APA style, *see* American Psychological
    Association (APA) style
Appeals, 103–105
    See also Critical thinking
Arabic numerals, using in formal outline,
    134
Arresting statement, in introduction, 155
Art
    As audiovisual sources, 62
    See also Artwork
Articles, *see* Encyclopedias; Newspaper
    articles; Periodical(s)
Artwork
    APA entry form for, 240–241
    Chicago note form for, 277–278
    evaluation of, 79
    MLA citation form for, 188
Artwork (Online)
    Chicago note form for, 285
    evaluation of, 79
    MLA citation form for, 203–204
Assigned-topic research papers, 9–11

MLA Works-Cited Entries

...mat consistently:

...of the entry at the left margin and indent subse-
...he half-inch.

...the author's name so that it appears last name first.

... When no author is named, list the source by title.

4. Cite the complete title; include full subtitles following a colon.

5. Use periods and one space to separate author, title, and publication information.

6. Double-space entries.

Gather information for complete citations before leaving the library, logging off the computer, or returning a source. See pages 165–209 for additional information and examples.

Sample Entries

A Book by One Author

Barr, Stephen M. *Modern Physics and Ancient Faith.* Notre Dame: U of Notre Dame P, 2003.

A Book by Two or More Authors

Fagan, Jay, and Glen Palm. *Fathers and Early Childhood Programs.* Clifton Park: Delmar, 2003.

Tucker, Susan Martin, et al. *Patient Care Standards: Collaborative Planning and Nursing Interventions.* 7th ed. St. Louis: Mosby, 2000.

An Edition Other than the First

Forging the American Character: Readings in United States History. Ed. John R. M. Wilson. 4th ed. Upper Saddle River: Prentice, 2003.

A Work in a Collection

Corrigan, Timothy. "Which Shakespeare to Love? Film, Fidelity, and the Performance of Literature." *High-Pop: Making Culture into Popular Entertainment.* Ed. Jim Collins. Malden: Blackwell, 2003. 155–81.

An Article in an Encyclopedia or Other Reference Book

Abrams, Richard M. "Theodore Roosevelt." *The Presidents: A Reference History.* Ed. Henry F. Graff. 2nd ed. New York: Scribner's, 1996. 325–46.